Praise for The Lie that Binds

"In vivid detail, Hogue lays out exactly how the radical right infected our democracy and our institutions to reverse social progress – and in doing so, teaches us how to most strategically fight back. This is a must-read for every legislator who is serious about protecting their constituents' civil and reproductive rights."

Senator Kirsten Gillibrand, NY, Founder and Author of *Off the Sidelines*

"*The Lie that Binds* is an unflinching look at the true origins of the right wing obsession with keeping half of the population "in their place." From the very beginning, the purpose of anti-choice movement was to maintain and consolidate power in the hands of a few white men. Hogue sticks to the facts and lays out the only effective path forward. Fight like hell!"

Zerlina Maxwell, author of *The End of White Politics*, MSNBC Political Analyst, SiriusXM host

"This is a must read account of how the Radical Right's quest for domination ultimately led to the country electing a race baiting, misogynist in Donald Trump. Hogue unravels for the reader decades of careful machinations of a movement hell bent on keeping women in their place and using abortion as a weapon to do so. To all feminists who dream of overthrowing the patriarchy: start here."

Alyssa Mastromonaco, NYT Best Selling author & co-host of Crooked Media's #Hysteria podcast

D0958198

Praise for The Lie that Binds

"Hogue makes a powerful and disturbing contribution to the literature on historical links between the domination of women and protecting white supremacy. The 'culture war' the evangelical right mounted around abortion has it's origins as a wedge issue to protect a privilege rooted in racial segregation. Women of color and low income women are the most vulnerable to the abuses of both. It is an important read that reminds us that the original sins of our founding will harm us all until they are repented."

   Maya Wiley, NBC News and MSNBC Legal Analyst

"Hogue lays bare how far-right extremists have taken over our government all while hiding in plain sight. This untold history details years of insidious schemes that enabled a creeping right-wing corruption of our political system, court system, and information systems and ultimately gave us a reality TV star in the White House. This book speaks to the true endgame of the forces opposing reproductive freedom so that we know exactly how to arm ourselves and, ultimately, win our country back."

   Joe Lockhart, CNN political analyst

The Lie

That Binds

Ilyse Hogue

Ellie Langford

WASHINGTON D.C.

Book Design & Cover Design: Adam Dines

Copy Editor: Alex Abbott

Managing Editor: Troy N. Miller

Printed in the United States of America
First Edition

Published by Strong Arm Press
www.strongarmpress.com
Washington, DC

ISBN-13: 978-1-947492-50-9

Acknowledgments

This book was many years in the making and was built on the amazing trove of research from the NARAL Pro-Choice America research team who doggedly monitors, aggregates, and analyzes raw content from anti-choice, right-wing, and alt-right media sources on a daily basis. The work is hard, and it can be disturbing and depressing. We're grateful to them for all of the valuable insight they provided for this book and contribute to the political and cultural analysis of our world.

This project stands on the shoulders of dozens of incredible researchers, experts, and thought-partners who illuminated key aspects of this story and helped shape our own understanding of this critical history. Our research is one piece of a much larger puzzle, and without the ongoing work of our friends and allies, we would not be able to see the full picture. Thank you all for sharing your expertise, for pushing us to think bigger, and for helping us to connect the dots. We're thankful for everything you've done and we're committed to continuing this work with you. We understand it's far from over.

Special thanks to Loretta Ross — you have consistently challenged us to expand our analysis of our opposition, shared your own wisdom and experience with us, shaped our thinking, and encouraged us to tell this story. Your efforts to bring people together, strengthen our collective work, and to push us all toward a stronger shared analysis of the threats we face were all critical in jump-starting this project. We're grateful for your continued friendship and thought partnership. Thank you for your work to ensure the progressive movement is consistently growing, reflecting, and innovating.

This project was made possible with support from the Open Society Policy Center. Thank you to the OSPC team for your partnership as this project developed. With your support, this work has grown far beyond what we originally hoped, and, we hope, will have a much greater impact.

Deep thank you to the NARAL Pro-Choice America Board of Directors, for continually believing in the idea that we need to understand our opposition better in order to formulate long-term strategy for durable change. Hannah Groch-Begley, the founding member of NARAL's opposition research team, once told Ilyse, "the best conclusions come from following the research where it leads you." The NARAL Board and staff has stayed true to this axiom in developing the department, the discipline, and the products of the research.

Thank you to all the friends, colleagues and contributors whose direct work made this project possible and without whom we might not have brought this project over the finish line: Becca Lewis; Mutale Nkonde; Dr. Megan Squire, and the team at CounterAction, who contributed insights and expanded our knowledge of digital threats to our democracy; Bushra Sultana Ahmad; our editors, Kathleen Collins, and Michael Eberhart; Evelyn Schlatter, Melissa Ryan and Charlotte Clymer, who shared their expertise and waded through early drafts; Adam Dines, our designer; Sally Rifkin, Gabriela Rico, and Caroline Resnick, who contributed research; Andy Barr and Sophia Tesfaye, who helped us wrestle the massive amount of research into a consumable narrative; and Spencer Collet, our diligent fact-checker. Thanks to Angelo Carusone for being a thought-partner and co-conspirator, always helping think through how this knowledge fit into the larger puzzle. Thanks to Elizabeth Schoetz whose remarkable commitment to excellence and to NARAL created space for this process.

At times, as with all long projects, we began to feel like we were rolling a boulder uphill and our confidence faltered in believing we could ever bring the project to completion. Three special people got us through those moments: Ryan Grim, at Strong Arm Press, who always believed this was a story that needed to be told and made himself available as not just a publisher but as a thought-partner and editor. Kelly Sackley, whose endless spreadsheets kept us on track when it felt overwhelming and whose prolific enthusiasm buoyed us on our dark days. Judy Estrin, who contributed endless hours of volunteer time to review drafts and interrogate us to make sure we were making the most precise points possible. Judy, your friendship, mentorship, and commitment to this story insured that we had not just a product to show, but one that met a standard of excellence that you set.

Ilyse wants to thank her husband, life-partner and father of her children, John Neffinger. For many early mornings of solo parenting while she found time to write. For coaching her through writer's block and crises of confidence. For always being a cheerleader and a best friend. For always making her greater. She wants to thank her parents, Ynette and Jim, for teaching her early on to never shy away from the hard fights if they were the righteous ones. For teaching her to always tell the truth, even when people didn't want to hear it. And for always loving and supporting her no matter what.

Ellie wants to thank her best friend, teammate, and husband, Max, for serving as a sounding board and thesaurus throughout this project, for his unshakable confidence that this work matters, and particularly, for everything he shouldered to make space for that work to happen. Thank you to her parents, Jenny and Joe, who taught her to ask tough questions, to run toward problems, and to always believe things can be made better. And to Ilyse and Adrienne, thank you for your mentorship and your trust.

Contents

Prologue

Ellie and I did not set out to write a book, but, as we were reviewing the research that was part of our normal business of the organization where we work, the story that was coming into focus was too compelling and too important not to share. Once we started, the book became almost impossible to finish as we raced to keep up with unfolding events in the world around us. As we go to print, America is in the grip of COVID-19 and the administration's dangerously inept response. We are in the middle of one of the most significant social uprisings in history, catalyzed by yet another death of another Black person at the hands of a police officer. In lesser, but still significant news — a documentary had just come out in which Norma McCorvey — aka Jane Roe in *Roe v. Wade* — confessed that her high profile conversion to the Religious Right was a sham.

For many, those may seem like disparate events. For those of us who have been studying the evolution of the anti-choice movement and their alignment with well-known white nationalists, misogynists and anti-science disinformers in support of Trump, it feels like convergence.

Several years ago, we set out to research a set of very specific questions. How instrumental was the support of what we commonly refer to as an anti-choice movement in electing Trump to the presidency? What did he promise them? What did he deliver? How could we use that knowledge to work to prevent his re election?

Simultaneously, our research department was routinely tracking incidents of disinformation, misinformation, and hate speech throughout anti-choice media and on social media platforms. Venues and leaders that are often minimized or overlooked by mainstream media and political consultants due to their "pro-life" brands, were routinely preaching not just anti-abortion gospel to their audiences but also parroting Donald Trump's anti-science, racist and xenophobic messages on everything from immigration to COVID-19 to voter suppression.

This made sense to us. Yet, as I traveled the country speaking to supporters about the tenuous state of reproductive freedom or organizing on behalf of progressive candidates, it became clear that many people don't know the real origins of the Religious Right — that the fusion of modern conservatism and anti-choice ideology was truly rooted in the fight to preserve school desegregation and white supremacy. In order to strategically fight against both Donald Trump and reproductive oppression, we have to also understand and communicate the full history and context of their fight: how it was always about maintaining rigid social order and a privileged class comprised primarily of white Christian men, and how it still is today.

Trump's election — and all the forces emboldened and facilitated through it — was hardly an anomaly; it was a culmination of a decades-long strategy by the Radical Right. The anti-choice movement that had successfully cloaked itself in a veil of "family values" was in fact born of the same aspirations and held the same beliefs as the new Alt-Right that was given so much credit for Trump's victory.

Trump's presidency is commonly and accurately described as a backlash by predominantly white voters against a changing society. But that's only a snapshot of this moment in time. The research that drove us to write this book paints an undeniable picture of a small group of Radical Right leaders who — beginning almost a century ago — saw movements for freedom and equality as an existential threat to their grip on social, economic, and political power. They fomented fear as a strategy to maintain control and privilege through a carefully architected and resourced campaign. They found utility in weaponizing abortion, which ultimately became a key component of their strategy. Understanding and unpacking that part of the Right's strategy is one key to dismantling their power.

At the center of this narrative is an inarguable fact: The overwhelming majority of Americans support, and have always supported, a woman's right to end her pregnancy. This is the story of how a small group of individuals adeptly manipulated politics to their own advantage by weaponizing deeply personal issues of pregnancy, parenting, and family and how they have, so far, gotten away with it.

That they have been so successful speaks to their own ability to use disinformation, a moral mantle, and a willingness to force a binary viewpoint on situations that by their very nature are anything but. Any individual decision to terminate a pregnancy factors in innumerable considerations: job status and prospects, financial savings, existing family concerns, individual faith, current health and well-being, partnership status, just to name a few. A million calculations go into making the best decisions that we can, in any given moment, about how to live our lives.

While the consensus is clear on the operative question of who should get to decide, we are a people with complicated feelings about abortion and often full of judgements about other people. We can agree that politicians should not be making the decision and still have conflicted feelings about the decision itself. In fact, data show that many of us do. In a political and policy world of black and white, a fair number of us live in the emotional gray zone.

The Right recognized and stepped into that breach, cravenly capitalizing on internal ambivalence, largely fueled by misunderstandings due to silence and social stigma around abortion. This book is a story of a small group of people who quite methodically set out to take a personal, often complex decision and turn it into a weapon in service of establishing an unpopular right-wing agenda — to wrap their cynical quest to build and maintain power for a privileged few in a cloak of morality. It's a story of a Trojan horse built with disinformation, propaganda, and social stigma, grounded in a blunt idea that God's intention was for white Christian men to be in charge and that the maintenance of a rigid family structure is necessary to enforce that God's will.

This book seeks to expose that the agenda of the Radical Right — in most ways indistinguishable from the institutional anti-choice movement — is and has always been about resisting any progress in America. The goal is the maintenance of a social order in which men have control over women and white Americans have control over people of color with a concentration of economic wealth that reinforces that order.

This book does not tell the other sides of the story. It doesn't detail the efforts of generations of feminists, advocates, and leaders of movements who have long sought to bring intersectional analysis to this conversation. We were inspired to write this book to set the record straight on the other side's historic motivations, but also to prompt people not immersed in these stories to start a journey of exploration and discovery. This book mentions, but doesn't dive into, many interrelated issues including the depth of complicity of funding sources and social media platforms in protecting the status quo — topics that have filled books on their own. We hope readers will think about how their own personal struggles or discomfort with thinking or talking about abortion might prevent them from fully engaging in the fight for freedom, racial and gender justice and democracy that lays before us. We hope readers will rethink the tired political commentary that excuses so-called "single-issue" voters and candidates from engaging in deeper questions about structural racism and misogyny or about the dangerous forces that supposed "moral" conservatism has enabled. It's our greatest hope our readers will seek out other voices, books, and stories out. They are plentiful and we've learned so much from them.

Reproductive oppression and anti-abortion activism make for potent tools in the opposition's toolbox. We must confront them outright to make social and political gains. This book seeks to offer some tangible solutions and ways to blunt and dismantle their power.

The greatest power of all, though, lies in our ability to reassert empathy as central to the American experience. Effective policy and political solutions have always and will always follow periods of mass empathy in our culture. True understanding of the complexity of real, lived experience in an unjust world can be a powerful catalyst for change and for realizing a commitment to dignity as a basic human right. We hope we are in one of those moments.

Chapter 1
The Trojan Horse

Paul Weyrich was frustrated. As one of the godfathers of the Religious Right, he had spent a good deal of the 1970s and 1980s building infrastructure that we recognize today as the power-centers of the modern conservative movement. The shadowy leadership group the Council for National Policy, the American Legislative Exchange Council (ALEC), and the powerhouse Heritage Foundation all sprang from Weyrich's unusual ability to envision unlikely alliances.[1] He even helped coin the term "moral majority" as part of his campaign for power that brought him into the inner-circle of a new rising movement.

But standing before the men-only Ethics and Public Policy Conference in 1990, it was clear to those in the audience that despite three straight GOP presidential victories, Weyrich was deeply unsatisfied.

According to eyewitnesses, Weyrich unloaded to the gathered attendees, lecturing that they knew little about the origins of their own movement or what it had taken to build the radical right into the political powerhouse it had become. He admonished the foot soldiers of the movement that they had spent so much time repeating the myth they originated from backlash to the 1973 *Roe v. Wade* decision, that they had come to believe it themselves. They had lost sight of the reality of their coalition's foundation.[2] As a result, the careful strategies Weyrich and his contemporaries had developed to build power on the back of abortion for the purpose of their true agenda were slowly being distorted. Don't get distracted by believing your own rhetoric, he seemed to warn.

Weyrich, born in Racine, Wisconsin, as the son of German immigrants, had always been a behind-the-scenes kind of guy.[3] He held no political aspirations for himself, and became politically active as a student at University of Wisconsin–Parkside supporting Barry Goldwater in the early 1960s. He dabbled in journalism before finding his way to Capitol Hill in 1967 working as an aide to a Republican senator from Colorado.[4] [5] [6]

Like many conservatives at the time, Weyrich believed that in the aftermath of the New Deal the United States was being derailed by investment in a government-supported social safety net. Still, he stood out among his peers for his fervent conviction that the country needed to be ruled by evangelical Protestants with an adherence to their interpretation of biblical law, an idea that stood in stark contrast to the traditional American ideal of maintaining the separation of church and state.[7]

After his 1990 lecture at the conference, one young attendee, historian Randall Balmer, was so startled that he approached Weyrich to be sure he had heard him correctly. He had, Weyrich assured him, reiterating that the purpose of the movement organized heavily around abortion politics was to undergird a system in which social order and status were rigid, grounded in the fundamentalist belief that God placed white, male Christians in charge[8] — all of it based on an ideology called "dominionism," which seeks to enforce Biblical law.[9] Weyrich wanted everyone to remember that they had broader aspirations than banning abortion: they had built a political movement designed to halt progressive cultural change and maintain power for a privileged minority.[10]

The story of Weyrich's movement — today the dominant force within the conservative establishment, the Republican Party, and the Trump administration — is ultimately not a story of true believers. It is not a story about religion or philosophy or medicine. It is a story about a marriage between wild-eyed zealots and cynical political operatives who have long sought to profit from inflaming the anger, resentment, prejudice, and fear of a small minority of Americans. It's the story of a quiet yet relentless assault on American democracy, where attacks on reproductive freedom are often the thin edge of the wedge. Weyrich and his cohorts were the architects of the strategy.

This is also the story of the "true believers," generations of right-leaning, largely white Evangelical Americans who were convinced through design, propaganda, and a lot of disinformation that abortion — a procedure they already believed to have personal and moral complexity — is the absolute root of all evil. Finally, it's the story of the establishment Republicans who walked a tightrope between the need to add new constituencies to their waning coalition and the sober reality that outright opposition to abortion and reproductive freedom could permanently put them on the wrong side of popular opinion.

The architects spent hundreds of millions of dollars to build infrastructure, mobilize previously disconnected people, and weave a narrative about cultural decline, all while catapulting the issue of abortion from relative political obscurity in the 1970s to the center of the conversation for the ruling political party in the United States. Their efforts were designed to preserve privilege and control, and our current political reality is the result of their social experiment.

Donald Trump is president. The Radical Right has absconded with the judicial branch. The national agenda reflects the priorities of a small minority of Americans. Much of this can be attributed to their efficacy. Only by understanding how their movement began, how it grew through exploiting issues of race and gender, and how it operates today, can we stop them from writing the next chapter in the story of our country.

———

This story actually begins with a Supreme Court case that predates *Roe v. Wade* by twenty years. In 1954, the Supreme Court ruled in *Brown v. Board* of Education that state laws used by segregationists to maintain structural inequality in the nation's schools violated the Constitution. The decision, heralded by so many as a long-overdue remedy for disparities between Black schools and white schools, resulted from decades of organizing and litigation by civil rights activists seeking to right historic wrongs born of slavery and Jim Crow.

Not everyone was so thrilled by this societal progress. Just as happened in the North, many white Southerners actively looked for a workaround to keep their children from having to go to school with Black children. They found a champion in fundamentalist preacher Jerry Falwell, who decried the court's decision as evidence that Chief Justice Earl Warren and the court were deaf to God's will. "The facilities should be separate. When God has drawn a line of distinction, we should not attempt to cross that line," he argued in a 1958 sermon from his Thomas Road Baptist Church.[11]

At that time, American evangelicals were largely disengaged from politics and were known as unreliable voters. Falwell himself was outwardly anti-political and preached that politics was a tainted realm. Still, he did have a history of delving into politics when it came to opposing civil rights — elevating racists like segregationist Alabama Gov. George Wallace through his radio show and consistently making spurious accusations about Martin Luther King Jr.'s motives.[12] [13]

After the Brown decision, Falwell saw a way to shield his racist views behind his religious credentials to sidestep the court's ruling. And he wasn't alone. Other white, Evangelical leaders were beginning to fear the potential loss of white supremacy and were starting to flex their political muscle.

Invoking a cry of "religious freedom," Falwell led an effort to set up all-white, church-affiliated schools that became known as "segregation academies" across the South. Since private schools were exempt from the Brown decision, many Evangelical leaders were able to use their ties to nonprofit religious institutions to get generous tax subsidies for all-white schools.[14] By some accounts, segregation academies like Falwell's enrolled up to 750,000 students over the next decade.[15]

For a while, Falwell seemed content to focus on his own Lynchburg Christian Academy, set up in 1967 and associated with his church.[16] In 1971, he expanded his empire by establishing Liberty University, still one of the largest Christian universities in the world and a dedicated training ground for right-wing activists who go on to Capitol Hill and conservative think tanks like the Heritage Foundation.[17] [18] But in 1968, a group of Black parents in Mississippi brought suit against segregation academies, asserting that their discrimination should not be tax exempt. This little known case, *Green v. Connally*, resulted in then-President Richard Nixon ordering the Internal Revenue Service to formally revoke tax exemptions for any remaining segregated schools.[19] This was the tipping point for the Rev. Falwell.

As the IRS began to dispense questionnaires asking for disclosures on racial policies and minority enrollment, Falwell grew incensed. His public statements show a deep sense of victimhood. "In one fell swoop, the heirs of slaveholders became the descendants of persecuted Baptists, and Jim Crow a heresy the First Amendment was meant to protect," political scientist Corey Robin wrote of Falwell's perceived persecution.[20]

With Falwell's backing, the South Carolina fundamentalist college Bob Jones University went to court over the order, kicking off a legal battle that lasted years. They argued that racial segregation was a religious matter, mandated by the Bible. They lost. In 1976, the IRS rescinded the school's tax-exempt status. But it became a cause celebre when Bob Jones didn't give up. The university finally exhausted all appeals in 1983.[21] Even then, it chose to forfeit its tax exemption rather than change its policies. Bob Jones University prohibited interracial dating as late as 2000.[22]

Bob Jones University administrator Elmer L. Rumminger later told Balmer, the young historian who sought to reconstruct Weyrich's history after that fateful conference, that desegregation was a political awakening for disengaged white Evangelicals. They were furious. According to Rumminger, the tax exemption fight "alerted the Christian school community about what could happen with government interference" and was "the major issue" attracting this group to politics.[23]

Weyrich had been probing for just this type of shift. Since the Goldwater campaign of the mid-1960s, Weyrich had been actively looking for ways to expand the conservative wing of the Republican coalition. He became convinced that activating evangelical voters was the way to do it. He had already tried to politicize the Equal Rights Amendment, school prayer, and even tested abortion as a way to activate Evangelicals, but up until that point, nothing had clicked until *Green v. Connally* sparked outrage.[24]

The GOP's "Southern Strategy" is a familiar element of 20th-century American political history. It goes something like this: When the Democratic Party aligned itself with the civil rights movement, segregationist Democrats fled into the arms of a Republican Party willing to trade its dwindling support among socially liberal, business-oriented Rockefeller types for a new base that was white, Southern, and culturally conservative. Lyndon B. Johnson famously declared after signing the Civil Rights Act into law in 1964: "We've lost the South for a generation."[25] But while that spark indeed accelerated the realignment, it didn't produce enough momentum to complete it.

As Angie Maxwell and Todd G. Shields write in their 2019 book, *The Long Southern Strategy*, the initial influx of segregationists "was not enough voters to be the sole cause of sustained realignment."[26] The Right needed to establish a novel and deeper connection with their new base, particularly as explicit opposition to racial equality became less politically tenable. As the conservative movement "went hunting for disaffected white southern voters, they bagged a flock of evangelicals whether they originally intended to or not," as Maxwell and Shields put it.

Until the 1970s, the correlation between religious affiliation and partisan identity was relatively weak. Catholic voters were a core block of the Democratic New Deal coalition, favoring workers' rights while holding socially conservative views on gender, sexual health, and religious issues. Evangelicals, meanwhile, were drifting towards the Republican Party, compelled by the hard-line stance right-wing Republicans took against the Soviet Union. They bought the idea that "godless Communism" was an existential threat to their way of life.[27] Evangelical leaders like Falwell and Billy Graham maintained close public relationships with Republican Presidents Eisenhower and Nixon.

Paul Weyrich later pinpointed the debate around segregation and Bob Jones University as the moment when evangelicals finally joined him at the barricades. He told Balmer in a 1990 interview that what changed was "Jimmy Carter's intervention against the Christian schools, trying to deny them tax-exempt status on the basis of so-called de facto segregation."[28] In a classic revisionist move, Weyrich elided over the inconvenient fact that Nixon, a Republican, had started the intervention against Bob Jones. Still, Weyrich's main point was striking. He had been looking for a political issue to activate evangelicals, but had missed that what would truly drive conservative activism wasn't any one issue, but an underlying fear of loss of the privilege they felt entitled to. Weyrich and his allies had stumbled on a formula for building political power that they learned could be repurposed time and time again.[29]

Falwell led the initial charge. In 1976, he launched a series of "I love America" rallies as a way to raise his profile and acculturate his followers to the idea of political engagement.[30] He preached that since the Christian way of life was under threat, they must disavow former beliefs that devout Christians should eschew politics. With his trademark zeal, he proclaimed that separation of church and state was "invented by the devil to keep Christians from running their own country."[31] In 1977, Falwell went to Florida to join former Miss America contestant and orange juice ambassador Anita Bryant in a campaign against an anti-discrimination measure protecting LGBTQ people.[32] The measure was repealed. He realized he was onto something. He wanted to scale. Two years later, with support from Weyrich, Falwell founded the Moral Majority, his primary vehicle to organize fundamentalist Evangelicals in politics. The Moral Majority went on to play an outsized role in the election of President Ronald Reagan in 1980.[33]

Tellingly, abortion appeared to be nowhere on Falwell's radar. As *Roe* became the law of the land, abortion clinics popped up around the country to serve patients. Falwell organized no protests. Pastor Ed Dobson, who was present at the founding of Moral Majority, said abortion was never mentioned as a reason for engagement.[34] Falwell didn't even mention the word "abortion" in a sermon until 1978, five full years after *Roe* was handed down.[35]

Falwell was not alone in his indifference to legalized abortion. In response to the Supreme Court's decision in 1973, W.A. Criswell, leading Evangelical and former president of the Southern Baptist Convention, applauded the decision, saying:

I have always felt that it was only after a child was born and had a life separate from its mother that it became an individual person, and it has always, therefore, seemed to me that what is best for the mother and for the future should be allowed.[36]

The Southern Baptist Convention never registered formal opposition to *Roe* until 1980, two years after the formation of the Moral Majority.[37]

―――――――

The 1960s had brought great turmoil to the country and into the living rooms of many Americans. The Civil Rights Movement coincided with the popularity and affordability of television, so millions were suddenly bearing witness to fellow citizens beaten and terrorized in the streets of the South. Graphic images of the war in Vietnam electrified an anti-war movement and shocked a system acculturated to the national unity forged in World War II. Multiple overlapping social movements were challenging the status quo: women's liberation, gay liberation, the black power movement. What felt electrifying to many felt overwhelming to others. Many people were nervous at what felt like an explosion of attacks on everyday norms.

Weyrich and Falwell saw that unease as opportunity. And they had company in their plotting a Far Right movement able to punch above its weight in the political arena. In 1971, a corporate lawyer named Lewis Powell wrote an eight page memo for the U.S. Chamber of Commerce titled "Attack on American Free Enterprise System." His diatribe was a call to arms for corporate America to defend its interests against criticisms of unchecked "capitalism emanating 'from the college campus, the pulpit, the media, the intellectual and literary journals.'" He held special vitriol for Ralph Nader, "whose model of public interest litigation and publicity was then at its height." Powell laid out a blueprint for a wide-reaching political infrastructure that would "build a group of scholars-on-call to defend the system; [monitor and critique media];" and construct legal organizations to advance litigation and shape the legal cannon in their favor.[38]

This system would allow the conservative movement to wield disproportionate political power in the face of ongoing cultural and demographic change.[39] Powell proselytized that the Right invest heavily in textbooks and professors who would train young people on right-wing ideology; in television and news programming, paid advertisements, scholarly journals, and books that would shift the national conversation to the Right; in political lobbying and shaping legislation; and critically, in controlling the court system.[40] Powell's focus was on propping up corporate power and elevating the interests of the U.S. Chamber of Commerce, but his ideas were a natural fit with Weyrich and Falwell, who were already putting the pieces into place. Powell was appointed to the Supreme Court by Nixon just a few months after he wrote his memo. Weyrich and Falwell would work hard to manifest his vision, even though Powell disappointed them many times on the Court.

Falwell's Liberty University, founded the same year as Powell wrote his memo, was the cornerstone to branding their work as fundamentalist Christian morality. Years later, the *Washington Post* would describe Liberty as a "bastion of the Christian right" and "a stage of choice in Republican presidential politics."[41] While Falwell focused on Liberty, Weyrich founded The Heritage Foundation with the help of conservative major-donor Joe Coors.[42] Heritage was designed as a think tank to feed both Republican elected officials and the conservative elite their new ideological construct, and it quickly became a juggernaut because of its relentless focus on message discipline. Edwin J. Feulner, who became president of the organization in 1977, later described its vision this way: "We have set out to make conservative ideas not just respectable but mainstream. To set the terms of national policy debate."[43]

To directly shape conservative legislation, particularly at the state level, Weyrich founded the American Legislative Exchange Council (ALEC) in 1973, which drafted and spread pre-packaged model bills to state legislators across the country.[44] ALEC burst into mainstream consciousness decades later as the architects of a policy known as "Stand Your Ground," which gained public notoriety when George Zimmerman killed Trayvon Martin in 2012, yet was not initially charged.[45][46] ALEC has spawned hundreds of right-wing bills over the years and provided extensive support to state legislators who carry the mantle. A very early ALEC leader was an Illinois state representative named Henry Hyde.[47] Hyde would go on to be the first public champion of anti-abortion policy in Congress and the author of the Hyde Amendment, which still exists today.[48] [49]

For grassroots power, they relied on Falwell's Moral Majority, founded in 1979 with strong support from Weyrich and other top conservative strategists including Richard Viguerie, Terry Dolan, and the Rev. Tim LaHaye.[50] Falwell hit the road making speech after speech flatly disowning his own prior views against political engagement and mobilizing his flock. In 1981, LaHaye, Weyrich, and others would go on to found the powerful and secretive conservative leadership group the Council for National Policy (CNP), which to this day gathers a "powerful organizing force" of top Republican leaders from Kellyanne Conway to Trump judicial nominations advisor Leonard Leo, offering a venue for conservative leaders and politicians to "collaborate on achieving their shared goals."[51] [52] [53] [54]

By combining the Powell corporate conservatives with their growing wing of fundamentalists and disaffected white Southerners, the godfathers of the Radical Right had hit upon a winning equation. The flock was gathering. The network of organizations was growing. What came next is not so much a story of true believers as it is about a group of people dedicated to preserving the status quo in a changing world. Religion and philosophy were contorted to give a moral sheen to their agenda, but their real power came from inflaming a targeted group of Americans who were terrified of losing economic and social status in an increasingly diverse and tolerant country. They were mainstreaming bigotry.

Throughout the 1970s, things continued to fall into place for the newly formed cabal. The Radical Right was beginning to look more and more like the insidious political powerhouse it is today, with one glaring exception. Despite the right's attempts to rewrite history and claim *Roe v. Wade* as a catalyst for what they pretend is a deeply ideological movement driven by moral imperatives — it was not. At the time when Weyrich, Falwell and others like Powell were laying the foundations of a movement, the GOP had not yet set their sights on politicizing abortion. In the 1970s, even in the years after *Roe*, abortion just wasn't a major political issue — it was a personal one.

———

To set the stage, it is important to take a look further back in time to before Weyrich began his campaign to consolidate power. Abortion had been illegal in the United States since it declared independence and adopted English Common Law on the issue of ending a pregnancy. Even as those punitive laws led to more and more deaths of and injuries to women, the issue was, at most, a sideshow in a political debate largely defined by men. In the mid-20th century, subsets of the Women's Liberation Movement made it their business to minimize the damage of the restrictive laws. Groups like the Army of Three and the Jane Collective taught women about self-managed abortion or connected them with willing and vetted medical professionals, who did the work at great risk to themselves.

As the need outstripped the resources available and women were becoming more outspoken about the risks they faced in back alley abortions, people across the country became more vocal about wanting abortion to become legal. Women's empowerment movements picked up the call, arguing that criminalizing abortion was dangerous, regressive and at its core, a strategy to scare women about the consequence of pre-marital sex and the social stigma that came along with it.

In 1967, Colorado Gov. John Love broke new ground when he signed the first state law liberalizing abortion.[55] While he reportedly wrestled with the decision, the story of a local pregnant woman who shot herself in the stomach rather than carry her pregnancy to term made headlines. Love ultimately believed his decision was a question of reducing harm and limiting government interference in personal decision-making and chose to afford women that freedom. Even though Gov. Love's decision was groundbreaking, there was surprisingly little backlash. Many more states followed suit in the six years before *Roe*.

The loosening of abortion laws wasn't controversial — and neither was it partisan. Love was a Republican.[56] Most Republican leaders of the time were staunchly pro-choice, including 1964 Republican presidential nominee Barry Goldwater, who was otherwise responsible for so much of the rightward shift of the party.[57] Both of the GOP's top primary candidates in 1964 were pro-choice, and runner-up Rockefeller went on to preside over the liberalization of New York's abortion laws as a pre-*Roe* governor.[58] A 1969 poll found that Republicans actually led Democrats by 10% in their support for legalized abortion in the first trimester, and a 1972 Gallup poll found that 68% of Republicans believed abortion to be a private matter between a woman and her doctor.[59] [60] Indeed, it wouldn't be until after Reagan's second term that Gallup polling showed Democrats' support surpassing Republicans on the question of legal access to abortion.[61]

The Roman Catholic Church, with its long-standing doctrine against abortion and contraception, was the most prominent opponent of legalizing the procedure. However, even Catholic leaders at the time had a more diffuse set of priorities, working on issues like funding parochial education and ending capital punishment. Conservative Catholics like William F. Buckley took a nuanced stance. Buckley, founder of the right-wing National Review and an avowed Catholic, criticized the church's rigid stance on abortion in 1966, arguing that religious freedom required a more flexible stance on abortion in cases of "maternal health, rape, [and] defect in fetus."[62]

Across denominations, Christian Americans didn't rank abortion near the top of their agenda. Evangelicals were "overwhelmingly indifferent" to the issue.[63] Randall Balmer describes a 1968 symposium where both the Christian Medical Society and Christianity Today condoned abortion in cases in which terminating the pregnancy would result in better outcomes for "individual health, family welfare, and social responsibility."[64]

Before the *Roe* decision, the Southern Baptist Convention passed a resolution in 1971 that encouraged its followers to work for legislation to legalize abortion. The convention's resolution outlined a wide-ranging set of cases in which abortion should be legal, including "rape, incest, clear evidence of severe fetal deformity, and carefully ascertained evidence of the likelihood of damage to the emotional, mental, and physical health of the mother."[65] The Southern Baptist Convention further reaffirmed this resolution post-*Roe* in 1974 and 1976.[66]

Evangelicals' disinterest in anti-abortion advocacy in this era was plain to see in the Bible Belt, where Christian Evangelicals wield the most political power today. As laws loosened across states before *Roe*, the Bible Belt was home to more places to access abortion than much of the rest of the country. In 1967, North Carolina liberalized its abortion laws, and Georgia followed suit shortly thereafter. At that time, Alabama offered women greater access to abortion than New York. These states received little backlash to liberalizing their abortion laws.[67] No massive protests occurred at the health-care clinics. There was no wave of politicians losing their seats over these votes. It must have seemed that an era of pain and shame for women was coming to a graceful close.

So what changed? A conservative movement built on maintaining white privilege began to lose steam, and went looking for a new boogeyman to keep its people engaged. Meanwhile, one woman with a cynical vision for how to gain power for herself stepped up to the plate.

———

Falwell's crusade against school integration was losing favor with the general public around the same time it was activating their base. While they continued to stoke the outrage of the devoted, he and Weyrich saw the writing on the wall. Society was accepting school integration as the norm, even as leaders struggled to effectively implement it. The movement architects needed a new focus.

Weyrich was already casting around for new ideas. Never short on ambition, he wrote about plans to build a "new political philosophy" that would be "defined by us [conservatives] in moral terms, packaged in non-religious language, and propagated throughout the country by our new coalition." He believed that, if successfully "blended and activated," the moral majority "could well exceed our wildest dreams" and "re-create this great nation."[68]

He didn't have far to look. By the early 1970s, conservative author and political activist Phyllis Schlafly was already hard at work mapping an entirely new way to stoke right-wing fear, outrage, and political activism. The Republican Party was solidly supportive of equal rights for women. Both Presidents Nixon and Ford championed the ERA and most leaders were pro-choice, but Schlafly saw an opportunity to change that. As former Republican activist Tanya Melich put it, Schlafly "unearthed the political gold of misogyny."[69]

Phyllis Schlafly was a longtime Republican political activist who aspired to be a leader on national security. She had spent the 1950s agitating against communism,[70] which she believed was the primary threat to the United States. She had backed Barry Goldwater's 1964 presidential campaign, and supported the rightward lurch in the party sparked by Goldwater's candidacy.[71] She found an early modicum of fame in the conservative movement for her 1964 book, "A Choice, Not An Echo," which decried GOP "kingmakers" who she blamed for undermining far-right populism and moderating the party.[72] The self-published book sold a surprising three million copies and helped drive support for Goldwater from the right against the more socially liberal, business-friendly Nelson Rockefeller.[73] [74] Schlafly parlayed her book into a monthly newsletter with a wide-distribution called The Schlafly Report.[75] Despite her reach, she hit walls in trying to position herself in the old boys club of politics.

Schlafly desperately wanted to find a foothold within the Republican Party establishment.[76] Though she was an elected delegate to every Republican National Convention from 1952 onward, she lost elections for both a congressional seat and for the role of president of the National Federation of Republican Women.[77] [78] As the Equal Rights Amendment was gearing up for easy passage, Schlafly's work to establish herself and to force the party to the Right finally gained traction with a subset of male Republicans who wanted to fight the ERA. She finally won an audience on the Right when she was willing to be the face of fighting on "women's issues."[79]

The fight had felt hopeless to these right-wing male electeds. More and more women were working outside of the home. The women's liberation movement focused on creating space for women to achieve economic independence and social parity and appeared to be succeeding in changing minds about the role women could play in society. In 1972, the Equal Rights Amendment — introduced originally in 1923 — passed through Congress and was sent to the states for ratification.[80] Polls showed that three in four Americans supported the ERA.[81]

Schlafly understood, though, that this change was provoking undercurrents of deep discomfort in a society where dominance was organized around heterosexual marriage. The structural reforms towards gender equality gained theoretical support and even popularity. But it was a different story once those reforms manifested in places where men had forever held power — workplaces and, most acutely, in the home.

Researcher Susan Faludi wrote that the feminist movement that grew out of the 1960s had succeeded in shifting norms. Both men and women consistently gave "lip service" to supporting women's equality but, Faludi cautioned, "when the issues change from social justice to personal applications, the consensus crumbled."[82] This wasn't just a policy difference. It was intimate, individual, and it went to the core of masculine identity. If a man could not be assured of success in the workplace due to challenges of newfound freedom for women, how could he possibly remain king of his own castle?

Faludi pointed to social science research that suggested traditional masculine identity is deeply reliant on traditional ideas of femininity. Researchers also found that "violating sex roles" has traditionally had "more severe consequences" for men, and that men often "view even small losses of deference, advantages, or opportunities as large threats."[83] "Maleness in America is not absolutely defined," anthropologist Margaret Mead wrote. "It has to be kept and reearned [sic] every day, and one essential element in the definition is beating women in every game that both sexes play."[84]

The Yankelovich Monitor Survey, which spent decades tracking social attitudes, consistently found that most men held one core definition of masculinity: being a "good provider for his family."[85] The greatest threat to male primacy in the workplace was not actually policies promoting equity. It was expanded reproductive freedom — access to contraception and abortion and a robust cultural conversation about family planning that allowed women to take control of their own lives and created conditions for professional advancement. The pill had become legal for unmarried women in 1972, the year before *Roe*, and more and more women were remaining in the workplace rather than dropping out because of unintended pregnancy.

Schlafly was consumed with containing communism and promoting the United States as a nuclear superpower, but she saw her contemporaries increasingly shaken by the cultural tumult. The milieu in which she lived was concerned that the sexual revolution of the 1960s would be "devastating" to American society.[86] Schlafly could not ignore the growing alarm among her peers that feminism would denigrate their privileged role in society. She was a shrewd operator of politics and culture, and she seized upon the Equal Rights Amendment as the symbol of the angst. As the ERA was sent to the states for what most believed would be a speedy ratification process, Schlafly realized threats to gender norms were now an imminent reality.[87] Suddenly — after years of being patronized and sidelined — Schlafly became sought after by right-leaning GOP leaders as a woman willing to organize women to crusade against other women.

Schlafly knew firsthand about dignity and the loss of it when a financial downturn struck women who believed privilege was their birthright. Her father lost his job in the Great Depression and her mother had to work to support the family.[88] She would go on to become the most notorious opponent of the Equal Rights Amendment, relishing the opportunity to undermine the crown jewel of the second wave feminist movement.[89]

Schlafly launched "STOP ERA" in 1972. "STOP" was an acronym for the very unapologetic "Stop Taking Our Privileges." She founded The Phyllis Schlafly Report to communicate nationwide to housewives like herself about the terrible threat the ERA posed to their way of life.[90] The women involved were overwhelmingly white, church-going and from the rural and suburban middle and upper class. By definition, they had privileges to lose, benefitting by association with the white male Christian power structure. These women quickly embraced Schlafly's core message that the push for equality would erase legal differences between men and women. They even bought her more tenuous message that the ERA would lead to supposed "horrors like 'homosexual marriage,' unisex bathrooms, or women in combat."[91] Soon, she had activated a grassroots army to zealously fight to maintain their privilege at the expense of other women's political, social and economic equity. They cast these other women — often unmarried, single moms, gay women, and women of color — as deserving of shame because of their own life choices.

Weyrich and Falwell took note of Schlafly's political prowess and her ability to organize new voices in the conservative coalition. They didn't dwell on the differences between her public-facing messages about gender equality and their own, still centered on religious freedom and school segregation. They saw the harmony in their ideology and their narratives. Both factions, after all, were warning their audiences that the new buzzwords of equality — whether they were applied to Black people, gay people, or women — were tantamount to attacking your family, your way of life, and your privileged status.

The movement architects had a clear target audience for this message. They had no viable path to gain political dominance with zero support from women. Given the racist underpinnings of the movement, that meant they needed a good portion of white women. Evangelical white women were already primed, since many of them had been involved in the fight against desegregation. White women had always been critical in driving a lot of the behind-the-scenes organizing of the white supremacist movement. "A political platform of family autonomy and parental rights — a kind of white supremacist maternalism" is how Elizabeth Gillespie McRae described this grassroots movement in her book "Mothers of Massive Resistance: White Women and the Politics of White Supremacy."[92]

Schlafly deftly steered these white women towards more public acceptance and folded them into the effort to fight gender parity measures. She never asked them to check their racism at the door. If anything, she told adherents who balked at the racist tendencies of their fellow warriors to swallow their displeasure for the sake of the cause. For her, these issues were two sides of the same coin. As STOP ERA and the Eagle Forum cemented themselves as the new right's "ladies' auxiliary," they found a sphere where they could raise their voices and flex some power without threatening the men in their lives. They used their collective weight to use women's issues to whitewash the racist underbelly of the movement and shore up traditional power systems.[93]

STOP ERA was extremely brand conscious. They knew their value was in the perfect combination of fierce advocacy wrapped in unapologetic traditional femininity. They were known for baking pies and breads to hand out to lawmakers with the slogan, "From the bread makers to the breadwinners." They shamelessly flattered male lawmakers as a core part of the lobbying strategy. There's no way to overstate the impact of Schlafly's work. As the Eagle Forum was getting off the ground, the ERA was sailing toward the victory line and 30 states quickly ratified of the required 38.[94] As the Eagle Forum focused laser-like intensity on the ERA, Schlafly's effort found its legs and progress slowed. Over the next few years, only five more states ratified. Then, four of the original 30 states rescinded their ratification.[95] As the 1979 deadline for ratification arrived, the ERA was three states short of the requirements to become a constitutional amendment.[96]

Schlafly basked in the attention and credit for this stunning defeat. It paved her path to the center of power in the new Radical Right, with stalwarts like Weyrich and Falwell heralding her as an indispensable force.

———

People like Weyrich and Falwell have always drawn political benefit from stoking racial animus to sow cultural discord. This cynical exploitation never stopped, but efforts became more coded in the 1970s as the successes of the Civil Rights Movement showed quickly growing public support for at least the theory of racial equality. So, when the movement architects saw Schlafly's accomplishments, they understood it as a ripe opportunity to add gender concerns to their efforts to defend the preservation of white patriarchal systems of control or, as they called it, "the natural family."

Schlafly's mastery at using identity politics provided a blueprint for the future of the new Radical Right. Maxwell and Shields underscored her influence in "The Long Southern Strategy":

The politicization of these southern white conservative and, more often than not, religious women in opposition to Second-Wave Feminism resuscitated and kept the GOP strategy alive. The cult of southern white womanhood had primed this audience for generations; thus, the anti-feminism rallying cry became as successful as the well-known dog whistles of race and religion. It is, in fact, a bridge between the two.[97]

Schlafly's work was proof of concept. The Evangelicals that Weyrich and Falwell had managed to activate were sensitive to more than just a loss of white supremacy. Weyrich and Falwell were convinced that at a moment when civil rights leaders were making advances and overtly racist appeals were losing their power, they would soft-pedal their racism and persuade more Americans to fear the impact of giving freedom and power to women. Since racism and misogyny have always been tangled in American society, finding the right balance that kept just enough women on board was key to success. And that is where adapting messaging to appeal to fundamentalist religion came in.

As Maxwell and Shields wrote:

> This southern white way of life... is not based solely on white superiority. Rather, it is best viewed as a triptych with religious fundamentalism and patriarchy standing as separate hinged panels that can be folded inward—bent to cover or reinforce white supremacy throughout much of the region's history.[98]

As the Moral Majority was gaining steam in the late '70s, other leaders of the Radical Right caught the wave and set about building their own "women's auxiliary." Moral Majority board member Tim LaHaye— who would later become something of a cult sensation as the author of the apocalyptic Christian series "Left Behind" — encouraged his wife, Beverly, to launch a complementary effort targeting women.[99] In 1978, Beverly founded Concerned Women for America, an organization that still exists today.[100]

By that time, President Jimmy Carter had officially enacted new IRS rules to strip segregation academies of their tax-exempt status for good, capping the decade-long legal and political battle. The age of government-sanctioned segregation was supposed to be over, although the struggle for equality in schools continues to this day. Schlafly's campaign had effectively defeated the ERA by the 1979 deadline for ratification. The architects of the Radical Right found themselves in a conundrum. They knew they could energize a coalition of millions by stoking fear of cultural change and lost privilege, but their pet issues were losing relevance. They needed a new focus, a "hot-button" cultural issue that could channel social conservatism into real political allegiance. They needed an issue that was hot enough to resonate with an energized base but not too hot that it would burn the Republican Party.[101]

In the late seventies, Weyrich joined a conference call for evangelical leaders to debate what could replace segregation as their focus for the next rallying cry of their new movement. A number of ideas were batted around, but none of them were just right. They probed for a hook that triggered a powerful emotional reaction against the cultural changes underway, something that tapped into the deep wells of racism or misogyny without coming off to the public as obviously racist or misogynistic. They wanted to bake their cake, and eat it too. Finally, someone on the end of one of the lines made a fateful suggestion: "How about abortion?"[102]

That singular voice forever changed the landscape of American politics.

Chapter 2
The Tightrope

In the summer of 2012, conservative Republican Rep. Todd Akin held a slight edge over Democratic incumbent Claire McCaskill in his race to take her Missouri Senate seat. Polling from the blog FiveThirtyEight had shifted its prediction for an outcome in his favor.[103] Akin was a well-liked businessman from St. Louis and had beat out several other candidates to win the GOP nomination.[104] He had a long track record of serving in the Missouri state House and represented Missouri in Congress, where he was awarded a 97% rating from the American Conservative Union.[105]

William Todd Akin was also an anti-abortion crusader who routinely promoted anti-choice myths and disinformation. He referred to abortion providers as "terrorists" and bizarrely claimed that doctors performed abortions on women who were not pregnant.[106][107] A former board member of Missouri Right to Life, he'd been arrested eight times over a three-year period in the mid-1980s for trespassing at clinics in Missouri and Illinois.[108][109] Frustrated by stalled progress of the direct action wing of the movement, Akin pivoted to politics. He wore his past activities as a badge of honor, but, as he entered politics, he noticeably adopted a less strident tone and changed his first name from William to Todd.[110] In 1988, Todd Akin won his first state House seat, where he served until he went on to the U.S. House of Representatives in 2000.[111][112] He had a good run in the House before he decided to run against McCaskill for her Senate seat in 2012.

Democrats were nervous. They had lost the House of Representatives two years earlier to the Tea Party revolution.[113][114] olding the Senate was a political necessity for them to have an impact in President Barack Obama's second term, and a victory in Missouri was key. But it didn't look promising. Then, three months before the election, Akin gave what should have been a routine interview to Charles Jaco, an anchor at a local Fox affiliate, and everything changed.

Jaco asked Akin if he believed abortion should be permitted in cases of rape or incest. Akin didn't miss a beat. "If it's a legitimate rape, the female body has ways to try to shut that whole thing down," he said.[115][116] With a singular comment, Akin attacked women on multiple fronts — wielding a discredited anti-choice myth about biology to justify a zero tolerance position on abortion, while also implying that people who get pregnant as a result of rape must be lying about their assault.[117]

Public condemnation was swift and loud. Akin's opponent shot back with the strength of true conviction. "I have a hard time imagining a woman uttering the phrase 'legitimate rape,'" McCaskill said. "It is not something that would ever come out of a woman's mouth, because it is something every woman is fearful of. I think every woman knows someone who has had to deal with sexual assault."[118]

The outrage did not stop at the Missouri borders. The *Washington Post* editorial board declared Akin's comments "loathsome" and leaders from his own party denounced him, some even calling for him to withdraw.[119] [120] National Democrats saw an opportunity to paint the GOP as out of touch to coveted women voters. They held up Akin as the poster child of a party engaged in a "war on women."[121] GOP presidential nominee Mitt Romney perpetuated the perception when he responded to an October debate question about gender parity in Cabinet positions by claiming he had "binders full of women."[122] Juxtaposed against President Obama's signature achievement of healthcare reform and no-cost birth control, the Republicans were appearing at best patronizing and at worst hostile to women.

Akin seemed genuinely bewildered by the response to his comment. In a direct-to-camera message to voters, he issued a weak apology for using the "wrong words" — a sentiment he later rescinded.[123] But even as he back-pedaled in hopes of political salvation, Akin steadfastly stood by the disinformation that women's bodies have a way of preventing pregnancy from rape.[124]

He lost the election by a significant margin, and his gaffe was widely credited with influencing the outcome of the entire cycle.[125] Despite his treatment as an outlier, that same year Indiana Senate candidate Richard Mourdock — running in an open race in a red state after defeating the Republican incumbent in a primary — suggested that pregnancies resulting from rape are "something that God intended to happen."[126]

Both Republicans lost in-reach Senate seats, and their ill-considered words became their political epitaphs. The wide interpretation was that Republicans paid a political price for stating truths steeped in both a misogynistic worldview and a rejection of sound science. This precise rejection of scientific facts would become so pervasive that the term "health disinformation" was coined to categorize it. But in 2012, Akin's ill-fated run seemed at best to be a footnote of modern politics.

In the era of Donald Trump, there's widespread recognition of the Radical Right's use of disinformation, lies, and propaganda to erode democracy, civil discourse and stifle individual freedoms. But Trump is neither the inventor nor the sole proprietor of that strategy. Nor was Todd Akin. Akin's genuine surprise at the response to his comment stemmed from his deep belief in the truth of it, despite mountains of scientific evidence to the contrary.[127] Akin was part of a subset of America's culture that had been taught to actively reject science and instead believe the teachings that, since the 1970s, had been churned out of institutions in the Weyrich camp. And he was far from alone.

By the turn of the millennium, health disinformation was widespread and the federal government was populated with true believers—people like Akin who came up in the wake of the movement architects' decision to center abortion. Akin was one of 215 Republicans and 11 Democrats in Congress who attempted to enshrine the phrase "forcible rape" into federal law.[128] [129] They included the term, inherently suggesting some rape survivors are less deserving, in an abortion measure. One of those who lobbied for the measure restricting access for victims of sexual assault was future Speaker of the House Paul Ryan. While that specific provision was ultimately stripped from the bill, the entire Republican House caucus was on record alongside Akin embracing junk science in their quest to judge rape survivors and deny them abortion care.[130] [131] [132]

Republicans did suffer high-profile losses that fall. Both Akin and Mourdock went down, the Democrats retained control of the Senate, and President Obama beat Romney to hold a second term.[133] But despite the political outcry, none of Akin's fellow 226 co-sponsors abandoned their efforts to limit access to abortion for rape survivors, a fact lost amidst the noise of the election. Far from negatively affecting Paul Ryan, his support for the measure in Congress actually helped him consolidate conservative allies on his march to the speakership.

The lesson for the GOP was that some of their people were just better at messaging, anticipating where the line was, and identifying which buttons to push. Even at the time, it was obvious that Ryan was happy for lesser candidates like Akin to be the public face of the extreme views that were more quietly promoted by the broader Right. Ryan's own equally extreme views were fully embraced by the party leadership and had been for some time.[134]

Despite losses and brand damage, the GOP did not see the need to shift the party's underlying agenda. When Republicans seized control of Congress in 2014 and Ryan became Speaker of the House, they attempted to undercut gains on birth control access and put paid parental leave out of reach. They attached measure after measure restricting abortion access for low income women. The obvious net effect of their efforts was to make life harder for anyone living outside the bounds of what Schlafly and Falwell defined as the natural family. They kept the tip of the spear squarely on women, specifically women who have sex. In retrospect, it's obvious that in the eyes of the party, Akin and Mourdock's sins were rhetorical, not substantive. All they were really guilty of was saying the quiet part loud.

Just four years after Akin and Mourdock imploded, establishment Republicans rallied behind a presidential candidate who bragged about committing sexual assault and was openly anti-science. That candidate, Donald Trump, would take the Radical Right's insidious playbook to new heights, leaning on anti-democratic disinformation and voter suppression efforts while stoking fear and hate to gain the fervent support of the Radical Right's critical base. He taught them how to say the quiet part out loud more effectively.

For many people experiencing whiplash from Donald Trump's election, this transformation seemed like it happened overnight. Some people reported not even recognizing their own country in the aftermath of 2016. But for the architects of the Radical Right, this was a tipping-point moment for which they had been laying the groundwork for decades. In the multidimensional chess that shapes public opinion, the radicals in the party recognized that sustained progress is less about winning each individual election and more about the long game to mainstream transformative ideas.[135]

———

In the 1970s, the Radical Right used fear, stigma, and the threat of lost privilege to generate political fervor. Just as the battle of Bob Jones University's tax status had demonstrated how fears of racial equality could move white, religious voters to the right, Phyllis Schlafly's work to rally white women and Evangelicals against the Equal Rights Amendment showed that feminism could also be a potent boogeyman. Yet neither segregation nor the ERA proved a sustainable issue on their own, and the work of cultivating racism and misogyny as political tools carried significant risks of backlash by a general public who liked to think of themselves as neither.

Falwell, Weyrich, and their co-conspirators knew they were walking a political tightrope and that they needed a symbol, a dog-whistle, to demonstrate to their inner circle of supporters that they were serious about preserving a Christian patriarchal system while presenting their views as just mainstream enough to not imperil their candidates' prospects come elections.

When abortion was suggested to fill this role during that fateful conference call, it seemed an unlikely issue to meet their needs.[136] The American public was overwhelmingly in support of legalized abortion. Through much of the 1970s, before the architects of the movement kicked around this idea, Republicans typically polled as even pro-choice than Democrats. It wasn't until 1988 that Gallup polling began to consistently show Democrats as more pro-choice than Republicans.[137][138][139]

But this crew of movement architects saw something that others didn't. They saw that for all the talk about equality and liberation, many remained uncomfortable with--even threatened by — a new class of women who were unabashedly sexual. Despite the dominant narrative in liberal and media cultures, they saw a growing discomfort about what this loosening of norms and mores meant for them, their understanding of family, and the privilege they believed was their birthright.

They saw a political arena riddled with sexism, where women were underrepresented and largely sidelined in conversations about their own freedoms and bodily autonomy. They saw that the procedure of abortion was largely supported as a solution to an existing problem, but they knew that abortion as a concept encapsulated all sorts of complicated feelings about women, sexual promiscuity, and sin.

In order to effectively politicize their new hobby horse, they knew they had to shift the focus from the women who risked and lost their lives to end pregnancies to the actions of those women that put them in that situation in the first place. Whereas pre-*Roe* consequences of premarital sex might be too harsh, in the story of the Radical Right, abortion allowed these women to get off scot-free for their own irresponsible actions and selfish rejection of motherhood. They bet that by wielding morality as a weapon, they could unearth enough judgement and stigma to buy the silence of the majority who supported legal abortion. The silence was key to success.

Then, by tapping into latent but growing resentment many held for women who were by then actively rejecting rigid sexual mores of chastity, motherhood, or sacrifice, they believed they could expand the Schlafly coalition and bring more people into the fold. This strategy required careful messaging and a complex campaign of disinformation, straight-up lies, coded racism, and misogyny. The fact that data showed limiting family planning and abortion led to entrenched poverty and oppression, especially in Black communities, was not lost on the movement architects.

———

It's fair to say that, in the aftermath of *Roe*, there was a small but vocal constituency that was truly opposed to abortion. Some, mostly Catholic, activists were using a religious lens to campaign against premarital sex, contraception, and abortion. The Roman Catholic Church was always firmly opposed to sex outside of the intention to procreate.[140] It also remained committed to a strict hierarchy of control with men at the top, a belief shared with the new Radical Right movement.

The first March for Life, held in 1974 and attended by approximately 20,000 people, was an early effort to lift up abortion and frame it as a stand-alone organizing theme.[141] [142] The march was the hook for a small number of congressmen to field an anti-abortion constitutional amendment, which failed overwhelmingly.[143] Their effort found zero traction with either party and was never even given a hearing.[144] Sen. Bob Dole became the first high-profile candidate to run an explicitly anti-abortion campaign post-*Roe* in his 1974 reelect and narrowly beat his challenger, a doctor who had performed abortions. The issue was given outsized credit for his win, even though Dole won by a much slimmer margin against Dr. Bill Roy than in his prior race in 1968.[145] [146]

The broader political conversation around abortion was finally jump-started by a relatively unknown freshman member of Congress named Henry Hyde. Hyde was Weyrich's partner in founding ALEC and represented the kind of voter the architects of this new effort hoped to sway with their focus on abortion. Brought up Irish-Catholic, Hyde was raised in a Democratic household in the era of the New Deal, but switched parties in 1952 driven by fears of communism.[147] The year after *Roe*, he ran for Congress as a Republican and won a seat representing the western suburbs of Chicago.[148]

Henry Hyde was one of the first candidates that the Radical Right experimented with throwing its political weight behind. Seeing many Republican candidates "going down the drain in the '74 election," Weyrich started a Political Action Committee (PAC) to help support a handful of conservatives. "We weren't able to save many," Weyrich recounted in a 2005 interview. "We did help some people like Henry Hyde and Bob Kasten."[149] With that support, Weyrich helped launch an early test case of whether the Right really could politicize abortion.

In 1976, Hyde began his one-man congressional crusade to limit the freedoms afforded by *Roe*. Backed by a small number of anti-abortion activists, he proposed an amendment to a standard appropriations bill that would prevent all low-income Medicaid participants from using their insurance to pay for abortion, no matter the reason.[150] His frustration by the lack of public interest in banning abortion was tempered by the daunting public opinion against him. He opted for an incremental approach. "I certainly would like to prevent, if I could legally, anybody having an abortion, a rich woman, a middle-class woman, or a poor woman," he admitted. "Unfortunately, the only vehicle available is the...Medicaid bill."[151] Hyde was well aware of the disparities in rights, in care, and in social and economic outcomes he would create by targeting low income women with his plan. During one congressional debate, Hyde wryly commented: "If rich women want to enjoy their high-priced vices, that is their responsibility."[152]

The debate around the original Hyde Amendment illustrated how a small group of men were able to manipulate the legislative process to move narrative goalposts. Although the goal of the legislation was an incremental approach to end all legal abortion, Hyde's arguments were anything but incremental. He was aggressive and uncompromising, and most of his colleagues were caught off guard, believing that Roe had settled a matter they were not anxious to revisit.

Because the legislature was overwhelmingly dominated by men and the ensuing debate was so unscripted, the episode offered a peek into the dominant attitudes of men in power. Among the Republican lawmakers Hyde rallied to support the measure, this question at hand was not one of medicine, science, or facts. They unabashedly approached it as a question of preference with disregard for public health data. Through the debate, they expressed unfiltered assumptions about women and pregnant people, and any concern for women in the equation was secondary at best.

The testimony from medical professionals that had been crucial to shifting state laws in the late 1960s and early 1970s was completely absent from the Hyde conversation. Nevermind that the Roe decision was actually about doctors' rights and privacy as much as those of pregnant people. Congress refused to allow doctors or researchers to testify, so the ensuing discussion was devoid of data, research, or a medical perspective that could illuminate real-world impacts of the ill-considered policy. This fact did not go unnoticed by Senate Appropriations Committee Chairman Warren G. Magnuson:

This is an amazing thing. Here we are passing on a piece of major legislation on which neither the House nor the Senate committees heard one single witness. We have no figures, we have no facts, we have no medical testimony; we did not hear a single witness on a matter of this grave importance.[153]

There were only 19 women in the House of Representatives at the time and none serving in the Senate.[154] [155] These women and the real-life experience they brought were sidelined throughout the debate.

The House spent a little time on the specific language of exemptions: women facing "severe OR long-lasting physical health damage" versus "severe AND long-lasting physical health damage." The Senate would be torn over this question for longer.[156] But, as The Economist reported in 1977, "House conservatives decided... the damage would have to be permanent" to merit an exception.[157] House Republican Rep. Robert Bauman candidly justified this more severe position, saying "severe and long-lasting can be any number of conditions which would not in any way affect the birth of the child"[158] putting to rest any question about his perception of the primary role of women in this equation.

The men then moved on to discuss a different exception to Hyde's ban on funding for abortion: the cases of rape or incest that would later bury Todd

Akin's career. Young girls were singled out first. House members demanded "forced rape" language be inserted into the amendment as a way to exempt statutory rape from any exceptions.[159] Marital rape did not even merit a mention since the default definition of "rape" in the penal code explicitly stated forced sexual intercourse by a male with a female not his wife.[160] Spousal rape was not a crime in all 50 states until 1993.[161]

The House spent official time airing their fears that conniving women would cry wolf about sexual assault in order to get an abortion. They discarded evidence that false reports of sexual assault are exceedingly rare and underreporting is the norm. Bauman again argued, "The problem you face with rape or incest is that several months later anyone can claim that they have been a victim of this type of attack and it would be almost impossible for anyone to prove that."[162]

Finally, GOP Rep. Robert Michel offered a proposal to end the debate. He argued the bill should include the "forced rape" terminology, and — as an extra precaution — "spell out that the instance of rape or incest must have been reported promptly to a law enforcement agency or public health service."[163]

The women's lives being affected by the measure merited almost no discussion, and there was only passing discussion of how punishing this was to entire classes of low-income women and women of color. Rep. Daniel Flood (D-PA), the longtime chairperson of the House Appropriations Subcommittee on Labor, Health, Education and Welfare, lifted his voice in an exceptional protest, saying, "A vote on this amendment is not a vote against abortion. It is a vote against poor people."[164] But his cries fell on deaf ears and his dissent was quickly quelled by the small group of true believers assembled by Hyde and his team. They had planned for a naysayer and wanted to make a quick example, so the response to Flood was swift, public, and harsh. With no commensurate counter-pressure from a disorganized pro-choice majority, Flood changed his position and voted for the amendment.[165]

Most members of Congress were blindsided by the energy of the small band of Hyde supporters. It didn't help that Congress was still trying to find its footing in a post-*Roe* world on abortion, an issue no one had ever talked much about. The legislators were shaken by the noise of this sanctimonious minority, so they wrongly concluded that the political ground was hostile to reproductive freedom when in fact most Americans had actually accepted that freedom as the norm. The Hyde amendment passed in 1976 by a 34-vote margin.[166]

By all accounts, most felt they had found a good compromise and hoped this would put the issue behind them. Of course, nothing could be further from the truth, but it wouldn't be the first time the majority would hold out an olive branch to a zealous minority who had no intention of stopping. The net effect of this "compromise" cut off millions of American women from a right they had just achieved. It established a baseline in law that accepted putting burdens on rape survivors and requiring doctors to allow pregnant women to reach the brink of death before allowing abortions. It showed that science, data, and research could be discarded in public policy if the conditions were right. Most fundamentally, the debate over the Hyde Amendment offered a snapshot into the views of legislators on the values of women's lives, particularly those who, in their minds, had fallen from grace.

In 1977, Rosie Jimenez became the first woman to die as a direct result of the Hyde Amendment. She was a Texas resident and Medicaid recipient who sought an abortion in Mexico because the amendment blocked her from receiving safe and affordable abortion care in the United States. An investigation by the Centers for Disease Control and Prevention found that her death could be directly attributed to the new policy.[167][168] Henry Hyde flatly rejected the CDC conclusion and called any statements linking Rosie's death to his law "hysterical characterizations."[169] The Right has adopted similar blanket rejections of consequences as their staple response to countless deaths and injuries of women around the world where abortion is illegal. And the term "hysterical" has continued to dog women who raise alarms about attempts to dismantle our rights.

———

Weyrich and Falwell watched Hyde's machinations with keen interest. They were familiar with Catholic doctrine and knew its broad application of the "pro-life" label that included anti-war, anti-poverty, and anti-death penalty stances among anti-abortion and anti-contraception positions.[170] Weyrich, Falwell, Schlafly, and their ilk were not interested in the whole package that fought hunger, supported immigrants, and sought world peace, but they saw a lot of promise in the moniker. Hyde's test-run also provided proof points that underlying cultural attitudes about women, particularly women's sexuality, could be weaponized beyond the Equal Rights Amendment battle.

Critically, Hyde's fight in Congress showed that it was possible to suppress the voices of abortion patients in the debate, those potent stories that so powerfully moved public support for *Roe*. The architects of the Radical Right could see a tenuous path forward, but they knew the broader political and cultural shifts wouldn't take place in the controlled, male-dominated environment of Congressional budgetary debate that had allowed Hyde to flourish. With public opinion and actual science working against them, they needed a way to control the terms of the broader debate. A massive propaganda and disinformation campaign would be required to shift natural compassion away from the pregnant people and to taint women who refused to conform to their rigid norms.

John C. Willke was already finding ways to thread that needle. Willke was widely referred to as a "father of [the] anti-abortion movement," but a more accurate moniker for him is the godfather of anti-abortion disinformation.[171] A physician by trade, Willke rejected science on this subject and chose to focus on building the language and propaganda that would undergird a new movement.[172] His "Handbook on Abortion," co-authored with his wife Barbara in 1971, served to advance ideas that would be crucial to the success of Weyrich and Falwell's future project.[173]

In it, he tackled the movement's thorniest problems head-on and offered key innovations that still define anti-choice messaging today. Willke argued the pregnant person must be erased from the narrative in order to move unobstructed focus onto the embryo or fetus. If women's inconvenient stories of hardship threaten to penetrate that focus, his followers would be trained to deny any hardships and cast doubt on their motives.

Todd Akin's 2012 comment that sparked such phenomenal backlash had its roots in Willke's work. In fact, Willke rushed to defend the embattled candidate forty years later.[174] "This is a traumatic thing — she's, shall we say, she's uptight," Willke theorized about a rape victim to the New York Times in the ensuing debate. "She is frightened, tight, and so on. And sperm, if deposited in her vagina, are less likely to be able to fertilize. The tubes are spastic."[175] The science on this question is clear: the percentage of women who become pregnant by rape is roughly the same as those who do so through consensual intercourse.[176] But scientific rigor was not Willke's concern. His concern was selling an ideology, and he was good at it.

In one messaging guide, Willke instructed: "Words are important. Words are powerful. The words we or the pro-abortion activists use very clearly and frequently shape the value system of those who listen." He issued such directions as: "I suggest you not speak of them 'doing' abortions, but rather of 'committing' abortions. To do so immediately places a cloud or stigma over that abortion being done."[177] The guide also included a long list of terms to use and avoid, for example:

> You should say: assault rape, forcible rape
> You should not say: rape
> Using the word rape alone includes statutory rape, which is intercourse, consensual or otherwise, with a minor. To use assault or forcible also separates it from the more vague and specious terms of marital rape and date rape.
>
> ...
>
> You should say: mother
> You should not say: pregnant woman
> Mother is a much softer word, calling for love and compassion by the reader.
>
> ...

You should say: womb

You should not say: uterus

Womb is a warmer, maternal term. Uterus is coldly medical.[178]

Author Susan Faludi, whose book "Backlash" explored the cultural rejection of feminism through the 1980s, credits Willke with hijacking the feminist claim on rights of women to own their bodies. He cynically applied it to the potential life of female fetuses, who he claimed were being denied their own theoretical rights.[179] Willke focused diligently on humanizing the fetus as a way to move focus from the woman. He suggested using terms like "little guy," no matter how new the pregnancy was, and using phrases like "place of residence" instead of uterus to remove the humanity of the pregnant person.[180]

It's hard to discern where Willke's work crossed the line from unscientific to straight-up disinformation, but much of it falls into the latter category. As documented in The New Republic, Willke dismissed an 1987 American Journal of Obstetrics and Gynecology study concluding that women's health outcomes rose significantly after *Roe* legalized abortion. He similarly ignored all medical consensus when he pushed claims that abortion causes cancer and severe emotional damage. All of these themes became staples for the Right's campaign against abortion.[181]

Willke was hardly shy about what he was doing. He often boasted of his innovations, talking of the difficulty he had convincing people to care only about the fetus and trying to break through a natural allegiance to the woman involved. He spoke to dismantling that barrier by using props and pictures of babies. The images he used were laughably disconnected from the actual gestational stage of the fetus in his story, but he paid that no mind.

But perhaps his most public legacy was the one that later doomed Akin and the GOP's chances of taking the Senate in 2012. In a 1999 article originally published in anti-choice magazine Life Issues Connector, Willke laid out in great detail his baseless argument that pregnancy cannot result from rape:

> Every woman is aware that stress and emotional factors can alter her menstrual cycle. To get and stay pregnant a woman's body must produce a very sophisticated mix of hormones. Hormone production is controlled by a part of the brain that is easily influenced by emotions. **There's no greater emotional trauma that can be experienced by a woman than an assault rape. This can radically upset her possibility of ovulation, fertilization, implantation and even nurturing of a pregnancy.** So what further percentage reduction in pregnancy will this cause? No one knows, but this factor certainly cuts this last figure by at least 50 percent and probably more.[182]

Willke's work to craft new, more fundamentalist anti-choice messaging grew in tandem with the nascent Radical Right. He caught the attention of movement stalwarts in 1976, during Ronald Reagan's first presidential run amidst the Hyde debate. But the partnership never gained real traction until 1980, after the fateful conference pinpointing abortion as the focus of efforts.

The relationship proved to be fruitful for both sides. Weyrich and Falwell would drive almost $15 million in new funding to Willke's organization National Right to Life, and Reagan would repeatedly call on Willke to shore up his alliance with the Religious Right.[183] [184] [185] Willke even later claimed credit for converting then-vice presidential candidate George H.W. Bush — a well-known advocate of family planning — to anti-choice ideology in preparation for the 1980 election.[186] [187] [188]

Willke's keen insight into the ability of words to shape reality was a powerful weapon against a pro-choice movement overly reliant on legal arguments and scientific facts to defend *Roe*. His success in framing the debate and keeping opponents on defense is evident in language that became mainstream in legislative and court battles alike — rhetoric like "abortifacient," "partial-birth abortion," "fetal pain," and "heartbeat" bills. All of these terms fly in the face of medical reality and scientific consensus, but the movement architects knew that if they owned the language, they owned the Story. They were effectively painting a picture — grounded in misinformation and disinformation — to a target audience they needed to win. It was also critically and effectively designed to compel silence from the majority they could never convert.

———

Willke's innovations in anti-choice disinformation and propaganda spawned an entire cottage industry. His tactics became a critical element of the Radical Right's playbook, providing the edge they needed to compete in a political arena where public opinion and science were against them. When facts get in their way, adherents have always been willing to craft alternative realities, even creating their own "science."

In 1991, Willke created an institution solely dedicated to the crafting and dissemination of anti-choice propaganda. He called it the Life Issues Institute and focused efforts on what it called the "confused middle," those who supported the right to access legal abortion but had complicated feelings about the ending of a pregnancy. Through focus groups and polling, the Institute zeroed in on undercutting the deep misgivings these people had about handing over control to politicians in order to elevate their internal emotional conflict.[189] Life Issues knew they had to solve this equation to overcome natural compassion for the woman involved. The Institute was eventually absorbed by Susan B. Anthony List, an organization dedicated to politicizing these messages.[190] [191] Today, SBA List is a key source of anti-choice disinformation, feeding anti-choice candidates, organizations, and publications with a steady stream of propaganda.

SBA List also built its own self-professed "research" arm, Charlotte Lozier Institute, which promotes the junk science that feeds many of the modern Radical Right's disinformation campaigns.[192] Charlotte Lozier coached a small number of far-right true believers and willing charlatans to give a professional face to carefully constructed disinformation and invented claims. A Rewire investigation found that the Charlotte Lozier Institute and other anti-choice research groups rely on a small set of self-proclaimed "experts" who systematically promote junk science in front of state legislatures, at policy conferences, and in the media. A *Rewire.News* report in 2014 found these claims have been "publicly discredited in episodes ranging from lying to the public, presenting false data in scientific journals, and being forced to retract articles that proved to be works of fiction presented as fact."[193]

A prevalent claim these "experts" peddle purports a negative correlation between abortion and mental health. This line of argument was designed to position the movement as one concerned about the women in its crosshairs. Vincent Rue is a legal consultant who invented the bogus illness "Post Abortion Syndrome" in the 1980s. He travels the country to this day testifying before conservative state legislatures that abortion should be banned on the basis of impacts to women's mental health. His claims were reviewed and discounted by the American Psychological Association, among others, yet they persist in being used to influence state-level legislation and taint the national anti-choice debate.[194]

Rue is not the only con artist on the circuit. WECARE founder Priscilla Coleman also promotes claims that abortion is connected to mental illness. Her organization works with a number of discredited or dubiously qualified anti-choice researchers, giving them a voice in legislation and a national profile.[195] David C. Reardon, founder of the Elliot Institute, also latched onto the idea that abortion causes depression. The Elliot Institute pushes pseudo-science created by Rue, Coleman, Reardon, and others to anti-choice protesters and fake women's health clinics. The groups' claims have influenced legislation and been cited at the Supreme Court by former Justice Anthony Kennedy.[196] These are all direct descendants of Wilke's philosophy of shaping narrative to shift reality.

Despite their assertions, the scientific consensus is clear: Abortion is a safe medical procedure, with no significant physical or mental consequences.[197] In fact, it is lack of access to abortion care that threatens harm to women's mental and physical health. The most exhaustive study in the field was published in 2020 by Professor Diana Greene Foster at UCSF. The "turnaway study" showed that women who were denied abortions suffered effects that ranged from anxiety and loss of self esteem all the way to debilitating conditions like eclampsia and death. They were more likely to stay with abusive partners and remain in poverty, and the children they already had were likely to suffer as well.[198]

But the anti-choice movement has refused to let this reality stand in its way. With Willke and his disciples, the Radical Right created infrastructure to construct and promote disinformation on abortion. Alongside climate deniers and tobacco apologists, these efforts paved the way for the acute war on truth that plagues this country and laid a foundation for ongoing efforts to undermine democracy for political gain.

━━━━━

In August 2019, Congress' best-known and most controversial white supremacist, Republican Rep. Steve King from Iowa, defended his plan to implement a total abortion ban with no exceptions. He argued that without rape and incest, human culture might face extinction:

What if we went back through all the family trees and just pulled those people out that were products of rape and incest? Would there be any population of the world left if we did that? Considering all the wars and all the rapes and pillages taken place and whatever happened to culture after society? I know I can't certify that I'm not a part of a product of that.[199]

The outrage was swift, and even members of his own party felt forced to distance themselves. But this comment was consistent with a long line of right-wing thinking. Hyde and Willke, Akin and King; none of these individuals are outliers. They're simply the ones who said the quiet part loud.

Behind closed doors, even more cautious strategists align themselves with extreme views. President of the SBA List, Marjorie Dannenfelser, has argued for the Radical Right to temper their public arguments, but she has not had substantive objection to the core premise. "I agree that the rape exception is abominable," she told the anti-choice LifeSiteNews. "I reject that, but I also know that we've found a sweet spot that we can get common ground on, and it's a place where the country is, and it's a place that we can actually get the legislation through."[200] As *Right Wing Watch* has documented, Dannenfelser also told a conservative talk radio show that she considered a rape exception "'regrettable,' 'just wrong,' and 'completely intellectually dishonest,' but that politicians sometimes require them for 'political' reasons."[201]

Activists like Dannenfelser bring a palatable sheen to the extreme views, and as such serve as a bridge to the more wary GOP establishment. Balancing carefully crafted disinformation and propaganda with a strategic distancing from overtly extreme language is the tightrope that the Radical Right walks. If they get it right, they reap the rewards of a fervent minority and maintain the silence of a passive majority. When they slip off, they get tarred by the Steve

Kings and the Todd Akins among them.

Republican leaders rushed to denounce King, but they were careful to affirm their anti-choice bona fides in doing so. When asked, a spokesperson for Sen. Chuck Grassley (R-IA) emphasized that "Senator Grassley is proudly pro-life. ... It should go without saying that rape and incest are never justified."[202] Sen. Joni Ernst's (R-IA) "spokesman Brendan Conley had similar comments: 'Sen. Ernst is proudly pro-life but it is without question that instances of rape or incest should be condemned.'"[203]

Through the decades since their inception, the anti-choice movement has learned to disguise its intentions and moderate its rhetoric, divorcing style from substance in walking the tightrope to advance its agenda without incurring backlash. They've gently but methodically worked to move the goalposts and normalize their fringe ideas. Even the Akins play a role in softening the ground for more public declarations of extremism. Finding that balance early on required a special kind of messenger. And in the late 1970s, Ronald Reagan emerged as just the front man to prove just how effective this approach could be.

Chapter 3
The Prototype

A Republican Party wanders in the wilderness after losing its grip on power. A charismatic showman with a background in entertainment rises as a potent political force on the strength of his relationships with Radical Right activists. His appeal is rooted less in a set of carefully considered policies than in his persona. As he becomes the surprise front-runner, establishment Republicans recoil — but a new coalition sees opportunity.

Sound familiar? This may sound like the story of the unlikely ascension of Donald Trump, but it is also the story of Ronald Reagan.

Reagan's rise to helm the GOP and win the presidency was the Radical Right's first real success flexing their muscle on the national stage. Reagan was the first candidate to run with their full backing, and the first to run on an overtly anti-abortion platform. Yet, he also exposed the limits the GOP faced in walking the tightrope of pandering to its new far-right factions without frightening more moderate members of its traditional base. Over his eight years in office, Reagan began to model how to politicize abortion and mold the topic into a partisan issue, but his early efforts were halting and imperfect. Reagan's rise showcased a political party in transition — eager to reach for new sources of power, yet still feeling for the guardrails.

As candidate and president, Reagan was clearly aligned philosophically with the emergent Radical Right and committed to maintaining a white male status quo. From early on, though, movement leaders detected his reticence in directly attacking abortion rights. His posture clearly illuminated their work to shift the political risk calculation in doing so, even at the end of Reagan's presidency.

In a 2016 interview, Reagan's close confidant and campaign adviser Stu

Spencer recounted the faithful annual trek Reagan would make to see Falwell. Every year, Falwell would implore the president to take a direct run at *Roe*. On one trip back, Spencer asked whether Reagan was actually considering Falwell's suggestion. The president looked at him and asked, "Stu, do I look insane to you?"[204] Spencer breathed a sigh of relief.

Reagan was all too happy to otherwise prove his loyalty to the agenda of the movement architects. He also rarely, if ever, objected to his friends advancing their goals on their own. The Schlafly/Falwell coalition was able to include explicit opposition to abortion for the first time in the 1980 party platform over the objections of many women in the party. As the nominee, Reagan tacitly granted his approval.[205] He also moved the political norms in more tangible ways. He signed draconian, albeit remote, policies like the Global Gag Rule, denying American aid to any health facility internationally that even spoke the word "abortion."[206] This rule has resulted in decades of untold damage to the poorest women around the world and remains a baseline for the GOP to this day.[207]

But perhaps the most indelible piece of Reagan's legacy was his cementing of the Radical Right's regressive ideology into the mainstream of the GOP. Reagan illustrated throughout his career, his campaign, and his presidency his inherent comfort with appeals grounded in long-established gender and race constructs.[208] [209] A tape released in 2019 of a conversation between Reagan and Nixon provided a proof point for his unabashed racism in reference to United Nations delegates from Tanzania. Reagan's daughter cried when she heard the tapes, and shortly after, the president of the Reagan Presidential Foundation professed surprise and offered a tepid apology.[210] [211] But many members of the Black community were far from surprised. Famed baseball legend Jackie Robinson wrote an opinion piece in 1968 warning the Black community about the negative impact of a Reagan presidency.[212] Meanwhile, his career in Hollywood was powered by his unapologetic machismo and those who worshipped it.

Reagan's intuitive grasp on how to move people allowed him to bring those views front and center in politics through the combination of political theater and coded language required for success in post-civil rights America.[213] Reagan and his advisers embraced the analysis that stoking fears of lost privilege would drive sufficient numbers of men and white women to propel the embattled GOP to electoral victory. For the movement architects, Reagan's candidacy represented their most significant triumph to date.

———

In the years following the Watergate scandal and President Richard Nixon's resignation, the GOP was stuck. The party had lost credibility. The Southern

Strategy had faltered.[214] President Jimmy Carter recaptured a segment of traditional Southern Democrats by leaning into his Southern roots and religious identity.[215] Many who felt the pull of the GOP's new fundamentalist approach were comforted by Carter's authenticity and modesty, and they remained hesitant to identify as Republicans, especially given Nixon's actions.

Maxwell and Shields noted that "though the GOP had taken a sharp right turn on civil rights enforcement in order to attract white southerners, Carter was authentically one of them. And for white southerners, identity, when absent an impending threat, trumped everything."[216] Republican strategists began to worry that their incursion into white, religious Southern voters had only been temporary.

Schlafly's work to vilify the feminist movement was promising, as was Hyde's early attacks on abortion coverage. The combination of efforts exposed a political establishment disorganized on gender issues and apparently disinterested or incapable of mounting a firm defense of reproductive freedom.[217] As Maxwell and Shields concluded, the Radical Right's strategy was coming together: "In order to cross from racial politics to religious politics, they built a bridge on the backs of feminists."[218] Weyrich, Falwell and their allies knew they could seize the strategic vacuum in the GOP if they found the right front man. And so the search began.

Heading into the 1976 election, Ronald Reagan was certainly well known. He was a two-term governor of California and a leading voice of the right wing of the party, but his candidacy for the GOP presidential nomination was considered a long shot at best.[219] Gerald Ford, who had succeeded Nixon as president after his resignation, was considered a lock by the GOP establishment and the best choice to beat Carter.[220] [221] [222] Reagan's popularity seemed strongest among self-identified conservatives and former segregationists, but he hit a pretty low ceiling among other GOP constituencies.[223] The party's intellectual elites didn't take him seriously. They thought his campaign might play well enough in California, where his background as governor and as a Hollywood actor burnished his brand, but saw no way voters across the country would elect a movie star — no matter how handsome — to run the nation.[224]

But not everyone was so dismissive. I.A. Lewis, who ran polling for the *Los Angeles Times,* agreed with conventional wisdom that Carter should beat Reagan by a large margin, but argued that Reagan would upset normal partisan dynamics and create some turbulence for the Democratic coalition.[225]

Reagan narrowly lost to Ford in the 1976 presidential primary, but Lewis' insight was spot on.[226] Reagan's exposure through his acting career combined with his popular radio show gave him an audience and a platform that exceeded most people's expectations.[227] [228] He hit a cultural sweet spot in the moment, as a 1982 *Rolling Stone* profile retroactively pinpointed. Amid a culture change that evoked deep insecurities, the piece noted the crux of

Reagan's appeal:

> Ronald Reagan looks like a 'real man.' He stands up to the commies. He loves rockets. He even dresses up like a cowboy. In every dimension, his political personality embodies the nostalgic idea of masculinity — with an important additional virtue. He looks happy. In an era when men are struggling with their own definition of masculinity, Ronald Reagan seems totally content with his. He's a real man who makes no apologies for it.[229]

A candidate embodying the "nostalgic idea of masculinity," who was not afraid to be a "real man" sparked endless possibility in the minds of Weyrich and Falwell. They had found their guy. They breezed past the fact that Reagan personally signed a high profile bill liberalizing abortion in California as governor.[230] His underlying philosophy was a match and, if anything, Reagan's messy stance on the issue would hopefully tell a story of evolution on the issue that they could compel the Republican Party to mirror. They knew that an ardent conversion would suffice in the minds of a base still coming around to focus on the issue and who loved nothing more than a good redemption story. Reagan had already planted the seeds for the story, stating on record that his decision to sign the bill had been a result of "inexperience."[231] If he was open to adopting their playbook, they reasoned that the moral posturing could be taught.

Overall, the movement strategists saw him as something of a policy blank slate, a politically savvy candidate who shared their worldview of holding fast to the traditional order of society. They thought they could broker a deal: adopt their platform in exchange for their enthusiastic support. Ed McAteer agreed.

Ed McAteer was a manager at Colgate-Palmolive in Memphis for most of his career, and a devout Evangelical for his entire life.[232] He was an early adopter of Falwell's call to arms and left the private sector to pursue politically organizing his fellow fundamentalists, founding the group Religious Roundtable.[233] He talked endlessly to these voters about political remedies for a world awash in sin and moral decay. His laundry list included opposing abortion, but the issue didn't get any more air time than ending pornography, getting prayer in schools, and fighting LGBTQ rights.[234] Even though most of his brethren agreed with his cause in principle, his pursuit to move them to action was slow going. John C. Green, a professor of political science at the University of Akron and expert in religion and politics, later noted, "Reforming this world didn't seem to appeal much to people whose whole goal was to get to the next world."[235]

While McAteer front-loaded his concerns about moral depravity with his church community, like Schlafly, he really believed in the existential threat of godless global communism to the American way of life.[236] He felt it needed to be confronted strongly, and he thought Ronald Reagan was just the man to do it.[237]

McAteer, Weyrich, and Falwell joined forces to test drive Reagan's appeal through Falwell's popular TV show, "The Old Time Gospel Hour."[238] Falwell, duly impressed by Reagan's interpretation of the Book of Revelation, agreed that Reagan offered an opportunity to engage evangelical voters in the world order.[239] The three then founded the powerful Moral Majority to transform their ideas into political power with Reagan's candidacy in mind.[240]

Reagan's obvious commitment to rigid social order resonated deeply with his new friends and was central to his public presentation. Reagan took to the pages of Christian publications, arguing that "the cultural excesses of the Sixties had been an aberration and that it was time to go back to a more traditional way of life."[241] Republican congresswoman Bobbi Fiedler, who rode Reagan's coattails to defeat her opponent on an anti-bussing platform in 1980, wrote that his views were "frozen in time."[242] [243]

Throughout his political career, Reagan had been open about his strong personal beliefs that a woman's place was in the home and that government should not be used to encourage women to consider options beyond the domestic sphere. As political theorist Zillah Eisenstein observed, "antifeminist politics ...was central to Reagan's platform."[244]

As Reagan and his new allies in the Radical Right geared up for his 1980 presidential run, they ensured that gender would become a centerpiece of his pitch to white Evangelicals. He eagerly agreed to reject the Equal Rights Amendment if elected.[245] Then, in a show of deference to the Moral Majority, he pledged to support a constitutional amendment banning abortion nationwide. He even outlined a proposal to force a constitutional convention if the ban failed in Congress.[246] [247] As Ronald Reagan sailed towards the GOP nomination in 1980, a fervent and organized Radical Right overwhelmed the remaining moderates in the party and passed extreme changes to the platform. They dropped support for the ratification of the ERA, added support for the anti-abortion constitutional amendment, and committed to the appointment of federal judges who would uphold those priorities.[248] The movement architects had fully arrived, and an unprepared GOP establishment had a bad case of whiplash.

Within months, the *Washington Post* noted Reagan's growing support from evangelical leaders who by now were full throated in the call to politicize abortion. "After waging war for months against candidates they oppose, antiabortionists are mounting a coordinated effort in support of Ronald Reagan, the most outspoken abortion foe of the remaining presidential hopefuls," it wrote. "The tone of their political effort has switched from predominantly 'anti' various candidates to a heavily pro-Reagan campaign."[249]

The summer of 1980 was a seminal moment for the new movement. McAteer organized the National Affairs Briefing Conference in Dallas, Texas, designed to take the unprecedented step of urging pastors to politicize their pulpits.[250] All the big names were there, from Paul Weyrich to Jerry Falwell, Tim LaHaye to Phyllis Schlafly. Also in attendance was James Robison, a young and charismatic preacher who was mentored by Billy Graham and was one of the most popular television ministers in the late 1970s.[251] [252] [253]

Like movement founder Weyrich, Robison was a committed dominionist who was outraged by the changes taking place in society.[254] He equated the cultural tolerance of the 1960s and 1970s with the downfall of America. Unabashedly outspoken about what he perceived as the evils of homosexuality, he was dumped by the Dallas station that hosted his television program in 1979 amid protests following a particularly hateful sermon.[255] As Robison took the stage that August night in Dallas to open the rally, establishment GOP campaign consultants Ed Meese and Mike Deaver implored Reagan to stay backstage, worried that the direct affiliation would tarnish their candidate.[256]

Reagan ignored these pleas, instead sitting front and center as Robison fired up the crowd. He struck familiar chords by saying, "I really appreciate the fact that I know you are not applauding men tonight. I am convinced that you are applauding the greatest country on the face of this earth, and you want it to remain the greatest country on the face of this earth."[257] Reagan publicly and enthusiastically applauded as Robison proceeded to excoriate communists, gay people, liberals, and anyone or anything else he considered a threat to "traditional family."[258] [259] His handlers sat cringing backstage.

Reagan directly followed Robison and brought down the house with his opening line, "I know you can't endorse me. But...I want you to know that I endorse you."[260] The crowd was enraptured as he proceeded to echo all of their critical concerns, reaching a crescendo when he criticized affirmative action and blasted the IRS for enforcing the rule that penalized segregation academies, affirming Falwell's journey to this moment. Reagan's speech ended with a plea to take action not just in the pews but also at the polls: "If you do not speak your mind and cast your ballots, then who will ... vote to protect the American family and respect its interests in the formulations of public policy?"[261] [262]

Reagan's historic speech made zero mention of abortion, yet no one complained.[263] [264] In fact, the Southern Baptist Convention's Richard Land described the event as "a transformative moment" when "the evangelical involvement in public policy" fully manifested.[265]

Completing a 180 in the GOP on women's equality, the ERA, and abortion access was a massive change to make in just one election cycle. Like Meese and Deavers, many of Reagan's established advisers were concerned that this shift to embrace anti-feminist arguments, and Reagan's full-throated embrace of the ascendant Radical Right, would tank their election strategy. Research at the time showed that many women voters already found Reagan unpalatable, and his advisers worried he'd struggle to find enough support among women to carry the election. [266]

Schlafly's work showed how to mobilize women to stand up for patriarchy and white privilege, but there was no proof her numbers would translate into enough votes to make the electoral math work. Reagan's GOP consultants went into overdrive working to put an approachable face on the GOP's aggressive anti-feminist pivot. They feverishly tried to create photo-ops with women and coached Reagan on updating his vernacular, urging him to drop favored terms like "women's libber" and "ladies" and to replace them with more neutral phrases.[267] They fashioned an anti-feminist Reagan, but one who would still be pro-woman — in an old-fashioned, chivalrous way that glorified traditional roles for white women. That sleight-of-hand was drawn straight from the Schlafly playbook.

It didn't appear to be enough, and the GOP establishment was nervous. With two months to go before the election, the GOP needed a Hail Mary play to convince voters that Reagan wasn't totally anti-woman. The campaign recruited women from the GOP party establishment to defend the Reagan campaign against accusations of sexism. They stood up a new Women's Policy Advisory Board (WPAB) "to advise the campaign on women's issues."[268] The WPAB was staffed with prominent Republican women, many of whom identified as feminists and almost unanimously supported the ERA, affirmative action, and abortion rights — all issues rejected by the Republican Party's new standard-bearer.[269] According to historian Katherine Rymph, the WPAB "made suggestions for policy statements regarding women's issues, advised the campaign on ways to eliminate sexist language from campaign materials and speeches, and encouraged the campaign to engage more female speakers."

Even though the campaign largely ignored the board's suggestions, they still faced almost immediate outrage from the Radical Right for spotlighting women from the party establishment. Scrambling to stay on the tightrope, the campaign created the parallel Family Policy Advisory Board (FPAB) staffed by Schlafly devotees to counterbalance the WPAB.[270] [271]

As the party increasingly turned away from its past support of *Roe* and gender equality, the handful of women who held onto jobs in Republican politics found themselves in a catch-22. Lose their jobs and standing within the party, or protect what privilege they had by helping the party deflect criticism about the rising anti-feminist power structure. Many chose their jobs and social standing over the possibility of true equality. In no time, the women of the campaign's policy advisory board found themselves working to "redefine Republican feminism," as Rymph put it, and dilute the feminist arguments that they and the Republican Party had previously embraced.[272]

The visible betrayal of these white women of gender equality for their own power and privilege left an indelible mark on what was a multicultural feminist movement even before the succesful impact of their campaign to influence undecided women voters was known. The effect of their pursuit of anti-feminist interests to maintain an economic and social order that benefitted them left an indelible impact in the minds of Democratic women of color and consequently bisected the female vote by race.[273]

———

Reagan's victory in the 1980 presidential election was credited to an unprecedented political coalition: a cross-section of newly mobilized evangelical voters, bigoted extremists thrilled by his subtle appeal to misogyny, and traditional Republicans voting their economic interests — including many white women — who accepted his anti-feminist, pro-traditional woman sleight of hand.[274] But the group that got the most attention were the "Reagan Democrats," a subset of working class white men, predominantly in the Rust Belt, who felt that their economic woes coming out of the 1970s were taking a backseat to the demands of other rising Democratic constituencies.[275]

The GOP's anti-feminist pivot was perfectly timed for this group, who were competing with women and people of color for jobs for the first time.[276] In the late 1970s and early 1980s, the economy faltered and went into recession. Men's wages shrank dramatically and numbers of male "breadwinners" fell to new lows.[277] "To some of the men falling back, it certainly looked as if women have done the pushing," Susan Faludi later noted.[278]

Weyrich's new right-wing infrastructure kicked into gear to drive that message home. Any failures of Reagan's corporate-friendly economic policies could be pinned directly on women fighting for gender equity. One Heritage Foundation research fellow later recalled that feminism became the go-to scapegoat. He explained, "In retrospect, I'd have to say they blamed the feminists for an awful lot more than they actually deserved....The feminists certainly didn't have anything to do with disastrous economic policies. But the feminists became this very identifiable target."[279]

Reagan's team worked the blame of feminism into core messaging strategies. Defending his terrible unemployment rate in 1982,[280] Reagan diverted attention from his botched economic policy by saying, "Part of the unemployment is not as much recession as it is the great increase of the people going into the job market, and — ladies, I'm not picking on anyone but — because of the increase in women who are working today."[281]

The plan worked so well that social scientists dubbed Reagan's key audience "Change Resisters," describing them as "disproportionately underemployed, 'resentful,' convinced that they were 'being left behind' by a changing society, and most hostile to feminism."[282]

The scapegoat strategy did not stop with working women. In the heat of the 1980 campaign, Reagan gave a speech at the Neshoba County Fair in Philadelphia, Mississippi.[283] [284] The fair was a familiar stomping ground for segregationist politicians, and the backdrop spoke volumes to both white racists and Black voters.[285] [286] Philadelphia was the site where three civil rights workers, one of whom was Black, were murdered for registering Black voters in 1964. The case and the town were later made famous by the film "Mississippi Burning" depicting the federal agents who took over the investigation after local officials were unable or unwilling to pursue justice.[287] [288] Reagan's speech in Mississippi was a blistering defense of states' rights, a well-known code for Jim Crow to most in the rural South.[289]

Even in his 1976 campaign, Reagan used fabricated stories to stoke racial resentment amid feelings of economic insecurity. He spoke to crowds about people buying steaks with food stamps, and housing projects with swimming pools and cathedral ceilings. He infamously twisted one woman's story of fraud into an indictment of low-income Black women by popularizing the term "welfare queen."[290] The symbol was designed to tap into racist and sexist tropes, as well as to perpetuate the myth that there were legions of single Black mothers ripping off good, hard-working taxpayers to live a life of luxury.

Reagan's attempts to stoke racial animus relied heavily on disinformation, and the tactic worked. He won popular support for his devastating economic policies that slashed housing benefits, aid to children in poverty, and food stamp programs.[291] In a 1981 interview, GOP consultant Lee Atwater described this as an evolved Southern Strategy, outlining the introduction of loaded terms like "states' rights" and "forced busing" to trigger the same responses that had previously only been incited by openly racist epithets.[292]

—————

If the 1980 election was proof of concept for the Radical Right's blueprint to power, it also surfaced its inherent risks. Although Reagan ultimately won the presidential race, his losses among women of color, self-identified feminists, and white women in Northern states were dramatic.[293] [294] The 1980 election was the first time in the history of the country that a partisan gender gap emerged, with Reagan netting 56% of male voters but only 47% of women.[295] It also marked both the end of motions by the GOP toward genuine gender equality and introduced a racial and geographical split among women voters — dynamics that have continued in every subsequent election.[296] Meanwhile, Reagan's budget cuts exacerbated economic pain among women and minority communities, which bore the brunt of his destructive economic program. In his first term, almost five million women and two million families led by women were pushed below the poverty line.[297]

Reagan's view of women continued to dog him into his first years in office. Despite the fact that over two-thirds of American women were in the workforce, women accounted for only 8% of his nominees to federal positions, and were almost exclusively relegated to child care and other family-related fields. Reports of Reagan's patronizing relationship with the few women on his staff began to leak out. According to one person familiar with the new administration, "When they disagreed with him, he called them in private 'pretty aggressive gals'; but when they supported his policies, they became 'good little girls.'"[298]

His image was turning into a real problem. News reports stated, "Reagan's advisers consider his continued lack of support from women to be one of his most persistent and disturbing political problems — a peril that has grown in concert with the impact of women's voting."[299] Presidential aide Lee Atwater warned that the gender gap could be "one of the most severe challenges facing the [Reagan] administration" and "could lock the GOP into permanent minority status."[300]

Almost immediately after the 1980 election, some on Reagan's team began to worry about how to maintain enough women voters to win reelection. In 1981, Reagan pollster Richard Wirthlin and a team of conservative analysts began a systematic research project focused on understanding women's voting preferences.[301] They polled 45,000 American women and concluded that no substantive change was required. The campaign could peel off critical blocs of female voters by doubling down on the efforts to burnish Reagan's shallow "pro-woman" brand.[302]

The strategy focused almost exclusively on optics. Reagan's team invested in elevating GOP women candidates and elected office-holders in the president's travels, taking care to choose ones aligned with his platform. They took extra care to keep the president from attacking female adversaries using gendered terms, instructing him to not refer to Democratic vice presidential candidate Geraldine Ferraro as a woman but instead as a "New York liberal," an epithet they reasoned needed no explanation.[303] White House Deputy Chief of Staff Mike Deaver doggedly pushed his recalcitrant boss into taking pictures when being briefed by women.[304] Other members of his team suggested Reagan issue "special awards for women," advocated for more women to be visibly included on Reagan's Secret Service detail, and called for footage that could be publicized of Reagan speaking in front of female audiences.[305] On top of that, they tried to get more female input on his speeches to cast the president as more compassionate and caring. None of these efforts were designed to affect how Ronald Reagan governed.[306]

While more seasoned GOP operatives struggled to hold together their older, more centrist coalition and win an election, the Radical Right worked to deepen their influence in the Reagan administration. As their power grew, so did their demands. Reagan threw them bones by focusing efforts to limit abortion in tailored ways that might not attract as much mainstream attention. He targeted American Indian reservations, further limiting access for a population of women already largely ignored in mainstream media. He attempted to require minors to notify their parents before getting an abortion, though that effort was ultimately blocked by the courts.[307] In his first year in office, Reagan also led the charge to remove the rape exception in the Hyde Amendment, which was not restored until 1993.[308] Around the tenth anniversary of the *Roe* decision, Reagan released the first book ever written by a sitting president. "Abortion and the Conscience of the Nation" was Reagan's contribution to the propaganda that continues to shape the Radical Right today.[309] In it, he popularized and embraced the language promoted by Weyrich and Willke, using inflammatory phrases like "abortion-on-demand," comparing abortion to slavery, and leveling false claims of infanticide.[310] All of these efforts signaled progress to the Religious Right while minimizing backlash from the primarily white women voters he needed to hold.

Still, movement leaders were dissatisfied. Emboldened by their successes and growing influence, they began to ratchet up their expectations. They found Reagan's support for the promised anti-abortion constitutional amendment tepid and when it failed, they grumbled that he never really tried.[311][312] The nomination of C. Everett Koop, the co-creator of an anti-abortion propaganda series "Whatever Happened to the Human Race?" as Surgeon General also fell short of expectations.[313][314] Koop's steadfast belief that abortion was a moral issue, not a political one, meant he resisted pleas to use his prestigious platform to advance disinformation to attack abortion.[315]

The Radical Right was also concerned about Reagan's female appointments. Early in his first term, establishment GOP advisers pushed Reagan to put Elizabeth Dole in charge of the Office of Public Liaison. Then in 1983, she was appointed as the first-ever female secretary of transportation.[316] Former Republican Rep. Margaret Heckler of Massachusetts was also tapped by the Reagan administration to be secretary of Health and Human Services.[317] Radical Right leaders began to gripe that Reagan had appointed "aggressive feminists" to high positions.[318]

Fissures really surfaced with Reagan's 1981 nomination of Sandra Day O'Connor, who would become the first female Supreme Court justice.[319] The president's advisers argued convincingly that this move alone would alleviate the perception that his administration was anti-woman and shore up female votes in 1984.[320] The Religious Roundtable set was not pleased. Despite Reagan's repeated assurances that he trusted O'Connor's positions on abortion and the Equal Rights Amendment, they called her nomination a direct rebuke of the GOP platform and of Reagan's promises.[321] They mounted a furious lobbying campaign to block her nomination,[322] but O'Connor was confirmed unanimously by the Senate.[323]

The movement had reached its ceiling. In order to advance, they needed to grow more power.

———

Reagan and George H.W. Bush went on to handily beat the Democratic ticket of Walter Mondale and Geraldine Ferraro in the 1984 presidential election. Despite their frustrations, the Radical Right had a discernible impact on the outcome. A majority of both men and women voted for the Republican ticket, but the Republican votes came almost exclusively from the white women they had targeted. Black voters overwhelmingly rejected the GOP with approximately 90% in favor of the Democratic ticket.[324] Reagan had successfully politicized the Schlafly play. He was able to appeal to the key segment of white women in the South, many of whom feared the "feminist" label and refused to risk what privilege they had. As Maxwell and Shields documented, many white Southern women were lured by Schlafly's type of "masked misogyny, which served to protect their privilege whether real or aspirational."[325]

The strategy was more than sufficient to hold evangelical voters' allegiance to the GOP. Despite their leaders' frustrations with the president, the alternatives seemed worse. According to Maxwell and Shields, "The transformation of evangelical fundamentalists from politically inactive to a 66 percent self-reported turnout rate in 1984 remains one of the most radical shifts in modern American politics. Nearly three-fourths of those voters chose Ronald Reagan despite the fact that only half claimed a Republican affiliation."[326]

———

Just a few years before Reagan's election, what would become known as the anti-choice movement had been little more than an artificial construct, an invention of right-wing extremists desperate for a way to keep evangelical voters motivated in the wake of the Civil Rights Movement of the 1960s. Now, a powerful Radical Right with a tactical focus on abortion could credibly claim responsibility for the elevation, election, and strategic direction of a two-term United States president. Over the eight years of Ronald Reagan's presidency, this group consolidated its power and, in doing so, undermined civil rights, stood in the way of economic opportunity for Black people, and undermined the gains made by the 1970s feminist movement. As Reagan prepared to leave office, they held more political power than ever, but they were far from satisfied.

Evangelical leader Pat Robertson's failed presidential run in 1988 reinforced what the polls consistently showed — the movement lacked enough popular appeal to stand on its own.[327] It had to settle on increased dominance within the GOP. But the movement rank and file had also become an indispensable part of the GOP coalition. Republican politicians who followed in Reagan's footsteps were required to prove their loyalty now in exchange for public support. The mutually reinforcing dynamic created a feedback loop that kept moving the GOP right.[328]

After George H. W. Bush was tapped to be Reagan's running mate in 1980, Willke did pay a visit to Bush as he later boasted. Describing a 1980 conversation at the Republican campaign headquarters, Willke recalled saying: "Well, Mr. Bush, you're the running mate of our favorite person and we'd like to like you folks. But I said it occurs to me that you've had a pro-abortion position."[329] Willke recalled offering to give Bush "a full briefing" on the Radical Right's priorities and issued a stern incentive to fall in line. "Look, we're the National Pro-Life group and you'll need every one of us to get elected," Willke said, continuing:

> I then [arranged it] so that I'd spend the morning with him, and then we'd invite some other pro-life people in for the afternoon...I brought my slide projector, put it on a coffee table between the two of us and it took me at least two and half hours to go through that slide set. Barbara Bush was sitting over there in the other room about ten feet away knitting and listening. When it was over, Barbara served us some little stuff for lunch. Over lunch then, I said, 'Now, Mr. Bush, now I'm going to ask you where are you on our issue?' He sat back and he said in effect, 'When I came in here this morning, I was not on your side, but I think you've changed my mind.' He said, 'I'll go with you folks on an amendment to reverse that Supreme Court decision and send it back to the states where it used to be.'"[330] [331]

For aspiring Republican figures, a new threshold had been established to unlock support. Rank and file Republicans continued to support abortion access and reproductive freedom, but candidates who did not relish going to war to limit abortion and contraception were rapidly drowned out. The die had been cast.

———

Now, over forty years after the Radical Right's initial rise, anti-choice orthodoxy has become a critical credential not just for candidates, but for anyone aspiring to hold a position of influence within the GOP or the Right. An arms race has emerged on who can be the most fervent basher of abortion rights. When studiously anti-choice Newt Gingrich emerged from retirement to run for president in 2012, he was almost immediately attacked by competitor Michelle Bachmann, who claimed that Gingrich failed to deliver anti-choice priorities as House speaker in the 1990s.[332] It's a race to the bottom we saw again as states raced to criminalize abortion in 2019.

The litmus test established through Reagan has even seeped into right-wing media. Nothing shows how sacred the anti-abortion creed is than the contrasting career paths of far-right pundits Tomi Lahren and Ben Shapiro. Lahren, a young commentator for *The Blaze* — a platform founded by Glenn Beck — seemed unstoppable in early 2017. Her videos shredding liberals and their policies were lighting up right-wing corners of the internet, and her unyielding defenses of President Trump made her a go-to on the mainstream media circuit.

Then one morning on ABC's "The View," Lahren suggested that the GOP's laser-like focus on ending legal abortion was in conflict with her own commitment to limited government. Almost overnight, she was excommunicated from the right-wing media club. Her mentor Glenn Beck immediately mocked her on-air, and her contracts were canceled despite her millions of followers on social media.[333] The damage was lasting. Lahren was relegated to Fox Nation, Fox News' online streaming service.[334] It was a tremendously public and sudden fall from grace.

Then, there's Ben Shapiro. A right-wing prodigy, Shapiro had a nationally syndicated column by the time he was 17 and published two books by the age of 21.[335] Though not initially known for espousing anti-choice viewpoints, he was savvy about the priorities in the landscape he aspired to occupy. He gave his full-throated support to the Radical Right orthodoxy of banning abortion even in cases of rape and incest, only making an exception for imminent death of the woman.[336] His career soared as he was lifted up by the vast right-wing infrastructure, and he is currently one of the most sought-after right-wing pundits in the world. Shapiro was even the keynote speaker at the 2019 March for Life.[337]

―――――

The threshold that was established was profound, but so was the disappointment among the Right when Reagan failed to meet it. The growing ranks of true believers were frustrated, while the movement architects were emboldened and craving more influence. As Willke's prolific abortion propaganda saturated the information environment of the Right, followers saw more lip service than action on an issue they were told was of monumental importance. The leaders who primarily sought out abortion as a rhetorical and tactical device to advance their broader agenda grappled with mainstream Americans, who stubbornly clung to the belief that politicians shouldn't decide what to do in a matter as personal as pregnancy. The political calculus was still not on their side. Instead of giving up, the leaders made a fateful decision to double down.

Willke had taken over the National Right to Life Committee in 1980.[338] From his position at NRLC, he worked with other associated groups to pump up the volume on anti-abortion propaganda and disinformation. He partnered with Bernard Nathanson in 1984 to promote a film called "The Silent Scream," which claimed to depict the experience of abortion from the fetus' perspective.[339] [340] Nathanson was a convert to the anti-choice cause who was previously an OB-GYN who performed abortions and even an attendee to the conference at which NARAL Pro-Choice America was founded.[341] The film was widely panned by medical professionals as having no grounding in science.[342]

Despite that inconvenient reality, Jerry Falwell premiered it on his television show.[343] Excerpts were then shown on major networks more than three times over the next month. Reagan invited his friends on the Right to a White House screening and remarked afterward that every member of Congress should view the film.[344] While the movement leaders claimed the film inspired many to convert to its cause, there's no evidence to prove that. What does seem clear, however, is that it inspired the converted to even higher levels of determination.

Cue Randall Terry, a disillusioned and relatively unknown activist who became convinced that political pressure was not sufficient to end what he called the scourge of abortion. In 1986, Terry founded his own group named Operation Rescue and christened it with the motto "If abortion is murder, then act like it."[345] What followed would permanently change the face of the anti-choice right in the United States.

Chapter 4
The Visionaries

On October 23, 1998, Dr. Barnett Slepian returned to his home in Amherst, New York, after offering prayers in memorial to his late father at a synagogue nearby.[346] As he stood in the kitchen chatting with his wife and sons, a sniper's bullet shattered the kitchen window, tearing through his body.[347] He died a few hours later.[348]

Slepian was an OB-GYN who also provided abortions to women in the greater Rochester-Buffalo area, many from working class backgrounds.[349] He had been a frequent target of extremists in the Radical Right coalition.[350] His wife Lynne, a nurse, had forwarded a threat to the local police earlier that day.[351] When news spread that a sniper had shot Slepian from the woods behind his house, no one doubted that it was an assasination for his work as an abortion provider. Slepian's murder capped a violent decade in which six Americans who worked at abortion clinics had been murdered in cold blood.[352] Clinics all over the country had been terrorized by countless instances of arson and vandalism.[353] Staff and patients alike had been harassed, bullied and intimidated.[354]

In the wake of Slepian's murder, some leaders on the Right called for calm and a ratcheting down of rhetoric, but not Randall Terry's Operation Rescue.[355] The group urged supporters to take to the streets in rallies nationwide, calling pleas for nonviolence a "pitiful philosophy and vision." Flip Benham, who would later take over the helm of the organization, wrote, "Mr. Barnett Slepian had murdered thousands of baby boys and girls and last night was murdered himself. Everybody wants to point the finger at someone else, but until the finger is pointed in the right direction, we are in store for more bloodshed in the streets — the likes of which will sicken even the sturdiest among us."[356]

The country was stunned and terrified. Twenty years after the architects of the Radical Right came up with the plan to weaponize abortion for political gain, they had lost control of their movement. Their plan had worked too well. The extremists they created were threatening to upend their hard-won gains through their terror campaign and erase hard-won gains in their political influence.

———

The Reagan years had mostly felt like a political home run to the architects of the Radical Right. Their ideas had dominated the 1980 and 1984 elections, and their influence in the White House had grown steadily. Though they had failed to force sweeping action to restrict access to abortion, they had demonstrated effectively politicizing the issue and stirring up grassroots anger to bolster their influence. Extreme groups like Operation Rescue began to crop up and push limits on the ground, but were still very fringe within the growing coalition.[357]

Meanwhile, the GOP establishment was feeling nervous about their odds going into 1988. Despite Reagan's popularity, no party had won three consecutive terms in the White House since 1948.[358] No question the Radical Right had brought new energy to the Republican Party, but their influence meant ever higher demands of Republican leaders. The tense detente between the factions threatened to unravel as a new election approached.

Despite Willke's overtures, movement leaders still had an inherent distrust of Reagan's vice president and assumed successor, George H.W. Bush. He might have sufficed for the second slot on the ticket, but vying for president was a different thing altogether. From the beginning of George H.W. Bush's run, the Radical Right treated him more as a political opportunist than a true believer in the cause. Plus, despite his public profile as a Texas oilman, Bush was widely viewed as an Ivy League-educated elite who summered in Kennebunkport, Maine.[359] He offered none of the populist swagger of his predecessor and showed an independent streak when it came to governing. Bush was a strong old-school conservative, but he had broken ranks early with the emerging Evangelical leadership by overtly supporting both birth control and the Civil Rights Act.[360][361] Bush moved to the right as vice president, even endorsing the Human Life Amendment — the constitutional amendment that had become the litmus test under Reagan.[362] Still, the movement's leaders were unconvinced and decided to run one of their own against him in the Republican primary. They wanted to fully occupy the power and momentum they had gained during the Reagan years, and they chose movement godfather Pat Robertson to be their standard bearer.

Robertson was the founder of the Christian Broadcasting Network and host of the popular show The 700 Club which intermixed religious and political content in just the way Falwell and Weyrich had prescribed.[363] Robertson took to the airwaves to garner support and succeeded in getting 3 million followers to commit to him before even launching his campaign.[364] Robertson campaigned on the platform pushed by the Moral Majority and emphasized the decay of American culture through the erosion of family values, using all of the code words that had activated and inspired the early movement.[365] He surprised most Republicans by finishing second in the Iowa primary, behind Kansas Sen. Bob Dole but ahead of Bush. The presumed nominee came in a distant third.[366][367] Robertson faltered in the next contest in New Hampshire and never regained his footing, but his early strength as a long-shot candidate made a deep impression on a party still grappling to articulate its new identity.[368]

Bush worked with right-wing commentator Doug Wead to develop his own strategy to convince evangelical voters to not sit the election out. Dubbed the "Red Memo," it included a list of 200 must-win evangelical leaders. The previously pro-choice Bush reversed his position.[369] He consolidated his lead as the establishment money and infrastructure gave him an advantage in many state primaries. He honed a message centered on continuing Reagan's policies but also presented a "kinder and gentler" face to win those rankled by the radical turn of the Republican base and Reagan's pandering to them.[370][371] Once again, some GOP leaders felt the tension of the tightrope. Bush's commitment to what he considered a more civil debate may have comforted moderates, but it played into the skepticism of the party's new base, a constituency operatives knew they needed. This delicate balance was front of mind going into the Republican National Convention in 1988. Taking the stage in Louisiana, Bush was careful to hit right-wing talking points in his keynote speech, but made a lone, single reference to "abortion."[372] Like Reagan before him, though, he carried a platform which committed the party to banning abortion with no exceptions at all.[373]

Bush surprised many by further feinting right when he chose his running mate. Dan Quayle was a young, attractive and deeply conservative second-term senator from Indiana who had the potential to bridge between the concerns of the Radical Right and the energy of young Republicans who had joined the party in support of Reagan.[374] Over the course of his tenure, Quayle would become known for stoking the fires of the culture wars with remarks defending traditional family structure. He attacked a popular television show, Murphy Brown, for portraying single motherhood in a favorable light and called homosexuality a "choice" — the "wrong choice."[375][376] His far-right positions were calming to a nervous radical base and he created a sense of unity across the party by consistently attacking the "liberal" Democratic ticket of Michael Dukakis and Lloyd Bentsen.[377][378]

Still, the Democrats led in the polls coming out of the conventions in

1988.[379] Bush's outward commitment to more civil politics crumbled as his team — led by Lee Atwater and with key input from future chairperson of not-yet-formed Fox News Roger Ailes — went back to the same old toxic and dirty well to give its candidate the edge.[380] That fall, the campaign launched the infamous Willie Horton ad, using the image of a Black convicted murderer who committed additional violent crimes after a weekend prison furlough that was part of a Massachusetts program. They once again used racial tensions to paint Dukakis as more concerned with his liberal principles than with the safety of good, law-abiding American citizens.[381] The ad was a turning point: Bush and Quayle won by a landslide.[382]

———

The movement architects now had enough power to demand fealty from even the top of the party, but they fell short of the necessary influence to field their own candidates or demand follow through on key components of their agenda. Access to abortion and contraception simply continued to hold too much popular support to attack head on, and other pieces of the puzzle were failing to get maximum traction as a result. They knew they needed more credibility in the elite echelons of DC, so they set out to strengthen a wide-reaching network of institutions built around their ideology to lock in their influence in Washington and ensure they would always punch above their weight.

Weyrich's Heritage Foundation continued to be a crucial piece of that puzzle. It had volumes of policy proposals waiting for Ronald Reagan on Inauguration Day in 1981, and was able to control much of the policy of the Reagan administration.[383] Heritage later trumpeted that nearly two-thirds of its recommendations — mostly on the core issues of ending affirmative action and enacting policies favoring the rich — were moved by the administration.[384] Upon leaving office, Reagan reflected that Heritage was a "vital force" in Washington.[385]

Hyper aware of the power of theater in politics and wanting to cement the perception of their power in the public mind, Falwell and Weyrich declared their movement a success in 1989 by officially shuttering Moral Majority, claiming that it had achieved its stated mission.[386] They turned their attention to their growing web of remaining institutions as they entered a new phase in their quest for power.

Their long game had three strategic prongs: First, they would erode legal precedent and judicial incentives and ultimately take the Supreme Court for right-wing adherents. Second, they would utilize state legislatures to normalize unpalatable ideas. Finally and above all, they would continue toward gaining national power over the politics and messaging of the right. They knew completing their plan might take decades, but they were prepared.

The quietest, though ultimately the most influential, prong of this strategy was the Radical Right's all-out assault against the independent judiciary.

In the early Reagan years, Weyrich and Falwell knew they could not solely rely on fickle politicians to implement their plan on a national scale. They didn't have public opinion on their side — certainly not on legal abortion nor on other elements of the plan designed to maintain their privilege and power. In order to implement their anti-democratic policy agenda and political philosophy, they needed the influence and power of a court system impervious to the will of the voters. In that pursuit, an institution named the Federalist Society became their main vehicle.

In 1982, a group of conservative students and professors gathered over a weekend at Yale Law School giddy with the opportunity offered by Reagan's presidency. They spent the time discussing the perils of federalism, decrying the cultural influence of coastal elites, and listening to speakers who excoriated everything from "New Deal" politics to the legalization of abortion and its impact on "acceptable sexual behavior."[387] This relatively small crew of around two hundred began the process of building a language and culture around constitutional originalism, a designed approach to interpreting the Constitution very narrowly based on what the Framers – all men, all white, all Christian – supposedly meant at the time they wrote it.[388] [389] They named the new group the Federalist Society, as a bit of an inside joke. One of the organizers wrote to invite future Supreme Court nominee Robert Bork to help them, saying "...our group out here settled on Federalist Society as a name, which I suppose makes up in euphony what it lacks in accuracy. If you have any brilliant ideas for a better name, however, that would be splendid."[390]

Legal scholars from Bork to future Solicitor General Ted Olson and future Supreme Court Justice Antonin Scalia — then a law professor just months away from his first federal judgeship — spent the weekend deep in conversation with adoring students. They were all convinced that there was a desperate need for an antidote to what they believed was insidious left-wing bias in law schools. One of the student organizers, Steven Calabresi, recalled that "part of Reagan's policy was to build up forces in battleground nations in order to help topple enemy regimes, and I thought of us as kind of the same equivalent in law schools."[391]

The weekend was a smashing success, with one prominent attendee comparing it to Woodstock for right-wing legal activists.[392] The attendees left convinced that they were a silent majority, despite all evidence to the contrary. They believed that if they could make it socially permissible, many more students on college campuses would come out against liberalism. They emerged from that weekend energized to build the Federalist Society, a new effort to train and promote conservative-minded lawyers into prominent positions, with an eye toward installing far-right judges. Backed by a who's who of right-wing money, the fledgling group quickly grew from a handful of grassroots chapters on university campuses into a million-dollar organization with headquarters in Washington, D.C., and at least 75 campus affiliates.[393] [394] One of its initial backers was the Olin Foundation, the force behind the establishment of business-friendly law and economics programs at law schools throughout the country.[395]

The Federalist Society scoped out the legal aspect of Falwell and Weyrich's new strategy, and it found that abortion proved to be an excellent litmus test for likely members of the Radical Right.[396] It turned out that young and ambitious legal minds who held an antipathy to *Roe v. Wade* were far more likely to also adhere to the broader philosophy and policy preferences of their movement. As its leaders built their cohort of up-and-coming legal minds, the expression of hostility toward abortion from the prospects was an excellent signifier that they were on board with the full agenda to assert control and maintain the status quo of power.

Edwin Meese, counselor to President Reagan, hired many "Federalists," as they came to call themselves.[397] [398] Other GOP operatives helped young Federalist Society lawyers just graduating from law school to find jobs. The movement was riding high when Chief Justice Warren Burger informed Reagan of his intent to retire in 1986. Reagan, in his second term with no reelection to plan for and chastened by the backlash to his O'Connor nomination, did two things: first, he moved to elevate right-wing ideologue William Rehnquist to occupy the position of Chief Justice. Then, he nominated Federalist Society superstar Antonin Scalia to replace Rehnquist.[399]

The fight over Rehnquist's ascension was bitter and divided. He had served on the Court since 1972, having been nominated by Nixon.[400] Rehnquist was a stalwart conservative, cut from the same cloth as Weyrich. As a clerk for the Supreme Court he wrote a memo arguing against mandated school desegregation as the Court considered *Brown vs. Board of Education*.[401] He consistently argued for prayer in school and capital punishment, and against equal rights extending to gender and abortion rights — dissenting in the *Roe* case. His ascension was an affront to the many causes and issues that Democrats had come to champion and many fought his nomination bitterly.[402] A witness testified to Rehnquist's efforts to suppress minority voting in the early 1960s and, in a heated argument, Senator Strom Thurmond overruled requests of Ted Kennedy and others demanding more transparency and fact-finding.[403] Rehnquist was finally confirmed by a count of 65-33, and the Democratic holdouts were defeated.[404]

They were also exhausted. They voted to confirm Scalia on the same day as the vote on Rehnquist. The Democrats had little fight left in them and had spent all their political capital. Besides, the junior nominee was relatively unknown outside of his own conservative legal circles, without an established paper trail on hot button issues — a profile that became a staple of Federalist nominees.[405] Scalia was confirmed unanimously by the Senate[406] and went on to be one of the most right-wing Justices in the history of the Court, upending norms by using oral arguments as political theater and writing scathing dissents in cases where he was outnumbered.

The following year, Justice Lewis Powell — of the infamous Powell memo — announced his intention to step down, giving the president yet another opportunity to shape the Court. Reagan drew again from that same well, nominating Federalist Society founding father Robert Bork.[407] The man who had used that original conference to decry "the gentrification of the Constitution" and to claim states should be able to ban abortion and define "acceptable sexual behavior" was up.[408] The new legions of Federalists were ecstatic by the possibility of having two of their own on the Supreme Court.

But Democrats and progressives were not going to be caught flat footed again. Opposition to Bork's nomination came fast and hard from civil rights and women's groups. Sen. Ted Kennedy from Massachusetts, who led the opposition, responded to the nomination by saying:

> Robert Bork's America is a land in which women would be forced into back-alley abortions, blacks would sit at segregated lunch counters, rogue police could break down citizens' doors in midnight raids, schoolchildren could not be taught about evolution, writers and artists could be censored at the whim of the Government, and the doors of the Federal courts would be shut on the fingers of millions of citizens for whom the judiciary is — and is often the only — protector of the individual rights that are the heart of our democracy ... President Reagan is still our president. But he should not be able to reach out from the muck of Irangate, reach into the muck of Watergate and impose his reactionary vision of the Constitution on the Supreme Court and the next generation of Americans. No justice would be better than this injustice.[409]

The extreme ideology on display at Bork's initial Federalist speech came back to haunt him in the lengthy confirmation battle. Bork's nomination was defeated in a bipartisan vote after months of bitter fighting.[410] The seat ultimately went to Justice Anthony Kennedy in 1988.[411] The Federalists were enraged and took a solemn vow to never let one of their people be sunk again.[412]

Other groups were also hard at work using the law and the courts to tilt culture in the direction of the Radical Right's goals. In 1990, Christian televangelist Pat Robertson created the American Center for Law and Justice (ACLJ) specifically to go head-to-head with the liberal American Civil Liberties Union.[413] ACLJ held a stable of attorneys ready to jump into high-profile battles worldwide focused on its version of family values.[414] The organization, today led by Donald Trump's personal attorney Jay Sekulow, has fought changes to the Kenyan Constitution that would allow abortion, supported the government of Zimbabwe in its effort to criminalize homosexuality, and, closer to home, effectively blocked the construction of an Islamic cultural center near the World Trade Center Memorial.[415] [416] [417]

In 1993, prominent evangelical Christian ministries stood up the Alliance Defending Freedom (ADF) to advance "religious freedom, sanctity of life, and marriage and family"[418] through legal advocacy and funding court cases that tested liberal precedent.[419] [420] In 1994, a Catholic lawyer named Kevin J. "Seamus" Hasson used seed money from the Knights of Columbus to round out these efforts with the Becket Fund, a non-profit law firm solely devoted to promoting "religious liberty."[421] All of these groups shared a fundamental belief that their way of life was under attack and aimed to use the courts to impose a traditionalist, Christian ideology on the American public, echoing the demands for "religious liberty" that the Radical Right had first tested in its pro-segregation work of the 1960s.

They've joined in common cause to choose a series of high profile cases they believed would cement the idea that liberal reforms around civil rights and gender equity amounted to an attack on traditional religion. In California, ACLJ and its allies aggressively defended Proposition 8, the anti-gay ballot measure designed to ban same-sex marriage in the state.[422] [423] Their rhetoric presented out-of-touch elites trying to foist a liberal agenda on the rest of the nation. In 2018, Alliance Defending Freedom advocated in the Supreme Court case *Masterpiece Cakeshop v. Colorado Civil Rights Commission*, which dealt with religious business owners' ability to refuse service to people based on their sexual orientation case, for similar reasons.[424] [425]

Perhaps the feather in the cap of the movement architects — some of whom didn't live to see the day — was their victory in the 2014 Hobby Lobby Supreme Court case. President Obama's Affordable Care Act had mandated a long overdue reform that birth control be covered by insurance at no extra cost to the employee. The owners of the craft supply chain Hobby Lobby sought to deny their employees this contraceptive coverage, using their go-to claim that it violated their religious beliefs.[426] Core to the plaintiff case was the claim that the owners of Hobby Lobby believed that some forms of contraception were "abortifacients."[427] This term was straight out of John Willke's propaganda playbook. It suggested, with no grounding in medical fact, that birth control was tantamount to abortion.[428][429] In a hotly contested 5-4 decision, the court ruled for Hobby Lobby, opening the door to the erosion of all sorts of gains in the name of moral objection. Tellingly, the court's majority wrote that the fact that the birth control did not actually cause abortions was irrelevant in this context. For a violation of religious liberty to occur, the plaintiff must only believe that it could happen.[430] Four of the five justices that ruled in Hobby Lobby's favor had Federalist Society ties.[431]

The Hobby Lobby case was a massive triumph for the Radical Right, underscoring the effectiveness of the mutually reinforcing strategies. The movement had effectively used abortion as a Trojan horse to move the goal posts, limit access to contraception, and enshrine disinformation into the legal canon. For them, it was icing on the cake that the victory undercut the ACA, a crowning achievement for the much-loathed Obama administration. They had effectively reversed one of the most significant national steps forward for gender equity in decades.

———

Capturing the courts could help blunt potential electoral impacts for carrying an unpopular agenda, but a conservative judiciary would be useless without the right docket to review. So the second prong of the leaders' plan targeted the states, advancing conservative priorities quickly through the state legislatures where more extreme legislators operated with relatively little attention. There, they could pass legislation that — when inevitably challenged — would serve the courts strategic cases to cement gains.

Americans United for Life (AUL) was founded in 1971 to advocate against a plethora of advances it felt undermined a fundamentalist biblical view of life. They focused on abortion, embryonic stem cell research, death with dignity efforts, contraception, and what it deemed to be unnatural methods of child bearing, including in vitro fertilization.[432][433][434] AUL co-evolved and sometimes overlapped in the early days with its counterpart ALEC, the similar organization spawned by Weyrich to focus on a right-wing corporate agenda.

While clear on its ideology, AUL had initially cast about for a clear mission and role in the emerging movement. It rose in defense of the Hyde Amendment as it met court challenges in the late 1970s and found its niche in advancing state legislative efforts and strategically countering legal attacks.[435] The general public was mostly ignorant of the nuances of the Hyde Amendment. The media establishment still treated women's issues as a sideshow when a Medicaid recipient in New York named Cora McRae brought the case against Hyde. AUL saw opportunity to publicize the case in ways that cemented right-wing narratives in the legal canon and — by virtue of being largely uncontested — in the common understanding of abortion rights.

When the Supreme Court returned a 5-4 decision in the 1980 case *Harris v. McRae* siding with Hyde supporters, it affirmed key tenets of Radical Right ideology that would become cornerstones to its strategy moving forward.[436] The court ruled that although *Roe* guaranteed a right to abortion, it did not guarantee access to that right through public funding or other accommodations.[437] Embedded in that ruling was the decision that being poor did not give you protected class status, which had far reaching application. In other words, rights that were not accessible to those who lacked resources did not violate equal protection.[438] Finally, the Supreme Court ruled that denying access to abortion did not violate the establishment clause protecting against enshrining religion in our national law. To the concurring justices, the fact that opponents consistently invoked religion in their own opposition was a coincidence, not establishment.[439]

For AUL and its allies in the Radical Right, the Supreme Court decision underscored their prescience in centering abortion in their strategy. The decision enshrined the right-wing coda that some people were not deserving of rights — even fundamental ones like the right to control your own body. Ditto the idea that poverty was not structural and poor people didn't merit equal protection. Finally, and crucially, the case confirmed that the separation of church and state was not as sacrosanct as people might believe.

AUL moved quickly to expand on the victory in *Harris v. McRae*. Looking to ALEC's success advancing right-wing economic policy for cues, AUL launched a program to write and distribute model legislation to state legislatures. With a laser-like focus, it used propaganda and disinformation to craft legislation and legal strategies that would minimize backlash from a wary public during the mid-to-late 1980s. AUL adherents began to move these pieces of legislation through state houses in earnest.

When *Planned Parenthood v. Casey* came in front of the Supreme Court in 1992, it had eight Republican appointed justices. The case was framed as a question of states' rights — that familiar dog whistle to the conservative base — in this instance to restrict abortion. The Court examined the constitutionality of laws like requiring women to notify their husbands before getting an abortion, required reporting for abortion clinics, and subjecting patients to waiting periods before ending a pregnancy.[440] Advocates on both sides held their breath, wondering if this would be the end of *Roe*. Ultimately, the Court disappointed the Radical Right and upheld the precedent of legal abortion across the country, while allowing each state broad power to set restrictions on clinics, on patients, and — in a move that severely encroached on doctor's autonomy — on the procedure itself.

The fact that *Roe* itself withstood the challenge seemed enough to satisfy a supportive but largely passive public. The specifics of the case, however, were a gold mine of opportunity for AUL, which went into overdrive churning out new laws for willing legislators in the states. Over the next several decades, they sparked a tidal wave of far-right bills and served as advisers to state legislative caucuses and on court cases defending their legislation. AUL was instrumental in moving anti-abortion legislation framed around medical disinformation like "partial-birth abortion" and "heartbeat bills."[441] They knew, despite the outcry from the medical establishment, that focusing attention away from the person who was actually pregnant and onto the fetus was crucial to winning their unpopular agenda.

Nearly every anti-choice policy passed at the state level in recent years bears AUL's fingerprints, from the forced vaginal ultrasound bill in Virginia to a bill Mother Jones described as "trying to shut down all the abortion clinics in Kansas." AUL legislators and leaders have worked to end legal access to abortion and, where they fall short, to shame and humiliate anyone who wants to end a pregnancy.[442] Bills passed in both Arizona and Arkansas require that women be told that medical abortions can be reversed despite the unequivocal stance of the American College of Obstetrics and Gynecology that "claims of 'reversal' are unsupported by medical evidence."[443][444] In an effort to stem momentum of "abortion reversal" bills, scientists at UC Davis undertook a study in 2019 to determine the effects on patients of the course of treatment references in the bills.[445] The study had to be terminated early after women subjects had to be rushed to the hospital. Again, the Radical Right showed that adverse impacts to women were a price they gladly paid to move their agenda.

———

Undergirding the entire effort was a coordinated messaging campaign that relied heavily on disinformation. Their attempts to radicalize their new base of voters and politicize the issue of abortion had driven their early victories, and the lies they told helped bind the movement together as Reagan handed off power. The fear and anger they had stoked was catching fire among the grassroots. That fervor could be channeled into partisan politics, but as the 1990s would prove, it could also burn dangerously out of control.

From Willke's efforts to train a new generation of conservatives to Weyrich's early investment in the Fox News predecessor Television News Inc. (TVN) — a project backed by GOP mega-donor Joe Coors and guided by future-Fox News head Roger Ailes — the Radical Right built channels to amplify their propaganda and to try to shift public opinion toward their way of thinking.[446] As the GOP entered its third consecutive term in the White House, it faced a growing threat from within. The extremists in the party were heeding the word of the right-wing propagandists, and an entire generation had bought into the Radical Right's talking point that abortion itself was the ultimate evil.

Movement leaders were so focused on their fabrications and political goals that they were slow to realize the mesmerizing effect their language was having on the rank and file. They failed to grapple with the ultimate implications. The extreme slogan "abortion is murder" made sense to an audience of supporters who had been taught so effectively to focus solely on fetuses. Not read in on the broader strategy, this group of true believers found the lack of urgent action by leaders discomforting and perplexing.

Operation Rescue gained traction in this void. Its leader Randall Terry increasingly rallied his followers to physically block women from accessing abortion clinics and create confrontations with attending physicians and clinic staff. Operation Rescue staged a series of protests at the 1988 Democratic National Convention, dubbed "the siege of Atlanta."[447][448] The event brought together some of the country's most aggressive anti-choice extremists and culminated in hundreds of arrests.[449] It was a frightening experience for delegates to walk the gauntlet into the convention center. The viciousness of the protesters made them seem larger than they were.

An even more insidious effect of the protests was that arrested activists ended up jailed together for weeks. It is believed that during this time, a core group of them formalized the anti-choice terrorist organization Army of God. They adopted code names and drafted the Army of God manual, explicitly calling for the murder of clinic workers and doctors who provided abortions. The manual included detailed descriptions of an escalating series of tactics, from blockading clinic entrances to attacking buildings and individuals through arson, and acid attacks. Individuals linked to the Army of God were involved in shootings.[450] Over the next many years, the Army of God became the primary face claiming credit for numerous clinic bombings and death threats, as well as kidnapping and murder.[451]

Meanwhile, Operation Rescue set out to escalate the clinic protests by organizing the 1991 "Summer of Mercy" protest in Wichita, Kansas. The goal was to set up high-visibility, highly confrontational events that profiled the group's extreme followers and shook up the old order. The campaign organized thousands of anti-choice activists to block the entrances of three clinics in the city over six weeks. The protests resulted in at least 2,600 arrests, and all targeted clinics were closed for over a week.[452][453]

Wichita was chosen because it was the home of Dr. George Tiller, a Kansas native and OB-GYN who had inherited his father's practice in 1970 after serving in the military as a doctor. Tiller treated women later in their term whose pregnancy had become unviable or even a significant threat to their life.[454] He became the unrelenting focus of the protests and vitriolic rhetoric. Tiller's clinic had been bombed in 1986.[455] Reporter Mary Mapes described what had become a regular scene in 1991 outside Tiller's clinic, with protesters terrifying patients and making work almost impossible (emphasis added):

Tiller's clients often included couples who had been hoping to become parents but had their hearts broken late in pregnancy when they received horrifying medical news about their much-wanted babies. ... They were hounded and harassed, shoved and shouted at on the most heart-breaking day of their lives. In order for patients to make it to their appointments, clinic supporters had to coordinate each woman's arrival with walkie-talkies. They shielded the patient by forming a flying wedge of bodies that rushed through the crowd to escort her into the building. I watched one woman sobbing as she and her husband were helped into the clinic. Her tears went unnoticed by the hundreds of protestors surrounding her who shrieked and wailed and tried to trip the people escorting her to the door.[456]

The protesters' tactics included taking pictures of the patients and employees as they entered the facility and mailing gruesome photos to friends and neighbors of clinic workers. They exacted economic costs to ancillary businesses, boycotting construction firms that did work for the clinics and landlords who rented them space. Activists began to stalk doctors everywhere they went, following them through grocery stores and generally making life unlivable.[457] Dr. Tiller's resolve was strong, but extremists saw the impact of their strategies as other doctors were driven from providing abortions by the constant harassment.

The rhetorical violence inevitably gave way to the real thing. Dr. Tiller had survived the firebombing and kept practicing despite the threats and violence he faced through the 1990s. Then, in 2009, in a resurgent wave of violence that coincided with Barack Obama's presidency, he was gunned down in the pews of his church by a man associated with Operation Rescue.[458][459]

In 1993, Dr. David Gunn was shot outside his clinic by Michael Frederick Griffin. The murder followed months of Operation Rescue stoking the anti-abortion movement's anger against Gunn by printing his photo and phone number on a widely distributed "wanted" poster that was even displayed at the school his daughter attended.[460] Gunn's murder was celebrated by far-right zealots, and Griffin was considered a martyr of the movement, someone the most committed activists could emulate.[461]

Over the course of the nineties, extremists murdered at least six more people around the country in the name of their cause, including Dr. Slepian in Rochester.[462] The country was stunned and appalled. The public never wavered in support for legal access to abortion, but the escalating violence and grotesque images had the intended effect of psychological intimidation. With some exception, the reaction of the silent majority was mostly to turn away from the horror.

The Republican establishment sought to distance themselves from the violence. They knew better than to underestimate how easily a discomforted electorate could spell defeat for them. Mainstream America continued to broadly support abortion rights and had deep sympathy for these doctors and their families. But the GOP's now intractable alliance with the more professional side of the anti-choice movement — whose tepid response to the violence was notable — continued to drive party Republicans, creating a challenge as they evaluated the potential of a Bush second term.

Their fear of violence came on top of increasing skepticism about the openly misogynistic tone of many in the GOP coalition. The more real estate the Radical Right occupied within the Republican Party, the more they began to speak their minds. In the midst of the wave of violence, John Willke — by then president of the National Right to Life Committee — argued that pro-choice women "do violence to marriage" because they "remove the right of a husband to protect the life of the child he has fathered in his wife's womb."[463] The polarization was growing. One national poll found that men who "strongly agreed" that the family should be "traditional" — defined as a male breadwinner and a female homemaker — suddenly jumped four percentage points between 1986 and 1988, the first rise in nearly a decade."[464]

It was in the middle of this bubbling cultural cauldron that Bush nominated Clarence Thomas to fill a vacancy on the Supreme Court left by Thurgood Marshall.[465] The previous year, Bush had nominated David Souter, and the Radical Right's deeply negative reaction left a lasting scar. Souter had been confirmed easily in 1990, but those on the Far Right who had never trusted Bush's conservative bona fides now demanded that the president choose a member from the Federalist Society, their movement's crown jewel.[466] The president seeking a second term needed to mollify the base, and so made his decision, not knowing it would make a bad political situation ultimately untenable.

For a short time, everything looked good. Movement leaders were thrilled with the decision to nominate Thomas, who they believed would be a rock-solid vote for their agenda. They gambled correctly that Senate Democrats would be loath to challenge a Black nominee. Leading Democrats seemed cautiously warm to the idea of Thomas despite concerns about his record and ideology. The protests of women mobilized by Thomas' opposition to Roe largely fell on deaf ears. NPR reported, "In truth, it seemed every bit as improbable that the Democrats would reject a Black nominee as that Bush would replace Marshall with anyone else."[467]

When law professor Anita Hill came forward to accuse Thomas of sexual misconduct, it threw both parties into disarray.[468] Members of the Radical Right wanted to protect their nominee at all costs. The more establishment GOP members were committed. The Democrats felt pressure to go to bat for Hill to maintain their own base of women voters, but the overwhelmingly male Senate Democratic caucus was unprepared to truly buck norms and practices to oppose their colleagues across the aisle. The Senate had been a fraternity since its inception; it was a hard habit to break.

GOP pundits and politicians mounted a strategy to smear Hill's credibility by targeting the media and their colleagues. They simultaneously painted her as a spurned lover and a mentally unstable underling. David Brock, a right-wing hatchet man at the time, coined the phrase "a little bit slutty and a little bit nutty" to smear Hill. Brock, who later converted to become a progressive leader, recanted his claims, and apologized.[469] The hearings became ugly, with women around the country protesting the senators' refusal to hear from corroborating witnesses, bristling at the overt sexism of Thomas' supporters, and railing against the absence of women on the committee responsible for vetting Thomas.[470]

After an incredibly acrimonious process — which the country would see an almost identical rerun of in 2018 — Clarence Thomas' nomination was sent to the full Senate without a clear recommendation from the deadlocked Judiciary Committee.[471] Vice President Quayle was called in to cast a tie-breaking vote, but it never became necessary. Thomas was narrowly confirmed as 11 Democrats crossed the aisle to side with their GOP colleagues.[472] Members of the Radical Right were elated by their victory on the Supreme Court, blithely ignoring the wake of destruction they left behind.

———

The Radical Right's overreach of the 80s and 90s and the resulting chaos sowed by their true believers were the tipping point to mobilize previously apathetic women. Already worried about threats to *Roe* and now outraged by the treatment of Anita Hill, female voters rallied together to support a record number of women running to unseat Republicans. A new professional class of women opened their pocketbooks in record numbers to donate to political candidates. Many supported EMILY's List, an organization that had formed in 1985 to support pro-choice women candidates.[473] Founder Ellen Malcolm recognized that organizing around the fear and frustration about the attacks on *Roe* was not just important for gender equity, it was a good political strategy.

Meanwhile, a nascent group of new movement leaders joined the old movement architects to push the GOP even further right. Failed presidential candidate Pat Robertson founded a new operation called the Christian Coalition in 1989, just after his primary loss to George H. W. Bush. The new organization was led by up-and-comer Ralph Reed.[474] Reed had come to the attention of movement leaders after being arrested protesting abortion clinics in North Carolina and founding the group Students for America with the help of segregationist Sen. Jesse Helms. At the helm of the Christian Coalition, he put his organizing skills to use, growing the membership from almost nothing to over a million members and filling 300 of the roughly 2,000 delegate spots at the 1992 Republican National Convention in Houston, enough to decide the party's presidential nominee.

Pat Buchanan — an adviser to Nixon and Reagan — had run an insurgent primary challenge to Bush's reelection, claiming Bush was soft on everything from abortion to crime to immigration. Buchanan was a self-described "paleoconservative," an ideology that combined Weyrich's dominionist thought with the overt nationalism that was popular with the Southern right-wing.[475] Using his growing stature among the Far Right following Reagan's presidency, Buchanan denied the devastation of the Holocaust and vilified the Central Park Five — five young Black men wrongfully convicted in 1989 of raping a white woman.[476][477] He had stunned the GOP when he took 38% of the vote in the 1992 New Hampshire primary, and the party worked to accommodate those voters through the rest of the race.[478] Buchanan snagged the coveted opening night keynote at the Republican National Convention that year.[479]

His speech, the curtain raiser for millions of prime-time viewers, railed against "the agenda Clinton and Gore would impose on America — abortion on demand, a litmus test for the Supreme Court, homosexual rights, discrimination against religious schools, women in combat," and more.[480] It was a speech so over-the-top that Texas humorist Molly Ivins joked that "it probably sounded better in the original German."[481]

For many listeners, Buchanan's tone and tenor mirrored that of the protests at abortion clinics making the news for the last few years. The next few days were full of speeches that beat the same drum. Marilyn Quayle, Pat Robertson, and others regaled listeners with the threats natural families would face by embracing the liberal agenda of abortion rights, gender equity, and LGBTQ equality.[482] RNC chair Rich Bond capped the event to approving roars by proclaiming: "We are America! They are not America" — othering everyone who would challenge the status quo of power.[483]

Buchanan's address was the first major national convention speech to elevate opposition to abortion as a central defining characteristic of the GOP. Despite increasing trepidation from Republican women and political operatives, the Radical Right had successfully pressured Bush to keep the draconian plank banning abortion in the platform. And in November of 1992, the skeptics were proved right.

Voters went to the polls to register massive backlash against the turn the GOP had taken, handing a decisive victory to Bill Clinton. Even Bush's supporters pointed to the tone of the convention as a core reason for his defeat. But that wasn't all. With the help of crossover voters, Democrats elected a record number of women to federal office in what became known as the "Year of the Woman." As Susan Faludi wrote, "The Democratic Party's emphasis on defending women's liberties — and the Republican Party's attack on the same — also inspired an unprecedented 28 percent of GOP women to defect from their own party at the polls."[484]

Republicans were cowed. Many knew they had gone too far, yet they also felt like they had passed the point of no return. Their coalition relied on an extreme base that left no room for moderates. They couldn't adjust on substance, so they set about to shift the optics by setting up a mirror image to the phenomenally successful EMILY's List. The Susan B. Anthony List was created in 1993 to run women opposed to legal abortion on the GOP ticket. Founder Rachel MacNair was a political neophyte who bought into the GOP story that they were not anti-women, only anti-abortion. She went so far as to state publicly that they were not looking for right-wing candidates: "We want good records on women's rights — probably not Phyllis Schlafly. [Candidates from the right wing] are precisely who we're not going to be supporting."[485][486]

The organization failed to gain traction amidst a general lack of enthusiasm for women candidates in the party, regardless of how anti-choice they were. Seasoned activists Jill Abraham and Marjorie Dannenfelser were brought in to build on MacNair's efforts. Dannenfelser had grown up Episcopalian and pro-choice in Greenville, North Carolina. She had been the "pro-choice chair" of the Duke University Republicans prior to spending a summer interning at the Heritage Foundation, where she was indoctrinated into the Radical Right and established her anti-choice bona fides.[487] She went on to work in the Reagan administration, as many Heritage graduates did, before helping to set up a professional "pro-life caucus" for the GOP on Capitol Hill.[488][489]

Dannenfelser surveyed the landscape and immediately amended the criteria for SBA List's support to allow the organization to back anti-choice men, as long as those men were running to defeat pro-choice women candidates.[490] She stripped her organization of everything but its anti-feminist core, all the while maintaining a careful "pro-woman" veneer. Under Dannenfelser's leadership, SBA List zeroed in on going head-to-head with vulnerable Democrats. The group especially focused on EMILY's List-endorsed candidates, aggressively making their position supporting abortion central to the race.

Public opinion had not shifted on abortion, but neither had people's discomfort with discussing it publicly. So despite the complete lack of data to support Dannenfelser's claim that her victories were attributed to the anti-choice positions of SBA List candidates, her loud proclamations made her a force to be reckoned with and a darling of the Radical Right. Money poured in, and the SBA List became a major hub of conservative electoral activity — from vetting and training far-right candidates to flooding campaigns with well-funded shock troops in closely contested elections.

As Clinton took office in 1993, the GOP struggled to regain its footing. Newt Gingrich, a controversial member of Congress from Georgia, had emerged as a new leader of the party, winning his first leadership position late in the Reagan years. As he rose through the ranks, the notoriously polemical and misogynistic Gingrich — famous for serving his first wife divorce papers as she lay in her hospital bed recovering from surgery — adopted the new conventional wisdom that the GOP had to at least appear more friendly to women. After the election, he filled five of the top seven posts in the National Republican Congressional Committee with women and curbed the external messaging on abortion and feminism. In the lead-up to the 1994 midterm elections, his disciplined message hid the Radical Right's social agenda in a platform that stressed fiscal constraint and cutting entitlements. However, he did continue the Radical Right's practice of vilifying their opponents, lobbing his trademark vitriol against Democrats. Among political scientists, Gingrich's attacks are often pinpointed as the origin in the breakdown of civility in modern federal politics.[491]

An onslaught of Radical Right attacks against President Bill Clinton helped the GOP win a commanding victory in the 1994 midterm elections under Gingrich's leadership. Moderates and white women voters — many of whom supported Ross Perot's third party bid in 1992 — came home to the Republican Party after the 1992 Democratic landslide.[492] [493] The victory put the House speaker's gavel in Gingrich's hand, along with the unenviable job of either bridging the fractious coalition that held the GOP together or watching it explode. For that, a whole new messaging approach would be required — and he knew just who to call.

———

Kellyanne Conway was a young law student when she first got bit by the political bug. She was a research assistant at a firm headed by Richard Wirthlin, President Ronald Reagan's primary pollster and strategist.[494] After graduating, she committed herself to politics, joining Frank Luntz's firm in the early 1990s.[495]

Luntz was taking the party by storm with his focus on using language to manipulate emotions, an approach that made him a perfect match for the Radical Right. He had worked with Pat Buchanan in his 1992 bid to upset Bush. After that failed, he became close to Newt Gingrich, helping him build the "Contract with America."[496] That effort served as the centerpiece of the GOP's quest to regain power after Clinton was elected, and it required women's support. It was through this project that Kellyanne Conway first impressed Gingrich. She helped him sell the Contract for America to women voters and, in 1995, he helped set her up in her own firm, The Polling Company.[497]

The Polling Company took on major corporate clients who wanted to focus on the expanding consumer base of women. Conway studied women's attitudes and trends on behalf of big names like Vaseline and American Express, gaining a deep understanding of what language moved them. She then translated that understanding into political strategies for a growing base of GOP clients who needed to close gender gaps to win, including Gingrich and Dan Quayle. Gingrich later recalled that Conway was unique from her male colleagues in her understanding women as whole beings with a multitude of interests.[498] This enabled her to construct language that appealed to women in ways that traditional GOP pollsters simply couldn't match.

From early on, Conway struck the perfect balance between reverence for the white men who ran the GOP and gentle reinforcement of messaging discipline when it came to women voters. Her reach and insights made Conway one of the most in-demand pollsters in the conservative movement. New York Magazine described her as a "beltway insider who has made something of a specialty out of teaching wild men how to be less threatening to swing voters, especially women."[499] As the movement's women whisperer, she began to achieve mainstream notoriety. She made regular appearances on Bill Maher's show "Politically Incorrect," and co-authored a 2005 book, "What Women Really Want," with Democratic pollster Celinda Lake.[500] Ultimately, her roster of clients listed top Republican leaders such as Jack Kemp, Michele Bachmann, Marsha Blackburn, Steve King, Fred Thompson, and Mike Pence.

Her meteoric rise and client base required Conway to go deep into how to sell a pro-choice public on an anti-abortion agenda. She was avowedly anti-choice and not challenged by the ethics of her task. She knew that core to her success was covering for unruly men who instinctively spoke about their desire to outlaw abortion as part of an effort to maintain a predominantly white, Christian system of control in society. She had to make sure they didn't say the quiet part out loud.

To thread this needle, Conway became the pollster of record for a wide variety of anti-abortion groups like the National Right to Life Committee, Family Research Council, and SBA List. She maintained contracts with movement stalwarts like the Heritage Foundation and the RNC and could thus provide a strategic bridge to more effectively build their Trojan horse of right-wing ideology.

By the turn of the century, all three strategic prongs of the Far Right's long-term strategies were in place. While Conway worked on the messaging, Marjorie Dannenfelser and SBA List honed their skills to get true believers of the Radical Right elected to state and federal office. Americans United for Life was hard at work enacting state-level restrictions on abortion, making enough progress to begin to quell the frustration that had fueled the earlier violence.

The Federalist Society had experienced setbacks during the Clinton years as the Democratic president added Ruth Bader Ginsburg and Stephen Breyer to the highest court.[501] As Clinton's tenure ended in scandal and impeachment proceedings, and the 2000 election was heating up, the balance on the

Supreme Court was up for grabs. Two Nixon justices predated the rise of the Radical Right, and thus were not reliable. The rest were split between Reagan-Bush appointees and Clinton's new justices. These nine disparate individuals together were about to be the faces of one of the most consequential cases to ever come before the court, one that would change the course of American history and give new meaning to popular democracy.

Chapter 5
The New Guard

The 2000 election was a bitter fight the whole way through. The Democratic nominee Al Gore inherited a tarnished mantle from the recently acquitted Bill Clinton. The Radical Right was wary of the younger Bush, just as they had been of the older one. Clinton survived his impeachment with acquittal in the Senate, but the ordeal took a toll on his presidency and the country.[502] The nation was further split by the fact that the entire spectacle had nothing to do with his job performance and instead revolved around personal conduct. Voters and pundits alike debated whether the impeachment was an egregious abuse of power or a necessary chastening of an amoral president.

The Radical Right found new energy for its message of faux family values among an electorate fatigued by the sordid scandal and offended by being subjected to intimate details of the president's sex life. The Democratic left — lukewarm on a President too moderate for their tastes — nonetheless saw the entire spectacle as one more act of a ruthless and hypocritical right. The fact that Newt Gingrich had been the driver of impeachment while having his own extramarital affair summed up the entire farce, unmasking Republicans' craven thirst for power veiled in moral superiority.[503]

The 1998 midterm elections served as a rebuke to the GOP. The party lost five House seats in a year when they were predicted to gain many, and Newt Gingrich resigned as the House speaker.[504] [505] As the 2000 presidential election was heating up, the real fight to head the GOP was happening far away from the nation's capital, in Texas. George W. Bush had an early lead in the Republican primary due to name recognition and establishment connections inherited from his father.

The Radical Right was conflicted. It had been disappointed by George H.W. Bush, and the younger Bush seemed to relish the neoconservative politics of his Ivy League background rather than the Southern conservatism made popular by Reagan. On the other hand, George W. Bush had been born again when he quit drinking.[506] His conversion seemed genuine and his faith devout, and he was not without his boosters in the movement.

Before Bush's conversion, his 1978 congressional campaign in Lubbock, Texas was an early failed attempt to walk the tightrope of the right.[507] In interviews, Bush enthusiastically opposed the Equal Rights Amendment, but he tried to strike a balance by distancing himself from the constitutional ban on abortion that was the litmus test for the far right. As the local newspaper reported at the time: "Bush said he opposes the pro-life amendment favored by [his opponent Jim] Reese and favors leaving up to a woman and her doctor the abortion question. 'That does not mean I'm for abortion,' he said."[508] His statement accurately reflected public opinion on the subject, but he lost the election nonetheless, and that quote dogged him almost two decades later as he ran for Texas governor against incumbent Ann Richards.[509] By then, the Right had consolidated power and Bush had both learned his lesson and become a devout Christian. He vowed to do everything in his power to restrict abortion if he was elected.[510] He was good on his promise in the Governor's mansion. Bush signed several pieces of legislation that made Texas one of the most difficult states in which to obtain an abortion.[511]

Still, the Radical Right had several candidates to choose from in the 2000 GOP primary. Pat Robertson was running again, and so were certified conservatives Tennessee's Lamar Alexander and Vice President Dan Quayle.[512] [513] Arizona GOP Sen. John McCain also ran, positioning himself as a moderate with some sharp criticisms of the candidates to his right. McCain criticized the younger Bush for drifting rightward, pointing to Bush's acceptance of an endorsement by Bob Jones University. McCain also called Pat Robertson and others "agents of intolerance."[514] Recognizing the limits of the coded racism and sexism that had come to define the party, McCain worked to focus the conversation in other places — an effort he would largely abandon as the Republican presidential nominee eight years later, succumbing to the political realities of an increasingly powerful Radical Right.[515]

Except for an upset by McCain in New Hampshire, none of the other candidates ever gained traction and Bush consolidated his lead early in the race to handily win the nomination.[516] Many voters and right-wing leaders rallied around Bush. Clinton's legacy of a booming economy and balanced budgets made most Americans feel financially secure, but the outgoing president drew low marks from voters on character. In their eyes, Clinton's moral failings were the Democrats' weakness and Bush — like his father — was widely perceived as an easygoing family man whose lovely wife and two daughters would be the perfect first family. Al Gore struggled to get out from under the scandal-ridden Clinton years. Consumer advocate Ralph Nader ran a third party effort that attracted many voters convinced that both parties were out of touch and peeled crucial votes away from the Democratic nominee.[517]

The election itself was too close to call. With irregularities reported in the crucial state of Florida, Gore requested a recount. For more than a month, the country was on edge with no clear outcome in what many believed to be the most consequential election in decades. Both sides mounted protests, and sent delegations to Florida to oversee the recount. The GOP establishment had learned a thing or two about the power of theater, and they mounted what came to be called the "Brooks Brothers riot." Dozens of screaming young Republican men in suits and ties, berated election officials in front of television cameras for the world to see.[518] On December 13, 2000, the Supreme Court put an end to the recount and handed down a decision that effectively gave George W. Bush the election, making him the 43rd president of the United States. The ultimate decision was 5-4, with the Federalist Society's justices in the majority.[519] *Bush v. Gore* is often pinpointed as the moment when many Americans came to believe that the Court was politicized and started to lose faith in our election system.[520] The movement architects' capture of the Courts and embrace of actively undermining democracy to hold power was once again successful.

George W. Bush's inauguration came at the end of a volatile decade. The clinic protests had labeled the movement as extremists and terrorists, and the Far Right's brand was in desperate need of adjusting.[521] Willke's hard work moving public sympathy toward the fetus was lost amidst images of terrified women running a gauntlet of screaming protestors and grieving families of slain doctors. The movement desperately needed a new touchstone, a way to move the focus and sympathy away from the victims of anti-choice terrorism.

A presentation at a 1995 medical conference described a new procedure for performing a safe abortion on a woman later in pregnancy — the type of procedure that Dr. Tiller often used in his Kansas clinic.[522][523] Where doctors saw offering safe care to patients in need, National Right to Life lobbyist Douglas Johnson saw an opportunity to reframe the debate.[524] Johnson drew creative, graphic pictures based on verbal description of the procedure, commonly referred to by physicians as "dilation and extraction." The fabricated depiction in Johnson's sketches were only rivaled by the term he coined to tell his story, "partial-birth abortion." Both were a wholesale concoction by the right-wing propaganda machine.[525] He laid his cards squarely on the table in a 1996 *The New Republic* interview where he said he hoped that by elevating a sensational story, he could finally entice a recalcitrant public to oppose abortion altogether.[526][527] OB-GYN Dr. Jennifer Gunter later referred to the creation of this phantom as "the thin edge of the wedge" of the Right's strategy explaining: "The anti-choice movement needs the idea of partial-birth abortions of a healthy fetus in the 'ninth month' just like they need the devil."[528]

The American College of Obstetricians and Gynecologists has routinely rejected the language as non-medical.[529] Doctors — many appalled by the idea that advocates and politicians would interfere in specifics of their treatment of patients — argued that the procedure is often the safest option for the women they are charged with serving.[530] Yet, once again, facts were of no consequence to a Radical Right by then firmly enmeshed, whether they liked it or not, with a rabidly anti-choice grassroots of their own making.

Working with AUL, the movement leaders simultaneously introduced state legislation in Ohio and federal legislation to ban what they called "partial-birth abortions."[531] They didn't care about how few people sought to terminate later in pregnancy. They turned a blind eye to the fact that most of these procedures involved wanted pregnancies that had gone terribly wrong. They ignored the many sad and harrowing stories of women who sought them. They actively sought to bury existing data that showed most later abortions occurred before the fetus was viable, and termination in the final month of pregnancy is virtually non-existent.[532]

The GOP was engaged in political theater that had nothing at all to do with health. The party establishment had effectively consented to play fast and loose with facts to score points with its base of voters depressed by Clinton's victory. It needed to show movement on an issue that had been stalled for years. Democrats were caught flat-footed by the introduction of this legislation. They were flummoxed by the obviously deceptive pandering of their counterparts across the aisle. The defenses of Democrats and the pro-choice movement almost entirely relied on facts and what they considered an obvious need to let doctors do their jobs. They also, like most Americans, had a visceral reticence to publicly discuss issues so obviously deeply personal.

Most were shocked when the Radical Right was able to capitalize on years of extremist rhetoric vilifying doctors and impugning their motives. While the movement leaders claimed to revile the assassinations taking place outside of clinics, they were happy to malign doctors' character in the hearing room. They also astutely judged that they had painted a picture so graphic and distasteful that Democrats, already reluctant to spend too much of their time defending abortion, would not want to engage. As a result, both the state and federal measures against so-called "partial-birth abortion" passed with a substantial number of Democrats crossing the aisle to vote with their Republican colleagues. President Clinton vetoed the federal version when it landed on his desk in 1996 and again in 1997.[533] Ohio's law was subsequently stayed by the court.[534]

When George W. Bush took office in 2001, the Radical Right knew they had an opportunity to hand their anti-choice grassroots their first legislative victory in decades.[535] When the "partial birth abortion" law was sent up to Bush in 2003, he signed it without hesitation.[536] The women whose lives hung in the balance didn't merit a mention. Surrounded by all-male members of Congress and a who's who of the Radical Right, Bush held a signing ceremony where he parroted anti-choice talking points. He proclaimed America "owes its children a different and better welcome."[537] He vowed to fight for the law all the way to the Supreme Court, speaking straight from Willke's script. "For years, a terrible form of violence has been directed against children who are inches from birth, while the law looked the other way," Bush said. "Today, at last, the American people and our government have confronted the violence and come to the defense of the innocent child."[538]

The Far Right had proved that a well-crafted message grounded in disinformation had the power to triumph over fact and good policy. They owned the narrative, struck another blow at *Roe*, and further solidified their central power within the GOP coalition. The Supreme Court upheld the law in 2007, overriding decisions from three separate district courts and a unanimous appeals court decision, all of which agreed that the law violated protections guaranteed in *Roe v. Wade*. Bush had recently put Samuel Alito and John Roberts on the court with the help of a newly formed right-wing group called the Judicial Confirmation Network.[539] [540] [541] [542] [543] [544] [545] In a 5-4 decision, Justice Anthony Kennedy joined Clarence Thomas, Antonin Scalia, and the two new Federalist Society members of the court.[546]

The movement's apparatus had hit its stride. The organizations that Weyrich and Falwell had put into place had shown that they could deliver on abortion as well as the GOP's corporate-friendly docket. The entire party was adopting a strategy of disinformation and propaganda to move an agenda increasingly out of sync with public opinion.

They had successfully blunted the momentum of the feminist movement by lobbying to undercut policies designed to help working women with families. The GOP had fought off long overdue action on everything from affordable child care to pay equity to humane social welfare programs. Simply by maintaining the status quo, the GOP handed the Radical Right a victory, while wage stagnation and their regressive tax policy disproportionately punished low income women, women of color, and the single moms who didn't meet their definition of worthy families.

The movement architects should have been basking in their achievements, but instead they were once again dissatisfied. There was widespread outrage by the Radical Right when Bush's second inaugural address contained references only to abortion and to none of their other priority issues. They were especially incensed that despite having backed and passed initiatives in 11 states banning marriage equality, Bush equivocated on the issue in interviews and declined to use his political capital to force the Senate to pass a federal ban.[547] Meanwhile, the fragile coalition that put the GOP in power was once again hemorrhaging women. White women were becoming more and more vital to electoral victory, as changing demographics combined with a draconian approach to social policies resulted in increased support for the Democrats among Black Americans and social liberals.

———

Under increasing pressure from both the true believers and the establishment, the actual founders of the Radical Right movement struggled to adapt to the evolving times and personally became more marginalized within their own movement.

After the Moral Majority was shuttered, Jerry Falwell largely retreated to the grounds of Liberty University. He used his platform there to rail against moral decay and made the institution a required stop for every aspiring politician. During the Clinton years, he continued to dabble in propaganda, spreading lies about White House counsel Vince Foster's suicide among other claims.[548] Falwell rose to infamy again after he blamed the attacks on September 11, 2001 on "...the pagans, and the abortionists, and the feminists, and the gays and the lesbians who are actively trying to make that an alternative lifestyle, the ACLU, People For the American Way, all of them who have tried to secularize America. I point the finger in their face and say 'you helped this happen." Later, amidst tremendous backlash, he backpedaled, drawing the outrage of his own followers who believed he should have stood firm.[549]

Weyrich, too, grew increasingly impatient and frustrated. During the later Reagan years, he had briefly considered forming a third party, but his disillusionment really manifested after George H.W. Bush took office.[550] While many in his world accepted Bush as an incremental step forward, Weyrich couldn't stomach a president who he believed to be another Rockefeller Republican at heart. Falwell also did not like Bush's well-known reputation as a family planning advocate. At a 1990 meeting of the Christian Coalition, Pat Buchanan told his depressed flock to ignore the sitting president and redouble efforts on electing a "pro-family" Republican majority to Congress, which would in turn help them elect a true believer to the presidency by the turn of the century.

Historians suggest that the Reagan years allowed stalwarts like Falwell and Weyrich to rise to power, and the elder Bush years cemented their belief that nothing short of a full takeover of the GOP coalition would achieve their goals.[551]

This was the backdrop against which Weyrich took the floor at the Ethics and Public Policy Conference in 1990 to give an inflammatory lecture lamenting that members of the new movement didn't even know their own history and relaying the origins of the Religious Right.[552] He excoriated them as being entirely focused on abortion while not knowing the true work that had gone into politicizing the issue as a means to secure a government focused on maintaining the power and privilege of the white male Christian class. Two years later, he joined other movement leaders in blaming Bush's 1992 defeat on his failure to adhere to conservative orthodoxy.[553]

In the aftermath of Clinton's victory and with lessons from his first media attempt at TVN, Weyrich launched National Empowerment Television (NET) as a platform to rail against apostates within the Republican Party. He warned, "Politicians who fail to recognize the significance of NET … will certainly do so at their own peril." He surrounded himself with extremists, prioritizing total adherence to his radical beliefs over efficacy. As one staffer put it, NET was full of "sound technicians who could spout the pro-life line but not plug in the microphone." Another said the building became full of "scared pessimists," even as the right-wing of the party was ascending. He eschewed any establishment Republicans and instead gave platforms to fringe actors like Bill Lind, who had won Weyrich's affection with a futuristic fantasy that showed the unfaithful being burned at the stake and women "given a bright red embroidered 'C' to wear over their left breast" as punishment for pursuing careers.[554]

No one was safe from Weyrich's ire. He publicly attacked Bob Dole for having a pro-choice chief of staff.[555] He ripped into Idaho's staunch right-wing Sen. Larry Craig for negotiating a balanced budget deal with President Clinton.[556] And Weyrich had a particularly tortured relationship with Newt Gingrich. He battled with the new House speaker just as Gingrich was racking up an impressive set of wins for the Far Right on everything from slashing the social safety net to lowering taxes to the Defense of Marriage Act banning gay marriage. In Weyrich's eyes, Gingrich was governing for incremental reform when it was time to wage a revolution.[557]

Weyrich's behavior alienated even movement stalwarts. Meanwhile, Gingrich and his brand of right-wing warriors — from Kellyanne Conway to Ralph Reed — became the center of gravity of the Radical Right. Conway was behind the scenes, organizing women and ensuring the rise of right-wing heroes like Gingrich and Michele Bachmann. Reed was increasingly the face of the new Far Right. In 1995, his image graced the cover of *Time* magazine with the headline "The Right Hand of God."[558] He was extolled as a religious leader with a softer hand and an ability to reach younger, more moderate people.[559]

By the time Fox News launched in 1996, Weyrich's NET was on the brink of financial ruin. Weyrich raided his Free Congress Foundation of revenue to keep it afloat. He complained that Gingrich conservatives could be seen on every major network pandering to the middle and robbing the true Religious Right of its place in the cultural conversation. After the Senate acquitted President

Clinton on impeachment charges in 1998, Weyrich seemed to give up his lifelong dream of capturing the government for the dominionist vision of a white, male, Christian power structure. He bemoaned that "cultural Marxism" was prevailing and said, "The question becomes, if we are unable to escape the cultural disintegration that is gripping society, then what hope can we have?"[560] In a move he later recanted, he counseled a complete withdrawal from the secular sphere stating inconsolably, "I no longer believe that there is a moral majority. I do not believe that a majority of Americans actually shares our values."[561]

Ironically, Weyrich's height of anguish converged with the fall from grace of his frequent target Gingrich. At almost the same time Gingrich resigned from leadership, right-wing wunderkind Ralph Reed resigned from the Christian Coalition, embroiled in a scandal about violating federal election law.[562] The Radical Right descended into disarray and became dispirited. Jerry Falwell died in 2007, followed a year later by his old friend and co-conspirator Paul Weyrich.[563][564] Neither would live to see the full manifestation, a decade later, of what they had put into motion.

———

Barack Obama's 2008 victory was spurred by a huge gender gap.[565] Republicans once again suffered a massive defeat despite their nominee, John McCain, abandoning his formerly more mainstream GOP views and adding right-wing darling Alaska Gov. Sarah Palin to the ticket.[566] Palin's unapologetic race-baiting, combined with her anti-choice orthodoxy, was red meat for a base that was still hungry for more influence. But in light of the historic candidacy of the first Black president, her approach proved toxic. In the immediate aftermath of the election, the Far Right scrambled to reorganize. Faced with headlines speculating about a "permanent Democratic majority," conservative leaders were "determined to engineer a political comeback."[567][568][569]

Disgraced Christian Coalition leader Ralph Reed, whose political reputation had suffered for his ties to corrupt lobbyist Jack Abramoff, saw an opportunity to remake himself.[570] He founded the brand-new Faith and Freedom Coalition, pledging to bring an army of grassroots power to the next right-wing crusader.[571] Former Reagan attorney general and Federalist Society board member Edwin Meese III stepped in to play statesman for a fractured movement, launching the Conservative Action Project to coordinate and align the increasingly unwieldy right-wing coalition.[572] The star consultant Meese hired was none other than Kellyanne Conway, who was called upon to help conduct the conservative movement's autopsy and chart a path forward. She began advising them on courting the necessary white women voters to win and putting a female face, once again, on their noxious aspirations.[573]

Conway recognized that as long as the right could be credibly attacked for being anti-woman, the GOP would remain in electoral purgatory. She set about reworking Schlafly's playbook for a modern era. The 1970s were over, and the women-libber scare tactics had gone the way of the older pro-segregation arguments, especially as the realities of GOP policies made life increasingly untenable for working women. Overtly running against feminism wasn't going to work.

Conway's strategy was brilliant in its simplicity. In a brazen act of gaslighting, she insisted that the GOP rebrand as pro-woman, while simultaneously accusing the Democrats of being the party obsessed with abortion. First, Conway used her unique expertise in polling to undermine decades of accepted data showing that the majority of Americans support legal access to abortion. Keying off of the victories during the Bush years, Conway's team crafted polling questions that used cartoonish and improbable hypotheticals about abortion to wedge public opinion. When Democratic and pro-choice leaders refuted her claims, Conway relentlessly branded their position as extreme. Her technique worked insofar as it confused people and the statistical noise made anti-choice positions seem more popular.[574] The fact that the strategy was dishonest was of no mind to right-wing leaders who had long accepted that dishonesty as the cost of doing business. They were thrilled with what they were seeing.

Obama's fledgling coalition was caught off-guard. As the administration began to advance its signature piece of legislation, the Affordable Care Act (ACA), the Right found a perfect vehicle to exacerbate tensions and advance its narrative. The ACA aimed to dramatically expand healthcare coverage to the tens of millions of Americans who remained uninsured. The legislation was grounded in progressive values and the needs of real people, but was built on a conservative framework from the start. Rather than seeking to directly expand healthcare through a government-funded single-payer system, the ACA was modeled on a market-driven plan popularized in Massachusetts by Republican Mitt Romney and drawn from concepts promoted by Weyrich's Heritage Foundation.[575] Democrats started from a position of compromise in an effort to seek common ground, while Republicans were ready to start moving the goalposts.

Throughout the debate, Democrats continued to believe they could win over the GOP if they were flexible on some key issues, namely abortion. Women and reproductive rights leaders argued that the ACA should cover abortion services for both ethical and strategic reasons. But both Congressional Democratic leaders and the Administration decided not to push for abortion coverage. Despite evidence that the Hyde Amendment increased the disparities in American healthcare, they didn't use the new law to challenge the longtime restrictions.[576] This olive branch was rejected by the GOP and the Right disingenuously claimed that the ACA would allow for taxpayer dollars to go toward abortion.[577] They specifically targeted vulnerable Democratic members of Congress, claiming that they were violating the religious freedom of Americans by voting for the bill.

Attempts to correct the record fell flat in the face of right-wing disinformation and a media that was, by then, well-steeped in propaganda that papered over the nuances of abortion policy, routinely disappeared the needs of pregnant people, and downplayed the sustained public support for reproductive freedom. Meanwhile, a small bipartisan group of conservatives and anti-choice Democrats submitted an amendment known as Stupak-Pitts.[578] The authors wrote the measure in such a way that it would have effectively ended abortion coverage in state health insurance exchanges and even jeopardized the private insurance coverage of abortion. The amendment prohibited subsidized individuals from purchasing health plans that included abortion coverage, even if they used their own money to pay most of their premium cost.[579] Far from a genuine compromise, the Stupak-Pitts Amendment was seen as a win-win by the Right. If the amendment passed, abortion was put out of reach for an expanded group of people handing the base a victory. If the Democrats held strong, the Right got to tank Obama's signature piece of legislation while blaming their rivals for holding healthcare hostage because they were obsessed with abortion. Either way, they got to split the progressive coalition. The strategy seemed to be ripped straight from Kellyanne Conway's playbook.

The amendment passed the House in a final floor vote of 240-194 with sixty-four Democrats crossing the aisle to vote with Republicans.[580] [581] The vote created massive backlash from women who were tired of being sold out, and the Senate countered with its own, slightly softer, version before Obama issued an executive order to bar any federal funding issued under the ACA from covering abortion. Only then were both amendments withdrawn.[582]

Obama's order did nothing to mollify his adversaries. For months, the GOP establishment and the Radical Right organizations leaned into a smear effort propagating all sorts of lies including that the ACA was a backdoor way to expand abortion and that Obama was secretly setting up death panels to decide who would live or die. The claims were preposterous but they nonetheless consumed the debate around the most significant piece of healthcare reform in generations. Even more insidious, they pitted different constituencies against each other weakening Obama's base of support.

The GOP carried the narrative into the crucial 2010 midterm elections, airing ads against Democrats running for reelection. Susan B. Anthony List targeted freshman Ohio Rep. Steve Driehaus with ads claiming he had voted for "tax payer funded abortions" when he voted for the ACA. Driehaus fought back in a case that ultimately went all the way to the Supreme Court. In the case, no side was arguing that the ads were truthful, only that the group in question had a constitutionally protected right to lie. Driehaus lost his bid for reelection in 2010, among many other freshmen Democrats. Many Democrats were so preoccupied fighting the lies about abortion coverage that they forgot that their pro-choice position was a political advantage, which — of course — was entirely the point.[583]

For the GOP and the Right, the ACA fight underscored the incredible value of Conway and her strategies of using lies and disinformation to fracture their opponents and subvert the power of a popular issue. For everyone else, it should have exposed a central lie of the Radical Right's long-term effort. While claiming to value life, they used manufactured concern about fetuses to undercut the most significant life-affirming legislation in decades. If that wasn't enough, the movement was about to show once again that the fight was never truly about abortion. The ACA finally gave them a concrete opportunity to hit at the heart of women's freedom and equality: advances in birth control.

Abortion coverage aside, Obama's effort did focus concerns of women in the new healthcare policy and was the most significant push in generations to address historic disparities. The policy prevented insurance companies from charging women more just for being women; the industry classified the entire gender as a "preexisting condition." In a barely concealed display of sexism, many Republican Congressmen bemoaned that men would have to shoulder more financial burden in the insurance risk pool for conditions they would never face — namely pregnancy. But nothing revealed their underlying motivations more than what came to be known as "no-cost contraception."

The name itself was a misnomer since all the policy did was bring contraception under the umbrella of most health insurance plan coverage without a copay. Women were still paying premiums on their plans so, like any other medication, there was an associated cost. But, once again, this fact made no difference to the right-wing propaganda machine. They simply couldn't stomach the idea of a policy that would save women collectively an estimated $1.4 billion a year on birth control and put previously cost-prohibitive forms — such as the IUD — in reach.

After the law passed, dozens of lawsuits were filed to block the expansion of contraception coverage, many backed by Alliance for Defending Freedom and the Becket Fund. Darrell Issa, a Republican member of Congress from California, called the mandate an attack on religious liberty: "While some Americans may not feel that government mandates forcing them to pay for contraception are an infringement on their religious beliefs, others consider it to be an assault against their freedom of conscience."[584] This line was parroted by most GOP candidates challenging Obama during his 2012 reelection campaign.

Issa was the chair of the House Oversight and Government Reform Committee and that year he held a hearing on contraception coverage with no testimony from women at all.[585] The Democrats had brought a young graduate student from Georgetown — Sandra Fluke. She had been moved to campaign on behalf of the contraception mandate and the ACA. A friend of hers had been prescribed oral contraceptives that she could not afford, lost her ovary to cysts, and entered early menopause, marring her chances of becoming a mother. The GOP refused to let Fluke testify, calling her not "appropriate or qualified," and instead gave unfettered airtime to right-wing male leaders.[586] In a dramatic showdown, the Democratic women at the hearing walked out of the conference room and into a sea of cameras where they gave Fluke a platform and decried the sham inside.[587]

Fluke was finally granted her day in Congress, where she testified about the implementation of the ACA's contraception coverage provisions and the importance of ensuring contraception access both to avoid unintended pregnancy and to treat medical conditions. After her hearing, right-wing shock jock Rush Limbaugh took to the airwaves to deride Fluke as a "slut" and a "prostitute" to millions of listeners.[588] While other major players were more delicate, they carried the same message. GOP megadonor Foster Friess made headlines when he said: "You know, back in my days, they used Bayer aspirin for contraception. The gals put it between their knees, and it wasn't that costly."[589]

It might as well have been the 1970s all over again. As the Radical Right and the GOP dug deeper into crude arguments that exposed their hypocrisy and illuminated for the nation how threatened they felt by even modest progress, the women on their team feared their hard work of honing messages to calm female voters was crumbling.

———

Of course, none of this was happening in a vacuum. The reaction to our country's first Black president was fierce. Racism and racial sentiment had been stoked throughout the campaign, first by right-wing pundits, then straight from the GOP ticket where vice presidential candidate Sarah Palin picked up the mantle. Many felt like the election itself was a triumph over centuries of racism and racist policies, but those attitudes were not going quietly into the night. The immediate rise of the Tea Party in the wake of Obama's 2009 inauguration gave the GOP something it had been wanting for some time: a countervailing grassroots force that could balance the influence of the religious right, which had come to dominate the party. Right-wing megadonors like Charles and David Koch poured money into organizations like FreedomWorks and Americans for Prosperity to capture the Tea Party's burgeoning energy and funnel it into stopping the momentum of the new, popular president.[590]

The Tea Party claimed to focus on libertarian economic issues like lower taxes and lower deficits, and they promised to be on the front lines fighting government tyranny. But almost from the beginning, it was beset by racism from within its ranks. Representatives in Congress reported hearing racial epithets thrown at them from Tea Party protesters. Rally signs telling the new president to "Go back to Kenya" became a common sight at Tea Party events. And Tea Party opposition to initiatives like extending unemployment benefits took on a markedly racist tone. A study showed that allegiance to the Tea Party coincided with holding racial animosity, particularly in Southern states.[591]

The new movement quickly became indecipherable from the old one. As some old guard institutions grappled with a new reality that sprung from defeat — Focus on the Family, for example, laid off a fifth of its staff and ousted its board chair after the 2008 election — savvier leaders saw reincarnation through the new movement. At the first Tea Party convention in Memphis, a year after Obama was sworn in, familiar Religious Right leaders outnumbered the libertarians that were the external brand of the new movement. Michele Bachmann mingled with guests gearing up for a 2012 presidential run. Alabama Judge Roy Moore made an appearance, an Alabama judge who was a folk hero in the fundamentalist set for restoring custody of three children to an abusive father because he deemed their lesbian mother's "lifestyle" to be a "crime against nature."[592] The new Tea Party and the old Radical Right became intertwined and evoked the pivotal moment in history when Phyllis Schlafly and Anita Bryant conspired with Jerry Falwell and Paul Weyrich about how to take over the GOP.[593]

As the 2010 midterms approached, Kellyanne Conway urged a return to discipline. She argued that Republicans could not afford to exacerbate the gender gap by highlighting the party's focus on reproductive oppression. In fact, she counseled to steer clear of abortion and birth control in order to emphasize the economy and foment acrimony around Obama's healthcare plan. Citing Sarah Palin as a model, Conway told CNN, "I think she's really engineering a huge moms mobilization to tell women that you don't have to listen to the traditional feminists when they pretend the only thing you want to talk about in politics is abortion."[594] Kellyanne knew that especially with a new Black president, stoking fears of government social engineering amid financial anxiety was a powerful elixir. Disaffected women, especially those in white rural and post-industrial communities that felt left behind, viscerally felt the loss of perceived social and economic privilege.

Amid Tea Party protests, chants about ACA "death panels," and a massive influx of right-wing spending due to the Supreme Court's Citizens United decision gutting campaign finance protections, the Republicans swept the midterms. In her post-election spin, Conway branded 2010 as "the year of the conservative woman."[595] Skewing facts and inserting her talking points to dismiss pro-choice views as an obsession, she said, "Women are rejecting labels and rejecting a collectivism based on their gender. It's also because the cost of admission ended up being too high, and abortion is the religion."[596] [597]

A closer look at the election revealed an even more troubling picture. Evangelical voters and the Tea Party had coalesced to combat the social progress embodied by the 2008 election, railing against what they believed was a tyrannical government designed to rob them of their rightful place in society.[598]

———

Kellyanne Conway was riding high and her refreshed brand of right-wing politics felt invincible until that summer day in 2012 when Todd Akin made his fatal mistake. A Conway client, Akin slipped up and revealed the truth about his beliefs. "If it's a legitimate rape, the female body has ways to try to shut that whole thing down."[599] Just days before the nomination of Mitt Romney for president, his comments shifted the entire public narrative away from attacking Obama on the economy and health care to focus once again on the GOP's position on abortion.[600] As the party struggled to regain control of the narrative and salvage the election cycle, Conway went into crisis mode.

At the Council for National Policy meeting the week before the convention, Akin was drilled on his vocabulary and positions, over two days, by a rotating cast of right-wing leaders. None were more diligent and frustrated than Conway and Marjorie Dannenfelser, who had spent years trying to teach the party's male candidates how to talk to and about women.[601] Under immense pressure, Akin apologized, but it wasn't enough.[602] Akin's collapse took with it any dreams the Republicans had of taking back the Senate that year.[603] Obama, meanwhile, handily won his reelection.[604] The House remained in the hands of the GOP, but the Democrats gained eight seats.[605]

Despondent leaders and operatives again turned to Conway and Dannenfelser to save them in the 2014 cycle and to prepare for the next presidential election in 2016. The pair began a series of bootcamps for GOP aspiring candidates. The women coached the mostly male audience to keep answers to questions about abortion as short as possible. Assure the base you are with them, they counseled, and move on. Two sentences maximum. Above all, remember that "'[r]ape' is a four letter word." The workshops also dedicated a fair amount of time to the power of their opposition's message. They urged right-wing leaders to try to muddy the waters for the segment of the public that, while supportive of legal abortion in general, was skeptical of it being lumped in with the rest of healthcare. Conway lectured, "Women's health issues are osteoporosis or breast cancer or seniors living alone who don't have enough money for health care."[606]

With their patented audacity, Conway and Dannenfelser didn't stop there. They went back to the well of medical disinformation and used junk science to claim that women are actually victimized by their own abortions, an allegation debunked by all credible data. Jeanne Monahan, president of the March for Life that year, emphasized the same themes, saying: "What we're seeing more and more is research... showing that many women do suffer emotional consequences after making a choice related to abortion. So for me, I do really like to emphasize that abortion is not good for women."[607]

This reframing of women as victims of abortion relied heavily on sexist tropes that women are helpless and need protection, especially from a feminist agenda that would divert them from their true purpose in life — being a mother. The Radical Right, led by AUL, reinforced this assertion with a raft of state legislation, which was being introduced and passed at a rapid clip — including mandatory ultrasounds, enforced waiting periods, and biased counseling mandating doctors read medically inaccurate scripts full of anti-choice propaganda to their patients. These laws all relied on a public willing to accept the idea that women were not capable of sorting fact from fiction or making up their minds without government intervention.

Meanwhile, Conway had also been working to divide the progressive coalition by shamelessly promoting an anti-choice crusade as a civil rights mission. She had worked with Priests For Life ahead of their "Pro-Life Freedom Ride" tour kick-off in Birmingham, Alabama.[608][609] They began a series of advertising campaigns suggesting that abortion providers were targeting Black women specifically by setting up shop in Black neighborhoods, a claim disputed by all evidence. The Far Right cynically exploited the very real history in this country of medical and reproductive coercion to deflect from their racism. Many Black reproductive justice allies called this another attempt to rob Black women of their agency.[610] The Radical Right, built on a history of racism and misogyny, deflected with a simple claim that the opposite was true. Up was down. In this case, right was left.

In the lead up to the 2014 midterm elections, Conway doubled down on her messaging. The party of intolerance relentlessly pushed a message that the Democrats were the unyielding ones. "Voters, including single women, need educating about what the Democratic Party stands for," she wrote in a 2013 National Review column. She sensationalized the Democratic position as "abortion, anyone, anytime, anywhere."[611][612] By that time, the GOP had effectively purged from its ranks all candidates and elected officials who supported protecting abortion access. Again to deflect, Conway took to the airways sparring with a Democratic pundit on CNN: "Can you — either of you name for me five prominent Democratic pro-life women in this country? There are none left. In 2007 — there are none left. You pushed them out."[613] She skipped the fact that Democrats were representing not just their own, but also the opinion of most independents and many Republicans as well.

This new strategy was effective. Conway received the lion's share of credit, with everyone from National Right to Life to her old mentor Newt Gingrich heaping praise on her ability to lead the GOP out of the wilderness. Even the Center for Medical Progress' David Daleiden, who had taken disinformation to a whole new level by releasing doctored and deceptively edited videos of interactions with Planned Parenthood employees, praised Conway's work. Conway, it turns out, did polling and focus groups to help shape the narrative around those infamous videos.[614]

The GOP won back the Senate in 2014 for the first time in eight years, putting the gavel and control of the upper chamber into the hands of right-wing darling, Kentucky Sen. Mitch McConnell. Daleiden would go on to be forced to pay Planned Parenthood millions of dollars in damages.[615] Conway was destined for a different future.

Chapter 6
The Natural

On June 16, 2015, real estate mogul and reality TV star Donald Trump descended via a golden escalator from the penthouse of his Manhattan skyscraper to announce his candidacy for president of the United States. In a speech that shocked even the most cynical figures in mainstream media for its overt racism and xenophobia, Trump promised to build a "great wall" along the southern border and to make Mexico pay for it. He called Mexican immigrants criminals and rapists, and flaunted his own wealth as a reason for Americans to vote for him.[616] [617]

Most pundits, who had watched Trump flirt with a run for public office for more than a quarter century, saw the speech as disqualifying. On the day of his announcement, Time magazine wrote, "There are about eight billion reasons Trump won't be president."[618] But the nation would soon learn that Trump knew his audience.

Seventeen months later, as America struggled to reckon with Trump's victory, experts flocked to cable news to offer opinions and theories about how they could have missed predicting what transpired. They scrambled to explain what felt inexplicable to so many. How did a political novice — an unapologetic misogynist who was caught on tape confessing to serial sexual assault, a friend of white supremacists who openly called for discrimination against Muslims and immigrants, and a wannabe autocrat with more respect for dictators than for American democratic tradition — manage to become a serious candidate for, much less win, the presidency of the United States?

Fingers pointed in every direction. Max Read at New York Magazine blamed fake news.[619] In the Washington Post, reporters continued to explore Russian meddling.[620] A columnist in the *New York Times* pointed to elite shaming of Trump supporters.[621] Tina Nguyen of *Vanity Fair* pointed to third party voters.[622] Many highlighted the fact that a majority of white women voted for the serial sexual predator committed to overturning *Roe*.[623] Filmmaker and cultural critic Michael Moore got extra credit for predicting the victory in advance, calling the 2016 election "The Last Stand of the Angry White Man." In what would prove to be an unfortunately prescient blog post in the fall of 2016, he wrote a tongue-in-cheek warning to a left he feared was asleep at the wheel:

> Our male-dominated, 240-year run of the USA is coming to an end. A woman is about to take over! How did this
> happen?! *On **our** watch!* There were warning signs, but we ignored them. Nixon, the gender traitor, imposing Title IX on us, the rule that said girls in school should get an equal chance at playing sports. Then they let them fly commercial jets. Before we knew it, Beyoncé stormed on the field at this year's Super Bowl (our game!) with an army of Black Women, fists raised, declaring that our domination was hereby terminated! Oh, the humanity!
>
> That's a small peek into the mind of the Endangered White Male. There is a sense that the power has slipped out of their hands, that their way of doing things is no longer how things are done. This monster, the "Feminazi," the thing that as Trump says, "bleeds through her eyes or wherever she bleeds," has conquered us — and now, after having had to endure eight years of a black man telling us what to do, we're supposed to just sit back and take eight years of a woman bossing us around?[624]

Pundits might have been blind to the white male rage that Moore zeroed in on, but leaders of the Radical Right weren't. They saw kinship and opportunity. They were successfully able to capitalize on this anger in support of Trump. In doing so, they exposed the failure of the political establishment to seriously comprehend the combined power of an established right-wing infrastructure, grounded in an anti-choice grassroots with a resurgent white power movement, topped off by men seething at lost privilege.

For decades, the self-proclaimed "pro-life" movement had been largely sidelined by mainstream pundits who seemed to have bought the story that its goals were relatively benign, if out-of-touch, and that it was narrowly focused on a moral objection to a singular medical procedure. As Trump's campaign shaped up, prominent political and media figures remarked how odd it was that a thrice-married walking embodiment of biblical sins ranging from greed to pride to lust would become the standard-bearer for a movement ostensibly rooted in a commitment to religious faith and traditional family structure.[625]

But Radical Right leaders saw promise in Trump's rise to advance and accelerate their core purpose by continuing to channel America's latent racism and misogyny into a viable political movement with seemingly no bounds.

On election eve 2016, Jerry Falwell Jr. was so confident of the win that he texted his good friend Sean Hannity early evening to say "I have a good feeling about tonight."[626] KKK leader David Duke crowed, "Make no mistake about it, our people have played a HUGE role in electing Trump!"[627] There were less familiar faces too. Breitbart reporter Milo Yianopolous joined Falwell to toast the victory in Midtown Manhattan. It was a motley crew that on the surface had little in common. While Falwell Jr. had become the stalwart at Liberty University succeeding his famous father,[628] Milo shot to infamy seemingly out of nowhere trolling mainstream media and penning articles for Brietbart like "Birth Control Makes Women Unattractive and Crazy" and "Would You Rather Your Child Had Feminism Or Cancer?"[629] [630]

In many ways, the 2016 GOP primary reflected the playbook of the movement's architects. Break the mold. Discredit gatekeepers. Go straight to the people using disinformation. Then, dominating the establishment with its unchallenged control of a loud and angry base driven by deep grievances. As the descendants of the movement architects watched Trump attack women, immigrants, communities of color, and other groups fighting to achieve equality in America, they observed his ability to easily traverse the tightrope that they had carefully walked for years. They didn't see a dangerous anachronism. They saw a natural demagogue. One they badly needed.

———

With the passing of Paul Weyrich and Jerry Falwell Sr. in the early Obama years, the Radical Right lost its strategic focal point and was loosely organized around several nerve centers. The Tea Party peaked after its victories in the 2010 elections.[631] The Family Research Council, a hate group founded during the Reagan years, picked up the mantle of the original Moral Majority and churned out policy papers objecting to abortion, LGBTQ rights, marriage and divorce, and anything else it deemed a threat to the traditional family.[632] [633] FRC President Tony Perkins was a regular staple on the now-dominant Fox News.[634] Susan B. Anthony List regrouped after the Todd Akin "legitimate rape" debacle and took credit for the 2014 GOP victory in the Senate.[635] [636] With the gavel now in Republican Sen. Mitch McConnell's hands and the House still under GOP control, the right-wing infrastructure kicked into gear to make life as difficult as possible for Obama in his final two years in office. Meanwhile, the Federalist Society worked with its friends on the Hill to hold Obama's judicial nominees hostage, slowing progress by forcing right-wing judges through along with the president's picks. By the end of his first term, Trump's nominees would make up a quarter of the federal appellate bench.[637] [638] [639]

During the 2016 election cycle, no one entity was influential enough to play power broker in the GOP primary. A record 17 candidates entered the race, from perceived moderates Jeb Bush and John Kasich to die hard Rightists Mike Huckabee and Rick Santorum.[640] Another eight flirted with the possibility before the start of the race.[641] And then there was Donald Trump. Arguably no one saw Trump's potential earlier than Ralph Reed. While Reed had made a comeback, he had failed to ascend to his prior level of power. He was looking to be a kingmaker, and by early 2011, he thought he had found his guy.

━━━━━

Donald Trump had begun promoting what became known as "birtherism" right after the 2010 midterms. Joseph Farah, a right-wing journalist turned conspiracy theorist, remembers getting an initial phone call from Trump in early 2011.[642] Farah had founded a website called WorldNetDaily (WND) — notorious for propagating fringe and baseless ideas — in the late-1990s after being exiled from mainstream journalism and later promoting the debunked claim that the Clintons were involved in the death of deputy White House counsel Vince Foster.[643] [644] [645] From his platform at WND, Farah peddled a panoply of disinformation, carrying forward Weyrich's contention that cultural Marxists were decimating the country and even arguing that soybeans caused homosexuality.[646] While no one knows the precise origin of the false assertion that Obama was born in Kenya, almost no one had done more to promote it than Farah's operation — until Trump joined in.

Journalists had vetted and rejected the allegation when it first popped up during the 2008 election.[647] The Obama White House first laughed at it, then denied it, then ignored it. Exploring a presidential run in 2012, Donald Trump wanted to revive it so he called Farah. Over the course of several phone calls, Trump repeatedly asked his new friend how they could turn the tide on the story and get to the bottom of it.[648] In the spring of 2011, Trump set off on a media tour and announced in a Today Show interview that he had "real doubts" about the president's citizenship and had personally sent investigators to Hawaii to uncover the truth.[649]

Trump was met with a combination of scorn and derision from the mainstream media. The Guardian called Trump's political aspirations "a punchline looking for a joke."[650] Later when he ultimately declined to run against Obama in 2012, the Washington Post's Chris Cillizza wrote that the decision "is likely to be greeted by a sigh of relief by most Republican Party strategists who viewed Trump as a major distraction for the more serious contenders for the nomination."[651]

But not everyone agreed. Sam Nunberg, a consultant helping Trump explore a 2012 run, argued that it was birtherism that allowed Trump to catch fire and consolidate a base.[652] He cited an April 2011 poll that showed Trump beating right-wing darling Newt Gingrich, in a dead heat with conservative stalwart Huckabee, and trailing just behind GOP establishment candidate Mitt Romney, who went on to win the nomination.[653]

The Rev. Jesse Jackson called Trump's efforts "coded and covert rhetoric for stirring up racial fears" about the first Black president.[654] NBC, which aired Trump's popular show, The Apprentice, warned him to back off for fear of alienating Black viewers. But Nunberg was not alone in egging Trump on. Right-wing consultant and Trump adviser Roger Stone saw how the base responded to Trump's claims. Stone, later convicted for witness tampering and lying to prosecutors in the Mueller investigation,[655] said, "Many of them believe the president is foreign-born, and Trump has an ability to interject any idea that is outside of the mainstream into the mainstream."[656] The disinformation campaign had its intended effect.

Ralph Reed was taken by Trump's willingness to play to the base even if he got some details wrong. Like his forefathers had seen in Reagan, Reed saw in Trump a natural showman, seemingly devoid of a guiding philosophy but with a raw instinct for projecting power. Trump's unapologetically racist message never deterred Reed and perhaps was further proof that their goals were aligned. He overlooked the novice's brash temperament, believing it might even be an asset to a modern campaign. In 2011, Reed invited Trump to his organization's annual Road to Majority conference, introducing him to leading movement players.[657] BuzzFeed News even reported that "Reed privately agreed to run Trump's campaign if he decided to enter the 2012 race."[658]

Meanwhile, Fox News enthusiastically promoted Trump's rise as a political figure. In 2011, he became a regular guest on its programs.[659] Trump even landed his own weekly segment on Fox News' morning show Fox & Friends, titled "Mondays with Trump." He used the platform to denigrate women, immigrants, and communities of color while the network trumpeted him as "bold, brash, and never bashful."[660] [661] The audience ate it up.

With Reed's guidance, Trump visited Liberty University, now under the purview of Jerry Falwell Jr., who took the helm after his father's death. The younger Falwell was in some ways more like his father's partner Paul Weyrich than his father. After inheriting the university, he embarked on a path of expansion that would ultimately turn the school from a $100 million operation to a $1 billion empire in less than a decade.[662] He was intrigued by Trump's ambition, unapologetic willingness to speak his mind, and tendency to lean into American exceptionalism.

Falwell Jr. hyped Trump's appearance, which drew record crowds. Trump took the stage with right-wing darling Michele Bachmann and the winners of the Miss Universe and Miss USA pageants.[663] [664] He worked to establish his Christian bona fides throughout his speech, claiming, "I really wanted to be here because I've heard so much about Liberty University, especially being Presbyterian, being a Christian, a very proud Christian ... and a real Christian."[665]

He went on to express grave concern about the direction that America was heading and its standing in the rest of the world. That day, Falwell Jr. described Trump as "one of the greatest visionaries of our time" and awarded him an honorary doctorate in recognition of his "unwavering and public commitment to our nation's founding principles."[666]

———

Falwell Jr. would later endorse Trump early in his 2016 bid, enraging many associates, students, and faculty at the fundamentalist Christian university.[667] It's not hard to see why. Those at Liberty were among the most devout. A decade and a half into the new millennium, the students were the second generation of Evangelicals to grow up with the idea that abortion was the central sin. They believed what they were taught and many were confused by what they saw as a bizarre endorsement when there were unimpeachable options in Huckabee and Santorum, whom many of these young people grew up lionizing.

Taken at face value, Falwell Jr.'s use of the term "unwavering" to describe Trump made no sense in a culture that had wrapped all of its aspirations around the mantle of ending legal abortion. If Trump had indeed been converted on the issue, his path had been pretty winding. On top of that, he was hardly fluent in the language of their movement.

In the 1980s and 1990s, Trump was mostly concerned with growing his empire in the unabashedly pro-choice culture of cosmopolitan New York. When Trump first dipped his toe into politics in the late 1990s, flirting with the idea of a presidential run on the Reform Party ticket, he pointed to his involvement with pro-choice fundraisers.[668] He even co-hosted one for NARAL, although — true to form — he never fulfilled his pledge. His position appeared to have been reflexively adopted from the world in which he operated and devoid of any real principle or philosophy. This was apparent in an NBC Meet the Press interview in 1999. "I hate the concept of abortion," he said. "I hate it. I hate everything it stands for. I cringe when I listen to people debating the subject. But you still — I just believe in choice."[669]

When Trump flipped positions in 2011, his answer was the exact opposite, but sounded familiar with its lack of fluency or conviction. When asked by Bill O'Reilly if he would outlaw abortion, Trump stammered through a tortured answer. "Something I don't like, I used to not be pro-life," he said. "I have become pro-life. I have seen friends that had children that they didn't want. And now they have children and they are the apple of the eye. So I really have changed in my views over the years but I am pro-life. I would — I would really

— I'm forming an opinion, I'm forming a very strong opinion but I'll let you know in about three or four weeks if I decided to."[670]

For ambitious right-wing leaders like Falwell and Reed, who saw Trump as an opportunity for ascendance, this answer was close enough. Reed later swore to NPR that he believed Trump was sincere in his commitment to anti-choice policies. "We became friends because I saw him on TV talking about the abortion issue in a way that I thought was compelling and transparent and based on his deep moral conviction," Reed said.[671] Later, he would claim, "I talked to him about it in 2010 and 2011, and he was unapologetically pro-life."[672]

Falwell and Reed seemed sure that Trump's positions and rhetoric were malleable. What was really attractive to these anti-choice leaders was his ability to tap into a deep-seated anger and anxiety that white Evangelicals felt about a country they saw as increasingly hostile to them, one where they were not in the majority and losing control of the debate.

Richard Land, the president of the Southern Baptist Convention's Ethics & Religious Liberty Commission, had pointed to so-called "anger points" to explain why the philandering Newt Gingrich was handily beating known family man Romney among Evangelicals in the 2012 presidential primary.[673] Gingrich had an affair while prosecuting the Clinton impeachment case and ultimately left his sick wife to marry a younger woman.[674] Yet for evangelical and far-right voters, his personal piousness was less important than his willingness to channel rage at anyone questioning the agenda of the Far Right. On this metric, the mild-mannered Romney couldn't compete. Going into 2016, Falwell and Reed knew that Donald Trump had cornered the market on anger points.

———

Trump centered raw racism in his campaign from the day he announced his run for president. "When Mexico sends its people, they're not sending their best," he belted out during his campaign announcement. "They're not sending you. They're not sending you. They're sending people that have lots of problems, and they're bringing those problems with us. They're bringing drugs. They're bringing crime. They're rapists. And some, I assume, are good people."[675]

To many in the Far Right, Trump's comment wasn't an embarrassing lapse in message discipline, but rather a successful audition. The political culture of the right in the United States often gets divided into subcategories like "corporatists," "nationalists," "pro-lifers," and the like, but, at its core, the Far Right is both so demographically and ideologically homogeneous that "activating that group is not rocket science," according to Public Religion Research Institute's Robert Jones.[676] "As our country transitions for the first time to a truly multicultural democracy, we are living through a tremendous backlash, and Trump really represents that," Southern Poverty Law Center senior fellow Mark Potok told *The Huffington Post*.[677] While mainstream pundits were laughing at Trump's campaign launch, his target audience was watching, listening, and applauding.

In just one month, Trump went from having the lowest favorability among Republicans to being at the top of the GOP field in many polls and a close second in others.[678] While pundits may have dismissed him, Trump and his team saw that his announcement speech paid dividends. His campaign quickly made his unapologetic anti-immigrant rhetoric and policies a focus of his messaging. Chants to "Build the Wall" became staples of Trump rallies as he brazenly promised that he would make Mexico pay for his promised barrier along the border and that it wouldn't cost American taxpayers a dime.[679] Establishment Republicans grew increasingly uncomfortable as his popularity surged among Tea Party voters, non-college educated voters, and those who held anti-immigrant views.[680]

By giving voice and credibility to these racist ideas, Trump became a gateway drug for those on the fringes who had never felt like politics was an effective means of advancing their agenda. Less than two weeks after his announcement, Trump won early support from The Daily Stormer, a neo-Nazi website. "Trump is willing to say what most Americans think: it's time to deport these people," the endorsement said. The site encouraged its white male readership to "vote for the first time in our lives for the one man who actually represents our interests."[681]

White nationalist activist Matthew Heimbach, who later helped organize the deadly 2017 Unite the Right rally in Charlottesville, Virginia,[682] said that Trump's candidacy was energizing disaffected young white men, "bringing people back out of their slumber."[683] David Duke praised Trump for going "all out" with anti-immigrant rhetoric and for "saying what no other Republicans have said, few conservatives say." He added that Trump is "certainly the best of the lot. And he's certainly somebody that we should get behind in terms of, ya know, raising the image of this thing."[684]

White nationalist leader Richard Spencer was all in as well. "Trump, on a gut level, kind of senses that this is about demographics, ultimately. We're moving into a new America," he told the *New Yorker*, going on to posit that Trump reflected "an unconscious vision that white people have — that their grandchildren might be a hated minority in their own country. I think that scares us. They probably aren't able to articulate it. I think it's there. I think that, to a great degree, explains the Trump phenomenon. I think he is the one person who can tap into it."[685]

Spencer had founded a white supremacist website in 2010 called AlternativeRight.com, which published content denigrating Jewish people, ethnic minorities, and women.[686] [687] He claimed to have invented the term "alt-right" and went on to take over the obscure National Policy Institute, aspiring to have an institutional think tank for white supremacist policies. He authored papers about how to establish a white ethno-state where women knew their rightful place and could not vote, and men could rule in peace.[688] [689]

That a presidential candidate from a major national party was endorsed by several prominent, avowed white supremacists should have raised some eyebrows. It should have been a moment for conservative leaders to distance themselves from such racism. Instead, many cheered Trump on. Ann Coulter breezily dismissed concerns about Trump's alliance with white nationalists: "They used to say the same thing about the pro-life Republicans and the pro-gun Republicans, and, 'Oh, they're fringe and they're tacky, and we're so embarrassed to be associated with them.' Now every one of them comes along and pretends they'd be Reagan."[690]

Of course, Trump himself openly revelled in the elite backlash to his support among extremists. Stirring up controversy to maximize attention is a trademark characteristic of his that has since become familiar. After Duke's endorsement, Trump was pressed to answer whether he would repudiate the known Klansman. He snidely answered, "If it made you feel better."[691]

———

Just as Trump's unapologetic embrace of bigotry excited racists who had never had a champion in mainstream politics, it did the same for a newly prominent group of misogynists.

Men's Rights Activists, or MRAs, weren't new. They had emerged in the 1970s as part of the reaction to feminism.[692] Decades later, a cohort of self-aggrieved men activated by women's equality found a new home online to "reclaim their natural manhood and usurp women's social, political, and economic power."[693] They gathered in chat rooms and radicalized a new generation around mostly personal issues, spending hours comparing notes on message boards about how they weren't getting their due in life and love because women had ceased to know their place.

Their culture revolved around trolling feminists and women who bucked their systems, but they rarely engaged with politics and so were relatively unknown to most Americans. But in 2014, the year before Trump launched his campaign, the movement burst into popular consciousness. During what would come to be known as Gamergate, hordes of MRAs harassed female video game developers and journalists, threatening them with rape and violence.[694] Their sin? Creating games with female protagonists that eschewed violence.

Gamergaters relished what they considered to be a provocative opposition to political correctness.[695] They saw a cultural malaise that had settled on a generation of disaffected white men entering a complicated world and wanted to shift it into anger. They operated in safety from secluded corners of the internet where conspiracy theories could blossom and they could test their offensive narratives with impunity. They delighted in misogynist rhetoric, egging each other on and lambasting those who tried to erect guardrails. "Are you triggered?!"[696] they would jeer at anyone who tried to curb their most hateful conversations. They referred to the converted as being "red pilled" in reference to The Matrix, a popular movie from the late 1990s in which the protagonist has to take a red pill to see the ugly truth about reality.[697]

In Trump, these online groups found a hero — someone who not only clearly shared their misogyny, but also was in on the joke against the liberals. Trump was willing to take their conversations out into the open, railing from the stump against political correctness and openly denigrating women he believed had wronged him.[698] [699] [700] [701] [702] The GOP establishment and the mainstream media pondered the wide field of 2016 primary contenders in search of a clear front-runner. But like the white supremacists, the MRAs had found their guy. They saw a kindred spirit and an opportunity to help propel Trump to electoral victory. As sociologists Pierce Dignam and Deana Rohlinger wrote in the book "Misogynistic Men Online," "The Red Pill forum was explicitly opposed to political involvement until the summer before the 2016 election. Users and forum leaders rejected political action because they associated it with 'mainstream' men's rights movements. This changed months before the election. **Leaders and elite users of the forum heralded Trump's candidacy as an opportunity to push back against feminism and get a 'real man' into the White House.**"[703] [Emphasis added.]

MRAs were fluent in the language of the internet and fought for Trump the same way they had fought against women in the video game industry: through mean-spirited inside jokes, especially homemade images. Purveyor of fake news and famous internet troll Chuck Johnson claimed, "The election was won by a bunch of people making memes. We memed the President into existence."[704] As the saying goes, "victory has a thousand parents;" however, there's no question that early support from MRAs not only boosted Trump's clout, but also encouraged his blatant sexism on the campaign trail. He had an army ready to leap into hand-to-hand combat with those who sought to temper it.

In May 2016, New York Magazine's The Cut, published a quiz inviting readers to guess whether various misogynistic quotes originated from Donald Trump or an MRA message board. The phrases it posted included "A person who is very flat-chested is very hard to be a ten" and "All of the men, we're petrified to speak to women anymore. We may raise our voice." It was hard to tell who said what.[705]

The MRA culture set the tone for Trump supporters to target Hillary Clinton in ways that would never have been socially permissible before. Time reporter

Charlotte Alter analyzed bestselling campaign merchandise in June 2016 and found that the most popular items almost always correlated with the most sexualized, base, and gender-specific messaging. She highlighted top sellers like buttons that read "Hillary will go down faster than Bill's pants" and "Trump that Bitch."[706] Alter's piece ended with an anecdote that captured the vice-like grip of emerging culture. "For [Etsy merchant Amy] Doughty, the money she makes from selling joke Monica Lewinsky buttons doesn't help her sleep easier at night. She's afraid her bestselling items mean that Trump is going to be president. 'When you sold a million pro-Obama things, you felt the energy that people loved him,' she says. 'When you sell all these Anti-Hillary things, it makes me so nervous.'"[707]

While memes were hardly new and all sides certainly used them, no one was as proficient at assuring their spread as the MRAs and the Radical Right. They quickly dominated large swaths of the internet and claimed it as Trump territory. In 2016, only 5% of the posts on right-wing propaganda site Breitbart were of images, but those images accounted for half of the site's most-shared posts on Facebook.[708] Memes helped spread toxic disinformation about Hillary Clinton's health and Democrats' positions on everything from national security to reproductive health. The Pizzagate conspiracy theory spread through the channels, perpetuating the lie that high profile Democrats were involved in pedophilia. The story led a disaffected follower to shoot up the pizza parlor falsely rumored to be the scene of the crime. A viral meme would often consume mainstream media cycles for days on end.[709]

Recognizing the potential in the digital content, Jeff Giesea — a consultant to the Koch brothers and Trump supporter Peter Thiel — teamed up with MRA leader Mike Cernovich to organize MAGA3X, a grassroots army of online trolls who worked to meme Trump into the White House.[710] As Jennifer Rubin, a columnist at the *Washington Post*, put it a few weeks before the election: "Donald Trump's campaign rhetoric is an extension of the crackpot right-wing media, his appearance paved by years of conspiracy theories, dog-whistles, paranoia and, yes, appeals to racism and ridicule of women."[711]

———

MRAs had a natural synergy with the Radical Right not only in their anti-feminist politics but also in their hatred of the mainstream media. When the Gamergate leaders were being criticized by journalists for their targeted harassment against women — particularly their ruthless attacks on women of color — they cried lazy journalism and media malfeasance.[712] Long before Trump made cries of "fake news" central to his campaign, his new allies had begun the work of delegitimizing the fourth estate in the eyes of their followers. For MRAs, the elite media was so captured by political correctness that they could not effectively do their jobs. White supremacists were notorious for their belief the media was run by their number one enemy — the Jews.

Christian Fundamentalists, also, had long felt persecuted by journalists and believed that liberal elites controlled the media and mocked their way of life. Newt Gingrich captured the anti-media sentiment — and the anger points — during his run for president in 2012. He was asked by CNN's John King how a prior extramarital affair squared with his religious beliefs. Instead of defending himself, Gingrich exploded with rage at King, "I think the destructive, vicious, negative nature of much of the news media makes it harder to govern this country, harder to attract decent people to run for public office. I'm appalled you would begin a presidential debate on a topic like that."[713]

Gingrich supporters in the audience leapt to their feet with applause. They had no trouble choosing sides in a contest between a sanctimonious hypocrite who supported their views and a mainstream media figure who they had been convinced looked down on them. The clip itself made rounds on right-wing news sites, with an overlay portraying Gingrich as a lion and King as a hunted zebra.[714] In their fight for their way of life, the Religious Right had long ago decided that the elite media was enemy number one.

In building their movement, Far-Right leaders included a prolific network of information sites to skirt the mainstream media. As early as 1973, National Right to Life created a series of publications talking directly to the converted and those they might convert. This included National Right to Life News and Choose Life, a "pro-life newspaper for the religious community" that was published every two months in English and Spanish for distribution through churches.[715] [716]

The movement was quick to adapt to the digital age and launched a series of platforms — including LiveActionNews, LifeNews.com, and LifeSiteNews. com — which pumped the internet full of phony information about abortion "reversal," the "abortion-breast cancer link," and "post-abortion syndrome" all in service of reinforcing its core ideology.[717] [718] Dedicated to advancing self-styled "pro-life" values, these sites have also elevated white supremacist tropes and disinformation to suppress the vote, as well as signal boosting plain old GOP talking points.[719] [720]

Of course, the same media outlet that had given Trump a platform during his birther campaign was also the centerpiece of the spread of anti-choice propaganda: Fox News. Often by the time other networks covered abortion-related content, they had been infected by the Fox-boosted disinformation. An in-depth study by Media Matters for America found that "CNN and MSNBC allowed Fox News to dominate abortion-related conversations with dangerous misinformation. Fox aired 94% of the three networks' statements about four common abortion-related topics, and it was wrong 85% of the time. When CNN and MSNBC did talk about abortion, they were wrong 67% and 40% of the time, respectively."[721]

Much like Trump himself, the purveyors of disinformation were handed Fox's megaphone to broadcast their claims and cry they were victimized by a supposedly biased mainstream media. Tucker Carlson and other prime-time hosts often invited Live Action's Lila Rose and other right-wing figures on-air to disingenuously claim that Twitter and other digital platforms were censoring their content. As a result, voters going into 2016 were confused and terrified by the constant denigration of mainstream media and baseless allegations of bullying by the left on social media platforms. From the beginning, the movement had been comfortable with disinformation as a key tenant of its strategy. Now more than ever, a proliferation of disinformation, hate speech, and racially charged content shaped the narrative and gave life to extremists who previously lived on the fringes of our culture and our politics.

———

Initially, not all right-wing leaders were as keen on Trump as Reed and Falwell Jr. On the heels of a successful midterm election for the GOP, Kellyanne Conway shrunk from Trump's claims when he was on his well-publicized birther tour in 2011. She dismissed his baseless claim, and said that if he wanted to win, he was going to have to do so "on the merits."[722] Conway was no more convinced when Trump dove into the 2016 race, believing that Trump couldn't win enough women to cross the threshold. She found his openly sexist views and rhetoric destructive to the carefully crafted message she had honed since the mid-1990s. Conway went all in for the safer, if equally extreme, bet.

Texas Sen. Ted Cruz was a Federalist Society member with a smooth presentation and an undeniable commitment to advancing the conservative agenda.[723] From her perch as chair of the Cruz SuperPAC Keep the Promise 1, Conway launched ads against Trump and told political newspaper Roll Call that he was too risky for female voters. "For every woman who is attracted to Trump as the non-political, non-traditional outsider, there are two or three women who say they don't like bullies," she said. "They don't like the attack on Bush's low energy, they don't like telling Rand Paul, 'I'm at 42 percent, you're at four.' They don't appreciate talking about Carly Fiorina by saying 'Look at that face, look at that face!'"[724]

She wasn't alone. As early as August 2015, Concerned Women for America President Penny Nance expressed concerns about Trump: "Does he have a problem with women? Three wives would suggest that yes, maybe there's a problem... Every presidential election since 1964 has been carried by women. Women don't like mean, and we certainly won't vote for men or women we don't trust."[725]

SBA List President Marjorie Dannenfelser, thrilled at the idea of electing a conservative woman, was an early supporter of GOP candidate and businesswoman Carly Fiorina. In December 2015, she and Nance co-wrote an op-ed for Time titled "Feminists Are Total Hypocrites When It Comes to Carly Fiorina."[726] In addition to Dannenfelser's praise of Fiorina's "poise under fire" and commitment to "principles and process," the pair saw her candidacy as an opportunity to continue presenting their anti-women agenda with pro-woman framing and actual women candidates.[727]

Indeed, in April 2016, the trio's missions converged after Cruz announced that Fiorina would be his running mate — Dannenfelser celebrated Fiorina as "the ideal choice for a Vice Presidential candidate."[728]

———

While these women remained skeptical, the men worked to help Trump aggressively cultivate relationships with key evangelical leaders.[729] They organized regular prayer sessions, often incorporating the topic of abortion to cover for his perceived weakness on this key issue.[730] Trump advisers sought help from influential community members like Family Research Council's Tony Perkins, who they tapped to incorporate Christian themes into Trump's speeches.[731]

Trump did his part. "If there's an evangelical on the plane, he wants them to sit beside him, and he just peppers him with questions," evangelical leader Richard Land told CBN's David Brody. "Peppers them with questions. Questions, questions, questions, questions, questions."[732]

Seemingly at Reed and Falwell's urging, Trump attended an October 2015 meeting of the secretive conservative leadership group the Council of National Policy (CNP). Trump prepared for the event under the tutelage of Eagle Forum President Ed Martin, a close associate of Phyllis Schlafly, and Martin briefed then-Trump campaign manager Corey Lewandowski on the mission of CNP, background on the organization, and how to work the crowd. Along with other aspiring GOP candidates, Trump had 30 minutes to speak and an additional 30 minutes for Q&A with the Far Right's top decision makers.[733]

Trump hit a home run. He delivered his practiced lines, emphasizing his commitment to hard-line, right-wing views and his support among grassroots evangelical voters. Far from kowtowing to the established leaders, Trump used his signature swagger to implore them to get onboard — leveraging his direct communication with the base via social media as a key strength. As one attendee summarized: "His message was, 'Your people are for me, and all you leaders ought to be for me too. You guys need to realize where your followers are, and get in line with them.' And he did that by reading poll results, line by line. He is a genius when it comes to using the bandwagon effect."[734]

Had anyone been paying attention, Trump's reception at the event offered an early sign that his candidacy wasn't a stunt or a fluke. Sources at the event described him as the "star attraction," noting, "While attendees shuffled in and out during other presentations, the room was packed and buzzing for the entirety of Trump's time on stage."[735] The crowd enthusiastically applauded as he worked his way through the required talking points, pledged to defund Planned Parenthood, and named Clarence Thomas as his favorite Supreme Court justice. One prominent conservative in attendance argued that the most significant proof point of Trump's viability was in his ability to disarm his opponents. With his popular appeal, not a single person at the conference rose up to challenge him.[736]

There was no love in these halls for the establishment candidate and presumed frontrunner, Jeb Bush. Though it would take mainstream media and conservative funders far longer to catch on, a conference attendee read the room, "The conservative movement is much more antagonistic toward Jeb Bush than Donald Trump. Coming out of this weekend, I see a conservative movement that would be more comfortable with Donald Trump as the nominee than Jeb Bush."[737] This group's disappointment in prior Bush presidencies would ultimately prove to be Jeb's undoing in the GOP primary.

Trump stood out as unapologetic in his views, while other candidates had modulated or moderated. For a movement that had formed its own identity around a combination of moral sanctity and claims of persecution from an agnostic society, Trump's no-holds-barred approach was a breath of fresh air.

While Trump viscerally aligned with his audience, he was far from fluent in their language. Early on, he struggled with a coded question from Charmaine Yoest, president of Americans United for Life, failing to recognize her language of "women's health funding" as a reference to abortion. But his willingness to rail against Planned Parenthood sufficed.[738]

Many evangelical leaders were willing to build a culture of permissiveness around Trump's candidacy. They treated his naiveté as the winsome charm of a new convert, not as a function of a lack of grounding philosophy. Small signs of Trump's ignorance were laughed off as he showered leaders with praise. Jerry Falwell Jr. invited Trump back to Liberty in January 2016, where the candidate famously referred to a Bible verse as "Two Corinthians" rather than "Second Corinthians."[739] When called out by skeptics, Trump went on *CNN* to redirect blame: "Tony Perkins wrote that out for me. He actually wrote out the 2. He wrote out the number 2 Corinthians. I took exactly what Tony said, and I said, 'Well, Tony has to know better than anybody.'"[740] That was enough. Falwell Jr. endorsed him.

Evangelical voters warmed to Trump's pitch. He wasn't perfect, they reasoned, but was eager to learn at the feet of their leaders and that was enough. David Brody, chief political analyst for Pat Robertson's Christian Broadcasting Network (CBN) and author of "The Faith of Donald J. Trump," interviewed Trump nine times ahead of the 2016 election — more than any other Republican presidential candidate in modern history. Brody identified the natural affection between the flock and their new candidate: "For all the media wondering why evangelicals are attracted to Trump's message, here's why: most evangelical Christians see the world and issues as black and white. They operate in biblical absolutes. They are also ripped by people for speaking out about their conservative biblical views. In much the same way, Donald Trump speaks out on his views and is ripped. He also sees the world as pretty much black and white and absolutely operates in non-negotiable absolutes. See the kinship?"[741]

———————

For the women of the Radical Right, who had spent decades carefully crafting messages to give their movement a shallow facade of respectability only to continually be tripped up by men who wouldn't heed their warnings, Trump's indelicate presentation was worrisome. Even as Trump aggressively campaigned to win over anti-choice voters, he had not learned how to walk their painstakingly constructed messaging tightrope. He kept slipping off it.

Trump committed a grievous sin in an August 2015 interview attempting to justify the Right's continual attack on Planned Parenthood funding. He said, "The problem that I have with Planned Parenthood is the abortion situation. It is like an abortion factory, frankly. And you can't have it. And you just shouldn't be funding it. That should not be funded by the government, and I feel strongly about that."[742] So far, so good. His comments — leaning on the disinformation that demonized Planned Parenthood and denied the fact that the Hyde Amendment's ban was still in effect — would have satisfied the Radical Right if he'd just stopped there. Instead, he rambled on, saying: "I would look at the good aspects of [Planned Parenthood], and I would also look, because I'm sure they do some things properly and good and that are good for women, and I would look at that, and I would look at other aspects also. But we have to take care of women."[743]

Right-wing leaders were apoplectic. Their effort to defund Planned Parenthood was about so much more than their performative objections to the medical procedure of abortion. They fundamentally objected to the organization's work to empower women through education and birth control. And as the organization had gained notoriety as a political powerhouse, they became an electoral threat that many in the GOP establishment agreed needed to be eliminated. Instead of bolstering the attacks on Planned Parenthood, Trump suggested that supporting the institution would be acceptable if it stopped providing abortions. Even more egregious to his new friends, Trump ceded the claim that Planned Parenthood provided critical healthcare services to women.

In a flurry of activity that almost sunk his campaign, anti-choice groups reacted swiftly and forcefully. SBA List's Mallory Quigley issued a statement saying, "We have always opposed federal funding for Planned Parenthood because they are America's largest abortion business and any dollars that they receive free up other funding, which is available for abortion."[744]

Alliance Defending Freedom's Kerri Kupec said, "I'm not quite sure what he was thinking when he said that, to be honest with you. To say, let's keep funding the quote unquote 'good aspects' - why are we making Americans and their hard-earned tax dollars complicit in this gross behavior that Planned Parenthood is engaging in, this callous disregard for human life?"[745]

Live Action's Lila Rose said, "Trump's vacillation on Planned Parenthood funding is deeply troubling, and reveals an ignorance about their horrific abortion practices."[746]

SBA List's Dannenfelser declared that Trump would be "unacceptable" as the Republican nominee, saying his opposition to abortion was unreliable and that he had "impugned the dignity of women."[747]

Trump was repentant. With the anti-choice movement gathering at the March for Life in Washington, D.C., Trump placed an op-ed in the Washington Examiner reasserting his position, "Let me be clear — I am pro-life... It is by preserving our culture of life that we will Make America Great Again."[748]

This was not enough for some. Days later, a group of 10 anti-choice leaders pushed back, declaring, "On the issue of defending unborn children and protecting women from the violence of abortion, Mr. Trump cannot be trusted."[749] Penny Nance characterized Trump as a "political opportunist," but left the door slightly open, noting that she was willing to hear Trump out and coach him on anti-choice ideology.[750]

For a while, there seemed to be a detente. Then, two months later, a different answer by Trump laid bare the stakes of his rhetorical missteps. MSNBC's Chris Matthews was probing the candidate on his desire to outlaw abortion and asked if women would then be criminally punished. Trump's uncertain response perfectly reflected both his observation of the anti-choice world and his lack of familiarity with its contrivances. "The answer is . . . that," Trump said, pausing briefly and glancing to the side as he considered his response, "there has to be some form of punishment." He punctuated the word "has" with a sort of karate chop.[751]

In response to calls from panicked anti-choice movement leaders, Trump walked his statement back within hours — but the damage was done. Doctors and pro-choice advocates noted that Trump's answer highlighted the reality of the Radical Right's position. Women were in fact already being punished by their policy proposals. Trump had said the quiet part out loud.

In Trump's comments, online feminists heard the familiar strains of the hordes of MRAs who stalked them. The mainstream media pointed to the obvious gaffe as further proof of Trump's inability to consolidate conservative support. They lifted up statements from Dannenfelser, who sternly lectured, "The pro-life movement has never, for very good reason, promoted the idea that we punish women." Dannenfelser declined to say exactly how the abortion bans her movement sought would be enforced without that effect.[752]

Kellyanne Conway took to CNN to defend her years of work. She told host Don Lemon, "the pro-life community is one mind on this. You do not punish the woman. She is looked upon as a victim."[753] And an outraged Penny Nance decried Trump's damage by saying, "He... became the caricature that the left tries to paint us to be."[754] His more devout opponents saw his error as an opportunity to redeem their own candidacy with voters. "Don't overthink it: Trump doesn't understand the pro-life position because he's not pro-life," tweeted Cruz spokesperson Brian Phillips.[755] Cruz went on to handily defeat Trump in the Wisconsin primary the following week, winning a majority of evangelical voters.[756] [757]

Trump's campaign staffers seemed to wonder whether this was a final blow against their quest to win over anti-choice advocates. The candidate skipped a planned address at the Priests for Life conference the following month, which caused Operation Rescue's Troy Newman to cast doubt on his authenticity. Newman said, "To me, that's just typical Donald Trump...we just don't know exactly what he believes or who he is."[758]

Frank Pavone, the head of the conference, minimized the incident, reminding people, "I far prefer the kind of mistake he made recently, and then corrected, regarding who should be punished, than the ongoing deliberate mistake of Clinton and Sanders who cannot seem to find an abortion they don't like." But the shine of Trump's candidacy was fading, as National Right to Life's Carol Tobias told *Politico*, "Pro-lifers like to support candidates that they know are going to be there...he would get, I think, more enthusiasm and more work out of the grassroots if he were a little more forthcoming on his position."[759]

———

Ultimately, Trump didn't need the consolidated support of anti-choice leaders to win the Republican nomination. In light of his massive rallies and vociferous online support, fueled by MRAs and white supremacists, just fracturing the right-wing leadership was sufficient. His growing list of supporters included stalwarts such as Sarah Palin, godmother of the movement Phyllis Schlafly, and Maine Gov. Paul LePage — who once justified his anti-choice position by claiming Maine was losing too much of its population to abortion.[760] [761]

As he had promised, Trump was able to skirt recalcitrant leaders and appeal directly to their followers and others who had considered themselves outsiders in the contemporary political environment. Indeed, according to a RAND Corporation study, "Among people likely to vote in the Republican primary, people are 86.5 percent more likely to prefer Donald Trump as the first-choice nominee relative to all the others if they 'somewhat' or 'strongly agree' that 'people like me don't have any say about what the government does.'"[762]

The same study found that Trump's primary supporters tended to be lower-income, less-educated males from states with a history of racism and, ironically, less likely to attend church.[763] They held stronger racist or sexist views than the general population, agreeing with statements like "immigrants threaten American customs and values" or "women who complain about harassment cause more problems than they solve."[764]

Although a minority voice within the party, voters with these sentiments decided the Republican primary contest. In July 2016, Trump accepted the nomination at the Republican National Convention in Cleveland, Ohio, to ebullient chants imploring the new nominee to "lock her up!" — referring to his general election opponent, Hillary Clinton.[765] Some Trump critics in the GOP facing reelection at home chose to skip the event. Sen. Steve Daines from Montana cited a fly-fishing trip with his wife, and Sen. Jeff Flake from Arizona claimed he had to mow his lawn.[766] Amid accusations of racism and sexism in the Trump campaign, corporate sponsors from Coca-Cola to Microsoft chose to scale back or withdraw their participation.[767] Trump's former rival Ted Cruz made a last stand during his convention speech, imploring delegates to "vote their conscience." He was booed off the stage and his wife Heidi was removed from the arena due to concerns for her safety.[768] [769]

Right-wing speakers paraded across the stage. Cultural celebrities like Duck Dynasty's Willie Robertson and religious leaders like Jerry Falwell Jr. extolled their candidate's virtues and prospects to best the right-wing nemesis, Democratic hopeful Hillary Clinton.[770] Establishment leaders like Senate Majority Leader Mitch McConnell were also all-in — a harbinger of what would become a dangerous complicity with the Trump administration.[771]

The speeches were punctuated by crowd pleasers like anti-immigrant icon Sheriff Joe Arpaio of Maricopa County, Arizona, and John Tiegen, veteran and Benghazi conspiracy theorist.[772] [773] Trump's personal pastor Mark Burns led the ecstatic crowd in a chant of "All Lives Matter."[774] But perhaps nothing symbolized the convergence of forces — and the synergy with the original vision of the founding fathers of the Radical Right movement — than the 2016 Republican platform.

While the disaffiliated rank and file put Trump over the top for the nomination, the movement faithful maintained control of the apparatus and saw an opportunity to concretize their agenda into GOP orthodoxy. The party platform underscored its commitment to ban most types of legal abortion, a mainstay since the Reagan years. But it did not stop there. Radical Right leaders focused diligently on reversing progress in other areas, confident it would meet no objections from the new nominee. Its leaders moved the party to the fringes on everything from guns to LGBTQ rights to immigration.[775] The GOP's platform committee prized rhetoric as much as policy, insisting on replacing every already objectionable reference to "illegal immigrant" with the more pejorative "illegal alien" and demanding lawmakers use religion as a guide for legislation, stipulating "that man-made law must be consistent with God-given, natural rights."[776] [777]

The LGBTQ movement was a focal point of vitriol, vindicating those who chafed at the omission in George W. Bush's second inaugural speech. Under the leadership of CNP's Tony Perkins, the platform committee adopted language affirming the primacy of the "traditional family." It committed to overturn the Supreme Court ruling affording marriage equality, stating that "natural marriage" between a man and a woman is less likely to produce drug-addicted offspring.[778] The platform affirmed the use of conversion therapy for LGBTQ youth, preached to the perils of allowing transgender people to use restrooms correlating to their identity, and committed the GOP to teach the Bible in public schools.[779] [780] [781] The disinformation campaign bled well beyond the LGBTQ realm, with the platform labelling carbon-intensive coal a "clean" energy source and calling pornography a "public health crisis."[782] Had they lived to see this day, Weyrich and Falwell would have been deeply gratified.

Anti-choice holdouts like Conway, Dannenfelser, and Nance had their backs up against a wall. The die was cast, but they were still not convinced that Trump could pull it off. If they went all in, his failure could set their movements back by years if not decades. But they also fretted that once in office, he would be unwilling or uninterested in delivering on their core issues.

Conway was the first to see the writing on the wall. Ever the pollster, she knew how to read the turning tide. Shortly after Cruz suspended his campaign in the lead up to the Republican National Convention, she had accepted a role to help the presumed nominee better appeal to women voters.[783] In August, she replaced Paul Manafort in running Trump's entire campaign and preached with the zealousness becoming typical of a Trump convert.[784] Ultimately, Conway would stand on the White House lawn and defend the fledgling administration's lies as "alternative facts."[785] But rolling into the fall of 2016, she had her work cut out for her persuading crucial allies to join the growing Trump coalition in order to secure victory for her candidate.

Chapter 7
The Alliance

Of the movement's original architects, only Phyllis Schlafly lived long enough to see Trump's rise. She made it clear that he was nothing less than the culmination of everything the Radical Right had been working toward. She endorsed him in early 2016 in a move so controversial that it prompted board members at her Eagle Forum, including her own daughter, Anne, to conspire to oust her.[786] Never one to shy away from unpopular decisions, Schlafly persevered, saying, "We've been following the losers for so long — now we've got a guy who's going to lead us to victory."[787]

Schlafly's endorsement was hugely symbolic. Alongside early supporters like Ralph Reed and Jerry Falwall Jr., it gave supporters permission to believe in a relative newcomer and it carried a formal stamp of approval on the candidate's chances from the old guard. What it didn't carry was much institutional power, as her Eagle Forum grassroots had atrophied and given way to new structures with a more overt focus on abortion.

Even with the nomination in hand, Donald Trump had a steep hill to climb. He had no political machine he could call his own and, as a GOP outsider, he could not count on marshaling its resources. A June 2016 *Atlantic* headline blared "There Is No Trump Campaign," reporting that despite raucous attendance at his rallies, Trump had failed to build any meaningful ground game.[788] The clock was ticking, and the Democratic apparatus was well resourced. It seemed basically impossible for his campaign to cover the shortfall. The fervent, vocal support of white supremacists and Men's Rights Activists had propelled him to the nomination, but these outsiders were not well-resourced or organized offline and had zero infrastructure for a real general election campaign.

When Trump became the nominee, he inherited the Republican National Committee's infrastructure, but it paled in comparison to Hillary Clinton's political organization and the Democrats' mobilization.[789] As Trump shrugged off calls to moderate his message and professionalize his approach in preparation for the general election, Republican leaders and funders shifted resources to focus their efforts on down-ballot races instead. Certain that their nominee would lose, they chose to save hard-fought gains from the impact of a disaster at the top of the ticket.

Trump needed a team, and the anti-choice movement — with all of its foot soldiers and political apparatus — was it. New guard leaders like Marjorie Dannenfelser or Concerned Women for America's Penny Nance were intrigued, but hesitant to put their credibility on the line for anyone less than a movement loyalist. If they were going to put themselves and their influence on the line, they needed more proof to be convinced that the risk was worth the reward.

His advisers knew he didn't have the full trust of the movement, and Trump didn't have years to prove his loyalty. Instead, they decided to sweeten the deal by promising massive rewards if he won. Trump was nothing if not transactional, and the Radical Right and anti-choice leaders proved willing to negotiate. They would drive a hard bargain as far as commitments on judges, pro-life positions, and staffing — including the vice presidential pick.

———

In February 2016, Trump was handed an unprecedented opening to prove his loyalty to the Radical Right — both by fate and by Mitch McConnell. Conservative Supreme Court Justice Antonin Scalia died suddenly, giving then-president Obama the opportunity to fill his third seat on the Supreme Court.[790] In the first two years of his presidency, Obama replaced David Souter and John Paul Stevens with Sonia Sotomayor and Elena Kagan, over the vehement protests of the GOP minority.[791] [792] But now, the GOP held the Senate and they were in no mood to give Obama a third seat, despite his nomination of the uniquely qualified Judge Merrick Garland to fill Scalia's seat.[793]

With an eye toward 2016, conservative donors, and a panicked right-wing, Mitch McConnell stepped in with a simple but high-stakes plan to ensure that the Radical Right's decades of plotting would not go to waste. He refused to grant the Obama nominee a hearing in the Senate Judiciary Committee, making a completely fabricated claim that a sitting president should not be able to nominate a justice in an election year.[794] It was a brazen move for the leader of a party that at the time was still embroiled in an ugly primary, circling around a nominee that no one believed was electable, with the Democratic frontrunner leading in every national poll.

McConnell knew that the Radical Right and the anti-choice movement had developed a wish-list of extreme policies they wanted a strong conservative president to pursue.[795] He also knew that owning the federal judiciary was the centerpiece of their strategy. He bet that Democrats — never known to rally around the Supreme Court and certain they would winwould be no match in his game of chicken for a zealous base who would rally around the opportunity to back a nominee fully committed to nominating the Federalist Society judges committed to overturning *Roe*.

McConnell was right. Trump turned out to fulfill that pledge and so many more, slowly winning over movement leaders with a series of unprecedented promises negotiated over time. With their allegiance came their resources, which the candidate desperately needed to propel him to his improbable victory.

———

Trump first signaled his endorsement of the federal 20-week abortion ban — a plum policy for the Radical Right — as early as July of 2015. In doing so, he turned a blind eye to something that made other leaders nervous; a massive public outcry that had followed Wendy Davis' thirteen-hour-long filibuster when Texas had passed the same measure just two years prior.[796] In an exclusive interview, he told The Christian Broadcasting Network's David Brody that he would happily enact SBA List's top legislative priority.[797] "We should not be one of seven countries that allows elective abortions after 20 weeks," Trump said, perfectly hitting talking points that demonstrated his adaptation to the movement's strategy to distract, deflect, and disinform. "It goes against our core values."[798]

By talking about the "seven countries," he glided over the fact that the vast majority of other countries make abortion services far more accessible in early pregnancy in order to push fewer people into surgery later in the process.[799] By talking about "our values," he discarded the mountains of testimony from doctors and patients that the bans were detrimental to the health and basic rights of pregnant women. And nowhere did he address challenges to the constitutionality of such a ban. All of this was music to the ears of movement leaders. SBA List took credit for Trump's announcement in its 2016 voter guide.[800]

Trump went on checking boxes. He registered a perfect score on the 2016 Federal National Pro-Life Alliance survey, by committing to the coveted litmus test for Supreme Court justices willing to overturn *Roe*. Trump even one-upped the ask by proclaiming support for legislation to completely remove the question of abortion from the jurisdiction of the federal courts, an extraordinary move that was considered fringe even by most anti-choice Republicans.[801] His enthusiasm to lean in and satisfy movement skepticism was strong enough for many to overlook his rhetorical errors.[802]

In February 2016, during one of his many repeat visits with CBN's Brody, Trump alternately excited and unnerved leaders by underscoring his deep commitment to reshape the federal judiciary in unorthodox and undisciplined ways. When asked, "Do you believe *Roe v. Wade* was wrongly decided back in the day, back in 1973?" Trump responded: "Well I do. It's been very strongly decided but it can be changed. Things are put there and they're passed but they can be unpassed with time but it's going to take time because you have a lot of judges to go."[803]

His potential as a vehicle to achieve their aims was clear, but his brash way of exposing their strategy unnerved more seasoned anti-choice leaders. In 2016, most people still felt certain that *Roe* could never be undone, believing it was too embedded in the social fabric and legal framework of our country. In early 2016, the media saw no merit covering such an outlandish idea coming from a candidate who no one believed stood a chance of winning.

SBA List's prior efforts to get presidential nominees to commit to anti-choice judges had met with little success.[804] [805] Following centuries of norms and practices, candidates resisted the call to apply litmus tests to judicial nominees. To avoid being "Borked," a term popularized in right-wing legal circles following the defeat of Reagan's nominee, the Federalist Society and the rest of the Radical Right's network of judicial groups had trained a new generation of conservative nominees to limit their paper trail on such issues and dogmatically adhere to evasive answers by invoking legal terms like "stare decisis" and "settled precedent."[806]

Never one to adhere to establishment practice, Donald Trump broke that barrier and joined McConnell's high stakes game of chicken with Democrats over Scalia's replacement. Trump made it clear during the primary that one of his first acts would be to appoint a Federalist Society-vetted judge committed to ending legal abortion. In an interview with Fox News' Chris Wallace in May 2016, he underscored his point: "I will appoint — judges that will be pro-life, yes. I will protect [the sanctity of human life] and the biggest way you can protect it is through the Supreme Court and putting people in the court."[807] Then Trump took the unprecedented step of releasing a full list of Supreme Court nominees he would consider. His claim was that every one of them was committed to gutting *Roe* and eviscerating reproductive rights. Many of their records showed a commitment to a whole host of other right-wing priorities. The Federalist Society litmus test was holding strong.[808]

Trump had essentially outsourced his judicial vetting process to core right-wing institutions like the Federalist Society and the Heritage Foundation.[809] The *National Review* was entirely accurate when it commented that "the timing of the list's release smacks of desperate pandering to conservatives," and both McConnell's gambit and Trump's proclamation had the intended effect. Major right-wing groups immediately circulated his pledge, and SBA List stated: "The battle lines have been drawn and the two sides are clear. SBA List is already making the case to pro-life voters that the Court matters and must be protected. This is not an election for pro-lifers to sit out."[810][811]

As he racked up primary wins and the nomination looked to be within grasp, Trump leaned on his longtime backers to help solidify this support. Far Right stalwarts and Trump boosters Ralph Reed and Tony Perkins were joined by other marquee names like James Dobson, Pat Robertson, and Gary Bauer to organize a private, invite-only meeting with key right-wing and anti-choice leaders.[812][813][814] The eight-hour event was called "A Conversation About America's Future With Donald Trump" and was intended as an intimate conversation to address any lingering concerns. Attendees at the event included Marjorie Dannenfelser of SBA List, Lila Rose of Live Action, Kristan Hawkins of Students for Life, Mike Gonidakis of Ohio Right to Life, and Troy Newman of Operation Rescue.[815] Jerry Falwell Jr. took to the stage to introduce Trump as "God's man to lead our great nation at this crucial crossroads in our history."[816]

Concerned Women for America President Penny Nance later wrote that the event included "a veritable who's who of Christian leaders." She described the "hopeful optimism" that permeated the event, noting, "As a major voting bloc, this was a room full of people appropriately prepared to be charmed and wooed."[817] At the conclusion of the weekend, Nance admitted to being one of those charmed and wooed by Trump's solid commitment on judges, but she was still holding out. She wanted more clarity on his intention to block funds for family planning clinics and to know his choice of running mate before formalizing her commitment. Mostly Nance, like other leaders, wanted a VP pick from the movement itself, an insurance policy to prove Trump's newfound loyalty.[818]

Internal chaos and personnel turnover had been a regular feature of Trump's campaign. As many of his loyal neophytes fell by the wayside, he used the opportunity to bring in increasing numbers of credentialed Radical Right operatives. Longtime GOP staffer John Mashburn, who had been an adviser to the late North Carolina GOP Sen. Jesse Helms, was hired as his campaign's policy director.[819] The Helms Amendment had long ago banned U.S. foreign aid from providing resources to health centers abroad if they offered comprehensive family planning services.[820] For skeptics like Penny Nance, Mashburn's appointment was a modest positive step, adding a recognizable name steeped in the movement's history and wisdom.[821] A few days after the "Conversation about America's Future," he shook up his campaign again. Even the most recalcitrant Trump supporters were visibly elated when the campaign brought on Kellyanne Conway in early July 2016.[822]

Now it was time to pick a running mate. Establishment Republicans, desperate to salvage their prospects, encouraged Trump to seek moderation on this ticket, floating names like Republican Governors John Kasich from Ohio or Chris Christie from New Jersey. While Kasich refused to be considered, Christie continued to lobby for a position. Knowing that his candidate needed someone familiar to and beloved by the Religious Right, Jerry Falwell Jr. encouraged Trump to reach out to then-Gov. Mike Pence of Indiana, an unpopular governor who was unlikely to win reelection in his own state.[823] [824] Pence's commitment to hard-line policies against women and the LGBTQ community had resulted in significant backlash from constituents and business leaders alike.[825] Unperturbed, Trump saw in Pence a kindred spirit who was willing to go against the grain of public opinion — and, importantly, a subservient running mate who would take orders and execute. On July 15, 2016, Pence was officially added to the ticket.[826]

"He was a key factor in why so many evangelicals supported Trump," Falwell said of Pence, who as the governor of Indiana oversaw both a draconian crackdown on gay rights in the name of religious freedom and a scorched earth approach to women's health. "It convinced people that if Trump was willing to pick somebody like Pence for vice president, he really was going to be a faith-friendly president."[827]

In August, settled in with a credentialed running mate and riding the convention bounce, Trump was squired by Conway around the far-right American Renewal Project's "Pastors and Pews" event in Orlando, Florida, where 700 faith leaders gathered to vet the new nominee. Evoking the Religious Roundtable meeting that introduced Reagan to the Religious Right, *Bloomberg News* trumpeted the story with the headline "Trump Goes Traditional With Florida Meeting of Evangelical Leaders." Conway was getting her candidate in line and on script. At this meeting dedicated to restoring a Bible-based culture, leaders were pleased to hear Trump's ardent support for lifting the Johnson Amendment, a federal policy barring tax-exempt churches from promoting political candidates. They'd long complained about not being able to fully use the pulpit to advance their political goals.

Still, top of mind at the gathering were recent rulings against vendors who refused to provide services for same-sex weddings. This group wanted to hear about how Trump would restore their rightful role in society and advance their vision of a Christian nation. Just two months after an attack in which dozens had been injured or killed at a gay nightclub in the same town, conference organizer David Lane declared, "Homosexual totalitarianism is out of the closet, the militants are trying [to] herd Christians there." If Trump disagreed, he didn't say anything to show it.[828] [829]

By then, the coarse, thrice-married Trump was polling among Evangelicals well ahead of where the devout Romney had been four years prior.[830] Most of the voters had made up their mind, but anti-choice leaders still scrambled to secure more concessions. In September 2016, Trump put the final seal on this alliance with a set of unprecedented commitments that met their every request.[831]

SBA List was given the honor of unveiling Trump's four pro-life policy promises committing to:

Nominate only pro-life justices to the U.S. Supreme Court.
Sign into law the 20 week abortion ban.
Defund Planned Parenthood as long as they continue to perform abortions.
Finally, make permanent the repressive Hyde Amendment.[832]

SBA List's Marjorie Dannenfelser took a victory lap, crowing, "For a candidate to make additional commitments during a general election is almost unheard of," she said. "The contrast could not be clearer between the two tickets."[833] The Trump campaign capped the deal by announcing that Dannenfelser would serve as national chairwoman of his campaign's newly unveiled Pro-life Coalition.[834]

Others in the Radical Right were similarly jubilant about their nominee. "Donald Trump has actually raised the bar for what pro-lifers can expect from Republican candidates," Alliance Defending Freedom (ADF) lawyer Matt Bowman wrote. Bowman, a former clinic protestor who would go on to work for the Trump administration's Health and Human Services Department, also boasted that "the movement has convinced Trump to accede to more of their demands than ever before."[835]

———

Trump had already sealed the deal with the Right by adopting their policies and hiring their people when he took the stage at the final debate of the general election. There, in a dramatic and unforgettable moment, Trump channeled the propaganda of John Willke when he viciously attacked Hillary Clinton for her position on abortion rights. After nervously stalking her around the debate stage, he flew into a tirade about how she would allow doctors to "rip the baby out of the womb of the mother just prior to the birth of the baby."[836]

Viewers were stunned. Fact-checkers rushed to correct Trump's claims, with the Vox headline proclaiming, "No, Donald Trump, Abortions Do Not Happen at 9 Months Pregnant."[837] [838] Doctors took pains to explain the facts about later abortion, fetal diagnoses, and clinical procedure. Clinton supporters rushed to point out that her position was grounded not only in Constitutional law but also her compassion for women's experiences.[839] And many women and families who had experienced the frequently agonizing situations that lead to abortions later in pregnancy shared personal stories, hoping to put an end to the politicization of their real lived experience.

In a parallel universe, Trump basked in adulation from members of a movement that was hearing their gospel come to life on one of the biggest stages in the world. Revved up, he began to center anti-choice themes in many speeches, with complete disregard for facts and feelings of those affected. With characteristic brashness, Trump frequently alluded to two unnamed friends who ended up deciding against aborting a child he described now as "a total superstar."[840]

Conway praised the effectiveness of Trump's blunt, if inaccurate approach: "I've been working on pro-life messaging for two decades in this town," she said. "And it took a billionaire man from Manhattan who had spent most of his life being pro-choice to deliver the most impassioned defense of life that many have ever heard."[841] Her allies followed suit, with SBA List's Mallory Quigley calling the debate moment "clarifying for voters." [842] Trump had cleared up any question that he intended to live up to his end of a bargain.

The once fractured and skeptical Far Right were now unified in their belief they could count on Trump's loyalty. They fully embraced his election as an unprecedented opportunity to bring the agenda of their movement's architects — both the Trojan Horse and everything it represented — to the center of the political agenda in Washington.[843] When the votes were later counted, it would become clear that leaders of the Radical Right had mobilized their own to put him over the top, an organizational feat that had once been predicted as almost impossible.

———

In late October, with weeks to go before Election Day, the Republican National Committee (RNC) was keeping its focus on down-ballot races.[844] [845] Trump and the Republicans had just over 1,400 staffers on the ground in battleground states, roughly a third of what Hillary Clinton and the Democrats had in place.[846] Reporter David Graham pointed to gaping holes in staffing in key states like Ohio and Colorado, explaining that "Trump has no state-level campaign director [in either state]." Across the map, Republican officials were awaiting marching orders from either Trump or the RNC but had been left wanting.[847] Rocky communication between the campaign and the party created chaos and confusion, compounded by the fact that almost no one believed Trump could win.

The anti-choice movement stepped up to fill the void. Two years prior, in the

2014 midterms, SBA List claimed to have visited half a million homes to get out the vote for their endorsed candidates.[848] The group had kept its operation active going into the 2016 presidential election cycle, boasting of access to more than 700,000 Americans.[849] Almost completely unnoticed by pundits and political elites, who had dismissed the growing strength of these forces for years, the voting bloc Dannenfelser created was leveraged in a moment when the situation seemed most dire for Trump's campaign.

SBA List would claim the largest ground game ever for the movement, ultimately spending more than $18 million in the 2016 election with over 750 canvassers knocking on 1.14 million doors to turn out the faithful for Donald Trump.[850] [851] Shamelessly coopting a feminist brand, SBA List's Women Speak Out PAC spent $2 million online to tear down Clinton, the first woman with a shot at the White House.[852 853 854 855 856 857]

Victory had always required them to undercut the inherent advantage Hillary had by being a pro-choice candidate in a pro-choice country. They knew they had to utilize the Kellyanne Conway strategy of deflection. In August 2016, SBA List launched a six-figure digital campaign specifically promoting disinformation about Hillary Clinton's stance on later abortion.[858 859] The ad was "designed to reach 550,000 pro-life, low propensity voters multiple times online" and used lies in an attempt to manufacture outrage and mobilize right-wing base voters.[860]

Their efforts to paint Clinton as an extremist on abortion were manifested in Trump's fact-free tirade at the debate. Now, they set about reinforcing his propaganda through social media and conversations while knocking doors to spread the word. SBA List amplified his disinformation with another heavy ad buy. Dropping during the last week of the campaign, the digital ad called "Not Okay" ran in the battleground states of Florida, Missouri, North Carolina, and Ohio targeting mostly white women deemed to be on the fence. Women Speak Out put out an urgent request to followers for funds to keep the ad up through Election Day, promising to boost the turnout of true believers and reach still undecided voters.[861 862 863 864]

Other movement organizations piled on. Penny Nance's Concerned Women for America state chapters campaigned for Trump, putting six teams in place in Florida to canvass an estimated 300,000 homes.[865 866] Nance ignored emerging concern about Trump's treatment of women, instead imploring all of the group's followers to turn out and vote for him: "Besides making decisions that affect our economy, Homeland Security, foreign policy, and the like, there's something else that president we elect in November gets to do. He or she gets to appoint judges. And just so we're clear, Supreme Court and federal judges are appointed for life. As in forever... Your vote for a presidential candidate on November 8th is also a vote for the men and women of the judiciary who make decisions that will impact America for years to come. Don't leave the future of our nation to chance. Make your voice heard on Election

Day."[867]

National Right to Life and its political groups claimed to have reached millions of pro-life voters in swing states and across key Senate and House races, becoming a top group to donate directly to anti-choice candidates.[868] [869] Ralph Reed's Faith & Freedom Coalition attested to have spent $10 million, knocked on 1.2 million doors, and distributed over 50 million pieces of campaign literature via churches and the mail.[870] The Family Research Council led a bus tour through 20 states and made more than 140 stops between September and the election.[871]

All of this election work came alongside a plethora of materials churned out by the institutions that Weyrich built. Priests for Life led the "Vote Pro-Life" Coalition, which included organizations like American Values, AUL Action, Heartbeat International, LifeNews, Life Site News, National Institute of Family and Life Advocates, Operation Rescue, and more.[872] [873] They collectively flooded the zone with propaganda and disinformation to compel voters to support their unlikely hero.

The Trump campaign itself did not invest in as many television ads as was traditional in a presidential race. It preferred to spend money on micro-targeted digital strategies and their signature large-scale rallies that received significant 'earned' TV coverage and allowed Trump to bask in the adulation of crowds as he denigrated minority populations, women, and the media.[874] However, the ads the campaign did run reinforced his core narratives. They played on fears that violent immigrants were stealing jobs from white people and terrorizing nice white communities.

Trump's grotesque debut ad of 2016 used images of the San Bernadino, California, mass killers, Syed Rizwan Farook and Tashfeen Malik, to call for a Muslim ban and closed borders.[875] Another Trump campaign ad literally depicted hordes of immigrants overrunning a border. When a fact-checker later pointed out that the border the ad showed was Morocco, not the United States, a campaign representative shrugged off the concern, saying: "No shit it's not the Mexican border, but that's what our country is going to look like if we don't do anything."[876] Outside operators seeking to affect the outcome of the US election through paying into fear and division had fertile ground from which to operate. A study of 2016 digital ads purchased by what turned out to be Russian groups seeking to influence the U.S. election showed that half of them sought to exacerbate tensions tied to race.[877]

Marjorie Dannenfelser, like Schlafly before her, thrived in this toxic stew of hate shaping the 2016 environment. While it's impossible to determine what drives individual votes, it's undeniable that white women in all four of the states targeted by SBA List broke for Donald Trump by significant margins.[878] The day after the 2016 election, SBA List took a moment to celebrate their victory, saying, "The pro-life movement is in the strongest position that it has been in in over 40 years since Roe v. Wade."[879] Weeks later, Dannenfelser said that the election "revolutionized the politics of abortion."[880] She never uttered a word of offense about the racism and misogyny that drove the campaign.

———

The willingness of the self-described "moral majority," including its women leaders, to tacitly encourage and provide cover for the scandal-prone president spoke to the underlying synergy between the Religious Right and the Trump campaign. Trump's support from white men grew and broadened from the early support of the online MRAs. His vocal racism and overt misogyny were a long awaited airing of deep grievances on behalf of those dreaming of the uncontested white male power structure of yesteryear.

We Hunted The Mammoth, a blog run by David Futrelle which tracks white male rage, explained the campaign's appeal, "Trump is, in many ways, their ideal alpha male, an arrogant, deliberately obnoxious asshole who treats women like shit but has a former model more than twenty years his junior as a wife.[881] Men's Rights Movement leader Daryush Valizadeh, who goes by Roosh V and authored an article advocating legalized rape, celebrated Trump's win as "a state of exuberance that we now have a President who rates women on a 1-10 scale in the same way that we do."[882] White nationalist James Allsup, who argued that women should not be able to vote, was invited to introduce Trump at a general election campaign rally and praised his promise to undermine contraception access.[883 884 885]

Going into the fall, white men with no college degree were breaking hard for Trump, with 76% reporting they were going to vote for him.[886] Most of these voters were in no way associated with the Men's Rights Movement or white supremacists, but these groups undeniably created a context for the election that reinforced a deep cultural angst that Trump cravenly tapped into. Instead of offering real solutions for so many who had been left behind in a post-industrial nation, the campaign's implicit message — like Reagan's in the eighties — was to blame others for taking what was rightfully theirs. Fueled by the Tea Party before them, their numbers amounted to real political power.

As for those in the Radical Right who had falsely claimed the mantle of feminism to advance a repressive agenda, they had multiple chances to pressure their nominee to temper his attacks and behave with more decorum. But true to form, their silence spoke volumes about what they were willing to tolerate and even support to maintain their privilege.

This was evident early on. At a GOP primary debate in the summer of 2015, in a question about presidential temperament, Fox News anchor Megyn Kelly reminded Trump of his long history of making sexist statements and objectifying women. "You call women you don't like fat pigs, dogs, slobs, and disgusting animals," she said, pointing to a comment he had made about a female contestant on his reality show looking better "on her knees." Trump turned the question into an attack on what he saw as humorless and rigid political correctness, saying: "I think the big problem this country has is being politically correct. I've been challenged by so many people and I don't frankly have time for total political correctness, and to be honest with you, this country doesn't have time either."[887]

He didn't stop going after Kelly when the debate ended. He continued to viciously attack her the following day with a rambling diatribe that took even the GOP establishment by surprise. He said Kelly had "blood coming out of her eyes. Or blood coming out of her wherever."[888] But while many scratched their heads at the inexplicable statement, his fans on the internet let out a raucous cheer. Finally, someone was standing up to uppity women. Future Trump adviser Steve Bannon used his platform as executive chairman at the alt-right *Breitbart News* to target Kelly. "We're gonna cull her out from the herd and just hit her nonstop," Bannon recalled later.[889] "That's when all war broke out." In a classic gaslighting move, Trump surrogate Newt Gingrich tore into the embattled Kelly in an interview, accusing her of being obsessed with sex for even asking the question.[890]

Kelly endured nine months of terror and harassment following the debate. The threats were so persistent that she had to increase security for her family, including her three small children. She finally left Fox News in January 2017, citing exhaustion and a desire to get out of the "snake pit."[891] The silence from the Radical Right was deafening.

Over the course of the campaign, more than 20 women came forward against Trump with charges of sexual assault ranging from uninvited kissing to grabbing genitals. Many of the stories were harrowing abuses of power, and the victims' accounts shared painstaking details. Trump went on the attack. He called every single one of the women a liar, sometimes mocking the accuser and her appearance, deeming them unworthy of his attention.[892] Right-wing movement leaders steadfastly refused to rebuke their candidate. The lack of defense of Kelly or the other women egged Trump on and he grew increasingly emboldened in his attacks[893] at the same time as he racked up endorsements from the Religious Right, wrapping himself more and more tightly in the "pro-life," "moral majority" veil.

Then on October 7, 2016, one month before the election, the *Washington Post* released a 2005 video of a conversation between Donald Trump and television host Billy Bush. The two were waiting in a trailer to film an episode of *Access Hollywood* when Trump started to describe how he went about seducing married women and even indicated he might hit on a woman that they were about to meet. He added, "I don't even wait. And when you're a star, they let you do it. You can do anything. ... Grab them by the pussy. You can do anything."[894]

The tape ricocheted around the globe and finally shocked and shamed establishment Republicans into voicing concern. Politicians from Mitt Romney to Paul Ryan condemned the comments. Republican National Committee Chairman Reince Priebus announced that the RNC would cease spending resources in support of Trump.[895] Arizona Sen. John McCain and several others rescinded endorsements.[896]

Trump, true to form, never retreated. With a wink and a nod to his base, he dismissed the tape as "locker room" talk and deflected that those who took offense had thin skins.[897] In an act of psychological warfare against his opponent, he threw the spotlight on three women who had accused Bill Clinton of sexual assault, insinuating the faux outrage was hypocritical and taking the spotlight off his own misdeeds.[898]

Many right-wing leaders — far from reviled — were awed by the audacity and effectiveness of Trump's move. While some establishment Republicans pulled back from the candidate, the Radical Right was largely unfazed. The tape might pose a problem for the public brand, but exploiting age-old tropes about women and sex, bad girls and worthy girls was a tried and true tactic for their movement. With their political machine fully operational, they believed the optics could be managed.

Trump's evangelical advisors convened an emergency meeting the day after the tape's release. They couldn't fathom risking the influence they had amassed within his campaign and decided to use their platforms as pious leaders to spin his candidacy as a redemption story. Johnnie Moore, head of My Faith Votes, explained to CBN's David Brody: "We had all the grace in the world for this man who had sacrificed his entire life, in my viewpoint, and supported us. How could we not support him? We all believed he was a different person, but even if he wasn't, it demanded all the more that we were people of grace with him."[899]

Jerry Falwell Jr. took it even further, suggesting that the tape was leaked by Trump's enemies within the GOP who were trying to derail his chances of winning the White House.[900][901] He unashamedly censored a Liberty University student's op-ed decrying the Access Hollywood statements and suggesting Trump was not fit to lead.[902] Falwell asserted that defeat was not an option and that the movement's support was justified if it would prevent "the Constitution being ripped apart by justices."[903] Ralph Reed shrugged off the entire affair, saying about the voters he represented: "I think a 10-year-old tape of a private conversation with a TV talk show host ranks pretty low on their hierarchy of... concerns." Reed reiterated his support for Trump, saying he prioritizes how Trump would "protect the unborn, defend religious freedom, [and] appoint conservative judges."[904] Pat Robertson simply chuckled indulgently that Trump was trying to appear "macho" and predicted that like the mythical phoenix, he would rise from the ashes.[905]

These leaders guessed exactly how Trump's blatant misogyny would play among their flock. There was no outcry from the pews or pulpits to withdraw support from Trump, and there wasn't much of a dent in his poll numbers.

The actions of the Radical Right not only mitigated the damage of Trump's statements, they also incentivized him to repay their support with an increase in his violent rhetoric when it came to abortion. It was just a few days later that he lit into Hillary Clinton at the third debate with his graphic, inaccurate description of a later term abortion.[906] A delighted Ralph Reed identified these few minutes of debate as "the third hinge point" of the campaign because it was about a topic that hadn't been the focus of attention by the media.[907] Trump learned early on that no scandal was too big to deflect by throwing the red meat of abortion disinformation at his base.

CBN's David Brody, a Radical Right stalwart himself, summarized: "The pro-life community, less concerned about the rhetoric and more concerned about the violence committed on the babies, asked themselves if 'Access Hollywood' was worth losing the election to Clinton with a candidate like Trump being willing to say things that respectable Republicans were unwilling to say."[908] The foundation upon which the movement was built held true. A study later conducted by Tresa Undem in 2019 found that the greatest predictor of holding "pro-life" views — defined as the desire to outlaw abortion entirely — is not religiosity, as many assumed, but hostility to gender equity.[909]

In the final days of the campaign, SBA List's Dannenfelser and Priests for Life's the Rev. Frank Pavone wrote an op-ed called "Dear pro-lifers: Trump is absolutely worth your vote." Hoping to assuage any lingering doubt, the letter didn't touch the sexual assault charges but rather focused on Trump's comments in the debates against Hillary Clinton's pro-choice positions and compared his stances to those of past Republican presidential nominees. "Could one imagine Mitt Romney or other past Republican nominees boldly describing late-term abortion and unapologetically proclaiming pro-life beliefs just weeks before the election?" the letter implored.[910]

―――――――

In so many ways, Trump's candidacy and the surrounding conversation underscored the culmination of a successful strategy put into place so long ago by movement architects. In an in-depth, exclusive interview with *Breitbart News*, the nonagenarian Schlafly unapologetically explained her support for Donald Trump in January of 2016. To the untrained eye, it might have been stunning that Schlafly never mentioned abortion in her ringing endorsement for the then underdog candidate. But those who understood the history of the Radical Right were not at all shocked that almost the entire interview focused on Trump's pet issue of immigration. Schlafly flaunted her own racist perception of immigrants, calling them people who "immediately go on welfare" and heralded Trump as America's last hope. Echoing strains from the

1970s, she complained that immigrants were destroying the nation and decried the fact that "good American children" were forced to go to school with them.[911] "The children go in our schools, and we've had to hire all of teachers who speak foreign languages to teach these foreign children — there's no reason why we we should do that at all." She said, "And these commentators who talk about the Constitutional rights of the immigrants — they don't have any Constitutional rights. They're not entitled to any U.S. Constitutional rights unless they're residents in this country, and they're not."[912] The movement had come full circle.

Phyllis Schlafly passed away almost two months shy of being able to see Donald Trump win the election.[913] Her final book, "The Conservative Case for Trump," was published the day before she died.[914] By then, the multiple accusations of sexual assault and harassment against her candidate were well known, even though the Access Hollywood tape had not yet come out.[915] Schlafly expressed no concern, and there's no reason to believe the tape would have swayed her. Schlafly was a long-time, frequent critic of protections against harassment. She once testified at a Senate labor committee that "men hardly ever ask sexual favors of women from whom the certain answer is 'No.' Virtuous women are seldom accosted by unwelcome sexual propositions or familiarities, obscene talk or profane language."[916]

Schlafly's book again reiterated her enthusiasm for a candidate she'd seen as the vindication of all her efforts to strengthen the Radical Right. Channeling the movement architects who had since passed, she brushed aside Trump's overt misogyny and accusations of sexual violence to praise him as "an old-fashioned man," the type her movement had always worked to uplift. "Critics can, and will, go on and on about Trump having been married three times, and about how, in the past, he boasted about his indiscretions," Schlafly and her co-authors wrote. "But anyone who meets him today will meet an old-fashioned man grounded in his two great priorities — hard work and family — and a man who in other respects has led a remarkably clean life." In the end, Schlafly's parting words underscored just how mercenary her movement truly was: "Trump has gone to great lengths to court national leaders in the social-conservative movement and has convinced many of the most prominent ones that he genuinely supports their policy positions."[917]

———

There are many reasons why Donald Trump now occupies the White House: arcane rules of the Electoral College, Russian interference, James Comey, tech fueled disinformation and conspiracy theories, voter suppression, third-party siphoning of votes, and more. When just 80,000 votes in three states determine the outcome, nearly any factor can seem to have been decisive.[918]

But without the enthusiastic, unshakable support of a Radical Right movement, its political infrastructure, and its perfectly honed messaging strategy combining Reagan's racial dog whistles with Kellyanne Conway's cynical faux-feminism, Donald Trump would not be president.

The Trump campaign was able to get 80% of the white evangelical vote share — precisely the target goal set by the RNC when it tried to figure out how a Republican could win in a post-Obama world.[919] [920] Trump overwhelmingly won white men, a victory lauded from the headlines of *Breitbart* to the dark corners of message boards like Stormfront and 4chan.[921] And as with his predecessor Reagan, Trump proved once again that the female majority could be split if a campaign played to embedded cultural prejudices.

The anti-choice movement could calculate the concrete contributions it delivered for Trump. Now its leaders had the capacity to translate victory into concrete gains for their unpopular agenda. But first, they had to claim credit.

Reed celebrated the high levels of evangelical and conservative Christian voter turnout, arguing that it was precisely because Trump wasn't afraid to lean into Radical Right positions and points: "Republicans have long courted Christians especially during the primaries, but Donald Trump won white evangelicals by a record 81% in last week's presidential election — unlike a lot of previous nominees who sort of backed away and kept those voters and their issues at arm's length."[922]

Students for Life President Kristan Hawkins applauded Trump's victory, writing to her followers, "It's now very easy to imagine a day when *Roe v. Wade* and *Doe v. Bolton* will be overturned and when Planned Parenthood, our nation's abortion Goliath, will be defunded of half a billion dollars in taxpayer money. This is possible, now. If... If we, the pro-life generation, hold President-Elect Trump to his promises."[923]

The movement leaders had wrapped Trump in their shroud of piety and put their credentials on the line to vouch for his moral character. They had provided a massive infusion of resources and cover when others shrank from his faltering campaign. Now, they expected payback.

They immediately zeroed in on Trump's need to deliver an anti-choice majority in the Supreme Court as an early test. After all, Mitch McConnell's high stakes gamble had paid off, and Trump would enter the White House with a vacancy to fill on the high court. Hawkins wrote, "We have to finish what we started. We need to ensure that only pro-life Supreme Court justices are appointed, period. ...We need to mobilize like never before and ensure our leaders in Washington will do what they have pledged."[924]

Many pundits retroactively gave at least partial credit for Trump's victory to his successful exploitation of underlying and persistent racism, misogyny, and xenophobia surfaced by social and economic anxiety among white working class voters afraid America was changing in a way that would leave them behind. Still, the media fell short of connecting the dots that allowed for those anxieties to be leveraged so effectively. The dots that pointed to a long and deliberate takeover of the Republican Party by a group erroneously labeled as single-issue voters. The Radical Right had become the kingmakers of the party, obfuscating their dominionist origins behind what came to be known as the "pro-life" movement. And while many noted that the GOP faithful turned out to the polls because of "abortion," almost none recognized the proxy that medical procedure had successfully become. The Trojan Horse of abortion now carried the weight of so much more. Trump understood. And the political landscape in 2016 was shaped — indeed, defined — by the deal he struck with the Radical Right.

For nearly half a century, the Radical Right had built towards this moment. Its leaders had convinced generations to have an almost Pavlovian response to the mention of abortion and had made their opposition to *Roe* an effective filter to keep out all but those most committed to their agenda. They had professionalized their operations and taken over the conservative establishment. They had prepared for a frontal attack on reproductive freedom as the tip of the spear in their agenda for control, the restoring of white Christian men to their rightful place in society as seen by Paul Weyrich, Jerry Falwell, and their fellow dominionists. And in the end, they cynically exploited their religious credentials in support of the most unqualified presidential candidate in American history — a man whose life was a rebuke of everything they claimed to value.

Their plan worked. And now America would pay the price.

Chapter 8
The Administration

On January 21, 2017, just one day after the inauguration of Donald Trump, millions of people marched in cities all over the globe — and the new president seethed.[925] [926] [927]

The Women's March was heralded as the largest single-day protest in American history.[928] People filled the streets in the nation's cities and gathered in small clutches in far-flung towns, with signs that read "my uterus is private property," "dismantle white supremacy," "glass ceilings are made to be broken," women's rights are human rights," and "we are stronger than fear" — just to name a few.[929] [930] Even the women at a research station in Antarctica huddled together for a picture with their signs.[931]

The largest and most visible gathering took place right outside the White House, where close to 500,000 people gathered in opposition to the new administration's agenda.[932] The mood was ebullient despite the devastation of the election results; the crowd roared its approval when a speaker announced from stage that their ranks dwarfed those gathered for the inauguration the day before. The march was an expression of outrage of the broad-based majority standing up to oppose a regressive and repressive president who had been elected by a significant minority of the popular vote.

Clearly rankled, Donald Trump sent press secretary Sean Spicer the next day into a scrum of reporters to insist — against all evidence — that the 2017 inauguration had drawn the biggest crowds in history.[933] Pundits and observers shook their heads and chuckled at what was an obvious lie. But that moment laid bare two important insights about this president: He intended to continue his assault against the truth, and nothing got under his skin like strong women challenging his power.

Trump's inauguration had been a clouded affair — the rancor of the election still stung for many people. The transition team and the inaugural committee were beset with scandal and allegations of cronyism, nepotism, and extreme incompetence.[934] [935] Shortly after the election, Trump fired former New Jersey governor and Trump loyalist Chris Christie from his position leading the transition into the White House and replaced him with Vice President-elect Mike Pence.[936] *Breitbart News* co-founder and Trump campaign adviser Steve Bannon moved up in the ranks.[937] The tone and tenor of the new administration were decidedly different from what the movement architects had envisioned so long ago, but it's reasonable to believe they would have been very pleased with the ideological philosophy of those moving into the White House.

Trump's inaugural speech never veered from his dark view of American society — a stark contrast to his predecessors who had used their inaugural addresses to uplift and unify.[938] True to form, he also never let facts get in his way. The *Washington Post* Fact Checker noted many places where the new president's dystopian description of the country didn't match reality; in fact violent crime was well below its 1991 peak and the economy during the Obama presidency led to an increase in jobs and a decrease in participation in social welfare programs.[939]

Perhaps nothing would foreshadow what was to come with this administration better than a moment on Meet the Press the Sunday morning following the inauguration and the march. Kellyanne Conway, once on the forefront of condemning Trump's approach to politics, went on television to frame Sean Spicer's lies about the crowd size as "alternative facts."[940] An incredulous Chuck Todd challenged Conway on the bizarre term, pointing out that, "Alternative facts are not facts. They're falsehoods."[941] But the Trump convert and perennial purveyor of propaganda stuck to her guns.[942] It was foreshadowing. Over the coming years, the Trump administration would lean into every element of the Radical Right's playbook: foment cultural racism and misogyny for political gain, use extreme rhetoric and disinformation, and justify later by whatever means necessary.

On January 23, 2017 — in what was perceived as a direct response to the Women's March — Trump reinstated the Global Gag Rule.[943] The policy effectively ended funding for organizations working in impoverished countries to help women access comprehensive reproductive healthcare.[944] [945] [946] It had been a mandate for every Republican president since Reagan established it, but Trump expanded it beyond previous administrations.[947] Anti-choice activists were delighted to find that their new president seemed eager to top his predecessors by attaching it to a much larger pool of funds.[948]

The new administration ignored plentiful data available from previous administrations that showed the Global Gag rule had led to more unintended pregnancies and women seeking abortions, many of them unsafe and some with devastating consequences.[949] The countries where women bore the greatest impact were those for which Trump made no effort to conceal his disdain. Later in his term, he famously called them "shithole" countries."[950] Obviously, reducing the number of abortions was not the goal for Trump and his new friends taking up residence in Washington. It was about asserting control over women's bodies — in this case, explicitly poor Black and brown women. Trump instinctively embraced the Henry Hyde principle: If you can't oppress everyone, start with those with the least power.

Next, the new Administration set about executing another long-held priority of the Radical Right. He signed an executive order undercutting the Johnson Amendment, a long-standing provision of tax law that prohibited churches from directly investing in or publicly supporting political campaigns.[951] With little coverage in the mainstream media, Trump made good on a promise to those who came to his rescue during the campaign: removing barriers to politicize the pulpit. In doing so, he declared: "We are giving our churches their voices back."[952] With one signature, Trump threatened the long-held value of separation of church and state, a bedrock of American democracy.[953]

Trump instructed all federal agencies to pay special attention to "religious freedom" in rulemaking and enforcement actions,[954] clearly indicating that it was safe to use that age-old concept to skirt antidiscrimination laws.[955] The new president may not have been able to recite the origin story of the Radical Right. He might not even have known that Bob Jones University invoked the same term to fight school integration, but he was a quick learner and fluent enough in his new language to strike this chord with his base. He proceeded to go beyond his campaign promises when he unexpectedly endorsed a move to add Bible literacy classes to public school curriculums,[956] something that surprised and thrilled his new supporters. Under Trump and the newly appointed Attorney General, Jeff Sessions, the Department of Justice also formed a new "religious-liberty" task force.[957] As a result, one of Trump's earliest impacts in office was the systematic dismantling of the legal architecture that had been set up by the Obama administration to protect LGBTQ and women's rights.[958]

The verdict was in. The gamble many in the Radical Right made in backing Trump was paying huge dividends. "I believe we've been on the phone with this president three times in the last four weeks," said one evangelical leader. "He's given us the most unprecedented access of any president in American history."[959] One prominent preacher went even further, saying, "I love him so much I can hardly explain it."[960]

A well-known political novice with few serious policy goals beyond subjugating immigrants and protecting privilege, Trump's ascension to the White House did not come with the normal circles of policy advisers, campaign staffers, or donors. The extraordinary incompetence of Trump and the small inner circle he brought with him created the perfect conditions for established Far Right forces to seize power of position in the fledgling administration. An early setback solidified their hold.

During the transition, Trump ignored warnings from his more establishment advisors — including an increasingly sidelined Chris Christie — and nominated Andrew Puzder to be labor secretary.[961] Andy Puzder had a long track record in right-wing politics.[962] Born in Cleveland, Ohio, he moved to St. Louis to attend Washington University law school.[963] He became active in Missouri politics as a lawyer, stumping loudly for right-wing causes from opposing labor laws to supporting laws restricting women's rights.[964] He was active in Lawyers for Life and pushed for laws in the Missouri state legislature that defined life as beginning at conception.[965]

Pudzer moved to the corporate world and ascended the ranks to become CEO of CKE Restaurants, parent company of Hardee's and Carl's Jr.[966] Trump liked him and saw in him a kindred spirit, a savvy businessman who wasn't afraid to speak his mind. Pudzer had drawn attention from feminists by defending what many believed to be sexist ads for his restaurant, saying, "I like beautiful women eating burgers in bikinis. I think it's very American."[967] Trump believed the GOP Senate would give him his pick, so he barreled ahead. This was around the time he fired Chris Christie, empowering Steve Bannon and his new team to get the Puzder nomination done.

Bannon and his crew failed. Democrats wildly objected to reports of worker mistreatment and Puzder's opposition to increasing the minimum wage.[968] Republicans balked at the fact that he had employed an undocumented immigrant to care for his children and not paid taxes on her services.[969] Both sides cited concerns about domestic assault charges filed by his ex-wife, despite the fact that she had recanted.[970] [971] As the Senate considered the nomination, elected officials were met in their home states by constituents protesting the nominee.[972] On February 15, the evening before the final vote, it became clear there would not be enough votes to confirm, so Puzder withdrew his nomination.[973] It was a political setback for the new administration, and a real offense to a president who didn't like to lose. A sullen Trump handed the reins over to the more seasoned operatives from the Radical Right who had set up shop in the Administration.

There was a natural affinity that allowed the new president to invest trust in this group. He liked their disdain for facts and premium on extreme loyalty. He welcomed them into the fold. And the lessons the Radical Right had learned through 40 years of empire building could now be put to use with a willing and malleable president. It was a perfect inside-outside game.

Advisers like televangelist James Robison, the very same who had lost his show in the late 1970s for calling homosexuality a sin and then presided over the rally that kicked off the Moral Majority — weighed in on key appointments.[974] [975] Robison, who prided himself on being a dominionist in the Weyrich mold, had been considered too fringe for either of the Bush presidencies, and he had retreated from politics in the post Reagan years.[976] In 2010, he re-emerged to fight against the reelection of Barack Obama, seeing new potential in the Tea Party revolution.[977] Robison had endeared himself to Trump in 2016 when he leaped to the then-candidate's defense after the release of the Access Hollywood tapes.[978]

After the inauguration, Robison boasted that Trump had "asked me to check out some of the people he was looking at and asked my opinion," noting he had suggested Rick Perry for energy secretary.[979] No matter that, as part of his own 2012 bid for the GOP presidential nomination, Perry had promised to abolish the entire energy department. Perry was a true believer on the issues that mattered to the Radical Right: maximizing power, control, and profit for a small number of like-minded people. So, he got the job.

Perry wasn't the only one. The list of Trump's nominees for plum positions read like a who's who of Radical Right stalwarts. Diehard evangelical conservatives were picked for key positions to undermine reproductive health policy, civil rights and LGBTQ protections. Trump selected a slate of conservative hardliners to his cabinet, including Attorney General Jeff Sessions; Health and Human Services Secretary Tom Price, CIA Director Mike Pompeo, Environmental Protection Agency Administrator Scott Pruitt, Secretary of Education Betsy DeVos, Housing and Urban Development Secretary Ben Carson, Agriculture Secretary Sonny Perdue, and United Nations Ambassador Nikki Haley. The Christian Broadcasting Network's David Brody described this initial Trump Cabinet as a "Believers in Politics all-star team," referring to their very public evangelical identities.[980] The administration even instituted a weekly Bible study at HHS, which according to the head of Capitol Ministries Ralph Drollinger, "[hadn't] existed among cabinet members in at least a hundred years."[981]

———

Trump showed little personal interest in the judiciary, but followed through on his campaign promise to outsource his selection of federal judges, a crucial priority that bound together a wary GOP establishment and the Radical Right that had taken up residence in the Administration. To the delight of both factions, Trump swiftly brought on the Federalist Society's Leonard Leo to oversee the nomination process.[982] In the late 1980s, as a student, Leo had founded Cornell's chapter of the Federalist Society, and he was invited to join the staff at headquarters after he graduated.[983] He accepted the plum role and then delayed his start date to help shepherd Clarence Thomas' nomination through the Senate.[984] In his time with the Federalist Society, Leo raised more than $250 million for dark money groups in service of confirming Radical Right judges.[985] Pro forma, he was a committed anti-choice activist, serving as co-chair of the board for Students for Life.[986] Leo would go on to make some of the most significant, damaging, and long-lasting decisions of the entire Administration.

Trump also selected Ken Blackwell, a Family Research Council board member, to oversee the hiring of a domestic policy staff.[987] Blackwell was a key pick, given that these staff positions would not only be responsible for development of new policy, but they would take an active role in dismantling existing policy protecting women and vulnerable populations. They would also serve as the propaganda arm for the Trump administration's efforts at home.

In a move typical of the new Trump team, Blackwell promoted Republican Senate aide Katy Talento to manage health care policy.[988] [989] Talento, a veteran of the Trump campaign and a skeptic of birth control, had penned a 2015 op-ed for The Federalist that pushed disinformation about both birth control and abortion, asking, "Is chemical birth control causing miscarriages of already-conceived children? What about breaking your uterus for good?"[990] [991] That all reputable sources of medical information dismissed Talento's arguments as nonsense was of no consequence to a Trump administration that placed a low priority on accuracy in policymaking.[992] [993]

The deputy assistant secretary for population affairs — a position responsible for overseeing reproductive health policy — went to Diane Foley. Foley previously ran a string of fake women's health centers designed to deceive and shame women seeking help and keep them from accessing abortion care.[994] She had once suggested that demonstrating proper condom use in a classroom setting could be "sexually harassing."[995]

The list went on and on. These critical positions did not receive the public attention of the cabinet members and thus were below the radar of most of the country. Under Trump's largely indifferent leadership, Radical Right strategists seized their opportunity to infiltrate all levels of the federal government and consolidate their control over federal policymaking and the judiciary.

Almost no one would relish the opportunity to pervert reproductive health policy and civil rights protections more than Michael Richard Pence and, as Vice President, he was uniquely positioned to do so. Pence, like Trump, had shown a penchant for ignoring facts and data in pursuit of goals. In the late

1990s, Pence had famously mocked government regulators putting more stringent warnings on cigarettes, calling them hysterical and stating — against all evidence — "Time for a quick reality check. Smoking doesn't kill."[996]

Pence's religious evolution is a textbook example of conversion to the Radical Right. He was brought up in an Irish Catholic family,[997] and his mother was an ardent supporter of John F. Kennedy. The Vice President voted for Jimmy Carter as late as 1980. When he became a born-again Evangelical in college and shifted his political allegiance just as President Ronald Reagan rose to power, he became the prototype for the successful electoral efforts of the Radical Right. Pence became a true believer.[998]

A lawyer and conservative radio and television talk show host, Pence served in Congress from 2000-2012, where he billed himself as "a Christian, a Conservative, and a Republican in that order."[999] [1000] [1001] He eagerly joined the Tea Party caucus in 2010 to fight President Obama's agenda before leaving Congress to become governor of the state of Indiana.[1002] There, he had an executive platform from which to rule in line with his ideology, and he gave it his best shot. Governor Mike Pence became the poster child for the movement architects' efforts to weaponize abortion in the service of maintaining social order.

In March 2015, Pence signed a provision that enshrined discrimination into Indiana law in the name of "religious freedom."[1003] Deceptively named the Religious Freedom Restoration Act, the law allowed business owners to circumvent anti-discrimination rules and deny service to LGBTQ Hoosiers and others with the claim that their discrimination was part of a religious belief. The move, which rocketed Pence to infamy from relative obscurity, was an attempt to placate those on the Radical Right whose attempt to ban gay marriage through a constitutional amendment had failed.[1004] Widely hailed as a carefully crafted attempt to legalize discrimination against LGBTQ people, Pence's action sparked widespread cultural and economic backlash. Companies from Salesforce to Angie's List threatened to pull out of expansion plans in the state and conventions threatened to relocate.[1005] Against a backdrop of massive public outcry and under pressure from local business leaders, Pence reluctantly signed an amendment strengthening some protections for the LGBTQ community.[1006]

As Governor, Pence ruled by the roster of Radical Right priorities. He oversaw a massive expansion in funding for charter schools with a special focus on religious institutions.[1007] He lobbied for and signed a bill into law that curbed how much Indiana cities and towns could pay their workers.[1008] As the war raged in Syria and images of carnage flooded the airwaves, Pence attempted — unsuccessfully — to prevent Syrian refugees from being settled in Indiana.[1009] He relished restricting abortion and undercutting women's reproductive access. Between 2013 and 2016, he signed every anti-choice bill that crossed his desk.[1010] In 2016, shortly before leaving office, he signed a bill forcing women to carry pregnancies to term in cases where the fetus has a severe genetic abnormality or was not viable, a move so inhumane that some Republicans voted against it.[1011] [1012]

Scott County, Indiana, became a case study of the ways people suffered because of Pence's single-minded determination to advance his far-right agenda. One in five residents of the county lived below the poverty line and injection drug use was widespread, putting more at risk of HIV. As the local government grappled with remedies like needle exchange, the county's Planned Parenthood clinic became the front lines of HIV testing and referral of services for those infected. When right-wing state policies defunded Planned Parenthood and forced the local clinic to close, roughly 24,000 people were left without basic services and the county suffered an HIV outbreak, with 20 new cases being diagnosed each week.[1013] [1014] This did not cause Pence to rethink his position. In fact, the governor even doubled down on his opposition to the needle exchange program, allowing more and more of the people he served to get sick.[1015]

Pence and his allies brought this experience and the data that showed the negative impact of their actions to the capital with them. None of that caused them to shift course. Pence personified a willingness to sacrifice the health and well-being of his own constituents — most living in underserved and marginalized communities — in order to advance rigid ideas about social order and who deserved to be on top.

━━━━

Once installed as vice president, Pence was eager to promote Radical Right loyalists to as many positions of influence as possible within the new Trump Administration. Superficially, the vice president and the president seemed to have little in common, but they both had a penchant for disinformation and a tolerance for cruelty that would become hallmarks of the Executive Branch. Pence wielded enormous influence in areas where Trump was disengaged from detailed personnel and policy decision making. Nowhere was Pence's power more visible than in shaping Trump's Department of Health and Human Services.

Perhaps the most significant of Pence's home state cronies to come to Washington was Alex Azar, a top executive at Indiana-based drugmaker Eli Lilly when Pence served as governor of the state.[1016] Trump's original Health and Human Services Secretary Tom Price lasted only eight months, forced to resign after it was discovered that he diverted an estimated $400,000 of government resources toward luxury charter flights.[1017] In September 2017, Pence brought in Azar to lead the embattled department, which they would come to call the "Department of Life."[1018] Pence also pressed Trump to pick former Indiana public health official Jerome Adams as surgeon general.[1019] [1020] Medicaid and Medicare Chief Seema Verma, her deputy chief of staff Brady Brookes, and Rebekah Armstrong, a deputy assistant secretary, had all been hired to key roles at HHS after working for Pence in Indiana.[1021] [1022]

This team had more in common than being from Indiana: In their roles there, they had borne witness to, and in some cases presided over, the devastation of the GOP's scorched earth approach to undermining reproductive health care policy. Through the 2000s, GOP leadership in Indiana had successfully blocked Planned Parenthood from receiving Title X federal funding for non-abortion family planning services, had pushed to cut off Medicaid funding to Planned Parenthood, and had overseen the shuttering of abortion clinics. [1023] [1024] [1025] Indiana's maternal mortality rate had risen along with this divestment in reproductive health care and availability of services. In 2014, with Pence serving as Indiana's chief executive, one in every 2,150 pregnant women in the state died giving birth.[1026] Lack of action to reverse the trend, despite mounting data, demonstrated that Pence and his team's commitment was to the ideology of control, not public health.

In March 2017, Scott Lloyd, who had grown up in the far right movement, was also rewarded with an Administration appointment as the head of a little-noticed agency within HHS, the Office of Refugee Resettlement.[1027] Lloyd was born in 1979, just as movement forefathers were undertaking their propaganda project to label abortion as the ultimate evil, and he was a poster child for the success of that effort. He sat on the board of one of Virginia's most notorious fake women's health centers, and he argued vociferously against contraception.[1028] [1029] He worked directly with Terri Schiavo's parents in the famous Florida case to keep a woman on life support with no possibility of recovery and against her husband's wishes.[1030] Lloyd was the textbook model of the next generation of anti-choice activists. Lloyd had no qualifications for the position he assumed and no experience with refugees or immigrants.[1031] The decision to appoint Lloyd seemed entirely based on his long commitment to radical anti-choice politics.

The results of Lloyd's single-minded focus will perhaps go down as some of the worst travesties of the Trump administration. As White House senior policy adviser Stephen Miller implemented his "zero tolerance" policies at the border, Lloyd's office rocketed to prominence, overseeing a dramatic increase in the number of unaccompanied minors separated from their families.[1032] Lloyd expressed total disinterest in addressing the urgent and unfolding crisis before him, ignoring career civil servants' urgent warnings about everything from the lack of beds for babies to the long-term impacts on children deprived of their parents.[1033]

People in the agency grew desperate as their pleas went unanswered. When a federal judge later ordered families to be reunified, it came to light that Lloyd had ordered his department to stop keeping records of the locations and names of affected families.[1034] This grievous decision significantly delayed reunification efforts and, in some cases, may have prevented some children from ever getting back to their parents.

In sworn testimony to a congressional panel, Lloyd later admitted that he failed to inform his supervisors that the separation could have devastating health consequences.[1035] The panel pressed him on what, exactly, he was doing if not tracking families in his care. As it turned out, Lloyd was tracking the periods and pregnancies of immigrant minors under his watch. Pages and pages of spreadsheets later showed that he was keeping track in order to prevent them from terminating pregnancies. He continued this practice for months after he was ordered to stop by a federal judge.[1036]

"My priority is unborn children, and there will be no more abortions," Lloyd told staffers upon his arrival.[1037] He ordered them to use the tracked period data and immediately inform him of young women in their care who might be pregnant. He installed a policy that restricted the charges in his custody from leaving detention to seek reproductive health care, allowing them out only to send them to fake women's health centers, like the one on whose board he had served. Also known as "crisis pregnancy centers," these organizations were fronts for the anti-choice movement that peddled junk science to shame women out of terminating pregnancies.[1038] [1039]

If shaming from the fake clinics where Lloyd sent these women was not enough, he often followed up personally. It was not uncommon for traumatized young women separated from their families, some having experienced rape on their journeys, to get a call or a visit from Lloyd.[1040] In an egregious abuse of his power, he would berate his wards for seeking abortions, sometimes threatening to call their parents.[1041] In at least one case, using taxpayer dollars and with total disregard for the norms and policies of his office, Lloyd flew across the country to pull a young woman from her cell and admonish her for seeking to end her pregnancy.[1042]

Lloyd focused the tenure of his critically important position almost entirely on denying immigrants' access to abortion. When Lloyd was confronted by Congress with statistics showing that 60% of women and girls report being raped on their travels to cross the border, he claimed ignorance.[1043] Given the widespread knowledge of that data in his department, his ignorance — if true — would have amounted to professional malfeasance. It's more likely that he just didn't care. Lloyd's long-standing position was that it was "in the best interest" of rape survivors to carry their pregnancies to term.[1044]

Lloyd became a horrific symbol of the Trump administration's zealotry when he held a young pregnant woman at a facility in Texas against her will and a judge's orders.[1045] A local sponsor stood ready to provide transportation to a clinic and financial assistance to the woman. She had met every legal criteria required and a state judge had granted her the right to get an abortion, yet Lloyd ordered the staff of the facility not to release her, essentially imprisoning her.[1046] [1047]

The ACLU sued on behalf of this "Jane Doe," and the government appealed all the way up to the Circuit Court, where a panel of three judges split 2-1 agreed that the government could hold this girl against her will.[1048] The judge writing for the majority was Brett Kavanaugh, who steadfastly refused to grant the minor relief.[1049] The full circuit reversed his decision shortly thereafter, and Jane Doe was ultimately able to obtain an abortion.[1050] But Kavanaugh was widely hailed by the right and the anti-choice movement for his fiery dissent in the case.[1051] So much so that Donald Trump added him to his short list of potential Supreme Court nominees.[1052] As for Scott Lloyd, he was finally relieved of his duties overseeing immigrant children in November 2018. He left the administration six months later after having inflicted unprecedented cruelty and damage on an untold number of people in the name of "family values."[1053]

━━━━━

Within months of the new administration taking office, high-profile and heartbreaking stories of its policies dominated the news. Trump's policy banning entry to people from several Muslim-majority countries, his zero tolerance policies at the border, and his efforts to strip Americans of their healthcare all blended together in a flurry of cruel and misinformed decisions that mainstreamed feelings of insecurity once contained within marginalized and vulnerable communities. Tensions were on the surface, protests occurred nearly daily, and new relationships and coalitions formed in the wake of the shock.

Scott Lloyd was just one example of the way the Radical Right's twisted priorities had begun to dominate health policy within the Trump administration. The Department of Health and Human Services changed its strategic plan and mission to centralize protection of "life from conception to natural death."[1054] The head of the department's Office of Civil Rights, Roger Severino, declared that he would dedicate his time in office to ending what he called the persecution of Christians, who he claimed as an oppressed class. Severino also became the first HHS official in memory to speak at a National Right to Life convention.

"Times are changing," Severino promised.[1055] "We are institutionalizing a change in the culture of government, beginning at HHS, to never forget that religious freedom is a primary freedom, that it is a civil right. Our president is fearless when it comes to life and conscience."[1056]

In a crippling blow to ongoing scientific research, the department quickly implemented a broad new restriction on stem cell usage in medical inquiry, a practice that has led to breakthroughs in treating everything from rubella and rabies to HIV.[1057] The new rule abruptly pulled the plug on years of efforts at the National Institutes of Health and over 200 other government-funded projects, many which were on the verge of new discoveries. Devastated scientists watched their lives' work go up in flames while Pence and his friends stood and applauded.[1058]

Using its new found power to assert a rigid definition of gender norms, HHS announced it would bar questions about gender identity on its annual national survey and strip gender identity from the nondiscrimination protections in the Affordable Care Act.[1059] [1060] Doctors and nurses were now free to refuse abortion and other care to transgender and nonbinary patients. HHS also emphasized the role of faith-based organizations in public health programs and pushed abstinence-only sexual education, despite reams of evidence that it led to terrible public health outcomes. Where abstinence-only education programs were mandated, they have been shown to increase the rate of unintended pregnancies.[1061]

Then, HHS released a new version of Title X — modeled on the one that had such a devastating effect in Pence's home state of Indiana. The bill denied public funds to any healthcare service that provided abortion, referred patients to abortion providers, or even uttered the word abortion — even though under current law none of those funds could cover actual abortion services. Pence cast the deciding vote in a deadlocked Senate, and Trump signed the bill with Dannenfelser and Concerned Women for America's Penny Nance by his side.[1062] Under the new framework, HHS redirected funding and awarded $5.1 million in taxpayer dollars to the Obria Group — a network of fake women's health centers just like the ones that Scott Lloyd forced immigrant girls to visit.[1063] Of course, Obria's National Advisory Board read like a roster of Trump boosters from the Radical Right anti-choice movement: Marjorie Dannenfelser, Live Action's Lila Rose, Students for Life President Kristan Hawkins and many others.[1064] [1065]

Frustrated Democrats pointed out that health was taking a back seat to proselytizing, and Rep. Elijah Cummings argued that Trump was taking his marching orders from extreme right-wing interest groups.[1066] Of course, that was exactly the point. Legions of fundamentalists cheered as Trump delivered a long sought after goal. "There has never been anything like it," Dannenfelser crowed to Reuters. "The policy I believe can't get done without Vice President Pence and his team."[1067]

Dannenfelser and Pence were also with Trump as he signed an executive order that would widen the Hobby Lobby decision, and allow any employer to refuse contraception coverage to their workers for any reason.[1068] "It's very clear from how quickly we were able to hit the ground running that the vice president certainly had an influential role," said Hawkins.[1069]

The night before the March for Life in 2017, where Pence became the first vice president in history to speak at the event, the White House hosted a reception for leaders and allies.[1070] Pregnancy Help News reported that Pence told the group the reason he first ran for office so many years ago was for this movement. "I really do believe this is the calling of our time," he said.[1071]

―――

As swiftly as the Radical Right was consolidating control over critical parts of the federal government, they recognized the inherent limitations of using the Executive Branch to move unpopular policies. Elections could make their progress fleeting if they couldn't entrench them. They had obviously anticipated this — their focus on the courts and the muscle of the Federalist Society was their insurance policy. Elections came every two years, but controlling the federal judiciary would lock in conservative power for a generation.

A little over a week after taking office, Trump nominated Neil Gorsuch to fill the stolen Supreme Court seat that Mitch McConnell had held hostage for most of the previous year.[1072] During the campaign, Trump had promised to nominate someone "in the mold" of the late Antonin Scalia, the far-right justice who had helped mold the Federalist Society from its very beginning. Except for the fiery temperament, Gorsuch perfectly fit the bill.[1073]

Gorsuch had come up through the Federalist Society's networks and was listed as a Federalist Society "expert" prior to his nomination.[1074] He was a proponent of the Radical Right's "originalist" and "textualist" philosophies, which focused solely on interpreting the language of the constitution as it was understood at the time it was written, denying the relevance of any cultural change or the real-world consequences of hardline judicial decisions.[1075] At age 49 when he was confirmed, Gorsuch became the youngest member of the Supreme Court.[1076]

Trump was quick to connect the nomination to his earlier pledge of loyalty to the Radical Right. His team immediately released a memo entitled, "Doing What He Said He Would: President Trump's Transparent, Principled and Consistent Process for Choosing a Supreme Court Nominee."[1077] With a nod to the right's strategy for longevity, Trump remarked: "Depending on their age, a justice can be active for 50 years, and his or her decisions can last a century or more and can often be permanent."[1078]

Leonard Leo took a leave of absence from his work with the Federalist Society to shepherd Trump's nomination to victory.[1079] The New Yorker called Gorsuch the "latest achievement" in Leonard Leo's "generation of originalist elites."[1080] The Judicial Crisis Network poured in $10 million in advertising to ensure Gorsuch's confirmation went smoothly, and anti-choice groups, including Susan B. Anthony List, National Right to Life, and March for Life, advocated for his confirmation.[1081] [1082] Following Gorsuch's confirmation, Trump sent thank you notes to anti-choice leaders for "all of your efforts to help confirm our Supreme Court nominee Neil Gorsuch."[1083] Gorsuch himself later thanked the Federalist Society, telling the group: "I can report, a person can be both a committed originalist and textualist and be confirmed to the Supreme Court of the United States....Thank you from the bottom of my heart for your support and prayers through that process."[1084]

On June 26, 2018, just over a year after Gorsuch's confirmation, the Supreme Court handed down a decision in *NIFLA v. Becerra*.[1085] At issue in the case was a California law that advocates had fought hard for — a law that required anti-choice crisis pregnancy centers to post signs stating that abortion services were available in the state even though they were not available on site. These fake women's health centers — like the one Scott Lloyd championed, like the one that HHS forced pregnant detainees to go to — thrived on luring women in with the illusion that they could obtain abortions. Once they had a captive audience, they subjected them to shaming and scare tactics to dissuade them from terminating their pregnancies. California sought to ensure that all women were informed about services available in the state.

In an almost unnoticed 5-4 decision, the court affirmed the rights of these centers to lie to women in the name of free speech with then-Justice Anthony Kennedy — considered the swing vote — siding with the conservative wing.[1086] A strong dissent by the liberals showed how polarized the court was on this issue. Kennedy was the perpetual middle man providing some semblance of balance — but not for long.

Two days later, Kennedy announced his decision to retire from the Supreme Court, rocking the legal world and presenting conservatives a once-in-a-generation opportunity to dramatically shift the balance of the court.[1087] The brazen gamble by Mitch McConnell to stonewall Obama's nomination of Merrick Garland in 2016 combined with over 40 years of planning by the Radical Right was about to pay deep dividends.

Kennedy's decision was not as surprising as it seemed. According to reporting by the *New York Times*, his announcement was the culmination of a carefully orchestrated year-long campaign by Trump and the GOP to pressure the justice to retire. The GOP was desperate to motivate the president's right-wing base ahead of the crucial 2018 midterms.[1088] Trump had cultivated a close relationship with Kennedy's son, Justin, who had worked with the Trump Organization as Deutsche Bank's global head of real-estate capital markets. The president also nominated four of Kennedy's former clerks for judicial posts, including Neil Gorsuch. No one can fully know the reasons for Kennedy's decision, but there's no question the right relished the opportunity to cement power on the court with a younger, reliable radical.

Family Research Council President Tony Perkins called upon the White House to select a nominee who could mobilize Christian conservatives. "My counsel has been to make sure we get someone who has an impeccable record when it comes to the issue of life not one that is questionable or shaded," he told far-right news site The Daily Caller.[1089] Kennedy's retirement brought the ultimate vindication for many evangelical leaders who risked their credibility with their followers to support the candidate Trump, especially those who stood by his side after the *Access Hollywood* tape leaked. "Hold your nose and go vote," the Rev. Franklin Graham had exhorted a rally of over 10,000 Religious Right adherents in 2016. "This election is about the Supreme Court and the justices that the next president will nominate."[1090] For some, Justice Kennedy had been a moderating force. For the Radical Right, Kennedy had been an apostate, defecting on key abortion cases and allowing gay marriage.

At 9:00 PM on July 9, 2018, Donald Trump nominated Brett Kavanaugh to replace Kennedy on the Supreme Court of the United States.[1091] By 10:30 PM, the steps of the Court were filled with activists and advocates determined to beat back the nomination. Speaker after speaker railed against the nominee and his threat to everything from abortion rights to civil rights. They spoke in front of a raucous crowd on the warm summer night. Right-wing activists milled about chanting pro-Trump slogans, and in a preview of what was to come, screaming matches broke out among a handful of protesters with contrasting views. The air was tense as several Democratic senators joined the crowd. Sen. Jeff Merkley of Oregon addressed those gathered, saying, "This nomination tonight is all about power over the people. ... I can tell you this is the most political of possible appointments. This is a nominee who wants to pave the path to tyranny." Kavanaugh's nomination, the culmination of decades of Radical Right efforts, was a tipping point for the smoldering resistance among progressives.[1092]

Kavanaugh fit with the movement leaders' vision of the perfect jurist, with one glaring exception. Recall that the Federalist Society coached their lawyers and judges to avoid creating a record on controversial decisions so there was less to object to as they ascended the ranks. Kavanaugh had a long paper trail. Between his time as a Bush Administration lawyer and his fiery decisions from the bench, Kavanaugh was transparently activist in a way that gave his opponents credible ammunition in the fight. McConnell knew how hard a Kavanaugh confirmation would be. Right after Kennedy retired, he took the incredibly rare step to opine in the pages of the *New York Times* that of all the options on the table, Kavanaugh could be the toughest to move through.[1093] The GOP Majority Leader, like the Federalist Society, preferred his nominees to appear as a blank slate in order to limit dissent in the Senate. The judge had a documented history for Democrats to hang their skepticism on, just as his recent dissent in the Scott Lloyd case denying the young migrant woman an abortion — *Jane Doe v. City of Dallas* — was the exact decision that raised his stock in the eyes of the Radical Right.

We don't know why Trump diverged from McConnell's guidance, but many point to Kavanaugh's writings on presidential immunity from criminal prosecution. In fact, Sen. Chris Coons (D-DE) speculated, at the time of the nomination, that Trump had chosen Kavanaugh over others with equally right-wing qualifications with "an eye towards protecting himself."[1094] Sen. Mazie Hirono (D-HI) went further, saying Trump was first and foremost "committed to self-preservation every minute, every hour, every day."[1095]

Meanwhile, Kavanaugh certainly met the litmus test of hostility to *Roe*. As a former White House lawyer under President George W. Bush, Kavanaugh challenged the notion of *Roe* as "settled law of the land," according to a 2003 email obtained by the *New York Times*.[1096] "I am not sure that all legal scholars refer to *Roe* as the settled law of the land at the Supreme Court level since the Court can always overrule its precedent," Kavanaugh wrote.[1097] In his dissent on Jane Doe, Kavanaugh had used anti-choice rhetoric to complain that his colleagues had created "a new right for unlawful immigrant minors in U.S. government detention to obtain immediate abortion on demand," and promoted "a radical extension of the Supreme Court's abortion jurisprudence."[1098]

McConnell's concern that Kavanaugh's paper trail would be a problem was shared by other establishment leaders on the right. For many, Kavanaugh was a second choice behind Amy Coney Barrett, a right-wing ideologue who was a master at walking their messaging tightrope.[1099] It helped that she was a woman, who — like Schlafly and the many others before — would get some leeway in leveling attacks against women and reproductive freedom. Coney Barrett had just been confirmed to the U.S. Court of Appeals for the 7th Circuit amid great concern over her record.[1100] Coney Barrett had signed a letter affirming life as beginning at conception and marriage as being between a man and a woman.[1101] As a judge, she had ruled that a school's punishment of a sex offender violated Title IX protections.[1102]

After Trump's formal nomination, though, any remaining dissent in the GOP dissipated as the right fell in line. The true believers in the movement were jubilant and led the way in enthusiasm. Brian Fisher, president of Human Coalition — a network of fake women's health centers — praised the nomination, saying, "Kavanaugh gives great hope to the pro-life movement that the end of *Roe v. Wade* and legal abortion is in sight."[1103] Clarke Forsythe, a lawyer with Americans United for Life, told *Reuters* he was optimistic this was the future majority to overturn *Roe*.[1104] Concerned Women of America and Susan B. Anthony List began to organize a roadshow on his behalf. Despite these public statements and with no sense of irony, the GOP spin machine called the mounting protests decrying Kavanaugh's threat to *Roe* "hysterical" and the protestors "chicken littles" who could never be satisfied.[1105] [1106] It was a classic form of gaslighting that the GOP had become known for.

The organizations spawned by Weyrich kicked into full gear to support the culmination of their vision. The Federalist Society's Leonard Leo had given $4 million to a nonprofit called Independent Women's Voice, which now organized rallies, wrote online commentary, and appeared regularly on Fox News to promote Kavanaugh.[1107] The Heritage Foundation pledged to spend the bulk of its almost $12 million budget on confirming Kavanaugh.[1108] Judicial Crisis Network committed at least $10 million, the Trump-aligned Great America PAC and Great America Alliance together committed $5 million, and the list went on.[1109] A NARAL Pro-Choice America analysis found that anti-choice and conservative groups pledged to spend as much as $36,462,000 to advocate in favor of Kavanaugh's nomination.[1110]

Those resources were necessary. Progressive activists and women around the country had had enough. Organizations joined forces in new coalitions. Throughout the summer, protests, rallies, canvasses and lobbying campaigns occurred on an almost daily basis to urge senators — both at home and in Washington, D.C. — to block the nomination. Advocates raised alarms about Kavanaugh's threat to *Roe*, to civil rights more generally, and to his disturbing statements on presidential powers. The GOP senators didn't want to hear any of it. Many refused to even meet with their constituents on the matter. When Republican Senate Judiciary Committee Chair Chuck Grassley held a town hall in the northern part of his home state of Iowa, constituents packed the hall, peppering the senior senator with questions about the nominee. He finally waved his hands in frustration, asking if anyone wanted to ask a question that was not about Kavanaugh.[1111]

The protests were effective. The public was skeptical of Kavanaugh. By Labor Day, as Kavanaugh entered his highly contested confirmation hearings, he had one of the lowest approval ratings of any Supreme Court nominee in history. His ratings were comparable only to failed Reagan nominee Robert Bork.[1112] The right was worried as the protests grew. Dozens of activists were arrested for disrupting the hearings, loudly challenging the nominee on his position on *Roe* and other critical rights that hung in the balance. Women dressed as handmaids, from the popular dystopian *Hulu* series and Margaret Atwood novel "The Handmaid's Tale," lined the halls of the Senate to highlight the threat to reproductive autonomy presented by the nominee.[1113] Taking a page from their new president, the GOP senators refused to budge.

Then, Dr. Christine Blasey Ford stepped forward and into the hurricane. She asserted that Brett Kavanaugh sexually assaulted her years ago in high school, at a small gathering in suburban Maryland.[1114] Blasey Ford was a well-respected professor of psychology at Palo Alto University and a research psychologist at the Stanford University School of Medicine.[1115] For so many women, Blasey Ford's story was not only an affirmation of deep skepticism of the GOP and the judge, but also underscored a deep and innate connection between rape culture and anti-choice ideology. Women instinctively connected the charges of sexual assault with the anti-abortion stance, knowing the intertwined history of control over bodily autonomy and oppression. Through Kavanaugh's ascension to the highest court of the land, they also felt deep alarm at the offensive entitlement now rippling out from the Trump administration, the architects of his rise.

Kavanaugh's response the day Blasey Ford testified made things worse. As throngs of people filled the Senate building and the entire nation tuned in via live television, he raged in front of the Senate Judiciary Committee, not even trying to contain his anger and frustration.[1116] He sulked and dodged questions, and his lack of contrition was only matched by his aggression and commitment to revenge. In a performance that most presumed would sink his nomination, Kavanaugh attacked Democrats for questioning him, accused them of looking for payback because of Trump's victory in 2016, and pledged retribution.[1117]

The outpouring of anger and frustration among women and allies was unprecedented. Daily, people swarmed the halls of the Senate imploring senators to listen to their stories of sexual assault.[1118] Marches filled the streets of the capital and those of the home states of senators. Students at Yale Law, Kavanaugh's alma mater, staged a sit-in protesting his nomination.[1119] Some professors even canceled classes. The normally reticent Anita Hill penned an op-ed reliving her own testimony, decades earlier, in front of the same committee and calling for better investigations.[1120] Even Patti Davis — daughter of Ronald Reagan, lion of the movement — wrote an op-ed supporting Blasey Ford.[1121]

The GOP refused to budge. President Trump stood by his man, mocking Blasey Ford and dismissing her claims, just as he had his own accusers.[1122] Some senators preferred a softer attack on Blasey Ford's credibility — one all too familiar to women — claiming that something might have happened to her, but she was confused about who perpetrated the act. By any normal standard, this administration should have jettisoned its nominee and opted for a more sanitized and unimpeachable version of the Federalist Society brand, if only to save the legitimacy of the Court. But Trump's mantra was never retreat and, on this, McConnell and Trump saw eye to eye.[1123] McConnell feared capitulation would empower a resistance movement that had grown steadily since the first Women's March, and senators in his caucus were incensed that their privileged bubble had been punctured, albeit by their own constituents.

After two women confronted him in a Senate elevator, demanding he push for a serious investigation into Dr. Ford's claims, then-GOP Sen. Jeff Flake from Arizona threatened party unity. Ana Maria Archila and Maria Gallagher told Flake of their own experiences with sexual assault and described what it felt like for the Senate to be so dismissive of sexual assault allegations.[1124] [1125] Hours later, Flake called for an FBI investigation into the claims, delaying the confirmation vote for a week.[1126] The investigation was widely critiqued as inadequate and overly narrow in scope. Witnesses who wanted to share their memories were never contacted. The report was never shared publicly. However, the delay gave the GOP some much needed time to regroup and the optics of it gave some cover to increasingly nervous senators.

At the urging of advisers, Kavanaugh did a media apology tour. He sat for a long interview — unprecedented for an unconfirmed nominee — with friendly Fox News.[1127] He also wrote an op-ed for the *Wall Street Journal* that appeared in early October, just before the confirmation vote. Published under the headline, "I Am an Independent, Impartial Judge," Kavanaugh acknowledged that his "tone was sharp" at the Senate Judiciary Committee hearing and admitted, "I said a few things I should not have said."[1128]

"It's the culture war on steroids, an incredible divide and intense to the point where people won't talk to each other in some cases," Bill Bennett, education secretary under Ronald Reagan, told the *Washington Post*. "You have the anti-Trump resistance, the #MeToo movement and the Supreme Court making for a perfect storm of controversy."[1129] But the Radical Right leaders were correct in their instincts that their base would hold firm. A poll by YouGov and The Economist showed that a majority of Republicans — 55% — believed that Kavanaugh should be confirmed even if the allegations were true, as opposed to 28% overall and just 13% of Democrats.[1130] "Boys will be boys," they seemed to reason, and movement leaders saw no purpose in punishing that past behavior when they were on the precipice of owning the future.

The generation of true believers had grown up. In a chilling summary of the efficacy of the original strategy, a young man stepped off a bus emblazoned with "Women for Kavanaugh" banners to give an interview with days to go before the final vote. "Even if it turns out he's guilty," he explained, "I'm still going to support him and I hope he gets in. Cause this could be a good chance to overturn abortion."

On October 6, 2018, with thousands of protesters surrounding the Capitol, Kavanaugh was confirmed in the closest nomination vote since 1881. The final Senate vote was 50-48 along party lines with the exception of Republican Lisa Murkowski, who voted "present," and Democrat Joe Manchin, who voted "yes." Republican Steve Daines, an otherwise expected "yes" vote, was away at his daughter's wedding.[1131] Dispensing with any pretense that Kavanaugh would be an independent jurist, the Federalist Society's Leonard Leo stated immediately after the vote: "Brett Kavanaugh has seen how unforgiving the Left can be. So Justice Kavanaugh has every incentive to basically do what he wants to do and ignore the Left."[1132] At the time of confirmation, he was the least popular justice in modern history.[1133]

Winning the Kavanaugh fight was key to the GOP's plan for the November midterm elections. Trump knew he had to get the old band of supporters back together in order to compete. He had satisfied the anti-choice traditionalists with his policy wins and his capture of the courts. He used the Kavanaugh confirmation hearings to appeal to the angry misogynists who believed that Kavanaugh was victimized — just like Clarence Thomas before him — by "fake" accusations from a woman. Then, putting the final piece of the puzzle in place, Trump went back to his original well of racism and xenophobia. He trumpeted a caravan "descending" on America from the south with such aggressive fearmongering that *Politico* magazine felt compelled to fact-check him, writing: "President Donald Trump's remarks in recent days about a caravan of Central American migrants heading toward the United States have stirred up a political frenzy — in the process distorting reality and ignoring basic facts."[1134]

Trump's toxic strategy worked to hold the Senate, but women who make up the base of the Democratic Party channeled their frustration into elections around the country.[1135] Their energy combined with increasing numbers of women defecting from the GOP, propelled enough victories for Democrats to reclaim the House of Representatives and sweep state houses around the country.[1136] When Trump returned to Washington in January 2019, he faced the most diverse House ever.[1137] Nancy Pelosi was again speaker, presiding over a class with record numbers of Democratic women all committed to reproductive freedom and justice, forming a crucial bloc against the Trump agenda.[1138] [1139] Meanwhile, the number of Republican women in the House dropped from 23 to just 13 that same year.[1140]

Despite the electoral losses, or perhaps because of them, anti-choice activists emerged into a new legislative session emboldened in their efforts to end *Roe* protections and fully ban abortion. Once Kavanaugh was confirmed, right-wing activists advanced new state-level restrictions that went well beyond constitutional limits set by his predecessors.[1141] Convinced this was an endgame, Concerned Women for America President Penny Nance told NPR that reproductive freedom opponents "were talking about, starting to get together and think about the best cases to move forward, to put in front of the court."[1142]

"The state legislature for the past 10 years have been very fertile ground for moving the ball down the field on the issue of life," Nance said. "And so we will continue those efforts, and I think we will continue to see success."[1143]

Sue Swayze Liebel, state policy director for the anti-choice group Susan B. Anthony List, credited Kavanaugh with inspiring a raft of new state-level restrictions against abortion access. "This has been one of the most prolific legislative seasons that I've seen in many, many years in the abortion debate. I think that the Kavanaugh hearing and the potential maybe for one more seat on the court is putting states on notice that, likely, *Roe* may be overturned," she said.[1144]

"Pro-life states are more hopeful than they've been in a long time because they see some of this shifting at the federal level, so they're being more bold in their efforts to restrict abortion activity," Liebel added. "In some instances, they're rushing to out-pro-life each other."[1145]

Their observations shined a light on the most dangerous legislative session for women and pregnant people in modern history.

───────

For as much as Radical Right leaders have come to shape Donald Trump's political identity, he, in turn, has pulled back the veil on their core beliefs.

The movement architects spent decades taking pains to mask their roots of racism and sexism and cloaking their efforts in a sheen of moral superiority. For 40 years, it had succeeded in doing so like no other political movement in America; silencing dissent and moving its agenda — but the alignment with Donald Trump shifted and exposed them in monumental ways. His rise was proof that explicitly bigoted politics can be more powerful than they ever imagined, and its backlash can be mitigated more successfully than they expected.

A 2019 Pew Research poll found that 69% of white Evangelicals approved of Trump's job performance as president of the United States.[1146] Furthermore, another 2019 poll found more than forty percent of Republicans said there's virtually nothing he could do to lose their support.[1147] Leaders across the Right made a calculated decision to tie their fate to Trump's. They traded their carefully-cultivated brand for Trump's support for their ideological goals.

Marjorie Dannenfelser of Susan B. Anthony List spent years investing in an image as a pious leader who cared for women's well-being, life, and traditional values. But as the President and his administration committed travesty after travesty, she remained silent just as the rest did in the wake of the Access Hollywood tape.

When Trump called the neo-Nazis, one of whom murdered a woman in Charlottesville, Virginia, "very fine people," SBA List declined to criticize him or comment at all.[1148]

When parents wept and rallied to protest the Trump administration's inaction as life after life was claimed in the wave of gun violence, Dannenfelser ducked and weaved like a pro.

Only when Scott Lloyd was separating families and endangering children — a cause supposedly close to Dannenfelser's heart — was she forced to comment. Facing traumatized children locked in cages, devastating their loving parents, SBA List released a statement saying:

From its inception Susan B. Anthony List has been completely dedicated to protecting the first right without which no other rights matter: the right to life.

Our sole mission is to restore that profound right. Therefore, we refrain from public comment on immigration and many other topics, including other policies that impact families. It is not in our purview to speak on behalf of our members on other issues.[1149]

The movement's leaders made the decision in 2016 that the risk of being associated with Trump was worth the reward. And perhaps it was. They got the policies they wanted and the Supreme Court they always dreamed of. But they have also committed themselves to a man whose brand of politics threatens to rip off the mask they have carefully constructed, illustrating just how racist and misogynist their agenda is — not just in impact, but in intent.

Trump held up a mirror to a movement, and this is who they are.

Chapter 9
The Endgame

In late 2019, the House impeachment trial and subsequent acquittal of President Trump reinforced the reality that Senate Majority Leader Mitch McConnell and others were unwilling to put any checks on an increasingly out of control executive branch. The November 2020 election already loomed as the most significant in recent memory. Then the COVID-19 pandemic hit. The lack of expert leadership, the president's lies and propaganda, and the public polarization that had come to define the Trump administration suddenly took on a new risk as the country grappled with the crisis of the novel coronavirus. A dangerous disease that was highly contagious and more lethal than the common flu, this previously unknown virus sent countries into turmoil, requiring extensive quarantines and creating havoc with financial markets.[1150] [1151] [1152]

The administration was slow to respond, and when it did, the guidance was incoherent, self-serving, and often downright dangerous. Coming in an election year, the pandemic shook up the primary process, amplified fears about voter turnout and ballot access, and upended campaigns and grassroots organizing.[1153] As death tolls and unemployment rates rose, legislative fights over relief packages and protests against stay-at-home orders dominated the daily news. In the midst of this deadly chaos, the Radical Right's strategy of pushing through their goals by leveraging disinformation and using, or blocking, federal and state legislation did not let up.[1154]

Even in the early days of the pandemic, the GOP demonstrated steadfast adherence to their own ideology and political agenda over science-based public health policy. Decisions were driven by the interplay of their agendas of money, religion, and power — not what is best for people's lives. Some pushed fundamentalist doctrine over public safety. Others placed concern for the stock market and economic growth as the highest priority.[1155] And still, for others, their chief concern was the ability to hold onto an increasingly tenuous grasp of power come November.[1156]

A massive disinformation campaign was used to muddy history and deflect responsibility — blaming China, the World Health Organization (WHO), and the blue state governors while promoting magical cures to minimize the perceived threat.[1157] [1158] [1159] If anything, the COVID-19 pandemic pierced through a carefully cultivated brand of "pro-life" as politicians who claimed the moniker rushed to encourage policies and behaviors that risked countless lives.[1160]

Despite his horrific track record on public health, Mike Pence was tasked with leading the response.[1161] [1162] He relied on his core of like-minded allies: HHS Secretary Alex Azar, CDC Director Robert Redfeld, Medicaid & Medicare Chief Seema Verma, and Secretary of HUD Ben Carson, among others.[1163] These senior leaders were cut from the same ideological cloth; Azar and Carson participated in a weekly bible study that had been instituted early on.[1164] Sessions were led by Ralph Drollinger, a fundamentalist preacher who wrote that the virus was the "consequential wrath of God" angered by depraved secularists, environmentalists, and LGBTQ people.[1165] Attendees included not just Azar and Carson, but prominent decision makers like Betsy DeVos and Mike Pompeo.[1166]

While Trump made a show of credibility by showcasing the medical experts in his inner circle — Dr. Anthony Fauci and Dr. Deborah Birx — their voices were often drowned out, muted, or contradicted by the ideologues who had spent the last several years cultivating Trump's trust — and by the president himself when they got too much attention.[1167] So when — against all logic and medical advice — some of the president's core supporters began calling their flock back to public places, the official response was supportive.[1168]

Mega churches in many parts of the country held services against the orders of local public health authorities, some going so far as to suggest that the virus was the work of Satan trying to tear true believers apart.[1169] [1170] Trump booster Jerry Falwell Jr. called Liberty University students back to campus at a time when many colleges were sending students home.[1171] Pastor Franklin Graham, who had a history of homophobia, including saying "gays would burn in the flames of hell," was given permission to run a field hospital in New York City.[1172]

At each step, public health and medical expertise seemed a footnote to fundamentalism and self-dealing. In the early days of the outbreak, an acquitted and emboldened Trump continued to hold rallies and even suggested that COVID-19 was a plot by Democrats to use against him in the election.[1173] [1174] When he could no longer deny the public health threat, he moved his disinformation, deflection, and blame into the White House with daily press briefings, an important tradition that had been stopped by the administration in March 2019.[1175] [1176] What many hoped would be a briefing focused on how to guide the country through this crisis was in actuality a stage with a captive audience where Trump aired grievances, self-aggrandized, and pushed his own ideology.

Unsurprisingly, the administration asserted authority over states or individuals when it served their interests and hid behind individual liberty and state's rights when it did not. As the crisis reached an apex, there were reports of an epic battle in the situation room over a drug called hydroxychloroquine that Trump continually offered up as a treatment, despite a lack of medical evidence to back up the claim.[1177] [1178] According to reports, Dr. Fauci cautioned that the drug had not been tested sufficiently and carried real risks. He was attacked by Peter Navarro, Trump's director of trade, for advocating a more conservative approach.[1179]

In the end, the official administration position would be that the decision to take the controversial drug would be one left to doctors and patients — a position that was laughably ironic to anyone who had followed their positions on reproductive health care.[1180] True to form, anti-choice leaders lost no time exploiting the coronavirus pandemic to attack abortion access. Early in the pandemic, anti-choice governors from Ohio to Oklahoma claimed that abortion is an "elective" surgery and should be rendered off limits due to COVID-19.[1181] The American Medical Association was aghast.[1182] Data showed that similar actions in similar crises around the world had led to dismal outcomes among pregnant women.[1183] Even the New York Times Editorial Board called for more access to abortion during the crisis, not less.[1184] The GOP ignored them all. They continued their drumbeat to cut off access to doctors and clinics while, simultaneously, refusing to lift restrictions on medication abortions — two pills that can be safely taken at home to terminate pregnancies early on — which would help people stay quarantined while ending a pregnancy.[1185]

Scientists' entreaties to the administration to lift bans on fetal tissue research that might hold the key to treatment for the virus similarly fell on deaf ears.[1186] National leaders in the anti-choice movement petitioned HHS Secretary Azar to use the moment to end access to abortion and hold firm on these ideological bans.[1187] Early in the crisis, COVID-19 Czar Mike Pence even took precious time to hold a national conference call with leaders of the Religious Right to reassure them their agenda was secure.[1188]

As with so much about the Trump presidency, this entire effort was unprecedented and shocking, yet still entirely predictable to those who had followed or been victim to the machinations of the Radical Right. The unique characteristics of Trump's transactional, chaotic, self-serving style were complemented by the consistent forces that are the characters of this story: The Weyrich-era architects, and those that came after them, focused on their long-term goals of dominionism — protecting the dominance of white Christian men in our society; a base of true believers for whom abortion is the driving issue and the litmus test regardless of the context and a testament to the effectiveness of Weyrich's Trojan horse strategy; and the establishment GOP officials who continued to walk the tightrope to maintain electoral power.

For decades, these three factions of the movement have continued to find an uneasy balance to mutually coexist. The Radical Right has become increasingly more extreme in their rhetoric, their laws, and their candidates. Their power has grown as Trump has taken up their call. The cost is a yawning chasm between the movement leadership's positions and those of the people they are supposed to serve and, as a result, an increasing reliance on disinformation and suppression of democracy in order to hold their power.

───

Even before COVID-19, the right was in a delirious state. The true believers were driven by a heady sense of hubris derived from their victory in putting Kavanaugh on the Supreme Court. An emboldened leadership, engaged in frenzied activity, was laying cards on the table for everyone to see. And in doing so, the moral corruption at the heart of their movement and the impossible consequence of taking their extreme beliefs to their natural conclusion was on full display.

Take the case of Marshae Jones. In late 2018, the twenty-seven year old Black woman was five months pregnant when she was involved in a fight with another woman in a suburb west of Birmingham, Alabama.[1189] During the altercation, Jones was shot in the stomach, causing her to miscarry.[1190] As the case wound its way through the courts into the summer of 2019, a grand jury decided not to indict the shooter, but in a stunning turn of events, Jones herself was charged with manslaughter.[1191] Alabama had passed the nation's most draconian of abortion restrictions the month prior, enshrining into law the idea of "fetal personhood" — that life begins the moment of conception.[1192] Charging Marshae Jones in her own shooting was the logical conclusion of this law. The case also underscored the extent to which pregnant women in Alabama had been successfully defined as primarily a vessel for potential life.[1193] Massive public outrage greeted the news broke that Jones was facing twenty years in prison. The district attorney ultimately chose not to prosecute the case.[1194] It was practically and politically untenable to follow through.

In spring of 2019, right-wing Florida state Senator Dennis Baxley felt free to justify an anti-choice measure by arguing publicly that abortion was leading to a falling birthrate for Americans of Western European descent in the U.S., who were being outpaced by immigrants.[1195] "Civilizations do die if they have a low birth rate and don't replace themselves. A new society replaces them," Baxley said, parroting xenophobic propaganda known in the alt-right and neo-nazi movement as "replacement theory."[1196] [1197] Baxley is not the only abortion opponent to have used this debunked argument, adding himself to a long list with better known GOP officials like Maine Governor Paul LePage and soon-to-be-former Iowa congressman Steve King.[1198] The fact that the mass murderer who shot up the mosque in New Zealand around that same time was reportedly obsessed with the replacement theory conspiracy didn't cause Baxley to pause.[1199] Emboldened by the era of Trump, the true believers felt comfortable inserting their overt racism into the debate.

The Republican Party had made great strides in eradicating reproductive freedom in America. What's left of these rights were on the precipice. The rhetoric of their adherents and many of their elected officials was more extreme than ever, as was the ideology behind the alarmingly radical state-level restrictions being passed across the country. The movement was emboldened at a time when they assumed that their opponents were distracted and fragmented. Their original strategy — while working across multiple fronts — also required constant escalation that threatened to be their undoing.

The day Brett Kavanaugh was confirmed to the U.S. Supreme Court marked a sea change in the rhetoric of the Radical Right. Whereas the more cautious factions of their leadership used to rely on dog whistles and back room deals to exert their authority, in the final weeks of 2018 leading into early 2019, the tenor of their public statements began to shift — tentatively at first, and then dramatically as caution quickly eroded.

The language of true believers that had long bubbled around the fringes suddenly was adopted by electeds and visible movement leaders. The story shifted too. The story that painted women as victims of the "abortion industry" gave way to a new narrative in which women were the perpetrators of a crime.[1200] It was hard to miss the seething influence of the Men's Rights Advocates in the new version of the tale. Propaganda circulated in mainstream circles using terms like evil,[1201] soulless,[1202] and barbaric[1203] in describing patients, doctors, and elected officials who supported abortion access. There were now claims that abortion is worse than anything else — including the Holocaust,[1204] gun violence,[1205] childhood cancer and car crashes,[1206] racism,[1207] a lack of border security,[1208] rape,[1209] and terrorist attacks.[1210] These narratives had previously been tamped down for political expedience. Now, with the taste of victory on their tongue, even the most brand-conscious national groups embraced the vitriolic language.

They knew that their inflammatory rhetoric came with significant risks; this was a movement with a history of violence. In November 2015, as Donald Trump and Ben Carson topped GOP presidential polls, Robert Dear Jr. walked into a Planned Parenthood clinic in Colorado Springs and shot a dozen people, killing three, including a police officer.[1211] He called himself a "warrior for the babies," according to eyewitness reports.[1212] Despite warning signs about the deadly results, the anti-choice movement ratcheted up its rhetoric as Trump's campaign cozied up to extremists of all stripes. Threats of violence spiked again.[1213] Reports of threats to clinics, clinic workers and vandalism throughout the country reached historic highs in 2016, with over one third of all clinics reporting some kind of threat.[1214]

When Trump had named staunch abortion foe and Radical Right stalwart Jeff Sessions to the head of the Justice Department shortly after his election, the movement took note.[1215] The department oversees domestic terrorism issues, which includes politically motivated violence at abortion clinics. Operation Rescue's Troy Newman, who also served on the board of Daleiden's organization the Center for Medical Progress (CMP) exulted, "Under the Obama Administration, the Department of Justice turned a blind eye to abortion-related crimes, allowing abortion criminals to run amok over the lives of women and their babies. We look forward to a new era of justice where the laws of the land are enforced against those within the Abortion Cartel that have behaved as if they are above them."[1216] They were learning they could operate with impunity in the new world order.

For his part, the new president had learned that he could rely on his new friends to weather difficult political news cycles. When times became tough, Donald Trump inevitably threw a bone to the Radical Right to distract, deflect, and bask in their adulation.

In January 2018, the *Wall Street Journal* broke the news that Trump's former longtime lawyer Michael Cohen had paid $130,000 during the 2016 election to adult film actor Stormy Daniels to ensure her silence surrounding an affair with Trump.[1217] Just days later, the administration's rule to block funding for groups like Planned Parenthood was announced.[1218] [1219] Speaking to the March for Life crowd through a live video feed, Trump touted his administration's unprecedented move to curtail Title X dollars and promised to continue pushing to ban abortion at 20 weeks.[1220]

On April 9, 2018, the day Cohen's home, hotel room, and office were raided by FBI agents, the Trump administration made a very public move to waive penalties for ideologues who ignore the Affordable Care Act's requirement that private health insurance include coverage for abortion care.[1221] [1222]

In May 2018, only one day after the Senate Intelligence Committee affirmed the intelligence community assessment revealing an "extensive" Russian conspiracy to elect Trump, the Trump administration proposed expanded Title X restrictions on providers like Planned Parenthood.[1223] [1224] [1225]

That summer, when the Commerce Department was pressured to lower its estimate of economic growth, the president appeared in front of a crowd of true believers to loudly declare: "We are proudly defending the sanctity of life."[1226] The audience broke into a chant of "four more years!"

The president showed a clear pattern of escalation, as establishment influences waned within the administration and the feedback loop with the right grew stronger. In his first year as president, Trump had scaled way back, mentioning abortion in only one speaking engagement — in the context of the Global Gag Rule — through the entirety of 2017.[1227] Trump seemed to intuitively grasp that — now that the election was over — it was better to sate the right's fetish on these issues behind closed doors and in bureaucratic actions not noticeable to the general public. Trump invoked abortion mainly when stumping for another candidate, or making an appearance at a patently anti-choice event like the March for Life, a dinner for evangelical leaders, or the SBA List Gala

But as his 2018 troubles spiked, "abortion" appeared in eight speeches and rallies — about the same number of mentions as the previous election year when he was making his overtures to the movement.[1228] By 2019, Trump took no such political precautions. Tracking right alongside the emboldened movement, he railed against abortion at 18 public speeches and rallies, routinely working the themes into his regular rally speeches.[1229] By then, the riff was well-rehearsed: He would disingenuously claim every top Democrat supports "late-term abortion" and even "execution," of fetuses. He would go on to say that he's asked Congress to "prohibit extreme late-term abortion" because "Republicans believe that every child is a sacred gift from God." This part of the speech would often end with sweeping negative claims that the Democrats were the party of "high crime," "high taxes," "open borders," "late term abortion," "socialism," "intolerance," "division," "witch hunts," or "delusions."[1230] [1231] [1232] [1233] [1234] [1235]

Trump had good reason to ignore the facts and lean into the false narrative. While he was buoyed by his great victory with Kavanaugh, neither he nor his advisers were blind to the price they had paid at the ballot box in 2018.

White men and born again Christian or Evangelical church-goers remained the GOP's only reliable voting bloc.[1236] Many in these groups resonated with Trump's message that they were the victims of politically correct culture gone wild. They believed that minorities were favored in America and sexual harassment was not a serious problem. Meanwhile, white women overall and self-identified moderates were moving away from Trump and the GOP, and towards Democratic candidates, adding power to the multi-ethnic base that already made up the backbone of the party.[1237]

These new Democratic and independent voters were frustrated by the process around Kavanaugh's confirmation, worried about threats to *Roe v.*

Wade, and concerned by the tone and tenor of the country. Their rejection of the GOP proved powerful in 2018, flipping control to put the speaker's gavel back in the hands of Nancy Pelosi. Democrats gained 41 seats in the House of Representatives — many in districts won by Trump a mere two years prior.[1238] [1239] State houses changed hands with several governors' seats going to Democrats, even in deep red states like Kansas and key rust belt states like Michigan and Wisconsin.[1240] [1241] Six state legislative chambers flipped Democratic, and in even more states, Democrats picked up seats and eroded GOP supermajorities.[1242] [1243]

Trump was also facing a bigger problem. With the House back in Democratic hands, he knew that they now had the power to move forward on investigations into his presidency and even impeachment proceedings. True to form, his response was to vilify his opponents, and change the public conversation. Speaking directly to his base in his 2019 State of the Union address, President Trump falsely claimed that state-level legislation "would allow a baby to be ripped from the mother's womb moments before birth" or allow "execut[ing] a baby after birth."[1244] He then continued to push the boundaries of civil and political discourse by repeatedly using the term "execution" in relation to Democrats' stance on abortion in tweets and public addresses.[1245] [1246]

After his address to the nation, Trump hosted a "National Pro-Life Conference Call," where he spun the election and encouraged the extreme language, some of which was making establishment leaders nervous.[1247] "We used, in the State of the Union, 'executed the baby,' and that's exactly what it was, it was an execution.'" He then told his audience, "I think your popularity and your cause is going to be actually benefited by what happened."[1248]

On March 2, 2019, Donald Trump took the stage at CPAC, the Conservative Political Action Conference, a mandatory annual stop for all aspiring and established voices of the right-wing.[1249] For over two hours, he regaled the crowd with campaign rally talking points and half-truths, regularly veering into uncharted terrain. At one point, he made the outlandish claim that Democrats support infanticide, stating, "if they didn't want the child, who is now outside of the womb — long outside of the womb — they will execute the baby after birth."[1250] [1251] All credible fact checkers would dismiss Trump's claim as a lie. That would not stop the president from making it a regular talking point, whipping the crowds at his rallies into a frenzy by calling Democrats murderers.[1252]

As often is the case, Trump was signal boosting the extreme end of the movement. In this case, reaching for a bigger, bolder narrative to attract those looking to vent their frustrations at the feminists who opposed Kavanaugh and at Democrats who had won in 2018, energy bolstered by the belief on the Right the end of *Roe* was "in sight."[1253]

They weren't the only one concerned about the implications of the

Kavanaugh Court. In 2019, now-Democratically controlled state legislatures in Virginia and New York moved legislation to prepare for a post-*Roe* America.[1254] [1255] Some of this was cleaning up. Since the *Roe* decision overrode state law, many states like New York had never bothered to remove abortion from the criminal code.[1256] Bills in both states were essentially status-quo measures with some small but impactful tweaks to protect pregnant people. One measure that Virginia was considering was to remove a redundant requirement that a pregnant person with serious health risks have multiple doctors — versus only the one charged with their care — to certify that an abortion was medically necessary.[1257]

Radical Right operatives saw an opportunity to spin their narrative in this mundane proposal, suggesting that Democrats were insidiously working to legalize "infanticide."[1258] Their wild-eyed charges reached fever pitch when Virginia Governor Ralph Northam, a doctor himself, delved into details of infant palliative care in answer to an interview question. With clinical expertise not common in — or rewarded by — politics, he explained the truth of tragic cases. He said that a nonviable fetus could be "delivered...kept comfortable," and "resuscitated if that's what the mother and the family desired."[1259] With no sympathy for families facing this terrible situation, the Radical Right became more aggressive, claiming that "every abortion is infanticide."[1260]

This new rhetoric was a coordinated effort but opportunistic, not planned. In the initial weeks after New York's measure was introduced, the movement tested a number of extreme phrases, including claiming New York and Virgina were working to legalize abortion "up until birth,"[1261] abortion "seconds before" birth,[1262] abortion "after birth,"[1263] "leav[ing] babies to die,"[1264] "letting infants die,"[1265] a "death sentence,"[1266] and that allowing *Roe v. Wade* to stand was tantamount to supporting "infanticide." Early on, some anti-choice influencers periodically backed away from this extreme language, like Dannenfelser and Conway before them, concerned about alienating audiences they considered persuadable. Those were no match for the president who relished the theatrics and pushed his own embellished term "execution."[1267] Ultimately, variations of this charged rhetoric became commonplace among even the establishment operatives, though the coalition eventually settled on the term "infanticide."

The entire episode was a perfect encapsulation of the Willke propaganda strategy –– the language succinct, carries implications that a crime has taken place, and focuses attention entirely on an "infant." It reached a high level of saturation in popular media, in large part thanks to Fox News' ceaseless propagation.[1268] Throughout 2019, digital ads targeted Democratic politicians with this false attack in an obvious effort to suppress defections by women voters concerned about threats to *Roe*. Facebook's refusal to police, curtail, or do anything other than boost disinformation on its platform allowed the messages to spread rapidly among the hopped-up true believers, infecting even the mainstream discourse online.[1269]

Despite the clear perils of escalating rhetoric in a movement with a history of violence, the White House plowed forward, hosting a screening of the anti-abortion propaganda film Gosnell as part of the effort.[1270] It was, *Politico* reported, "a broader push by Trump to energize his devoted fans in the white evangelical community as he prepares for a tough reelection fight."[1271] A senior official had told the *Washington Post* that Trump's efforts were intended to distract and re-energize his base after a series of defeats, including the election and a budget standoff in late 2018."[1272]

———

Rich billionaires played their part too. In the 2018 Illinois gubernatorial primary, billionaire Richard Uihlein pumped $2 million into the race to back a candidate far to the right of GOP incumbent Bruce Rauner.[1273] Uihlein was cut from the Weyrich cloth and — like those who had come before him — felt real displeasure with how insufficiently-conservative he believed the current party to be. His pick against the moderate Rauner was Jeanne Ives, a little known state legislator from Wheaton, Illinois.[1274] [1275] Considered a fringe candidate before Uihlein breathed life into her faltering campaign, Ives ran against Rauner attacking his positions on immigration, abortion, and marriage equality — positions that Rauner justifiably claimed were in line with a largely blue state where Trump lost by almost a million votes.[1276] [1277] [1278]

Ives was what the movement architects dreamed of in a candidate. She supported voter suppression; she was one of five state legislators to vote against a state constitutional amendment guaranteeing the right to register and cast a ballot in Illinois regardless of "race, color, ethnicity, status as a member of a language minority, national origin, religion, sex, sexual orientation, or income."[1279] [1280] She helped stop a ban on dangerous "conversion therapy" for gay people — eschewing medical consensus and stating at the time, "We have no purview in this department. We have no expertise in this department. It's absolutely something that should not ever be legislated on. Let people decide for themselves what they need to have for themselves."[1281]

Of course, Ives made no such concessions for women having the freedom to end pregnancies. Ives staunchly opposed abortion, and she had no qualms openly fighting mothers who didn't fit the conservative mold. In an Illinois House floor debate in 2015, Ives rankled Democrats and voters. "I'm not interested in providing childcare to people where you don't even know the paternity. You better know who the daddy is and whether or not he can afford that child," she lectured.[1282] Called out as race-baiting and misogynistic, Ives laid bare her truth about just which children deserved support and which women deserved derision.[1283] She further enraged critics in the 2018 primary when she ran an ad widely hailed as transphobic and racist.[1284] [1285] Ives pushed too far and fell off the tightrope, but she may have, to mix metaphors, moved the goalposts. She lost to Bruce Rauner in the primary, but sufficiently weakened him with the base that he was defeated by Democrat J.B. Pritzker.[1286] [1287] Ives mounted a campaign for federal Congress in 2020, with Uihlein supporting her.[1288] [1289]

———

Before Ives, Uihlein jumped to the support of another candidate in the Weyrich mold named Roy Moore. In 2017, Moore was running to fill Jeff Sessions' Senate seat after Sessions went to lead the Department of Justice. In his primary bid against the more establishment Luther Strange, Moore earned endorsements from key Trump loyalists, including advisers Steve Bannon and Sebastian Gorka, an alt-right hero and outspoken Islamophobe.[1290] Moore appealed to these hardliners for his unyielding politics and history of defying higher authority. He wore his 2003 removal from his office as Alabama Chief Justice as a badge of honor, often touting his refusal to take down a marble statue of the Ten Commandments that led to his termination.[1291] Moore ran again a decade later and won. He was reinstated as Chief Justice in 2015, when he was suspended once again almost immediately for ordering Alabama state judges to refuse same sex couples marriage licenses, after the 2015 Supreme Court ruling legalizing gay marriage. Moore resigned in 2016, a hero to many in his state who refused to cede ground to the federal government accommodating a changing world.[1292] He then mounted his Senate run.

The Alabama primary illuminated tensions within the coalition that had thrust Trump into the White House. While Trump's militant deputies went all in for Roy Moore in early 2017, Strange had been appointed as acting senator by the sitting governor after Sessions went to Washington.[1293] Strange was deeply conservative by any account and had significant backing from the likes of Senate Majority Leader Mitch McConnell, who spent $10 million from his Senate Leadership Fund to support him.[1294] Initially, Trump took his cues from McConnell and Pence by backing the establishment candidate, but his misgivings were clear as Strange floundered, and at a rally in the final stretch of the campaign, Trump told a crowd in Alabama, "I might have made a mistake."[1295] Trump ultimately threw his weight behind Moore in the general election in the midst of an unfolding scandal that read like a precursor to the Kavanaugh nomination. Trump decided Moore's anti-choice, anti-LGBTQ credentials, his judicial nominees, and his typical racist, anti-immigrant rhetoric outweighed a growing series of accusations from women that streamed in as the campaign drew to a close.[1296]

With weeks to go before the Alabama special election, multiple women spoke of Moore harassing and assaulting them when he was a district attorney in his early thirties and they were in high school — at least one as young as 14 at the time.[1297] [1298] The accusations were corroborated by many who worked around Moore. Colleagues from the DA's office said everyone knew Moore liked young girls and thought it "was weird" that he hung out at high school football games and the mall.[1299] A retired detective from the police force in his town said that she had been told by superiors to keep an eye on him since he was known to harass young cheerleaders at athletic events.[1300]

Moore himself veered between denials and justifications, stating that he never dated young women "without their mother's permission."[1301] Some prominent Republicans pulled their support, but many chose to stay the course.[1302] Alabama State Auditor Jim Zegler even went so far as to use the Bible to say that Moore's behavior was acceptable, telling the Washington Examiner in an interview after the story broke: "There's nothing to see here... Take the Bible — Zachariah and Elizabeth, for instance. Zachariah was extremely old to marry Elizabeth and they became the parents of John the Baptist. Also take Joseph and Mary. Mary was a teenager and Joseph was an adult carpenter. They became parents of Jesus."[1303]

Pastor Flip Benham from the virulent anti-abortion Operation Save America remarked that when Moore returned home from a tour in Vietnam, many women his own age were already married. So he had to expand his search, and "there is something about a purity of a young woman, there is something that is good, that's true, that's straight and he looked for that."[1304] These defenses had traction in the Evangelical community, with a poll taken after the allegations showing that they made Evangelical voters in Alabama more likely to support Roy Moore.[1305] Many of these voters said his support for rigid anti-abortion laws was a top reason for conttinued support.

Moore's campaign brought together the money, power, and hypocrisy of the Radical Right. Uihlein, Jeanne Ives benefactor, was also the largest investor in a SuperPAC dedicated to Moore's candidacy. Jerry Falwell Jr. and Franklin Graham never swayed from their support of Moore.[1306] But perhaps no greater support came than from Bannon's old outfit at *Breitbart News*. CNN reported at the time that it was difficult to tell the difference between the homepage of Breitbart and the Moore campaign website. Breitbart's staff reported that the management there believed that the race was "everything."[1307] Nothing was more telling than an interview with Editor in Chief Alex Marlow, who said that Breitbart was fighting so hard to defend Moore because they believed that if Moore was disqualified based on this behavior, it would set a standard that President Trump himself could not meet.[1308] [1309]

On December 12, 2017, Moore lost to Democrat Doug Jones, who became the first Democrat elected to the senate from Alabama in over 25 years.[1310] [1311] Roy Moore never conceded the race and announced he would run again in the Republican primary for senate in 2020.[1312] [1313] He lost badly.

Ives and Moore tried to take a page out of Trump's book and lost their races. Others, like Ron DeSantis in Florida and Brian Kemp in Georgia won gubernatorial campaigns running on equally extreme platforms, admittedly without the scandals. Both governors had invoked racist dog whistles against their Black opponents.[1314] Both had used the issue of abortion to rile up their evangelical base.[1315] [1316] Both also had successfully used voter suppression and disenfranchisement to squeak out their narrow victories, providing living, breathing examples that undermining democracy goes hand in hand with pursuing an unpopular agenda.[1317]

Still, 2018 overall turned out to be a broad referendum on Trump, especially among women. The GOP now faced a clear choice and a crucial election in 2020. They could moderate their behavior to be more in line with voters or double down. Following Trump's lead, Republican leaders chose the latter. With the belief that they finally had a Supreme Court that would work for them, red states went on an anti-choice legislation binge through much of 2019, passing the dangerous and demeaning laws of an even greater scope and scale.

It was no coincidence that the most extreme measures were passed in states where voter suppression and gerrymandering efforts had been particularly successful. Georgia's Kemp had engaged in extraordinary acts of suppression in his gubernatorial bid against Democrat Stacey Abrams. As the secretary of state, he oversaw his own election in a race that included aggressive voter registration purges, stories of groups of voters being turned away at the polls, and fake robocalls that promoted racism and antisemetism.[1318] [1319] Kemp's management of his own election was considered a "textbook" example of voter suppression and was decried by groups like the NAACP as deliberately "silencing" the Black community.[1320] Even with all the anti-democratic machinations, Abrams' vote tally was so close the race was not officially called for days.[1321]

Kemp had run right and promised his base early action. So shortly after he took office, he pushed an aggressive law to ban abortion so soon after conception that most women wouldn't know they were pregnant before the law kicked in. The proposed law provoked such immense backlash and clashes in the state legislature that it barely passed.[1322] As many noted during the proceedings, Georgia already had one of the highest maternal mortality rates in the nation , and its proposed bill would only make that problem worse — a far cry from a "pro-life" position.[1323] Kemp became a walking poster child for centering cruelty in policy making and his actions made it clear that no amount of collateral damage was too high in the quest for control.

Almost a dozen states introduced or passed abortion bans, first at eight weeks, then six weeks, and then laughably at two weeks, mocking the reality of when and how people find out they are pregnant. A few years prior, these types of laws had not just been unconstitutional, they were unthinkable. The party establishment understood these measures pushed way past what the public would tolerate.

The idea of pushing extreme state-level abortion bans to force the Supreme Court to reconsider *Roe* wasn't new. A 2011 proposal in Ohio to ban abortion at 6 weeks had been supported by hardliners including John C. Willke — godfather of the anti-choice movement — but had been considered so risky that it had caused a fracture within the state's Radical Right coalition. Proponents of the move defected from the more recalcitrant Ohio Right to Life to spinoff an even more extreme organization, Ohio ProLife Action[1324]. Taking their cues from the Willke playbook, the bill's pushers had labeled their radical proposal a "heartbeat bill," a phrase that caught on in anti-choice circles and remains in use today. Experts and OB/GYNs have routinely explained that it's scientifically inaccurate to suggest a fetal heartbeat exists at such an early stage in pregnancy, but accuracy was never the point.[1325] Instead, the language was always an intentional effort to focus attention on a false image of fetal viability and obscure the person carrying the pregnancy.

For years, the Radical Right's lead strategists had largely opposed such early abortion bans, knowing they would be wildly unpopular and could tarnish the movement. After all, winning an abortion ban wasn't supposed to be the actual goal, as Paul Weyrich had reminded his audience years earlier. The Ohio GOP shelved the original bill but that didn't stop fringe state-level groups from promoting several similar bans in the next several years. They knew it would take time, and, meanwhile, the Willke strategy of disinformation and propaganda was showing signs of success. While public support for legal access to abortion never wavered, people demonstrated an emotional reaction to the invented term and often withdrew from the debate confused about the facts. In 2013, South Dakota finally passed the ban, and in 2015, the Supreme Court blocked the law from taking effect, creating a temporary chilling effect.[1326] [1327] That freeze thawed, however, when Brett Kavanaugh was confirmed to the Supreme Court. The true believers believed this was the endgame.

———

From the very beginning, the push for sweeping state-level abortion bans was deeply embedded in the larger Radical Right playbook. The author of the original Ohio bill was a woman by the name of Janet Folger Porter, who would later emerge on the national scene riding to the rescue of an embattled Roy Moore in his Alabama Senate run.[1328] One of her first appearances in support of Moore was an interview with CNN's Poppy Harlow that was so rife with disinformation, deflection, and dog whistles that CNN's Chris Cillizza dedicated an entire column to trying to deconstruct and debunk the interview.[1329] She opened by congratulating a visibly pregnant Poppy on her "unborn child" and then proceeded to spend the interview decrying non-existent issues like abortion "up until the moment of birth."[1330] She spent a good deal of the interview casting the women who had come forward about Moore's abuse as liars and the media as lazy enablers, finally saying that a vote against Moore was a vote for the "lynch mob media," George Soros, and Democrats.[1331] [1332]

Porter's rise followed the evolution of the movement. Starting early in her career, she had spent a decade serving as the legislative director for Ohio Right to Life, which was by then an established gateway for young radical activists on the right.[1333] Porter wanted a wider platform from which to rail against the full range of threats to a white Christian way of life. Her organization earned the designation of "hate group" by the Southern Policy Law Center for its anti-LGBTQ sentiments, including a proclamation that God flooded the Earth in the time of Noah to get rid of marriage between men and that Christians are targets of the "gay agenda."[1334] [1335] [1336]

Porter's approach fully embraced disinformation as a tool, not only pioneering scientific misnomers like "heartbeat ban", but also insisting that homosexuality is a choice that can be cured through conversion therapy.[1337] She became a regular contributor to the right-wing conspiracy news site, WorldNetDaily, where she used her platform to promote birtherism and claim that then-President Obama might be staffing up to establish internment camps for conservatives.[1338] In 2010, her radio show on Christian radio was cancelled for promoting dominionist theories, a charge she weakly denied.[1339] Prior to being kicked off the air, she used the platform to rage against everything from climate change legislation to immigration reform, once claiming, "you cannot be a Christian and vote for Obama."[1340]

After the Republican-led Ohio state senate failed to move the abortion ban forward in 2011, she aligned with the newly formed Ohio Pro-Life Action to target unsupportive Republicans, cleaning house to make way for electeds who rose from the ranks of true believers and movement architects.[1341] Movememnt Founder John Willke stunned followers by siding with Porter over the organization he helped found and resigned his board position at Ohio Right to Life.[1342] Willke died in 2015, just as his life's work was beginning to crescendo.

Porter's take-no-prisoners approach gained her national prominence among the far right. She became a clearinghouse for state legislators who wanted to introduce similar legislation and for activists who wanted to employ similar tactics. She was transparent that her efforts were designed to be a direct challenge to *Roe v. Wade*. "It's time to quit begging for crumbs," she said."[1343] [1344]

By 2019, it seemed the Republican Party had caught up with Janet, not the other way around. The Ohio state legislature had passed abortion bans twice since the original attempt in 2011, only to be vetoed by then-Governor John

Kasich.[1345] In 2018, far right Republican Mike Dewine was elected to replace Kasich, and as one of his first acts in office, he finally signed into law the six week abortion ban that Porter had worked toward for almost a decade.[1346] [1347] Ohio's action came at a time when the true believers of the Radical Right were energized after the Kavanaugh fight and increasingly willing to throw caution to the wind. One longtime anti-abortion lobbyist in Missouri — which was then pushing its own eight week abortion ban — lamented that the movement didn't care anymore for the advice of lawyers saying, "Sometimes, people just want something. Social movements can take on a life of their own."[1348] This movement wanted a lot.

In state houses around the country, the debates raged. Georgia's abortion ban promised to classify women who miscarried vulnerable to criminal investigations.[1349] Alabama established prison sentences of up to 99 years for doctors who violated the law and served their patients by providing abortion.[1350] Texas, not content with their existing restrictions, held a hearing on a measure that would mandate capital punishment for people who had an abortion.[1351] Ohio legislators didn't skip a beat after passing their ban, moving a bill that created a new felony called "abortion murder" and mandating life in prison for anyone who receives or performs an abortion.[1352] This particular law had a provision which would require doctors who remove ectopic pregnancies — embryos that implant in the fallopian tube instead of the uterus — to reimplant them in the uterus, a scientific impossibility.[1353] One doctor observed of the new law, "that is not medicine, that's magic."[1354] Almost all of these bills defined life as beginning at conception, inscribing a particular theological view of life into the legal canon of many states, in a breathtaking challenge to dearly held principles of individual freedom and autonomy and of separation of church and state. On a more practical side, attorneys scrambled to interpret the implications of these new "personhood" measures on everything from tax law to alimony.[1355] [1356]

It was against this chaotic backdrop that Marshae Jones was arrested in Alabama and politicians, like Baxley in Florida, were justifying their approach with racist conspiracies. Perhaps at no point since Falwell and Weyrich began their social experiment had the underlying desire to punish non-conforming women and keep racial minorities in their place been so apparent. The legislators who had been groomed for this moment couldn't help but show the underpinnings of their beliefs, driven by distrust of women and racial enmity. In South Carolina, a GOP lawmaker, pleading for a rape exception to her state's abortion ban, shared her story of sexual assault as a sixteen year old. She was told by a colleague that rape was a "misdeed of the parent" that doesn't justify an abortion.[1357]

These laws were so extreme that a mere 25% of self-identified Republicans agreed with them. If anything they drove more support for abortion access which reached an all-time high of 77% in early 2019.[1358] The aggressive action on so many dangerous and demeaning laws, over the cries of legislators and constituents alike, was so blatant and jarring that it provoked massive national backlash. In late May of 2019, tens of thousands gathered at statehouses around the country to demonstrate against the state bans and demand federal action.[1359] Hundreds of private sector CEOs signed an open letter in the *New York Times* demanding that politicians stop "banning equality," and there was talk of economic boycotts in states where they were passed.[1360] GGeorgia became a particular focus because Atlanta had become a top staging ground for the film industry. Prominent actors and directors pledged not to film there if the ban was enacted into law.[1361] Immediately after that bill became law, organizations announced the Reclaim Georgia fund to defeat every legislator who had voted for the ban in that state.[1362]

The protests made the GOP nervous. National Republicans took care to avoid discussing the bans. They could do the math, and were afraid of the electoral implications. Even in Georgia, it had been very difficult to maintain GOP unity to pass the bill after the protests began.[1363] A couple of GOP legislators even skipped the final vote so as to avoid going on the record supporting the ban.[1364] After months of silence on the issue, President Trump knew he needed to appear to back off a bit and set a new narrative direction in a series of three classic tweets.[1365] He positioned himself as the heir to Reagan, supporting exceptions for rape, incest and health; he attempted to pacify the far right by reminding them of the judges he gave them to gut *Roe v. Wade*; and he pivoted to his refrain of calling the Democrats the extremists.[1366]

It proved to be too little, too late. In November of 2019, the electorate once again rejected the GOP. This time, voters elected a pro-choice governor in the deep red state of Kentucky in a race where abortion played a major role.[1367] Democrat Andy Beshear beat far right incumbent Matt Bevin, who had just signed the Kentucky abortion bans into law.[1368] [1369] In the final weeks of the election, Beshear was hit with a slew of ads full of disinformation and calling him "pro-death" and followed up with the familiar racist charge that he would "allow illegal immigrants to swarm" the state of Kentucky.[1370] Despite that, Beshear won by a narrow margin, and once again, suburban women made the difference.[1371]

A few states over in Virginia — where Governor Northam's statements had become the bullseye of the Radical Right's attacks many months earlier — state legislative elections were also underway.[1372] The right set out to make good on their vow to take out the Democratic elected officials who had forwarded the state's Repeal Act in 2019. But Virginia Republicans knew the purple state's history of punishing extremists who stray too far from its values. GOP candidates were generally running as moderates on Second Amendment rights and healthcare, disappointing the right-wing base. Abortion was the only thing Republican candidates had left to feed the base, so they went all in, running dozens of ads in different districts accusing Democrats of "infanticide" as they had with Beshear. Despite their last ditch efforts, their loss was resounding.[1373] Democrats flipped the state Senate and achieved a trifecta in the state. In 2020, Virginia finally ratified the ERA and Governor Northam signed the Reproductive Health Act into law.[1374]

The elections in 2018 and 2019 showed just how vulnerable the GOP was going into 2020. Yet the right's realization of this made them more dangerous, not less. Their disinformation machine went into overdrive, as did their willingness to move closer and closer to the white supremacists who had been emboldened by the moment. Much like their early predecessors, the GOP establishment cooperated by staying silent and the self-proclaimed "Religious Right" gave a wink and a nod to neo-Nazi websites Stormfront and the Daily Stormer and white nationalist group Patriot Front as they took up the call. They creatively merged the new rallying cry of "infanticide" with their own deep lore about god "Moloch," demanding child sacrifice. The Moloch fable is a proxy for Jewish people and age old anti-Semitic charges of blood libel.

The Daily Stormer ran the headline "MOLOCH: New York Legalizes 'Any Time' Abortions if Mothers' Lives are in Danger."[1375] The piece went on to assert "Women exist as women for the sole purpose of making babies. If their purpose was any other, they'd be men, or maybe they wouldn't even exist."[1376] Using racial slurs and inflammatory language, the piece affirmed all of the underlying subtext of the messages the president and the Radical Right were sending: that women with too much power were part of a nefarious conspiracy to undermine the natural social order.

The claims sound outrageous and offensive. That didn't stop "mainstream" anti-choice activists from amplifying the messages. Just days later, Students for Life tweeted: "If Governor Moloch Northam was 'taken out of context', then all he needs to do is vow to veto any legislation that repeals prohibitions on third-trimester abortions and promise to #resistinfanticide."[1377] Students for Life wasn't the only anti-choice group to embrace the white supremacists' dog whistles.[1378] No major leader of the Radical Right stepped in to correct them.

Social media turbocharges the effectiveness of disinformation strategies, enabling insidious alliances by allowing extremists to find each other more easily. Facebook, thanks to its lax policies and unwillingness to antagonize conservative leaders and right-wing media, has been a huge facilitator of these disinformation campaigns, and will be particularly relevant in the 2020 election. Analysts expect approximately $3 billion to be spent on political digital advertising in the 2020 election, primarily on Facebook.[1379] [1380] The Trump campaign has already spent approximately $27 million on Facebook advertising, dramatically outpacing spending by the Democratic field.[1381] [1382]

Meanwhile, Facebook has continually refused to check disinformation, maintaining that doing so would be tantamount to censorship.[1383] The massive company has also been slow to shut down forums where extremist language turns to outright threats. Like the Men's Rights forums that facilitated "Gamergate" and left online feminists terrified for their safety, right-wing forums abound on Facebook in an age of COVID-19.[1384 1385 1386] Right-wing activists and anti-choice adherents mix and mingle with on-line misogynists, white supremacists and anti-government extremists in groups overtly dedicated to protesting quarantine orders.[1387] The disproportionate focus has been on women in power, specifically Gretchen Whitmer, governor of Michigan.[1388] Credible threats to the governor's life and a constant presence of phalanxes of armed men led to the Capitol of Michigan being shut down — while the spaces on Facebook, where the threats emerged and the protests were being organized, remained open.[1389 1390 1391] Other social media platforms have made overtures towards solving the problem, but none have put real mettle into it.

This lack of action has profound implications, not only for the 2020 election, but as a platform for voter suppression and conspircy theories, for the sustainability of our democracy and the public health of the nation. The right's disinformation campaigns pollute the public sphere, making facts almost impossible to discern.

The strategy has undeniable impact, be it perceptions of the threat of COVID-19, leading to risky individual behavior and policy making, or the fueling of right-wing extremism. Surveys conducted in the weeks after the President's State of the Union in 2019 found that more than half of Americans were aware of the "infanticide" claims.[1392] Many were confused and upset by the charge. The New York Times heralded the extreme infanticide messaging as a "unusually forceful, carefully coordinated" campaign and a major advance in anti-choice strategy.[1393]

The GOP was happy to capitalize on and foment the confusion. In February 2019, Senator Ben Sasse of Nebraska introduced legislation called the Born Again Abortion Survivors Protection Act.[1394] First introduced in 2017, Sasse's bill then failed to make it out of committee.[1395] His colleagues had expressed concerns that it was inflammatory and redundant with a 2002 bi-partisan bill that affirmed the legal rights of infants regardless of their state of development.[1396] Sasse's bill dictated specific medical interventions, overriding medical judgement, and it threatened criminal sanctions for doctors that veered from the prescribed path.[1397] The bill was tabled.[1398] By 2019, however, it was back with McConnell's support.[1399]

The Senate majority leader was as aware as anyone of the political price the GOP was playing for catering to their extreme base. He didn't like losing the House majority in 2018, and he knew his grip on the Senate majority was tenuous going into 2020. Undermining the ability of physicians to perform their duties and vilifying their intentions was apparently a small price to pay for a brazen attempt to hold onto power amidst declining public support. Sasse's bill was run again, this time put for a floor vote amidst language so outrageous that even Kaiser Health News felt compelled to release a piece in late February specifically debunking Sasse's core claims."[1400] The vote failed to pass.[1401]

So why do it? Almost immediately after the vote on the sham bill, in a craven political act, the right ran attack ads against Democrats who were up for reelection in 2020. The ads in question made outlandish claims that Democrats opposed medical care for infants. They were paid for by America's PAC, the far-right outfit that had spent $9 million alone in 2016 and 2018 to elect crusaders from the Radical Right bankrolled by none other than Richard Uihlein.[1402]

———

The GOP strategy of deflection, including building straw men arguments and pressuring the media to parrot them, complemented the disinformation campaigns. This rhetorical device is often referred to as "whataboutism," and it has documented roots in Soviet propaganda strategies.[1403]

Late night comedian and social critic John Oliver did a full episode explaining the Trump administration's reliance on this tactic. "It implies that all actions regardless of context share a moral equivalency," he explained in a 2017 show. "And since nobody is perfect, all criticism is hypocritical and everyone should do whatever they want ... It doesn't solve a problem or win an argument. The point is just to muddy the waters, which just makes the other side mad."[1404]

Trump used this rhetorical device to defend his pardon of Sheriff Joe Arpaio, who was convicted of criminal contempt for ignoring the law in going after undocumented immigrants in his jurisdiction.[1405] The president used it in standing by white supremacists who descended on Charlottesville, Virginia as "very fine people."[1406] Never mind the Nazi-inspired march resulted in the murder of counter-protestor Heather Heyer.[1407] Instead of condemning the actions outright, Trump pointed to fabricated claims that the left — Antifa — had provoked or even planned the rally themselves as a way to discredit him.[1408] These dangerous and thoroughly debunked claims rocketed through the right-wing echo chamber and were parroted by Alex Jones on the radical alt-right platform Infowars. Republican Congressman Paul Gosar went a step further, invoking anti-Semitism while claiming that the operations were bankrolled by Jewish philanthropist Geroge Soros.[1409]

———

The genesis of this entire decades-long saga can be traced back to the original architects of the movement betting that they could rely on a different kind of silent majority. Antiquated social mores about sex, sex outside of marriage, and women who have sex when they don't want a family combined to create a stigma around the entire issue of abortion and reproductive healthcare. That stigma resulted in silence, even among supporters of reproductive freedom, that the right has exploited successfully for many, many years. Whether because politicians believe the issues are risky to engage or that they can find common ground on other priorities if they give on this one, Democratic attempts to change the subject or deprioritize reproductive rights has only emboldened the right and allowed the GOP to move a raft of repressive and oppressive policies - often attaching or threatening to attach abortion provisions to completely non-germaine issues to gain the upper hand in negotiations.

The Stupak-Pitts amendment to the Affordable Care Act was, at least in large part, designed to scuttle the new president's signature piece of legislation and divide the progressive coalition through infighting.[1410] The GOP attached Hyde funding restrictions to the initial COVID-19 relief bill, daring the Democrats to vote against the modicum of relief they were offering a panicked and hard hit public or upset their base by throwing abortion, and especially abortion for low income women and women of color, under the bus.[1411] Some are tempted to concede, reasoning that it's better to stay focused and not get distracted. Others have an internal aversion to discussing these issues for personal reasons. Whatever the reason, the reticence to attack the GOP head on has allowed the right to own the narrative and keep Democrats rocked back on their heels.

But, in its own way, the current GOP strategy is also a recognition of defeat. They know that in order to maintain the upper hand, they have to keep escalating. As they got more extreme, a growing reproductive freedom and justice movement started to erase cultural shame around abortion and work with Democrats to embrace the public support that is already there. More and more people were speaking up and out against the GOP machinations.

So they again ratcheted up the psychological barriers to engagement, with Trump's escalation of rhetoric and the right's embrace of the claims of "infanticide," spending hundreds of thousands of dollars spreading the false and incendiary rhetoric. Democratic officials understandably held back in their response, believing the notion was so absurd that it was not worth responding to it.

They were underestimating the impact of how people are processing incendiary information in today's environment. Our ability to rationally judge the accuracy of an idea we are presented with most often has to get past our visceral emotional reaction first. The right was smartly placing their bets on the fact that a majority of the public would be so reviled by the charges that they would turn off from the conversation entirely.

SBA List, which has stated outright that "Every abortion is infanticide," told the *New York Times* that it had poll-tested the talking point for mass distribution in 2020: "The group says surveys it has conducted in swing states like Arizona and North Carolina show that portraying Democrats as supporters of infanticide — an allegation the left says is patently false — can win neutral voters to their side."[1412] [1413] While SBA List's claims of persuading voters to their side are almost certainly overblown, they have successfully sowed confusion and redirected resources, time, and energy to combatting their claims. The right couldn't win the argument on facts, but they could win it when the spectators forfeited watching.

Since we began writing this book in 2019, the implications of allowing them to silence the majority have become even clearer. We've learned we have everything we need to win on the merits of the argument and to expose the toxic lie that bound this movement together in the first place.

This is a moment in our country where so much hangs in the balance: reproductive rights, civil rights, human rights, and indeed even our belief in the promise that democracy holds. A loss in this moment would risk the end of so much more than a single medical procedure, although that in and of itself would be devastating. It would risk the end of social progress that has been such a long journey, fought by so many. A victory, on the other hand — one sparked simply by speaking up, calling the bluff of the Radical Right, knowing our history, and using it to hold those accountable who have used racism and misogyny to wield privilege as a weapon rather than a responsibility — that victory is our charge and the truth is our tool.

The Future

The modern conservative movement — the Radical Right as we've been calling it — built their entire power structure on a single massive lie. They've worked hard to convince themselves, their followers and the public that their movement is more than an anti-democratic power grab on a historic scale, that it's driven by deeply held moral beliefs about individual pregnancies.

They astutely chose a convenient fiction. Republican voters, like almost all people, want to believe that their chosen course is the moral one. At the same time, most people choose not to argue morality with others, believing it is a personal code, not a political one. The reticence to argue is especially acute when it comes to issues of abortion. Any individual decision to end a pregnancy involves so many different factors and circumstances that it inherently lives in the complicated grey zone of the mind The Right has always defined this as black and white, when — like most things in life, people are just making the best decisions they can for themselves at the time.

Forcing an overly simplistic view of the issues surrounding abortion rights and, more broadly, of reproductive freedom, also benefits the GOP brand. They demand the moral high ground without ever reckoning with the breadth of moral issues — from racial and economic inequality to climate change and more — that impact their privilege in society. They channel their frustration at a changing culture, or at perceived threats to traditional privilege or masculinity, into a crusade that feels not just morally justifiable, but morally superior.

Wrapping themselves in ostensibly Christian virtue also means that they're often given the benefit of the doubt in all aspects of public discourse. No matter the attack, the default of those around them is benevolent intent because they present as being driven by an unimpeachable and divinely inspired set of principles. They are often not asked about or held accountable for policies they propose, much less those that spring from their infrastructures and founding philosophy. They can ignore children in cages, promote self-serving tax policy, or deny healthcare to millions of Americans during a global pandemic simply by whistling "abortion."

As forces on the right moved from focus from maintaining segregationist policies to attacking the potential Equal Rights Amendment to the protections *Roe v. Wade* to the security offered by policies like the Affordable Care Act, it effectively used its facade of morality to stay perpetually on the offensive. Focused solely on maintaining power through winning and obstructing progress and they never developed a plan for governing. The movement's proposals were too often not subject to scrutiny, because who could question someone's deeply held religious or moral beliefs?

Try to ask a Republican to defend the abortion bans that moved through conservative states in 2019. Ask how exactly they enforce such a ban. Ask how potential violations would be investigated. Serious questions about the consequences of implementing their own policies often result in platitudes, promises, or dodges. Republicans don't have a governing philosophy around the issue itself and have not been effectively forced to reckon with the damage their poorly conceived ideological bills would wreak. Then, ask what they're doing to combat America's maternal mortality problem. Ask how they will help women who need to support their children. Ask about the uninsured kids, the lack of access to education, to food security, and to job opportunity.

In recent focus groups, we've found that when people are asked to think through current anti-choice policy proposals — how they work, who they would impact, and what measures would be necessary to enforce them — those people become increasingly opposed to those policies and the harsh realities they would impose. That holds true even for many people who initially supported much of the "pro-life" ideology.

———

We have focused on how the manipulative strategy of the Radical Right and GOP has been used to politicized the issue of abortion for their larger political gain. However, the effects don't stop there. They've consistently used similar techniques to undermine steps toward racial equality, LGBTQ equality, economic justice, and so much more. And they've been able to level those attacks despite overwhelming public support for more progressive policy in each and every one of those areas. What we're looking at is a wide-reaching effort to attack democracy and insulate white, male privilege from a changing society.

The issue of reproductive freedom may be best understood as a canary in a coal mine, though not the only one. Systematic attacks on reproductive freedom are one of the classic hallmarks of democratic backsliding.[1414] [1415] [1416] [1417] Advocates for reproductive freedom, health, rights, and justice have spent the last several decades combatting the elements of creeping authoritarianism — from disinformation and propaganda, to the ongoing efforts to undermine trust in science and medicine, to a relentless barrage of attacks on institutions designed to protect individual liberty or free and fair elections.

The Radical Right has never had popular support, but with the help of their relentless disinformation campaigns and a network of powerful institutions at their disposal, popular support can be overwhelmed. With the Supreme Court now under their control, they're stronger than ever.

We still live in a democracy and popular opinion still matters. But we are being held back on engaging on the critical issue of reproductive freedom by a fear of leaning in and taking a bold and public stance. That fear began in an era where white men led both parties and even the most progressive political leaders considered so-called "women's issues" a sideshow, but it has been proactively nurtured by the Radical Right. Our progressive political leadership is more diverse than ever, women and pregnant people have made their demands known, and policies that center the lived experiences of women and families are in line with what the vast majority of Americans want. The polling unquestionably demonstrates that protecting reproductive freedom is a core American value.

The underlying reality remains the same. Consistent research has shown that more than 7 in 10 Americans support legal access to abortion.[1418] Only 9 percent of voters believe abortion should be rendered completely illegal, now the mainstream GOP position. Even among self-identified Republicans, support for a full abortion ban is as low as 20 percent.[1419] [1420] Backlash to the draconian positions of the anti-choice right are now too visible to ignore. From the uprisings around the Kavanaugh nomination to the marches protesting the abortion bans of 2019 to the electoral outcomes since 2016, the evidence of overreach on the right is apparent.

Political flash points like the Women's March, or the backlash to Georgia and Alabama's draconian abortion bans show that, when the public is able to see through the Radical Right's shallow "moral" facade and understand the cruelty their proposals would impose, the public recoils. There's no reason Democratic leaders shouldn't lean in.

———

If 2016 was the culmination of decades of right-wing strategy to maintain and entrench power, 2020 is quite possibly our point of no return as a pluralistic democracy.

They continue to attempt wide-scale voter suppression tailored to the demographics of each state and county. And as the coronavirus pandemic has made it dangerous to wait in long lines at crowded polling places, the president and the GOP have invested massive resources into fighting vote-by-mail efforts.[1421] Beyond 2020, Republicans are preparing to implement a minority agenda through the use of gerrymandering in the 2021 redistricting process, going so far as to attempt to tinker with the 2020 Census to ensure that people in Democratic-leaning areas are undercounted.[1422] [1423] [1424]

Anti-choice operatives, signal-boosted by the president, enabled by right-wing media and social media platforms that have abdicated responsibility, intend to disarm the power of the majority and project a different reality. Our democracy has always relied on some commonly held commitments to an objective truth and on a robust system of fact-checking by a vigilante media. These pillars are crumbling under the wild west of social media frontiers and an aggressive assault on truth led by a president for whom power is the only guiding principle.

Key to asserting the power of the majority is learning from the past. The right has turned abortion and a debate about "choice" into a proxy for who has power and on whose behalf it is wielded and who will suffer. They are using it as the head of the spear — as a way to bind their coalitions. Democrats and progressives have been responding as though the issues of reproductive freedom are just one among many concerns, siloed among issue organizations.

———

The Radical Right's original architects succeeded beyond their wildest dreams. Few lived to see the results but they have effectively spawned the next generation to carry the torch. Abortion was and remains the tip of the spear, the Trojan Horse in which they can help move their bigotry.

Unraveling their central lie will take time, discipline, and practice. Perhaps most of all, exposing the fallacy at the center of their movement requires us to confront our own, deeply entrenched attitudes about race and gender that manifest individually, culturally, and politically. That's no easy task, especially when everything seems to be falling apart.

The manipulative strategy that has driven the Radical Right for so many decades only works when left uncontested. Countering those strategies requires a serious investment in better, bolder messaging; proactive efforts to fight disinformation both online and offline; long-term planning and coordination across the progressive coalition; a focus on the courts; and a more realistic political analysis that understands the ways the right has manipulated race and gender to activate their audiences and project their power.

They depend on our silence and our fragmentation. 2020 is the year to change this.

Our path forward is not easy but should be grounded in the principles of ending that silence, working together to take back control of the debate, forcing hard questions on our opponents, and unmasking the underlying ideology of an anti-choice movement, contrasting it with our own.

We must:

1) **Call the movement what it is:** This movement is, and always has been about an exclusive grip on power by a ruling class of white fundamentalist Christian men with zero tolerance for dissent. Wrapping their aims in the cloak of religiosity does not change this fact. We must overcome fears that critiquing them is tantamount to attacking faith. The rise of a faithful progressive movement helps in this work and should be supported and encouraged. Elevating the many voices of Christian leaders who chart a different vision is imperative to not force false choices among the many Americans who hold religious views.

2) **Embrace the values conversation:** We stand for freedom and equal opportunity. They stand for control and oppression of others. Starting the conversation from a values centered place is crucial to appeal to the hearts and emotions of the millions of Americans sifting through the noise and caught in the middle.

3) **Claim and use our own language:** Democratic elected officials and progressive organizations need to recognize and rebut the Willke strategy by refusing to repeat inaccurate terms like "heartbeat bills." Instead we have to call these measures what they are, "abortion bans" and "forced pregnancy laws."

4) **Confront disinformation and hypocrisy head on:** Ask the first question. Don't wait to respond to their claims. Do they stand with their party in wanting to ban abortion? Why do they distrust and disrespect their constituents' opinions? Why do they think they know better than their constituents when it comes to these very personal family matters? How do they plan to enforce the draconian restrictions they're proposing? Why won't reckon with the real-world issues they will create? Why are they focusing on banning abortion in places where infant and maternal mortality are highest? Why won't they use science and public health data to guide policy making? These are very difficult questions to answer and even GOP candidates running for office try hard to avoid them. We should force them on the record.

5) **Fight together by connecting our issues and efforts:** We need to

move beyond just fighting for issues. We're fighting for people, for commonly held values, like freedom, dignity, and equity. Start by exposing their history of oppression and contextualizing their present day efforts as part of that continuum. This is not just ethical solidarity; it's a good strategy to undercut their ability to play us off each other.

6) **Recognize that democracy is at the heart of our fight:** Voter suppression, gerrymandering and disenfranchisement affects everyone and everything, not just those who are denied their constitutional rights. Progressive principles and policies will never prevail as long as the majority is prevented from, or discouraged or disincentivized from, casting ballots. Make fighting against voter suppression efforts core to every strategy, overcompensating on voter engagement efforts.

Fighting together against white Christian male dominance is in the best interest of racial equality, gender equality, sexual equality, religious diversity, ethnic equality, immigration rights, and income equality. It is what starts to loosen their lock on power, create space for new and innovative solutions to advance our society and our country. At its very essence attacking their central lie and speaking the truth is what, indeed, shall set us free.

About the Author

When Ilyse Hogue took the helm of NARAL Pro-Choice America in 2013, she knew she had a challenge ahead of her. Anti-choice lawmakers in states across the country were implementing sweeping restrictions meant to legislate abortion access out of existence and it was clear that they wouldn't stop until they achieved their ultimate endgame of banning abortion completely. She got right to work, boldly pushing the national conversation around reproductive freedom and centering the ability to decide if, when, and how to raise a family as an issue fundamental to societal equity. Under her leadership, NARAL cemented its role as an organizing powerhouse — tripling its membership to 2.5 million people, advancing state and federal legislation to protect and expand abortion access, and fighting an unprecedented wave of abortion bans at the state level.

Understanding the importance of rejecting stigma around abortion care, Ilyse made history in 2016 when she shared her own abortion story on the national stage during the Democratic National Convention, explaining, "It's not as simple as bad girls get abortions and good girls have families. We are the same women at different times in our lives – each making decisions that are the best for us."

A lifelong activist and organizer, Ilyse is an expert in organizing and mobilizing grassroots support around social justice issues including reproductive freedom, climate change, and democracy reform. Her commentary has been featured in The Washington Post, HuffPost, The Nation, Cosmopolitan, and ELLE. She is a frequent guest in the media, appearing as a progressive pundit on MSNBC, CNN, and NPR. Ilyse holds a Master of Science from the University of Michigan and a Bachelor of Arts from Vassar College.

About the Researcher

Ellie Langford is Research Director at NARAL Pro-Choice America, where her team works to understand the radical right's efforts to chip away at reproductive freedom in America and sound the alarm about their growing influence within the Trump administration. Ellie has a deep background in audience research, qualitative data analysis and message development, and has built and tested communications strategies for major nonprofits and foundations. She has also worked in opposition research and media criticism, monitoring extremist ideologies online and writing about misinformation and disinformation in the media.

Resources

In our research, we've focused primarily on understanding our opposition and the threat they pose to reproductive freedom, to the broader progressive movement, and to American democracy. Our analysis builds on the insights of crucial thinkers in the reproductive justice movement and historians who have helped document the origins of the Radical Right -- including some who identify as part of the conservative movement. We have relied on primary sources where practicable, including writings by figures like Phyllis Schlafly, John Willke or Kellyanne Conway among many other extremists. The focus of this work means that many of the writers listed as sources here are not necessarily people we agree with on all -- or any -- issues. Their inclusion on this source list does not mean NARAL endorses their ideas. We are simply doing our best to present an accurate and well-documented picture of the conservative movement and the threats we and our allies face.

For a list of experts and thought partners we fully endorse, as well as other resources that expand on related issues including reproductive justice, racial equality, voting rights, anti-disinformation efforts and more, see our website at: https://theliethatbinds.com/.

1   "Paul M. Weyrich." *SourceWatch*, accessed March 9, 2020. https://www.sourcewatch.org/index.php/Paul_M._Weyrich.
2   Randall Balmer, *Thy Kingdom Come: How the Religious Right Distorts Faith and Threatens America*, (New York: Basic Books, 2007), pg 13.
3   Bruce Weber, "Paul Weyrich, 66, a Conservative Strategist, Dies," *The New York Times*, December 18, 2008. https://www.nytimes.com/2008/12/19/us/politics/19weyrich.html.
4   David Keene, "In Memoriam: Paul Weyrich, Conservative Trailblazer," *The Hill*, December 18, 2008. https://thehill.com/31602-in-memoriam-paul-weyrich-conservative-trailblazer.

5   Bruce Weber, "Paul Weyrich, 66, a Conservative Strategist, Dies," *The New York Times*, December 18, 2008. https://www.nytimes.com/2008/12/19/us/politics/19weyrich.html.

6   "US conservative activist Paul Weyrich dead at 66," The Associated Press, December 18, 2008, http://www.nbcnews.com/id/28299805/ns/politics/t/conservative-activist-paul-weyrich-dead/#.XsV_hBNKj_Q.

7   Ned Walsh, "God and Government: Christian Dominionism and the GOP," *The News & Observer*, April 10, 2015. https://www.newsobserver.com/news/local/community/smithfield-herald/sh-opinion/article18081173.html.

8   Randall Balmer, *Thy Kingdom Come: How the Religious Right Distorts Faith and Threatens America*, (New York: Basic Books, 2007).

9   Frederick Clarkson, "Dominionism Rising," *Political Research Associates*, August 18, 2016, https://www.politicalresearch.org/2016/08/18/dominionism-rising-a-theocratic-movement-hiding-in-plain-sight.

10   Randall Balmer, *Thy Kingdom Come: How the Religious Right Distorts Faith and Threatens America*, (New York: Basic Books, 2007).

11   Max Blumenthal, "Agent of Intolerance," *The Nation*, May 16, 2007. https://www.thenation.com/article/agent-intolerance/.

12   Max Blumenthal, "Agent of Intolerance," *The Nation*, May 16, 2007. https://www.thenation.com/article/archive/agent-intolerance/.

13   John Nichols, "The Old Time Hypocrisy Hour," *The Nation*, May 15, 2007. https://www.thenation.com/article/archive/old-time-hypocrisy-hour/.

14   Jonathan Merritt, "Segregation Is Still Alive at These Christian Schools," *The Daily Beast*, September 18, 2016. https://www.thedailybeast.com/segregation-is-still-alive-at-these-christian-schools.

15   Vanessa Williams, "Analysis | A White Southerner Confronts Her Schooling at a Segregated Private 'Academy' and Challenges Others to Do the Same," *The Washington Post*, November 8, 2019. https://www.washingtonpost.com/nation/2019/11/08/white-writer-confronts-her-schooling-segregated-private-academy-challenges-others-do-same/.

16   "About LCA," *Liberty Christian Academy*, accessed March 9, 2020, https://www.lcabulldogs.com/about-lca/.

17   "About Liberty." *About Liberty | Liberty University*, accessed March 9, 2020, https://www.liberty.edu/aboutliberty/.

18   "Top Internship Sites," Liberty University Washington Fellowship, accessed May 20, 2020, https://www.liberty.edu/media/1103/pdf/Top_Internship_Sites.pdf.

19   Randall Balmer, "The Real Origins of the Religious Right," *POLITICO Magazine*, May 27, 2014, https://www.politico.com/magazine/story/2014/05/religious-right-real-origins-107133.

20   Stephen Prothero, "Donald Trump Goes to Liberty U," *CNN*. Cable News Network, January 17, 2016, https://www.cnn.com/2016/01/16/opinions/prothero-trump-liberty/index.html.

21   Phil Gailey, "Bob Jones, In Sermon, Assails Supreme Court," *New York Times*, May 25, 1983, https://www.nytimes.com/1983/05/25/us/bob-jones-in-sermon-assails-supreme-court.html.

22   Randall Balmer, "The Real Origins of the Religious Right," *POLITICO Magazine*, May 27, 2014. https://www.politico.com/magazine/story/2014/05/religious-right-real-origins-107133.

23   Randall Balmer, "The Real Origins of the Religious Right," *POLITICO Magazine*, May 27, 2014. https://www.politico.com/magazine/story/2014/05/religious-right-real-origins-107133.

24   Randall Balmer, *Thy Kingdom Come: How the Religious Right Distorts*

Faith and Threatens America, (New York: Basic Books, 2007)

25   Chris Ladd, "Pastors, Not Politicians, Turned Dixie Republican," Forbes, March 27, 2017, https://www.forbes.com/sites/chrisladd/2017/03/27/pastors-not-politicians-turned-dixie-republican/#1011bbf1695f.

26   Angie Maxwell and Todd G. Shields, The Long Southern Strategy: How Chasing White Voters in the South Changed American Politics, (Oxford University Press, 2019) pg. 10.

27   Angela Lahr, "American Evangelical Politics During the Cold War," *Oxford Research Encyclopedias*, March 2020, https://oxfordre.com/religion/view/10.1093/acrefore/9780199340378.001.0001/acrefore-9780199340378-e-701.

28   Randall Balmer, *Thy Kingdom Come: How the Religious Right Distorts Faith and Threatens America*, (New York: Basic Books, 2007).

29   Stephen Prothero, "Donald Trump Goes to Liberty U," *CNN*. Cable News Network, January 17, 2016, https://www.cnn.com/2016/01/16/opinions/prothero-trump-liberty/index.html

30   Frances FitzGerald, "How the Christian Right Became a Political Force," *The New Yorker*, June 18, 2017,.https://www.newyorker.com/magazine/1981/05/18/a-disciplined-charging-army

31   Matt Stearns, "Jerry Falwell Brought Religious Conservatives into U.S. Politics," *The Mercury News*, August 14, 2016. https://www.mercurynews.com/2007/05/16/jerry-falwell-brought-religious-conservatives-into-u-s-politics/

32   John Tanasychuk Writer. "How Anita Bryant Fought -- and Helped -- Gay Rights," *Sun*, September 14, 2018.https://www.sun-sentinel.com/news/fl-xpm-2007-06-04-0706030236-story.html

33   Randall Balmer, *Thy Kingdom Come: How the Religious Right Distorts Faith and Threatens America*, (New York: Basic Books, 2007).

34   Linda Wertheimer and Randall Balmer, "Evangelical: Religious Right Has Distorted the Faith," *NPR*, June 23, 2006,.https://www.npr.org/templates/story/story.php?storyId=5502785

35   "God in America: 'Of God and Caesar," PBS, accessed May 20, 2020, https://www.pbs.org/godinamerica/transcripts/hour-six.html.

36   Linda Wertheimer and Randall Balmer, "Evangelical: Religious Right Has Distorted the Faith," *NPR*, June 23, 2006,,https://www.npr.org/templates/story/story.php?storyId=5502785

37   "Resolutions Search," Southern Baptist Convention, accessed May 20, 2020, http://www.sbc.net/resolutions/year/1980.

38   Mark Schmitt, "The Legend of the Powell Memo," *The American Prospect*, April 27, 2005, https://prospect.org/article/legend-powell-memo/.

39   Charlie Cray, "Greenpeace Analyzes the Lewis Powell Memo: Corporate Blueprint to Dominate Democracy." *Greenpeace USA*, November 5, 2015, https://www.greenpeace.org/usa/greenpeace-analyzes-the-lewis-powell-memo-corporate-blueprint-to-dominate-democracy/.

40   "The Lewis Powell Memo: A Corporate Blueprint to Dominate Democracy." Memo to the Education Committee, U.S. Chamber of Commerce, via *Greenpeace USA*, August 23, 1971, https://www.greenpeace.org/usa/democracy/the-lewis-powell-memo-a-corporate-blueprint-to-dominate-democracy/.

41   Nick Anderson , "Virginia's Liberty University: A mega-college and Republican presidential stage," *Washington Post*, March 23, 2015, https://www.washingtonpost.com/news/grade-point/wp/2015/03/23/virginias-liberty-university-a-mega-college-and-republican-presidential-stage/?utm_term=.d280f9c8a17b.

42   Paul M. Weyrich, interview by Bryan Lamb, *Q&A with Paul Weyrich*, CSPAN, March 22, 2005, https://www.c-span.org/video/?185929-1/qa-paul-wey-

rich&start=1240.

43   "Edwin Feulner," *The Heritage Foundation*. Accessed March 9, 2020, https://www.heritage.org/staff/edwin-feulner.

44   Rachel Weiner, "How ALEC Became a Political Liability," *Washington Post*, April 24, 2012, https://www.washingtonpost.com/blogs/the-fix/post/how-alec-became-a-political-liability/2012/04/24/gIQA3QnyeT_blog.html.

45   Rachel Weiner, "How ALEC Became a Political Liability," *Washington Post*, April 24, 2012, https://www.washingtonpost.com/blogs/the-fix/post/how-alec-became-a-political-liability/2012/04/24/gIQA3QnyeT_blog.html.

46   Elspeth Reeve, "ALEC, Group That Pushed Stand Your Ground, Quits the Culture Wars," *The Atlantic*, October 30, 2013. https://www.theatlantic.com/politics/archive/2012/04/alec-group-pushed-stand-your-ground-quits-culture-wars/329233/.

47   Rachel Weiner, "How ALEC Became a Political Liability," *Washington Post*, April 24, 2012, https://www.washingtonpost.com/blogs/the-fix/post/how-alec-became-a-political-liability/2012/04/24/gIQA3QnyeT_blog.html.

48   Barbara Lee, "The Hyde Amendment Denies Women Health Care. Yes, Abortion Is Health Care," *TIME*, August 23, 2019, https://time.com/5660018/hyde-amendment-abortion/.

49   Isaac Stanley-Becker, "Henry Hyde, Abortion Amendment's Namesake, Was a Culture Warrior with Some Surprising Causes," *The Washington Post*, June 7, 2019, https://www.washingtonpost.com/nation/2019/06/07/henry-hyde-abortion-amendments-namesake-was-culture-warrior-with-some-surprising-causes/.

50   Frances FitzGerald, "A Disciplined, Charging Army," *New Yorker*, May 16, 2007, https://www.newyorker.com/magazine/1981/05/18/a-disciplined-charging-army.

51   Robert O'Harrow Jr. and Shawn Boburg, "A conservative activist's behind-the-scenes campaign to remake the nation's courts," The Washington Post, May 21, 2019, https://www.washingtonpost.com/graphics/2019/investigations/leonard-leo-federalists-society/court-courts/.

52   "Policy Counsel," *Council for National Policy*," May 20, 2020, https://cfnp.org/policy-counsel/ ; Jake Tapper and Stephen Collinson, "Conservatives in secretive group 'slow walk' Trump support," *CNN Politics*, May 17, 2016, https://www.cnn.com/2016/05/17/politics/conservatives-slow-walk-donald-trump-support/index.html.

53   Heidi Beirich and Mark Potok, "The Council for National Policy: Behind the Curtain," Southern Poverty Law Center, May 17, 2016, https://www.splcenter.org/hatewatch/2016/05/17/council-national-policy-behind-curtain/.

54   Scott W. Stern, "How Powerful Is This Right-Wing Shadow Network?," *New Republic*, February 19, 2020, https://newrepublic.com/article/156431/how-powerful-council-national-policy-right-wing-shadow-network.

55   Gynecology: New Grounds for Abortion," *Time*, May 5, 1967. http://content.time.com/time/magazine/article/0,9171,899513,00.html

56   Mindy Sink, "John Arthur Love, 85, Governor Of Colorado and an Energy Czar." *The New York Times*, January 24, 2002. https://www.nytimes.com/2002/01/24/us/john-arthur-love-85-governor-of-colorado-and-an-energy-czar.html.

57   Joshua Tait, "How Did Evangelicals and Republicans Come to Oppose Abortion?" *Medium*. Arc Digital, May 22, 2019. https://arcdigital.media/how-did-evangelicals-and-republicans-come-to-oppose-abortion-dcd4ac56c333.

58   Sue Halpern, "How Republicans Became Anti-Choice," *New York Review of Books*, November 8, 2018, https://www.nybooks.com/articles/2018/11/08/how-republicans-became-anti-choice/.

59   Joshua Tait, "How Did Evangelicals and Republicans Come to Want to

Ban Abortion?" *Arc Digital*, May 21, 2019, https://arcdigital.media/how-did-evangel-icals-and-republicans-come-to-oppose-abortion-dcd4ac56c333.

60   Sue Halper, "How Republicans Became Anti-Choice." *The New York Review of Books*, November 8, 2018. https://www.nybooks.com/articles/2018/11/08/how-republicans-became-anti-choice/.

61   "Abortion Trends by Party Identification," Gallup, accessed July 17, 2019, https://news.gallup.com/poll/246278/abortion-trends-party.aspx?g_source=link_NEWSV9&g_medium=TOPIC&g_campaign=item_&g_content=Abortion%2520Trends%2520by%2520Party%2520Identification.

62   Joshua Tait, "How Did Evangelicals and Republicans Come to Oppose Abortion?" *Medium*. Arc Digital, May 22, 2019, https://arcdigital.media/how-did-evan-gelicals-and-republicans-come-to-oppose-abortion-dcd4ac56c333.

63   Randall Balmer, "The Real Origins of the Religious Right," *Politico Magazine*, May 27, 2014, https://www.politico.com/magazine/story/2014/05/religious-right-re-al-origins-107133.

64   Randall Balmer, "The Real Origins of the Religious Right," *Politico Magazine*, May 27, 2014, https://www.politico.com/magazine/story/2014/05/religious-right-re-al-origins-107133.

65   Randall Balmer, "The Real Origins of the Religious Right," *Politico Magazine*, May 27, 2014, https://www.politico.com/magazine/story/2014/05/religious-right-re-al-origins-107133.

66   Randall Balmer, "The Real Origins of the Religious Right," *Politico Magazine*, May 27, 2014, https://www.politico.com/magazine/story/2014/05/religious-right-re-al-origins-107133.

67   Joshua Tait, "How Did Evangelicals and Republicans Come to Oppose Abortion?" *Medium*. Arc Digital, May 22, 2019. https://arcdigital.media/how-did-evan-gelicals-and-republicans-come-to-oppose-abortion-dcd4ac56c333.

68   Randall Balmer, "The Real Origins of the Religious Right," *Politico Magazine*, May 27, 2014, https://www.politico.com/magazine/story/2014/05/religious-right-re-al-origins-107133.

69   Emily Crockett, "Phyllis Schlafly Started the War on Women. But It Will Outlive Her," *Vox*, 7 Sept. 2016, www.vox.com/2016/9/7/12817756/phyllis-schlafly-dies-started-war-on-women.

70   Emily Crockett, "Phyllis Schlafly Started the War on Women. But It Will Outlive Her," *Vox*, 7 Sept. 2016, www.vox.com/2016/9/7/12817756/phyllis-schlafly-dies-started-war-on-women.

71   Phylis Schlafly," *The Sunday Telegraph*, September 18, 2016, https://www.pressreader.com/uk/the-sunday-telegraph/20160918/282187945485622.

72   Donald T. Critchlow, "Phyllis Schlafly, the mother of right-wing populism," The Washington Post, September 8, 2016, https://www.washingtonpost.com/opin-ions/phyllis-schlafly-the-mother-of-right-wing-populism/2016/09/07/63862514-7539-11e6-b786-19d0cb1ed06c_story.html.

73   Adele M. Stan, "Goodbye, Schlafly: One of the Most Influential and Reviled Right-Wingers Has Passed On,," *Alternet*, September 6, 2016, https://www.alternet.org/2016/09/phyllis-schlafly-dies/.

74   Warren Weaver, "ROCKEFELLER - GOLDWATER CONTEST IS ASSESSED; Future of the Republican Party Is at Stake as Both Men Embark On a Bitter and Personal Campaign for the Nomination," *The New York Times*, 12 Jan. 1964, https://www.nytimes.com/1964/01/12/archives/rockefeller-goldwater-contest-is-as-sessed-future-of-the-republican.html.

75   "Phyllis Schlafly Bio – founder of Eagle Forum," Eagle Forum, accessed May 20, 2020, https://eagleforum.org/about/bio.html.

76   Adele M. Stan, "Goodbye, Schlafly: One of the Most Influential and Reviled Right-Wingers Has Passed On.," Alternet, September 6, 2016, https://www.alternet.org/2016/09/phyllis-schlafly-dies/.

77   Emily Crockett, "Phyllis Schlafly Started the War on Women. But It Will Outlive Her," Vox, 7 Sept. 2016, www.vox.com/2016/9/7/12817756/phyllis-schlafly-dies-started-war-on-women.

78   Donald T. Critchlow, "Remembering Phyllis Schlafly," POLITICO, December 31, 2016, https://www.politico.com/magazine/story/2016/12/phyllis-schlafly-obituary-eagle-forum-era-214559.

79   Adele M. Stan, "Goodbye, Schlafly: One of the Most Influential and Reviled Right-Wingers Has Passed On,," Alternet, September 6, 2016, https://www.alternet.org/2016/09/phyllis-schlafly-dies/.

80   Alice Paul Institute, "History of the Equal Rights Amendment," Equal Rights Amendment, Last Modified 2018, https://www.equalrightsamendment.org/the-equal-rights-amendment.

81   Mark R. Daniels, Robert Darcy, and Joseph W. Westphal. "The ERA Won. At Least in the Opinion Polls." PS 15, no. 4 (1982): 578-84. https://www.jstor.org/stable/419066?seq=1#page_scan_tab_contents.

82   Susan Faludi, Backlash: the Undeclared War against American Women, Three Rivers Press, 2006 pg., 74.

83   Susan Faludi, Backlash: the Undeclared War against American Women, Three Rivers Press, 2006 pg. , 76.

84   Susan Faludi, Backlash: the Undeclared War against American Women, Three Rivers Press, 2006 pg. 76.

85   Susan Faludi, Backlash: the Undeclared War against American Women, Three Rivers Press, 2006 pg. 79.

86   "The Pill and the Sexual Revolution - American Experience," PBS, Accessed July 17, 2017, https://www.pbs.org/wgbh/americanexperience/features/pill-and-sexual-revolution/.

87   Catherine Rymph, Republican Women, University of North Carolina Press, Chapel Hill, 2006.

88   Carol Felsenthal, "The Surprising Secret to Phyllis Schlafly's Success," Time, 8 Sept. 2016, https://time.com/4483234/phyllis-schlafly-parenting/.

89   Laine Kaplan-Levenson, "The Women Who Fought For And Against The ERA: Part I," WWNO, 20 Apr. 2017, https://www.wwno.org/post/women-who-fought-and-against-era-part-i.

90   Phyllis Schlafly Bio - Founder of Eagle Forum," Eagle Forum, eagleforum.org/about/bio.html.

91   Emily Crockett, "Phyllis Schlafly Started the War on Women. But It Will Outlive Her," Vox, 7 Sept. 2016, www.vox.com/2016/9/7/12817756/phyllis-schlafly-dies-started-war-on-women.

92   Elizabeth Gillespie McRae, Mothers of massive resistance: White women and the politics of White supremacy (Oxford: Oxford University Press, 2018) pg. 10.

93   Adele M. Stan, "Goodbye, Schlafly: One of the Most Influential and Reviled Right-Wingers Has Passed On," Alternet, September 6, 2016, https://www.alternet.org/2016/09/phyllis-schlafly-dies/.

94   Jone Johnson Lewis, "Which States Ratified the ERA and When Did They Ratify?" ThoughtCo, 7 Oct. 2019, www.thoughtco.com/which-states-ratified-the-era-3528872.

95   Robert Black, "Could the Equal Rights Amendment Become a Reality?" National Constitution Center – Constitutioncenter.org, https://constitutioncenter.org/blog/could-the-equal-rights-amendment-become-a-reality.

96   Robinson Woodward-Burns, "Analysis | The Equal Rights Amendment Is One State from Ratification. Now What?" *The Washington Post*, 20 June 2018, https://www.washingtonpost.com/news/monkey-cage/wp/2018/06/20/the-equal-rights-amendment-is-one-state-from-ratification-now-what/.

97   Angie Maxwell and Todd G. Shields, The Long Southern Strategy: How Chasing White Voters in the South Changed American Politics, (Oxford: Oxford University Press, 2019) pg. 8.

98   Angie Maxwell and Todd G. Shields, The Long Southern Strategy: How Chasing White Voters in the South Changed American Politics, (Oxford: Oxford University Press, 2019) pg. 8

99   Stephen Bates, "Tim LaHaye Obituary," *The Guardian*, July 28, 2016. https://www.theguardian.com/books/2016/jul/28/tim-lahaye-obituary.

100   "Our History," *Concerned Women for America*, accessed July 14, 2017, https://concernedwomen.org/about/our-history/.

101   Margery Evan, "Race, not abortion, was the founding issue of the religious right," *The Boston Globe*, February 5, 2018, https://www.bostonglobe.com/opinion/2018/02/05/race-not-abortion-was-founding-issue-religious-right/A5rn-mClvuAU7EaThaNLAnK/story.html.

102   Emory University, "True Origins of the Religious Right," YouTube (video), May 11, 2009, 35:29, https://youtu.be/_Gf4jN1xoSo?t=967.

103   Nate Silver, "In Senate Races, Politics Are Local Again," *FiveThirtyEight* (blog), *New York Times*, August 15, 2012, https://fivethirtyeight.blogs.nytimes.com/2012/08/15/in-senate-races-politics-are-local-again/.

104   "United States Senate elections in Missouri, 2012", Ballotpedia, accessed January 31, 2020 https://ballotpedia.org/United_States_Senate_elections_in_Missouri,_2012

105   Stephanie McCrummen and David A. Fahrenthold, "Akin's congressional legacy small, but his support among Christian groups is big," *Washington Post*, August 22, 2012, https://www.washingtonpost.com/politics/akins-congressional-legacy-small-but-his-support-among-christian-groups-is-big/2012/08/22/b2c-2d98e-ec75-11e1-aca7-272630dfd152_story.html.

106   Todd Akin, "Abortion is Unamerican," (speech, U.S. House of Representatives, Washington D.C., January 22, 2008), https://www.c-span.org/video/?c4876712/user-clip-abortion-unamerican.

107   Kevin McDermott, "Long before 'legitimate rape' comment, Akin alleged abortions on non-pregnant women," *St. Louis Post-Dispatch*, October 3, 2012, https://www.stltoday.com/news/local/govt-and-politics/long-before-legitimate-rape-comment-akin-alleged-abortions-on-non/article_f5f0c752-0d72-11e2-b591-0019bb30f31a.html.

108   Jodi Jacobson, "MO Senate Candidate Todd Akin Says Abortion Not Necessary Because Women's Bodies Can 'Shut Pregnancy Down' After Rape," *Rewire News*, August 19, 2012, https://rewire.news/article/2012/08/19/mo-senate-candidate-todd-akin-says-womens-bodies-can-shut-pregnancy-down-after-ra/.

109   Dan Friedman, "Akin was Arrested at Least Eight Times in 1980s," *Hotline On Call* (blog), *National Journal* (via WayBack Machine), November 3, 2012, https://web.archive.org/web/20121105005549/http://hotlineoncall.nationaljournal.com/archives/2012/11/records-show-ak.php.

110   Kevin McDermott, "Todd Akin was arrested at least three times during '80s abortion protests," *St. Louis Post-Dispatch*, October 23, 2012, https://www.stltoday.com/news/local/govt-and-politics/todd-akin-was-arrested-at-least-three-times-during-s/article_daebda70-1d5b-11e2-9adc-0019bb30f31a.html.

111   Allison Yarrow, "Who Is Mrs. 'Legitimate Rape'? Meet Todd Akin's Wife,

Lulli," *Daily Beast*, updated July 13, 2017, https://www.thedailybeast.com/who-is-mrs-legitimate-rape-meet-todd-akins-wife-lulli.

112   John Eligon, "A Politician Whose Faith Is Central to HIs Persistence," *New York Times*, August 21, 2012, https://www.nytimes.com/2012/08/22/us/politics/todd-akins-faith-is-central-to-his-politics.html.

113   Virginia Young, "Thune calls Missouri's 2012 Senate race key for GOP," *St. Louis Post-Dispatch*, February 26, 20122, https://www.stltoday.com/news/local/govt-and-politics/thune-calls-missouri-s-senate-race-key-for-gop/article_b57e57c2-4229-11e0-9afe-00127992bc8b.html.

114   Jeff Zeleny, "G.O.P. Captures House, but Not Senate," *New York Times*, November 2, 2010, https://www.nytimes.com/2010/11/03/us/politics/03elect.html.

115   Charles Jaco, "Jaco Report: Full Interview With Todd Akin," *Fox 2 Now*, updated August 20, 2012, https://fox2now.com/news/jaco-report/the-jaco-report-august-19-2012/.

116   John Eligon and Michael Schwirtz, "Senate Candidate Provokes Ire With 'Legitimate Rape' Comment," *New York Times*, August 19, 2012, https://www.nytimes.com/2012/08/20/us/politics/todd-akin-provokes-ire-with-legitimate-rape-comment.html.

117   Aaron Blake, "Todd Akin, GOP Senate candidate: 'Legitimate rape' rarely causes pregnancy," *New York Times*, August 19, 2012, https://www.washingtonpost.com/news/the-fix/wp/2012/08/19/todd-akin-gop-senate-candidate-legitimate-rape-rarely-causes-pregnancy/?arc404=true.

118   Sam Stein, "Claire McCaskill Reacts To Todd Akin's 'Legitimate Rape' Remarks," *HuffPost*, accessed May 19, 2020, https://www.huffpost.com/entry/claire-mccaskill-todd-akin-legitimate-rape_n_1810351.

119   Editorial Board, "The repugnant code behind Todd Akin's words," *Washington Post*, August 20, 2012, https://www.washingtonpost.com/opinions/the-repugnant-code-behind-todd-akins-words/2012/08/20/7e91ed12-eb08-11e1-a80b-9f898562d010_story.html.

120   John Eligon and Michael Schwirtz, "Senate Candidate Provokes Ire With 'Legitimate Rape' Comment", *New York Times*, August 19, 2012, https://www.nytimes.com/2012/08/20/us/politics/todd-akin-provokes-ire-with-legitimate-rape-comment.html.

121   Nancy L. Cohen, "Women fought the GOP's 'war on women' and won," The Guardian, November 7, 2012, https://www.theguardian.com/commentisfree/2012/nov/07/women-fought-gop-2012-waronwomen.

122   Emma G. Keller, "Mitt Romney's binders full of women just don't stack up," *The Guardian*, October 16, 2012, https://www.theguardian.com/world/2012/oct/17/romney-binders-full-of-women.

123   Sean Sullivan, "Todd Akin takes back apology for 'legitimate rape' comment," *Washington Post*, July 10, 2014,https://www.washingtonpost.com/news/post-politics/wp/2014/07/10/todd-akin-takes-back-apology-for-legitimate-rape-comment/.

124   Arit John, "Todd Akin Takes Back Apology Over 'Legitimate Rape' Theory," *The Atlantic*, July 10, 2014, https://www.theatlantic.com/politics/archive/2014/07/todd-akin-takes-back-apology-over-legitimate-rape-theory/374214/.

125   "Election 2012 - Missouri" *New York Times*, accessed May 19, 2020, https://www.nytimes.com/elections/2012/results/states/missouri.html?mtrref=www.google.com&gwh=185B3A52ACAB9083D007DC785D0990C8&gwt=pay&assetType=PAYWALL.

126   Annie Groer, "Indiana GOP Senate hopeful Richard Mourdock says God 'intended' rape pregnancies," *Washington Post*, October 24, 2012, https://www.

washingtonpost.com/blogs/she-the-people/wp/2012/10/24/indiana-gop-sen-ate-hopeful-richard-mourdock-says-god-intended-rape-pregnancies/.

127   Arit John, "Todd Akin Takes Back Apology Over 'Legitimate Rape' Theory," *The Atlantic,* July 10, 2014, https://www.theatlantic.com/politics/archive/2014/07/todd-akin-takes-back-apology-over-legitimate-rape-theory/374214/.

128   U.S. Congress, House, *No Taxpayer Funding for Abortion Act,* H.R. 3,112th Congress, 1st session, introduced January 20, 2011, https://www.congress.gov/bill/112th-congress/house-bill/3/cosponsors?q={%22search%22:[%22No+Taxpay-er+Funding+for+Abortion+Act,%22]}&s=2&r=1&overview=closed&searchResult-ViewType=expanded&KWICView=false.

129   Ian Millhiser, "How Todd Akin And Paul Ryan Partnered To Redefine Rape," *Think Progress,* August 19, 2012, https://thinkprogress.org/how-todd-akin-and-paul-ryan-partnered-to-redefine-rape-1958f57aae89/.

130   Ian Millhiser, "How Todd Akin And Paul Ryan Partnered To Redefine Rape," *Think Progress,* August 19, 2012, https://thinkprogress.org/how-todd-akin-and-paul-ryan-partnered-to-redefine-rape-1958f57aae89/.

131   "Roll Call Vote 292," 112th U.S. Congress, May 4, 2011, http://clerk.house.gov/evs/2011/roll292.xml.

132   Editorial Board, "The repugnant code behind Todd Akin's words," *Washington Post,* August 20, 2012, https://www.washingtonpost.com/opinions/the-re-pugnant-code-behind-todd-akins-words/2012/08/20/7e91ed12-eb08-11e1-a80b-9f898562d010_story.html.

133   "Live Coverage of Election Day," *New York Times,* updated November 29, 2012, https://www.nytimes.com/elections/2012/results/live-coverage.html.

134   Illyse Hogue, "The Danger of Laughing at Todd Akin," *The Nation,* August 20, 2012, https://www.thenation.com/article/danger-laughing-todd-akin/.

135   Illyse Hogue, "The Danger of Laughing at Todd Akin," *The Nation,* August 20, 2012, https://www.thenation.com/article/danger-laughing-todd-akin/.

136   Linda Wertheimer, "Evangelical: Religious Right Has Distorted the Faith," *National Public Radio,* June 23, 2006, https://www.npr.org/templates/story/story.php?storyId=5502785.

137   Anna North, "How abortion became a partisan issue in America," *Vox,* April 10, 2019, https://www.vox.com/2019/4/10/18295513/abortion-2020-roe-joe-biden-democrats-republicans/.

138   Daniel K. Williams, "The GOP's Abortion Strategy: Why Pro-Choice Republicans Became Pro-Life in the 1970s," *Journal of Policy History* 23, no. 4 (2011): 513-539, https://www.researchgate.net/publication/231752505_The_GOP%27s_Abortion_Strategy_Why_Pro-Choice_Republicans_Became_Pro-Life_in_the_1970s.

139   Lydia Saad, "Republicans', Dems' Abortion Views Grow More Polarized," *Gallup,* March 8, 2010, https://news.gallup.com/poll/126374/republicans-dems-abortion-views-grow-polarized.aspx.

140   Patricia Miller, "The Story Behind the Catholic Church's Stunning Contraception Reversal," *Rewire News,* July 24, 2018, https://rewire.news/religion-dis-patches/2018/07/24/catholic-churchs-stunning-contraception-reversal/.

141   Tara Isabella Burton, "The March for Life, America's biggest anti-abortion rally, explained," *Vox,* January 18, 2018, https://www.vox.com/identi-ties/2018/1/18/16870018/march-for-life-anti-abortion-rally-explained.

142   "Abortion History Timeline," National Right to Life, accessed September 18, 2019. https://www.nrlc.org/abortion/history/.

143   Joint Resolution Proposing an Amendment to the Constitution of the United States with Respect to State Laws Relating to the Termination of Pregnancy, S.J. Res.91, 94th Congress (1975), https://www.congress.gov/bill/94th-congress/

senate-joint-resolution/91.

144   Joint Resolution Proposing an Amendment to the Constitution of the United States with Respect to State Laws Relating to the Termination of Pregnancy, S.J. Res.91, 94th Congress (1975), https://www.congress.gov/bill/94th-congress/senate-joint-resolution/91.

145   Elizabeth Kolbert, "POLITICS: A POLITICAL LIFE; Abortion, Dole's Sword in '74, Returns to Confront Him in '96," *New York Times*, July 8, 1996, https://www.nytimes.com/1996/07/08/us/politics-political-life-abortion-dole-s-sword-74-returns-confront-him-96.html.

146   "KS US Senate," Our Campaigns, accessed May 19, 2020, https://www.ourcampaigns.com/RaceDetail.html?RaceID=6353.

147   Isaac Stanley-Becker, "Henry Hyde, abortion amendment's namesake, was a culture warrior with some surprising causes," *Washington Post*, June 7, 2019, https://www.washingtonpost.com/nation/2019/06/07/henry-hyde-abortion-amendments-namesake-was-culture-warrior-with-some-surprising-causes/.

148   Isaac Stanley-Becker, "Henry Hyde, abortion amendment's namesake, was a culture warrior with some surprising causes," *Washington Post*, June 7, 2019, https://www.washingtonpost.com/nation/2019/06/07/henry-hyde-abortion-amendments-namesake-was-culture-warrior-with-some-surprising-causes/.

149   Paul Weyrich, interviewed by Brian Lamb, "Q&A with Paul Weyrich," *C-SPAN*, March 22, 2005, https://www.c-span.org/video/?185929-1/qa-paul-weyrich&start=1240.

150   Isaac Stanley-Becker, "Henry Hyde, abortion amendment's namesake, was a culture warrior with some surprising causes," *Washington Post*, June 7, 2019, https://www.washingtonpost.com/nation/2019/06/07/henry-hyde-abortion-amendments-namesake-was-culture-warrior-with-some-surprising-causes/.

151   Zoë Carpenter, "The Next Big Fight for the Pro-Choice Movement: Taxpayer-Funded Abortions," *The Nation*, July 8, 2016, https://www.thenation.com/article/the-next-big-fight-for-the-pro-choice-movement-taxpayer-funded-abortions/.

152   Zoë Carpenter, "The Next Big Fight for the Pro-Choice Movement: Taxpayer-Funded Abortions," *The Nation*, July 8, 2016, https://www.thenation.com/article/the-next-big-fight-for-the-pro-choice-movement-taxpayer-funded-abortions/.

153   Planned Parenthood World Population Memo, 12/16/1977

154   "Women Members by Congress, 1917–Present," United States House of Representatives, accessed May 19, 2020, https://history.house.gov/Exhibitions-and-Publications/WIC/Historical-Data/Women-Representatives-and-Senators-by-Congress/.

155   "Women in the Senate," United States Senate, accessed September 18, 2019, https://www.senate.gov/artandhistory/history/common/briefing/women_senators.htm.

156   "The MacNeil/Lehrer Report; Abortion," National Records and Archives Administration, American Archive of Public Broadcasting (WGBH and the Library of Congress), November 8, 1977, https://americanarchive.org/catalog/cpb-aacip_507-tq5r786j1v.

157   "Abortion; The wages of sin?," *The Economist*, December 10, 1977 (via Nexis), https://advance.lexis.com/api/permalink/5e76cdb0-4a02-4f0e-a011-74c953e56d67/?context=1519360.

158   "The MacNeil/Lehrer Report; Abortion," National Records and Archives Administration, American Archive of Public Broadcasting (WGBH and the Library of Congress), November 8, 1977, https://americanarchive.org/catalog/cpb-aacip_507-tq5r786j1v.

159   "Abortion; The wages of sin?," *The Economist*, December 10, 1977 (via Nexis), https://advance.lexis.com/api/permalink/5e76cdb0-4a02-4f0e-a011-74c953e56d67/?context=1519360.

160   Deboarah C. England, "The History of Marital Rape Laws," Criminal Defense Lawyer, NOLO, accessed May 19, 2020, https://www.criminaldefenselawyer.com/resources/criminal-defense/crime-penalties/marital-rape.htm.

161   Deboarah C. England, "The History of Marital Rape Laws," Criminal Defense Lawyer, NOLO, accessed May 19, 2020, https://www.criminaldefenselawyer.com/resources/criminal-defense/crime-penalties/marital-rape.htm.

162   "The MacNeil/Lehrer Report; Abortion," National Records and Archives Administration, American Archive of Public Broadcasting (WGBH and the Library of Congress), November 8, 1977, https://americanarchive.org/catalog/cpb-aacip_507-tq5r786j1v.

163   Edmond Le Breton, *Associated Press*, December 12, 1977 (via Nexis), https://advance.lexis.com/api/permalink/4ba918bd-2e8a-44d4-806f-54a376e-37da3/?context=1519360.

164   "The dark, insidious history of Hyde: Why lawmakers must question their acceptance of this archaic policy," NARAL Pro-Choice America, Medium, September 29, 2017, https://medium.com/@NARAL/the-dark-insidious-history-of-hyde-why-lawmakers-must-question-their-acceptance-of-this-archaic-92cb5e82222d.

165   Maris A. Vinovskis, "The Politics of Abortion in the House of Representatives in 1976," *Michigan Law Review* 77, no. 7 (1979): pg. 1797, https://repository.law.umich.edu/cgi/viewcontent.cgi?article=3614&context=mlr.

166   *"On A Separate Vote In The House, To Agree To The Hyde Amendment To H.R. 14232, Which Prohibits The Use Of Funds In The Bill To Pay For Or To Promote Abortions,"* GovTrack, accessed June 1, 2020, https://www.govtrack.us/congress/votes/94-1976/h952.

167   Alexa Garcia-Ditta, "Reckoning With Rosie," *Texas Observer*, November 3, 2015, https://www.texasobserver.org/rosie-jimenez-abortion-medicaid/.

168   Lynn M. Paltrow, "Women, Abortion and Civil Disobedience," *NOVA Law Review* 13, no. 2 (1989): pg. 476, http://advocatesforpregnantwomen.org/20110819134644.pdf.

169   Helen Dewar, "Woman Dies After Mexico Abortion; Had Been Told of Medicaid Cutoff," *Washington Post*, October 27, 1997, (via Nexis),https://advance.lexis.com/api/permalink/7c019138-9c99-4f2a-ba8a-f0505097e71f/?context=1519360.

170   Linda Greenhouse and Reva B. Siegel, *Before Roe v. Wade: Voices that shaped the abortion debate before the Supreme Court's ruling* (New Haven: Yale Law School, 2012). http://documents.law.yale.edu/sites/default/files/BeforeRoe2ndEd_1.pdf

171   Emily Langer, "John 'Jack' Willke, a father of antiabortion movement, dies at 89," *Washington Post*, February 23, 2015, https://www.washingtonpost.com/national/john-c-willke-physician-who-led-movement-against-abortion-dies-at-89/2015/02/23/b3670848-bb70-11e4-bdfa-b8e8f594e6ee_story.html.

172   Kenneth R. Rosen, "John C. Willke, Doctor Who Led Fight Against Abortion, Dies at 89," *New York Times*, February 22, 2015, https://www.nytimes.com/2015/02/23/us/john-c-willke-doctor-who-led-fight-against-abortion-dies-at-89.html.

173   J.C. Willke and Barbara Willke, *Handbook on abortion* (Cincinnati: Hiltz, 1971). https://www.worldcat.org/title/handbook-on-abortion/oclc/4824830?referer=di&ht=edition.

174   Garance Franke-Ruta, "A Canard That Will Not Die: 'Legitimate Rape' Doesn't Cause Pregnancy," *The Atlantic*, August 19, 2012, https://www.theatlan-

tic.com/politics/archive/2012/08/a-canard-that-will-not-die-legitimate-rape-doesnt-cause-pregnancy/261303/.

175   Pam Belluck, "Health Experts Dismiss Assertations on Rape," *New York Times*, August 20, 2012, https://www.nytimes.com/2012/08/21/us/politics/rape-assertions-are-dismissed-by-health-experts.html?mtrref=undefined&gwh=A3A7AABECEE86F03188D618234881CC4&gwt=pay&assetType=PAYWALL.

176   Kate Clancy, "Here is Some Legitimate Science on Pregnancy and Rape," *Context and Variation* (blog), *Scientific American*, August 20, 2012, https://blogs.scientificamerican.com/context-and-variation/here-is-some-legitimate-science-on-pregnancy-and-rape/.

177   John C. Willke, "Words Are Important," Life Issues Institute, October 1, 2003, https://www.lifeissues.org/2003/10/words-important/.

178   John C. Willke, "Words Are Important," Life Issues Institute, October 1, 2003, https://www.lifeissues.org/2003/10/words-important/.

179   Susan Faludi, *Backlash: the Undeclared War against American Women*, (New York: Three Rivers Press, 2006), pg. 414.

180   Susan Faludi, *Backlash: the Undeclared War against American Women*, (New York: Three Rivers Press, 2006), pg. 429.

181   Molly Redden, "More Wisdom from the Guy Who Brought You 'Rape Can't Get You Pregnant,'" *New Republic*, August 21, 2012, https://newrepublic.com/article/106380/more-wisdom-guy-who-brought-you-rape-cant-get-you-pregnant.

182   John C. Willke, "Rape Pregnancies are Rare," Life Issues Institute, accessed May 19, 2020, https://www.lifeissues.org/1999/04/rape-pregnancies-are-rare/.

183   Facing Life Head On, "Where It All Began Part 1," YouTube (video), 22:05, June 22, 2015, https://youtu.be/x4-DTQ1uUt0?t=810.

184   Deana A. Rohlinger, *Abortion Politics, Mass Media, and Social Movements in America* (Cambridge: Cambridge, 2015), pg. 56, https://books.google.com/books?id=aZBEBQAAQBAJ&pg=PA56&lpg=PA56&dq=John+Willke+Reagan&source=bl&ots=ZEylqQbzR8&sig=ACfU3U2bC2J5T1CVIb4yct_eExRFu4D_jg&hl=en&sa=X&ved=2ahUKEwj-oOTStYXmAhVyUN8KHZZxBD0Q6AEwDXoECAoQAQ#v=onepage&q=Willke&f=false.

185   Robin Roner, "Reagan Exhorts Foes of Abortion at Capital Rally," *New York Times*, January 23, 1986, https://www.nytimes.com/1986/01/23/us/reagan-exhorts-foes-of-abortion-at-capital-rally.html.

186   "Dr. Jack Willke on President Bush's Pro-Life Conversion," Life Issues Institute, December 4, 2018, https://www.lifeissues.org/2018/12/dr-jack-willke-on-president-bushs-pro-life-conversion/.

187   Facing Life Head On, "Where It All Began Part 1," YouTube (video), 22:05, June 22, 2015, https://www.youtube.com/watch?v=x4-DTQ1uUt0&feature=youtu.be.

188   Facing Life Head On, "Where It All Began Part 2," YouTube (video), 21:57, June 22, 2015, https://www.youtube.com/watch?v=ZembF8dl0ro&feature=youtu.be.

189   *"Our Mission," Life Issues Institute, accessed May 19, 2010, https://www.lifeissues.org/our-mission/.*

190   Bradley Mattes, "'A Match Made in Heaven': Life Issues Institute becomes the Pro-life Grassroots Partner of Susan B. Anthony List," Life Issues Institute, June 18, 2018, https://www.lifeissues.org/2018/06/a-match-made-in-heaven-life-issues-institute-becomes-the-pro-life-grassroots-partner-of-susan-b-anthony-list/.

191   "About Susan B. Anthony List," Susan B. Anthony List, accessed May 19, 2020, https://www.sba-list.org/about-susan-b-anthony-list.

192   "About Us," Charlotte Lozier Institute, accessed May 19, 2020, https://lozierinstitute.org/about/.

193   Sofia Resnick and Sharona Coutts, "Anti-Choice 'Science': The Big Tobacco of Our Time," *Rewire News*, November 13, 2014, https://rewire.news/article/2014/11/13/anti-choice-science-big-tobacco-time/.

194   "False Witnesses: Vincent M. Rue," *Rewire News*, accessed May 19, 2020, https://rewire.news/false-witnesses/#vincent-rue.

195   "False Witnesses: Priscilla K. Coleman," *Rewire News*, accessed May 19, 2020, https://rewire.news/false-witnesses/#priscilla-coleman.

196   "False Witnesses: David C. Reardon," *Rewire News*, accessed May 19, 2020, https://rewire.news/false-witnesses/#david-reardon.

197   Jen Christensen, "The majority of women feel relief, not regret, after an abortion, study says," *CNN*, January 15, 2020, https://www.cnn.com/2020/01/12/health/women-abortion-emotion-study/index.html.

198   "Turnaway Study," Advancing New Standards in Reproductive Health, University of California San Francisco, accessed May 20, 2020, https://www.ansirh.org/research/turnaway-study.

199   Robin Opsahl, "U.S. Rep. Steve King: If not for rape and incest, 'would there be any population left?'", *Des Moines Register*, August 14, 2019, https://www.desmoinesregister.com/story/news/politics/2019/08/14/steve-king-abortion-rape-incest-westside-conservative-iowa-representative-birth-iowa-civilization/2007230001/.

200   Dustin Siggins, "Lindsey Graham on abortion after rape: 'I'm going to leave that to the family,'" *Life Site News*, June 11, 2015, https://www.lifesitenews.com/news/lindsey-graham-on-abortion-after-rape-im-going-to-leave-that-to-the-family.

201   Miranda Blue, "Anti-Choice Leader: Abortion Ban's Rape Exception Is 'Abominable' but Politically Necessary," *Right Wing Watch*, June 12, 2015, https://www.rightwingwatch.org/post/anti-choice-leader-abortion-bans-rape-exception-is-abominable-but-politically-necessary/.

202   Linh Ta and Nick Coltrain, "Steve King: 2020 Democratic presidential candidates, Republicans condemn 'rape and incest' remarks," *Des Moines Register*, updated August 17, 2019, https://www.desmoinesregister.com/story/news/elections/presidential/caucus/2019/08/14/steve-king-senator-offensive-rape-incest-comment-population-jd-scholten-randy-feenstra-4th-district/2010467001/.

203   Linh Ta and Nick Coltrain, "Steve King: 2020 Democratic presidential candidates, Republicans condemn 'rape and incest' remarks," *Des Moines Register*, updated August 17, 2019, https://www.desmoinesregister.com/story/news/elections/presidential/caucus/2019/08/14/steve-king-senator-offensive-rape-incest-comment-population-jd-scholten-randy-feenstra-4th-district/2010467001/.

204   Steve Lopez, "Review of Column: For Reagan Campaign Manager, This Election Is Tough to Watch" *Los Angeles Times*, September 7, 2016, https://webcache.googleusercontent.com/search?q=cache:F16rxgRSfM8J:https://www.latimes.com/local/california/la-me-0918-lopez-spencer-election--20160916-snapstory.html+&cd=1&hl=en&ct=clnk&gl=us.

205   "Republican Party Platform of 1984 | The American Presidency Project." n.d. Www.Presidency.Ucsb.Edu. Accessed May 12, 2020. https://www.presidency.ucsb.edu/documents/republican-party-platform-1984.

206   "Global Gag Rule: How U.S. Aid Is Threatening Health and Speech Worldwide." 2019, Open Society Foundations, 2019, https://www.opensocietyfoundations.org/explainers/what-global-gag-rule.

207   "INFOGRAPHIC: Which Women Are Hurt Most by Trump's Global Gag

Rule?" 2017, Global Fund for Women, October 26, 2017, https://www.globalfundfor-women.org/infographic-global-gag-rule/.

208   Valerie Scatamburlo d'Annibale, *Cold Breezes and Idiot Winds: Patriotic Correctness and the Post-9/11 Assault on Academe*, (Rotterdam: Sense Publishers, 2011): pg. 75.

209   Curtis Wilke, "A 'grand bargain' that secured the South for the GOP," *Washington Post*, August 16, 2019, https://www.washingtonpost.com/outlook/a-grand-bargain-that-secured-the-south-for-the-gop/2019/08/16/64166948-976a-11e9-830a-21b9b36b64ad_story.html.

210   Renee Graham, "Why is anyone surprised by Reagan's racism?" *Boston Globe*, August 2, 2019, https://www.bostonglobe.com/opinion/2019/08/02/why-anyone-surprised-reagan-racism/wVSXLxvnSXV2WlUJ3rbcQL/story.html.

211   Patti Davis, "The Ronald Reagan who raised me would want forgiveness for his 'monkeys' remark," *Washington Post*, August 1, 2019, https://www.washingtonpost.com/opinions/the-ronald-reagan-who-raised-me-would-want-forgiveness-for-his-monkeys-remark/2019/08/01/c3c2b66c-b40c-11e9-951e-de024209545d_story.html.

212   Louis Moore, Twitter post, August 1, 2019, 10:42 a.m., https://twitter.com/loumoore12/status/1156938222989172736.

213   Valerie Scatamburlo d'Annibale, *Cold Breezes and Idiot Winds: Patriotic Correctness and the Post-9/11 Assault on Academe*, (Rotterdam: Sense Publishers, 2011): pg. 75.

214   "Presidential Election of 1976." n.d. 270toWin.Com. Accessed May 12, 2020. https://www.270towin.com/1976_Election/.

215   Alec Ryrie, "The Weakness of the Religious Left: How Progressive Evangelicals Ceded Moral Authority to the Right Wing," *Salon*, April 9, 2017, https://www.salon.com/2017/04/09/the-weakness-of-the-religious-left-how-progressive-evangelicals-ceded-moral-authority-to-the-right-wing/.

216   Angie Maxwell and Todd G. Shields, *The Long Southern Strategy: How Chasing White Voters in the South Changed American Politics*, (Oxford: Oxford University Press, 2019): pg. 10.

217   Angie Maxwell and Todd G. Shields, *The Long Southern Strategy: How Chasing White Voters in the South Changed American Politics*, (Oxford: Oxford University Press, 2019): pg. 247.

218   Angie Maxwell and Todd G. Shields, *The Long Southern Strategy: How Chasing White Voters in the South Changed American Politics*, (Oxford: Oxford University Press, 2019): pg. 247.

219   Bill Peterson, "Reagan-for-President Committee Is Formed, But He Hasn't Announced Candidacy -- Yet," *Washington Post*, March 8, 1979, https://www.washingtonpost.com/archive/politics/1979/03/08/reagan-for-president-committee-is-formed-but-he-hasnt-announced-candidacy-yet/80d0d3ce-4e80-405a-9a2e-77e7f678caab/.

220   "1976: The Last Time Republicans Duked It Out To The Last, Heated Minute," *National Public Radio*, March 16, 2016 www.npr.org/2016/03/13/470271684/1976-the-last-time-republicans-duked-it-out-to-the-last-heated-minute

221   Andrew Glass, "Ronald Reagan Enters Presidential Race: Nov. 20, 1975," *POLITICO*, November 19, 2016, https://www.politico.com/story/2016/11/ronald-reagan-enters-presidential-race-nov-20-1975-231633.

222   "Another Loss For the Gipper," AllPolitics - Back in TIME (archive), *CNN*, accessed June 2, 2020, https://www.cnn.com/ALLPOLITICS/1996/analysis/back.time/9603/29/index.shtml.

223   "Another Loss For the Gipper," AllPolitics - Back in TIME (archive), *CNN*,

accessed June 2, 2020, https://www.cnn.com/ALLPOLITICS/1996/analysis/back.time/9603/29/index.shtml.

224   "Another Loss For the Gipper," AllPolitics - Back in TIME (archive), *CNN*, accessed June 2, 2020, https://www.cnn.com/ALLPOLITICS/1996/analysis/back.time/9603/29/index.shtml.

225   "Is Defeat Probable for GOP If Reagan Wins Nomination?," *Christian Science Monitor*, March 5, 1980, https://www.csmonitor.com/1980/0305/030542.html.

226   Lee Edwards, "Ronald Reagan vs. Gerald Ford: The 1976 GOP Convention Battle Royal," *National Interest*, April 16, 2016 https://nationalinterest.org/blog/the-buzz/ronald-reagan-vs-gerald-ford-the-1976-gop-convention-battle-15818.

227   Bill Peterson, "Reagan-for-President Committee Is Formed, But He Hasn't Announced Candidacy -- Yet," *The Washington Post*, March 8, 1979, https://www.washingtonpost.com/archive/politics/1979/03/08/reagan-for-president-committee-is-formed-but-he-hasnt-announced-candidacy-yet/80d0d3ce-4e80-405a-9a2e-77e7f678caab/.

228   T. R. Reid and Maralee Schwartz, "Reagan: A Life Built on Performing," *The Washington Post*, October 22, 1980, https://www.washingtonpost.com/archive/politics/1980/10/22/reagan-a-life-built-on-performing/2dff8097-9b26-43f0-b8ce-88174d43c560/.

229   William Greider, "Women vs. Reagan," *Rolling Stone*, August 19, 1982, https://www.rollingstone.com/politics/politics-news/women-vs-reagan-89061/.

230   Sam Brock and Kinsey Kiriakos, "Reality Check: Ronald Reagan Increased Taxes and 'Liberalized' Abortion As CA's Governor," *NBC Bay Area*, June 4, 2014 https://www.nbcbayarea.com/news/local/reality-check-ronald-reagan-increased-taxes-and-liberalized-abortion-as-cas-governor/1971524/

231   Françoise Coste, "'Women, Ladies, Girls, Gals...': Ronald Reagan and the Evolution of Gender Roles in the United States," *Miranda* (online), December 2016. https://journals.openedition.org/miranda/8602#bibliography.

232   Mark Wingfield, "Remembering Ed McAteer and the Jerusalem Embassy," *Baptist News Global*, May 16, 2018, https://baptistnews.com/article/remembering-ed-mcateer-and-the-jerusalem-embassy/

233   Los Angeles Times Staff, "Edward McAteer, 78; Founded Conservative Religious Roundtable," *Los Angeles Times*, October 13, 2004, https://www.latimes.com/archives/la-xpm-2004-oct-13-me-passings13.2-story.html.

234   Amy Black, "Evangelicals and Politics Where We've Been and Where We're Headed," National Association of Evangelicals, Fall 2016,https://www.nae.net/evangelicals-and-politics/.

235   Margalit Fox, "Edward E. McAteer, 78; Empowered Christian Right," *New York Times*, October 10, 2004, https://www.nytimes.com/2004/10/10/obituaries/us/edward-e-mcateer-78-empowered-christian-right.html.

236   Duane M. Oldfield, The Right and the Righteous: The Christian Right Confronts the Republican Party, (Lanham, MD: Rowman & Littlefield Publishers, 1996): pg 57.

237   Margalit Fox, "Edward E. McAteer, 78; Empowered Christian Right," *New York Times*, October 10, 2004, https://www.nytimes.com/2004/10/10/obituaries/us/edward-e-mcateer-78-empowered-christian-right.html.

238   Carolyn Gallaher, "Aberration or Reflection? How to Understand Changes on the Political Right," *Political Research Associates,* May 24, 2019 https://www.politicalresearch.org/2019/05/24/aberration-or-reflection-how-understand-changes-political-right.

239   Françoise Coste, "'Women, Ladies, Girls, Gals...': Ronald Reagan and the Evolution of Gender Roles in the United States," *Miranda: Revue pluridisciplinaire du*

monde anglophone / Multidisciplinary peer-reviewed journal on the English-speaking world, February 24, 2016, https://journals.openedition.org/miranda/8602.

240   Carolyn Gallaher, "Aberration or Reflection? How to Understand Changes on the Political Right," *Political Research Associates,* May 24, 2019 https://www.politicalresearch.org/2019/05/24/aberration-or-reflection-how-understand-changes-political-right.

241   Françoise Coste, "'Women, Ladies, Girls, Gals...': Ronald Reagan and the Evolution of Gender Roles in the United States," *Miranda: Revue pluridisciplinaire du monde anglophone / Multidisciplinary peer-reviewed journal on the English-speaking world*, February 24, 2016, https://journals.openedition.org/miranda/8602.

242   "Fiedler, Bobbi," *History, Art & Archives*, U.S. House of Representatives, accessed June 2, 2020, https://history.house.gov/People/Detail/13103.

243   Françoise Coste, "'Women, Ladies, Girls, Gals...': Ronald Reagan and the Evolution of Gender Roles in the United States," *Miranda: Revue pluridisciplinaire du monde anglophone / Multidisciplinary peer-reviewed journal on the English-speaking world*, February 24, 2016, https://journals.openedition.org/miranda/8602.

244   Marisa Chappell, "Reagan's 'gender gap; strategy and the limitations of free-market feminism," *Journal of Policy History,* 24, no. 1, (2012): 115-134. https://ir.library.oregonstate.edu/concern/articles/9s1616563?locale=en.

245   "Chronology of the Equal Rights Amendment, 1923-1996," *National Organization for Women*, accessed May 12, 2020, https://now.org/resource/chronology-of-the-equal-rights-amendment-1923-1996/.

246   Fred Barnes, "Ronald Reagan, Father Of the Pro-Life Movement," *Wall Street Journal*, November 6, 2003, https://www.wsj.com/articles/SB106808204063174300.

247   T. R. Reid, "Reagan Is Favored by Anti-Abortionists," *Washington Post*, April 12, 1980, https://www.washingtonpost.com/archive/politics/1980/04/12/reagan-is-favored-by-anti-abortionists/f89c94bf-4e00-4674-b91c-c1f10a6aea15/.

248   Catherine E. Rymph, *Republican Women: Feminism and Conservatism From Suffrage Through the Rise of the New Right,* (Chapel Hill: The University of North Carolina Press, 2006): 228.

249   T. R. Reid, "Reagan Is Favored by Anti-Abortionists," *Washington Post*, April 12, 1980, https://www.washingtonpost.com/archive/politics/1980/04/12/reagan-is-favored-by-anti-abortionists/f89c94bf-4e00-4674-b91c-c1f10a6aea15/.

250   "Building a Movement Party," Miller Center, November 5, 2018, https://millercenter.org/rivalry-and-reform/building-movement-party.

251   "Building a Movement Party," Miller Center, November 5, 2018, https://millercenter.org/rivalry-and-reform/building-movement-party.

252   Michael S. Hamilton, "How a Humble Evangelist Changed Christianity As We Know It," *Christianity Today*, accessed June 2, 2020, https://www.christianitytoday.com/ct/2018/billy-graham/how-humble-evangelist-billy-graham-changed-christianity.html.

253   "Robison Ascending," *Texas Monthly*, April 1981, https://books.google.com/books?id=ySwEAAAAMBAJ&pg=PA224&lpg=PA224&dq=%22james+robison%22+%22television%22+%22popular%22+%22seventies%22&source=bl&ots=wC2G0ZsxDh&sig=ACfU3U1dsCu1eSs3N9uyWHvc-MTMf_lC4XQ&hl=en&sa=X&ved=2ahUKEwjY_5at87_nAhVIlXIEHe2pBlMQ6AEwAHoECAoQAQ#v=onepage&q=%22james%20robison%22%20%22television%22%20%22popular%22%20%22seventies%22&f=false.

254   "Exposing Huckabee's Dominionist Sympathies," *Religious Right Watch*, January 19, 2008, https://www.religiousrightwatch.com/2008/01/exposing-huckab.html.

255   Ariel Levy, "Prodigal Son," *New Yorker*, June 28, 2010, https://www.newyo-

rker.com/magazine/2010/06/28/prodigal-son.

256   William Martin, *With God on Our Side: the Rise of the Religious Right in America,* (New York: Broadway Books, 2005): pg. 217.

257   "James Robison: National Affairs Briefing (James Robison / LIFE Today)," YouTube video, from a 1980 National Affairs Briefing, posted by "ifetodaytv," posted March 31, 2014, https://youtu.be/lH1e0xxRRbk?t=99.

258   William Martin, *With God on Our Side: the Rise of the Religious Right in America,* (New York: Broadway Books, 2005): pg. 217.

259   Daniel Schlozman, *When Movements Anchor Parties: Electoral Alignments in American History,* (Princeton: Princeton University Press, 2015): pg. 2.

260   Daniel Schlozman, *When Movements Anchor Parties: Electoral Alignments in American History,* (Princeton: Princeton University Press, 2015): pg. 2.

261   Daniel Schlozman, *When Movements Anchor Parties: Electoral Alignments in American History,* (Princeton: Princeton University Press, 2015): pg. 2.

262   "ADDRESS BY THE HONORABLE RONALD REAGAN THE ROUNDTABLE NATIONAL AFFAIRS BRIEFING DALLAS, TEXAS," Reagan Bush Committee, August 22, 1980, http://digitalcollections.library.cmu.edu/awweb/awarchive?type=file&item=684006.

263   "Ronald Reagan at the National Affairs Briefing," YouTube video, from a Dallas National Affairs Briefing, posted by "lifetodaytv," posted May 4, 2015, https://www.youtube.com/watch?v=5pclC1bAfLI&feature=emb_title.

264   "Ronald Reagan National Affairs Campaign Address on Religious Liberty (Abridged)," American Rhetoric, accessed June 5, 2020, https://www.american-rhetoric.com/speeches/ronaldreaganreligiousliberty.htm.

265   Brian Kaylor, "A 'Transformative Moment' in SBC Political Activity ·," *Ethics Daily*, July 25, 2019, https://ethicsdaily.com/a-transformative-moment-in-sbc-political-activity-cms-16555/.

266   Françoise Coste, "'Women, Ladies, Girls, Gals...': Ronald Reagan and the Evolution of Gender Roles in the United States," *Miranda: Revue pluridisciplinaire du monde anglophone / Multidisciplinary peer-reviewed journal on the English-speaking world*, February 24, 2016, https://journals.openedition.org/miranda/8602.

267   Françoise Coste, "'Women, Ladies, Girls, Gals...': Ronald Reagan and the Evolution of Gender Roles in the United States," *Miranda: Revue pluridisciplinaire du monde anglophone / Multidisciplinary peer-reviewed journal on the English-speaking world*, February 24, 2016, https://journals.openedition.org/miranda/8602.

268   Catherine E. Rymph, *Republican Women: Feminism and Conservatism From Suffrage Through the Rise of the New Right*, (Chapel HillThe University of North Carolina Press, 2006): Kindle location 4696.

269   Catherine E. Rymph, *Republican Women: Feminism and Conservatism From Suffrage Through the Rise of the New Right* (Chapel Hill: The University of North Carolina Press, 2006): 230.

270   Sidney M. Milkis and Daniel J. Tichenor, *Rivalry and Reform: Presidents, Social Movements, and the Transformation of American Politics,* (Chicago: The University of Chicago Press, 2019): pg. 233.

271   Catherine E. Rymph, Republican Women: Feminism and Conservatism From Suffrage Through the Rise of the New Right, (Chapel Hill: The University of North Carolina Press, 2006): Kindle location 4708.

272   Catherine E. Rymph, *Republican Women: Feminism and Conservatism From Suffrage Through the Rise of the New Right*, (Chapel Hill: The University of North Carolina Press, 2006): 230.

273   Alexis Grenell, "White Women, Come Get Your People," *New York Times*, October 6, 2018, https://www.nytimes.com/2018/10/06/opinion/lisa-murkows-

ki-susan-collins-kavanaugh.html.

274   Julian Zelizer, "Reagan vs. Carter holds a crucial lesson for 2020 Dems," CNN, February 22, 2020, https://www.cnn.com/2020/02/22/opinions/reagan-vs-carter-1980-what-democrats-can-learn-opinion/index.html.

275   Françoise Coste, "Ronald Reagan's Northern Strategy and a new American Partisan Identity: The Case of the Reagan Democrats," Caliban: French Journal of English Studies 31 (2012): pg. 221-238, https://journals.openedition.org/caliban/476.

276   Susan Faludi, *Backlash: the Undeclared War against American Women*, (New York: Three Rivers Press, 2006): pg. 81.

277   Susan Faludi, *Backlash: the Undeclared War against American Women*, (New York: Three Rivers Press, 2006): pg. 79.

278   Susan Faludi, Backlash: the Undeclared War against American Women, (New York: Three Rivers Press, 2006): pg. 81.

279   Susan Faludi, *Backlash: the Undeclared War against American Women*, (New York: Three Rivers Press, 2006): pg. 247.

280   Michael A. Urquhart and Marillyn A. Hewson, "Unemployment continued to rise in 1982 as recession deepened," Monthly Labor Review, February 1983, https://www.bls.gov/opub/mlr/1983/02/art1full.pdf.

281   Susan Faludi, *Backlash: the Undeclared War against American Women*, (New York: Three Rivers Press, 2006): pg. 81-82.

282   Susan Faludi, *Backlash: the Undeclared War against American Women*, (New York: Three Rivers Press, 2006): pg. 80.

283   David Kopel, "Reagan's Infamous Speech in Philadelphia, Mississippi," *The Volokh Conspiracy*, August 16, 2011, http://volokh.com/2011/08/16/reagans-infamous-speech-in-philadelphia-mississippi/.

284   "Reagan and Philadelphia," *Washington Monthly*, June 10, 2004, https://washingtonmonthly.com/2004/06/10/reagan-and-philadelphia/.

285   Jon Schwartz, "Seven things about Ronald Reagan you won't hear at the Reagan Library GOP debate," *The Intercept*, September 16, 2015, https://theintercept.com/2015/09/16/seven-things-reagan-wont-mentioned-tonight-gops-debate/.

286   Joseph Crespino, "Did David Brooks Tell the Full Story About Reagan's Neshoba County Fair Visit?" History News Network, Columbian College of Arts and Sciences, November 2007, https://historynewsnetwork.org/article/44535.

287   Wayne King, "FILM; Fact vs. Fiction in Mississippi," New York Times, December 4, 1988, https://www.nytimes.com/1988/12/04/movies/film-fact-vs-fiction-in-mississippi.html.

288   Joe Carter, "9 Things You Should Know About the 'Mississippi Burning' Murders," *Gospel Coalition*, January 13, 2018, https://www.thegospelcoalition.org/article/9-things-know-mississippi-burning-murders/.

289   Jon Schwartz, "Seven things about Ronald Reagan you won't hear at the Reagan Library GOP debate," The Intercept, September 16, 2015, https://theintercept.com/2015/09/16/seven-things-reagan-wont-mentioned-tonight-gops-debate/.

290   Gillian Brockell, "She Was Stereotyped as 'the Welfare Queen.' The Truth Was More Disturbing, a New Book Says.," *Washington Post*, May 21, 2019, https://www.washingtonpost.com/history/2019/05/21/she-was-stereotyped-welfare-queen-truth-was-more-disturbing-new-book-says/.

291   Renée Graham, "Why Is Anyone Surprised by Reagan's Racism?," *Boston Globe*, August 2, 2019, https://www.bostonglobe.com/opinion/2019/08/02/why-anyone-surprised-reagan-racism/wVSXLxvnSXV2WlUJ3rbcQL/story.html

292   Rick Perlstein, "Exclusive: Lee Atwater's Infamous 1981 Interview on the

Southern Strategy," *The Nation*, December 7, 2018, https://www.thenation.com/article/archive/exclusive-lee-atwaters-infamous-1981-interview-southern-strategy/.

293   Angie Maxwell, "Why Southern white women vote against feminism," *Washington Post*, September 10, 2019, https://www.washingtonpost.com/outlook/2019/09/10/why-southern-white-women-vote-against-feminism/.

294   Angie Maxwell and Todd G. Shields, *The Long Southern Strategy: How Chasing White Voters in the South Changed American Politics*, (Oxford: Oxford University Press, 2019).

295   Françoise Coste, "'Women, Ladies, Girls, Gals…': Ronald Reagan and the Evolution of Gender Roles in the United States," *Miranda: Revue pluridisciplinaire du monde anglophone / Multidisciplinary peer-reviewed journal on the English-speaking world*, February 24, 2016, https://journals.openedition.org/miranda/8602.

296   Angie Maxwell and Todd G. Shields, *The Long Southern Strategy: How Chasing White Voters in the South Changed American Politics*, (Oxford: Oxford University Press, 2019): pg. 20.

297   Susan Faludi, *Backlash: the Undeclared War against American Women*, (New York: Three Rivers Press, 2006): pg. 8-9.

298   Françoise Coste, "'Women, Ladies, Girls, Gals…': Ronald Reagan and the Evolution of Gender Roles in the United States," *Miranda: Revue pluridisciplinaire du monde anglophone / Multidisciplinary peer-reviewed journal on the English-speaking world*, February 24, 2016, https://journals.openedition.org/miranda/8602.

299   Norman D Sandler, "Reagan Still Wrestling Women Woes," UPI, September 18, 1983, https://www.upi.com/Archives/1983/09/18/Reagan-still-wrestling-women-woes/7387432705600/.

300   Marisa Chappell, "Reagan's 'Gender Gap' Strategy and the Limitations of Free-Market Feminism," *Journal of Policy History* 24, no. 1 (February 1, 2012).

301   Bill Peterson, "Reagan Did Understand Women," *Washington Post*, March 3, 1985, https://www.washingtonpost.com/archive/opinions/1985/03/03/reagan-did-understand-women/a710c0a0-38f0-4c04-ad3b-ae791371ccf2/.

302   Bill Peterson, "Reagan Did Understand Women," *Washington Post*, March 3, 1985, https://www.washingtonpost.com/archive/opinions/1985/03/03/reagan-did-understand-women/a710c0a0-38f0-4c04-ad3b-ae791371ccf2/.

303   Bill Peterson, "Reagan Did Understand Women," *Washington Post*, March 3, 1985, https://www.washingtonpost.com/archive/opinions/1985/03/03/reagan-did-understand-women/a710c0a0-38f0-4c04-ad3b-ae791371ccf2/.

304   Françoise Coste, "'Women, Ladies, Girls, Gals…': Ronald Reagan and the Evolution of Gender Roles in the United States," *Miranda: Revue pluridisciplinaire du monde anglophone / Multidisciplinary peer-reviewed journal on the English-speaking world*, February 24, 2016, https://journals.openedition.org/miranda/8602.

305   Marisa Chappell, "Reagan's 'Gender Gap' Strategy and the Limitations of Free-Market Feminism," *Journal of Policy History* 24, no. 1 (February 1, 2012).

306   Marisa Chappell, "Reagan's 'Gender Gap' Strategy and the Limitations of Free-Market Feminism," *Journal of Policy History* 24, no. 1 (February 1, 2012).

307   Françoise Coste, "'Women, Ladies, Girls, Gals…': Ronald Reagan and the Evolution of Gender Roles in the United States," *Miranda: Revue pluridisciplinaire du monde anglophone / Multidisciplinary peer-reviewed journal on the English-speaking world*, February 24, 2016, https://journals.openedition.org/miranda/8602.

308   Jessica Arons, "The Changing Status Quo On Federal Abortion Funding," *Kaiser Health News*, March 19, 2010, https://khn.org/news/031910arons/.

309   Françoise Coste, "'Women, Ladies, Girls, Gals…': Ronald Reagan and the Evolution of Gender Roles in the United States," *Miranda: Revue pluridisciplinaire du monde anglophone / Multidisciplinary peer-reviewed journal on the English-speak-

ing world, February 24, 2016, https://journals.openedition.org/miranda/8602.

310   Françoise Coste, "'Women, Ladies, Girls, Gals...': Ronald Reagan and the Evolution of Gender Roles in the United States," *Miranda: Revue pluridisciplinaire du monde anglophone / Multidisciplinary peer-reviewed journal on the English-speaking world*, February 24, 2016, https://journals.openedition.org/miranda/8602.

311   Steven V. Roberts, "THE NATION; Reagan's Social Issues: Gone but Not Forgotten," *New York Times*, September 11, 1988, https://www.nytimes.com/1988/09/11/weekinreview/the-nation-reagan-s-social-issues-gone-but-not-forgotten.html.

312   Angie Maxwell and Todd G. Shields, *The Long Southern Strategy: How Chasing White Voters in the South Changed American Politics*, (Oxford: Oxford University Press, 2019): pg. 292.

313   R. Scott Appleby and Martin E. Marty, *Fundamentalisms and the State: Remaking Politics, Economies, and Militance*, (Chicago: The University of Chicago Press, 1996).

314   Holcomb B Noble, "C. Everett Koop, Forceful U.S. Surgeon General, Dies at 96," *New York Times*, February 26, 2013, https://www.nytimes.com/2013/02/26/us/c-everett-koop-forceful-surgeon-general-dies-at-96.html.

315   Holcomb B Noble, "C. Everett Koop, Forceful U.S. Surgeon General, Dies at 96," *New York Times*, February 26, 2013, https://www.nytimes.com/2013/02/26/us/c-everett-koop-forceful-surgeon-general-dies-at-96.html.

316   "Elizabeth Dole: Files, 1981-1983," Reagan Library Collections, https://www.reaganlibrary.gov/sites/default/files/archives/textual/smof/dole.pdf

317   Adam Clymer, "Margaret Heckler, Lawmaker and Reagan Health Secretary, Dies at 87," *New York Times*, August 7, 2018, https://www.nytimes.com/2018/08/06/obituaries/margaret-heckler.html.

318   Steve Kornacki and Alan Nothnagle, "Liberals Are Not Uniquely 'Unreasonable,'" *Salon*, November 26, 2011, https://web.archive.org/web/20120502124642/http://www.politics.salon.com/2011/11/26/liberals_are_not_uniquely_unreasonable/singleton/.

319   Françoise Coste, "'Women, Ladies, Girls, Gals...': Ronald Reagan and the Evolution of Gender Roles in the United States," *Miranda: Revue pluridisciplinaire du monde anglophone / Multidisciplinary peer-reviewed journal on the English-speaking world*, February 24, 2016, https://journals.openedition.org/miranda/8602.

320   Françoise Coste, "'Women, Ladies, Girls, Gals...': Ronald Reagan and the Evolution of Gender Roles in the United States," *Miranda: Revue pluridisciplinaire du monde anglophone / Multidisciplinary peer-reviewed journal on the English-speaking world*, February 24, 2016, https://journals.openedition.org/miranda/8602.

321   Françoise Coste, "'Women, Ladies, Girls, Gals...': Ronald Reagan and the Evolution of Gender Roles in the United States," *Miranda: Revue pluridisciplinaire du monde anglophone / Multidisciplinary peer-reviewed journal on the English-speaking world*, February 24, 2016, https://journals.openedition.org/miranda/8602.

322   Françoise Coste, "'Women, Ladies, Girls, Gals...': Ronald Reagan and the Evolution of Gender Roles in the United States," *Miranda: Revue pluridisciplinaire du monde anglophone / Multidisciplinary peer-reviewed journal on the English-speaking world*, February 24, 2016, https://journals.openedition.org/miranda/8602.

323   Françoise Coste, "'Women, Ladies, Girls, Gals...': Ronald Reagan and the Evolution of Gender Roles in the United States," *Miranda: Revue pluridisciplinaire du monde anglophone / Multidisciplinary peer-reviewed journal on the English-speaking world*, February 24, 2016, https://journals.openedition.org/miranda/8602.

324   "Election Results 2008," *New York Times*, accessed May 12, 2020, https://www.nytimes.com/elections/2008/results/president/national-exit-polls.html.

325   Angie Maxwell and Todd G. Shields, *The Long Southern Strategy: How*

Chasing White Voters in the South Changed American Politics, (Oxford: Oxford University Press, 2019): pg. 129.

326   Angie Maxwell and Todd G. Shields, *The Long Southern Strategy: How Chasing White Voters in the South Changed American Politics*, (Oxford: Oxford University Press, 2019): pg. 262.

327   Susan Gilmore, "Pat Robertson's 1988 `Army': From Rebels To Gop Mainstream," *Seattle Times*, April 13, 1992, https://archive.seattletimes.com/archive/?-date=19920413&slug=1486177.

328   Angie Maxwell and Todd G. Shields, The Long Southern Strategy: How Chasing White Voters in the South Changed American Politics, (Oxford: Oxford University Press, 2019): pg. 292-3.

329   "Where It All Began Part 1" YouTube video, from Season 2, Episode 11 of "Facing Life Head-On," Life Issues Institute, posted by "Facing Life Head On," posted June 22, 2015, https://youtu.be/x4-DTQ1uUt0?t=1031.

330   "Dr. Jack Willke on President Bush's Pro-Life Conversion," Life Issues Institute, December 4, 2018, https://www.lifeissues.org/2018/12/dr-jack-willke-on-president-bushs-pro-life-conversion/.

331   "Where It All Began Part 1" YouTube video, from Season 2, Episode 11 of "Facing Life Head-On," Life Issues Institute, posted by "Facing Life Head On," posted June 22, 2015, https://youtu.be/x4-DTQ1uUt0?t=1067.

332   Emily Schultheis, "Anonymous group hits Newt on abortion," *POLITICO*, December 16, 2011, https://www.politico.com/blogs/burns-haberman/2011/12/anonymous-group-hits-newt-on-abortion-107790.

333   Matthew Haag, "Tomi Lahren Sues Glenn Beck, Saying She Was Fired for Her Stance on Abortion," *New York Times*, April 8, 2017, https://www.nytimes.com/2017/04/07/business/media/tomi-lahren-lawsuit-glenn-beck-blaze.html.

334   Tomi Lahren, "Final Thoughts," *Fox News*, https://nation.foxnews.com/final-thoughts-with-tomi-lahren/.

335   "Ben Shapiro Bio," Premiere Speakers Bureau, accessed May 12, 2020, https://premierespeakers.com/ben-shapiro/bio.

336   Seth Stevenson, "The Many Faces of Ben Shapiro," *Slate*, January 24, 2018, https://slate.com/news-and-politics/2018/01/is-ben-shapiro-a-conservative-liberals-can-count-on.html.

337   Bonnie Chernin, "Ben Shapiro Is Headlining the March For Life 2019, and one pro-life professor objects," *Renew America*, December 16, 2018, https://www.renewamerica.com/columns/chernin/181216.

338   "In Memoriam: John C. Willke, M.D.," *National Right to Life*, accessed May 12, 2020, https://www.nrlc.org/jcw/.

339   Karen Scoggins, "NRLC Vigorously Promotes 'The Silent Scream,'" *NRL News Today*, February 23, 2011, https://www.nationalrighttolifenews.org/2011/02/nrlc-vigorously-promotes-%E2%80%9Cthe-silent-scream%E2%80%9D/.

340   Ruth Marcus, "'Silent Scream': Loud Impact," The Washington Post, February 9, 1985, https://www.washingtonpost.com/archive/politics/1985/02/09/silent-scream-loud-impact/f8db85e8-d804-4b36-882f-4ae06303370b/.

341   William Grimes, "B. N. Nathanson, 84, Dies; Changed Sides on Abortion," *New York Times*, February 22, 2011, https://www.nytimes.com/2011/02/22/us/22nathanson.html.

342   Elizabeth Mehren, "Medical Group Cites Flaws in 'Silent Scream,' Response," *Los Angeles Times*, December 3, 1985, https://webcache.googleusercontent.com/search?q=cache%3AzhUeP9NXspkJ%3Ahttps%3A%2F%2Fwww.latimes.com%2Farchives%2Fla-xpm-1985-12-03-vw-12959-story.html.

343   Rickie Solinger, *Reproductive Politics: What Everyone Needs to Know*, (Ox-

ford: Oxford University Press, 2013): pg. 94.

344   Paul Houston, "'Silent Scream' Called 'Testament for Pro-Life' : White House Showcases Abortion Film," *Los Angeles Times*, Los Angeles Times, February 13, 1985, https://webcache.googleusercontent.com/search?q=-cache%3AusqOw227aAwJ%3Ahttps%3A%2F%2Fwww.latimes.com%2Farchives%-2Fla-xpm-1985-02-13-mn-4582-story.html.

345   Robin Abcarian, "The abortion battle within," *Los Angeles Times*, August 26, 2009, https://www.latimes.com/archives/la-xpm-2009-aug-26-na-operation-rescue26-story.html.

346   Patrick Rogers, "Ambushed," People, November 9, 1998, https://people.com/archive/ambushed-vol-50-no-17/.

347   Susan Sachs, "Stubborn Belief in Duty Guided Slain Doctor," New York Times, November 15, 1998, https://www.nytimes.com/1998/11/15/nyregion/stub-born-belief-in-duty-guided-slain-doctor.html.

348   Eyal Press, "My Father's Abortion War," The New York Times Magazine, January 22, 2006, https://www.nytimes.com/2006/01/22/magazine/my-fathers-abortion-war.html.

349   Jeff Stein, "Celebrating murder," Salon, April 17, 1999, https://www.salon.com/1999/04/17/abortion/.

350   "Profile of killer of abortion provider offered," CNN, October 28, 1998, http://edition.cnn.com/US/9810/28/shooter.profile/.

351   Patrick Lakamp, "Askey Says Amherst Police Responded Profession-ally," Buffalo News, October 29, 1998, https://buffalonews.com/1998/10/28/askey-says-amherst-police-responded-professionally/.

352   "Violence Statistics," National Abortion Federation, accessed May 12, 2020, https://prochoice.org/education-and-advocacy/violence/violence-statis-tics-and-history/.

353   "Violence Statistics," National Abortion Federation, accessed May 12, 2020, https://prochoice.org/education-and-advocacy/violence/violence-statis-tics-and-history/.

354   "Violence Statistics," National Abortion Federation, accessed May 12, 2020, https://prochoice.org/education-and-advocacy/violence/violence-statis-tics-and-history/.

355   Jeff Stein, "Celebrating murder," Salon, April 17, 1999, https://www.salon.com/1999/04/17/abortion/.

356   Jeff Stein, "Celebrating murder," Salon, April 17, 1999, https://www.salon.com/1999/04/17/abortion/.

357   "Operation Rescue's Big Break: How an Organization Rooted in the Radical Fringes of the Anti-Choice Movement Is Threatening to Shut Down the Govern-ment," Right Wing Watch, September 2015, https://www.rightwingwatch.org/report/operation-rescues-big-break-how-an-organization-rooted-in-the-radical-fringes-of-the-anti-choice-movement-is-threatening-to-shut-down-the-government/.

358   "Every US president listed," The Guardian Datablog, accessed May 12, 2020, https://www.theguardian.com/news/datablog/2012/oct/15/us-presidents-listed.

359   Randall Rothenberg, "In Search of George Bush," New York Times, March 6, 1988. https://www.nytimes.com/1988/03/06/magazine/in-search-of-george-bush.html.

360   Sean Sullivan, "George H.W. Bush embodied the Republican Party's de-cades-long struggle with race," The Washington Post, December 4, 2018, https://www.washingtonpost.com/politics/george-hw-bush-embodied-the-republican-

partys-decades-long-struggle-with-race/2018/12/04/1268ab08-f73b-11e8-8c9a-860ce2a8148f_story.html.

361   Allison Herrera, "Before he was president, H.W. Bush championed family planning," The World, December 5, 2018, https://www.pri.org/stories/2018-12-05/he-was-president-hw-bush-championed-family-planning.

362   Neil J. Young, "How George H.W. Bush enabled the rise of the religious right," Washington Post, December 5, 2018, https://www.washingtonpost.com/outlook/2018/12/05/how-george-hw-bush-enabled-rise-religious-right/.

363   "Pat Robertson," Right Wing Watch, accessed May 28, 2020, https://www.rightwingwatch.org/people/pat-robertson/.

364   Jeff Gerth, "Tax data of Pat Robertson groups are questioned," New York Times, December 10, 1986, https://www.nytimes.com/1986/12/10/us/tax-data-of-pat-robertson-groups-are-questioned.html.

365   Mary Schmich, "The Campaign of a Believer," Chicago Tribune, October 2, 1987, https://www.chicagotribune.com/news/ct-xpm-1987-10-02-8703140492-story.html.

366   "Caucus history: Past years' results," Des Moines Register, accessed May 12, 2020, http://caucuses.desmoinesregister.com/caucus-history-past-years-results/.

367   E. J. Dionne, "Dole Wins in Iowa, With Robertson Next," February 9, 1988, https://www.nytimes.com/1988/02/09/us/dole-wins-in-iowa-with-robertson-next.html.

368   Geoffrey Skelley, "The Modern History of the Republican Presidential Primary, 1976-2012," Sabato's Crystal Ball, January 21, 2016, http://centerforpolitics.org/crystalball/articles/the-modern-history-of-the-republican-presidential-primary-1976-2012/.

369   Angie Maxwell and Todd G. Shields, The Long Southern Strategy: How Chasing White Voters in the South Changed American Politics, (Oxford University Press, 2019).

370   Frank Bruni, "George H.W. Bush's Uncommon Grace," New York Times, December 1, 2018, https://www.nytimes.com/2018/12/01/opinion/george-hw-bush-kindler-gentler.html.

371   E.J. Dionne, "THE 1988 ELECTIONS; BUSH IS ELECTED BY A 6-5 MARGIN WITH SOLID G.O.P. BASE IN SOUTH; DEMOCRATS HOLD BOTH HOUSES How the Poll Was Taken," New York Times, November 9, 1988.

372   George H. W. Bush, "1988 Acceptance Speech," C-SPAN, August 18, 1988, https://www.c-span.org/video/?3848-1/george-hw-bush-1988-acceptance-speech.

373   "Republican Party Platform of 1988," The American Presidency Project, accessed May 13, 2020, https://www.presidency.ucsb.edu/documents/republican-party-platform-1988.

374   The Editors of Encyclopaedia Britannica, "Dan Quayle," Encyclopaedia Britannica, accessed May 13, 2020, https://www.britannica.com/biography/Dan-Quayle.

375   Jacey Fortin, "That Time 'Murphy Brown' and Dan Quayle topped the front page," New York Times, January 26, 2018, https://www.nytimes.com/2018/01/26/arts/television/murphy-brown-dan-quayle.html.

376   Karen de Witt, "THE 1992 CAMPAIGN: The Vice President; Quayle Contends Homosexuality Is a Matter of Choice, Not Biology," New York Times, September 24, 1992, https://www.nytimes.com/1992/09/14/us/1992-campaign-vice-president-quayle-contends-homosexuality-matter-choice-not.html.

377   "THE VICE-PRESIDENTIAL DEBATE; Transcript of the Debate on TV Between Bentsen and Quayle," New York Times, October 6, 1988, https://www.nytimes.com/1988/10/06/us/vice-presidential-debate-transcript-debate-tv-between-bentsen-quayle.html.

378   James Gerstenzang and Douglas Jehl, "Bush, Quayle Warn GOP of Danger in Divided Party: Republicans: Appeals for unity address a challenge from the right but avoid a direct attack on Buchanan," Los Angeles Times, February 22, 1992, https://www.latimes.com/archives/la-xpm-1992-02-22-mn-1944-story.html.

379   "Gallup Presidential Election Trial-Heat Trends, 1936-2008," Gallup, Internet Archive, https://web.archive.org/web/20170630070844/http://www.gallup.com/poll/110548/gallup-presidential-election-trialheat-trends-19362004.aspx#4.

380   Rebecca Harrington, "Roger Ailes produced one of the most infamous political ads of all time, and it helped George H.W. Bush win the presidency," Business Insider, May 18, 2017, https://www.businessinsider.com/roger-ailes-revolving-door-ad-bush-election-2017-5.

381   Doug Criss, "This is the 30-year-old Willie Horton ad everybody is talking about today," CNN, November 1, 2018, https://www.cnn.com/2018/11/01/politics/willie-horton-ad-1988-explainer-trnd/index.html.

382   "1988 Presidential Election," 270 To Win, accessed May 13, 2020, https://www.270towin.com/1988_Election/.

383   "Heritage Has Won Victories for Conservative Principles," Heritage Foundation, accessed May 13, 2020, https://www.heritage.org/about-heritage/impact.

384   Andrew Blasko, "Reagan and Heritage: a Unique Partnership," The Heritage Foundation, June 7, 2004. https://www.heritage.org/conservatism/commentary/reagan-and-heritage-unique-partnership.

385   Andrew Blasko, "Reagan and Heritage: a Unique Partnership," The Heritage Foundation, June 7, 2004. https://www.heritage.org/conservatism/commentary/reagan-and-heritage-unique-partnership.

386   Peter Steinfels, "Moral Majority to Dissolve; Says Mission Accomplished," New York Times, June 12, 1989, https://www.nytimes.com/1989/06/12/us/moral-majority-to-dissolve-says-mission-accomplished.html.

387   Michael Kruse, "The Weekend at Yale That Changed American Politics," Politico, October/September, 2018, https://www.politico.com/magazine/story/2018/08/27/federalist-society-yale-history-conservative-law-court-219608.

388   Michael Kruse, "The weekend at Yale that changed American politics," POLITICO, October/September, 2018, https://www.politico.com/magazine/story/2018/08/27/federalist-society-yale-history-conservative-law-court-219608.

389   Michael Stokes Paulson, "Originalism: A Logical Necessity," National Review, September 13, 2018, https://www.nationalreview.com/magazine/2018/10/01/originalism-a-logical-necessity/.

390   Michael Kruse, "The weekend at Yale that changed American politics," POLITICO, October/September, 2018, https://www.politico.com/magazine/story/2018/08/27/federalist-society-yale-history-conservative-law-court-219608.

391   Michael Kruse, "The weekend at Yale that changed American politics," POLITICO, October/September, 2018, https://www.politico.com/magazine/story/2018/08/27/federalist-society-yale-history-conservative-law-court-219608.

392   Michael Kruse, "The weekend at Yale that changed American politics," POLITICO, October/September, 2018, https://www.politico.com/magazine/story/2018/08/27/federalist-society-yale-history-conservative-law-court-219608.

393   "The Insidious Power of the Anti-Choice Movement," NARAL Pro-Choice America, accessed May 13, 2020, https://www.prochoiceamerica.org/report/insidious-power-anti-choice-movement/.

394   Michael Kruse, "The weekend at Yale that changed American politics," POLITICO, October/September, 2018, https://www.politico.com/magazine/story/2018/08/27/federalist-society-yale-history-conservative-law-court-219608.

395   Dylan Matthews and Byrd Pinkerton, "How charitable donations remade our courts," Vox, May 29, 2019, https://www.vox.com/future-perfect/2019/5/29/18629799/federalist-society-brett-kavanaugh-olin-foundation-jane-mayer.

396   Nan Aron, *Liberty And Justice For All: Public Interest Law In The 1980s And Beyond* (New York: Routledge, 2018)

397   Michael Kruse, "The weekend at Yale that changed American politics," POLITICO, October/September, 2018, https://www.politico.com/magazine/story/2018/08/27/federalist-society-yale-history-conservative-law-court-219608.

398   William J. Haun, "The Philosopher in Action: A Tribute to the Honorable Edwin Meese III," Engage 13, issue 1 (2012), Federalist Society, accessed December 4, 2017, https://fedsoc.org/commentary/publications/the-philosopher-in-action-a-tribute-to-the-honorable-edwin-meese-iii.

399   Bernard Weinraub, "Burger Retiring, Rehnquist Named Chief; Scalia, Appeals Judge, Chosen for Court," New York Times, June 18, 1986, https://www.nytimes.com/1986/06/18/us/burger-retiring-rehnquist-named-chief-scalia-appeals-judge-chosen-for-court.html.

400   John W. Dean, "The Rehnquist Choice: The Untold Story of the Nixon Appointment That Redefined the Supreme Court," Washington Post, November 19, 2001, https://www.washingtonpost.com/wp-srv/style/longterm/books/chap1/therehnquistchoice.htm.

401   "A Random Thought on the Segregation Cases," Memo from law clerk William H. Rehnquist to Justice Robert H. Jackson, written December 12, 1952, Government Publishing Office, accessed May 5, 2020, https://www.govinfo.gov/content/pkg/GPO-CHRG-REHNQUIST/pdf/GPO-CHRG-REHNQUIST-4-16-6.pdf

402   Linda Greenhouse, "William H. Rehnquist, Architect of Conservative Court, Dies at 80," New York Times, September 5, 2005, https://www.nytimes.com/2005/09/05/politics/politicsspecial1/william-h-rehnquist-architect-of-conservative.html.

403   Robert M. Andrews, "Former Prosecutor Says He Saw Rehnquist in Voter Confrontation Effort," Associated Press, August 1, 1986, https://apnews.com/499f-8c78d1235e4720aacaa008491969.

404   "Rehnquist Confirmed by Senate, 68␣26," New York Times, December 11, 1971, https://www.nytimes.com/1971/12/11/archives/rehnquist-confirmed-by-senate-6826-rehnquist-is-confirmed-as.html.

405   Bernard Weinraub, "Burger Retiring, Rehnquist Named Chief; Scalia, Appeals Judge, Chosen for Court," New York Times, June 18, 1986, https://www.nytimes.com/1986/06/18/us/burger-retiring-rehnquist-named-chief-scalia-appeals-judge-chosen-for-court.html.

406   "Supreme Court Nominations (Present-1789)," United States Senate, accessed May 13, 2020, https://www.senate.gov/legislative/nominations/SupremeCourtNominations1789present.htm.

407   Adam J. White, "Bork Won," Commentary Magazine, October 2012, https://www.commentarymagazine.com/articles/bork-won/.

408   Michael Kruse, "The weekend at Yale that changed American politics," POLITICO, October/September, 2018, https://www.politico.com/magazine/story/2018/08/27/federalist-society-yale-history-conservative-law-court-219608.

409   Julie Novkov, *The Supreme Court and the Presidency: Struggles for Supremacy* (Thousand Oaks, California: CQ Press, 2013), 106.

410   Linda Greenhouse, "Bork's Nomination Is Rejected, 58-42; Reagan Saddened," New York Times, October 27, 1987, https://www.nytimes.com/1987/10/24/politics/borks-nomination-is-rejected-5842-reagan-saddened.html.

411   Scott Bomboy, "How Justice Kennedy replaced Powell (and Bork) at the Court," Constitution Daily, June 27, 2018, https://constitutioncenter.org/blog/how-justice-kennedy-replaced-powell-and-bork-at-the-court.

412   Stuart Taylor Jr., "Of Bork and Tactics," New York Times, October 21, 1987, https://www.nytimes.com/1987/10/21/us/of-bork-and-tactics.html.

413   Mari Cohen, "Hillel Partners with Right-Wing Christian Law Firm," Jewish Currents, January 28, 2020, https://jewishcurrents.org/hillel-partners-with-right-wing-christian-law-firm/.

414   Mari Cohen, "Hillel Partners with Right-Wing Christian Law Firm," Jewish Currents, January 28, 2020, https://jewishcurrents.org/hillel-partners-with-right-wing-christian-law-firm/.

415   "Kenya's draft constitution under attack from religious NGO," BBC World Service, May 4, 2012, https://www.bbc.co.uk/worldservice/africa/2010/05/100504_kenya_ngo.shtml.

416   Kapya Kaoma, "Major Christian right actors seek to criminalize homosexuality in Africa," Political Research Associates, November 5, 2012, Internet Archive, accessed May 13, 2020, https://web.archive.org/web/20140223142117/https://www.politicalresearch.org/major-christian-right-actors-seek-to-criminalize-homosexuality-in-africa/#.

417   Chelsea Schilling, "WorldNetDaily - Stopping Ground Zero Mosque: Firefighter in 9-11 Attacks Fight to Preserve 'Landmark,'" American Center for Law and Justice, accessed May 13, 2020, https://aclj.org/ground-zero-mosque/worldnetdaily---stopping-ground-zero-mosque-firefighter-in-9-11-attacks-fight-to-preserve-landmark-.

418   "About Us," Alliance Defending Freedom, accessed June 1, 2020, https://www.adflegal.org/about-us.

419   "Alliance Defending Freedom (pka Alliance Defense Fund, Inc.)," MinistryWatch, accessed 5/13/20, https://briinstitute.com/mw/ministry.php?ein=541660459.

420   Brennan Suen, "ADF and friends: Hate group Alliance Defending Freedom is at the center of an anti-LGBTQ industry," Media Matters, September 28, 2017, https://www.mediamatters.org/alliance-defending-freedom/adf-and-friends-hate-group-alliance-defending-freedom-center-anti-lgbtq.

421   Amelia Thomson-DeVeaux, "God's Rottweilers," POLITICO, October 5, 2014, https://www.politico.com/magazine/story/2014/10/becket-fund-religious-conservatives-111468?o=0.

422   "FOX News - Glenn Beck - Constitution Under Attack: Prop 8 Under Court Review," American Center for Law and Justice, accessed May 14, 2020, https://aclj.org/traditional-marriage/fox-news---glenn-beck---constitution-under-attack-prop-8-under-court-review-.

423   "Alliance Defending Freedom," Southern Poverty Law Center, accessed May 14, 2020, https://www.splcenter.org/fighting-hate/extremist-files/group/alliance-defending-freedom.

424   Brief for Petitioners, David A. Cortman, Rory T. Gray, Nicolle H. Martin, Kristen K. Waggoner, Jeremy D. Tedesco, James A. Campbell, Jonathan A. Scruggs, Masterpiece Cakeshop, Ltd.; And Jack C. Phillips V. Colorado Civil Rights Commission; Charlie Craig; And David Mullins, No. 16-111, Supreme Court of the United States, SCOTUSblog, September 16, 2017, https://www.scotusblog.com/wp-content/uploads/2017/09/16-111-ts.pdf.

425   "Masterpiece Cakeshop, Ltd. v. Colorado Civil Rights Commission," SCO-TUSblog, accessed May 14, 2020, https://www.scotusblog.com/case-files/cases/masterpiece-cakeshop-ltd-v-colorado-civil-rights-commn/.

426   Jaime Fuller, "Here's what you need to know about the Hobby Lobby case," March 24, 2014, https://www.washingtonpost.com/news/the-fix/wp/2014/03/24/heres-what-you-need-to-know-about-the-hobby-lobby-case/.

427   Julie Beck, "What's So Controversial About the Contraceptives in Hobby Lobby," June 30, 2014, https://www.theatlantic.com/health/archive/2014/06/whats-so-controversial-about-the-contraceptives-in-the-hobby-lobby-case/373709/.

428   "Abortifacients: An Overview," Life Issues Institute, September 29, 2014, https://www.lifeissues.org/2014/09/abortifacients-overview/.

429   Joerg Dreweke, "Contraception Is Not Abortion: The Strategic Campaign of Antiabortion Groups to Persuade the Public Otherwise," December 9, 2014, https://www.guttmacher.org/gpr/2014/12/contraception-not-abortion-strategic-campaign-antiabortion-groups-persuade-public.

430   "Burwell v. Hobby Lobby Stores," Oyez, accessed May 14, 2020, https://www.oyez.org/cases/2013/13-354.

431   Jeffrey Toobin, "The Conservative Pipeline to the Supreme Court," New Yorker, April 10, 2017, https://www.newyorker.com/magazine/2017/04/17/the-conservative-pipeline-to-the-supreme-court.

432   "About," Americans United for Life, accessed May 14, 2020, https://aul.org/about/.

433   "About," Americans United for Life, accessed May 14, 2020, https://aul.org/about/.

434   Denise M. Burke, "Contemporary Threats to Healthcare Freedom of Conscience," Americans United for Life, Internet Archive, accessed May 13, 2020, https://web.archive.org/web/20080724171934/http://www.aul.org/ROC_Threats.

435   "Defending the Hyde Amendment: 30th Anniversary of Harris v. McRae," June 21, 2010, Americans United for Life, https://aul.org/2010/06/21/defending-the-hyde-amendment-30th-anniversary-of-harris-v-mcrae/.

436   "Harris v. McRae," Oyez, accessed May 14, 2020, https://www.oyez.org/cases/1979/79-1268.

437   "Harris v. McRae," Oyez, accessed May 14, 2020, https://www.oyez.org/cases/1979/79-1268.

438   Harris v. McRae, 448 U.S. 297 (1980), Legal Information Institute, accessed May 14, 2020, https://www.law.cornell.edu/supremecourt/text/448/297#writing-USSC_CR_0448_0297_ZO.

439   Harris v. McRae, 448 U.S. 297 (1980), Legal Information Institute, accessed May 14, 2020, https://www.law.cornell.edu/supremecourt/text/448/297#writing-USSC_CR_0448_0297_ZO.

440   "Planned Parenthood of Southeastern Pennsylvania v. Casey." Oyez. Accessed June 1, 2020. https://www.oyez.org/cases/1991/91-744.

441   Susan Roberts, "Surprised by all these abortion bans? Meet Americans United for Life — the most significant antiabortion group you've never heard of," Washington Post, May 31, 2019, https://www.washingtonpost.com/politics/2019/05/31/surprised-by-all-these-abortion-bans-meet-americans-united-life-most-significant-pro-life-group-youve-never-heard/.

442   Kate Sheppard, "Wham, Bam, Sonogram! Meet the Ladies Setting the New

Pro-Life Agenda," Mother Jones, September/October 2012, https://www.mother-jones.com/politics/2012/08/americans-united-for-life-anti-abortion-transvagi-nal-ultrasound/.

443   Molly Redden, "Arkansas Will Force Doctors to Tell Women Abortions Can Be 'Reversed,'" Mother Jones, April 7, 2015, https://www.motherjones.com/kevin-drum/2015/04/new-law-forces-arkansas-doctors-push-unproven-abor-tion-reversal-treatment/.

444   Sandhya Somashekhar, "In Arizona, Arkansas, women must be told that abortion can be 'reversed,'" The Washington Post, April 7, 2015, https://www.wash-ingtonpost.com/news/post-nation/wp/2015/04/07/arizona-arkansas-tell-wom-en-drug-induced-abortion-can-be-reversed/.

445   Mara Gordon, "Study Of Progesterone To Reverse Medication Abortion : Shots - Health News," NPR, December 5, 2019, https://www.npr.org/sections/health-shots/2019/12/05/785262221/safety-problems-lead-to-early-end-for-study-of-abortion-pill-reversal.

446   Jack Shafer, "Fox News 1.0," Slate, June 5, 2008, https://slate.com/news-and-politics/2008/06/revisiting-tvn-roger-ailes-first-stab-at-running-a-tv-news-operation.html.

447   Jerry Schwartz, "400 Are Arrested in Atlanta Abortion Protests," New York Times, October 5, 1988, https://www.nytimes.com/1988/10/05/us/400-are-arrest-ed-in-atlanta-abortion-protests.html.

448   David Treadwell, "250 Arrested in Anti-Abortion 'Siege of Atlanta,'" Los Angeles Times, October 5, 1988, https://www.latimes.com/archives/la-xpm-1988-10-05-mn-2866-story.html.

449   Jerry Schwartz, "400 Are Arrested in Atlanta Abortion Protests," New York Times, October 5, 1988, https://www.nytimes.com/1988/10/05/us/400-are-arrest-ed-in-atlanta-abortion-protests.html.

450   "Anti-Abortion Extremists," National Abortion Federation, accessed May 14, 2020, https://prochoice.org/education-and-advocacy/violence/anti-abor-tion-extremists/.

451   "Anti-Abortion Extremists," National Abortion Federation, accessed May 14, 2020, https://prochoice.org/education-and-advocacy/violence/anti-abortion-ex-tremists/.

452   Eric Harrison, "25,000 Abortion Opponents Cap Wichita Protests : Ral-ly: Speakers call on residents to continue their opposition. Operation Rescue is leaving the city," Los Angeles Times, August 26, 1991, https://www.latimes.com/archives/la-xpm-1991-08-26-mn-950-story.html.

453   Isabel Wilkerson, "Drive Against Abortion Finds a Symbol: Wichita," https://www.nytimes.com/1991/08/04/us/drive-against-abortion-finds-a-symbol-wichita.html.

454   Mark Zhang, "George Richard Tiller (1941-2009)," The Embryo Project Encyclopedia, July 16, 2012, https://embryo.asu.edu/pages/george-richard-til-ler-1941-2009.

455   Ed Pinkington, "For years anti-abortionists tried to stop Doctor Tiller. Finally a bullet did," The Guardian, June 1, 2009, https://www.theguardian.com/world/2009/jun/01/us-doctor-tiller-killing-abortions.

456   Mary Mapes, "No Mercy," The Huffington Post, May 25, 2011, https://www.huffpost.com/entry/no-mercy_b_209529.

457   Stephanie Simon, "Protesters Who Push the Limits," Los Angeles Times, February 14, 2004, https://www.latimes.com/archives/la-xpm-2004-feb-17-na-abortion17-story.html.

458   Mark Zhang, "George Richard Tiller (1941-2009)," The Embryo Project

Encyclopedia, July 16, 2012, https://embryo.asu.edu/pages/george-richard-tiller-1941-2009.

459   Laura Bauer and Judy L. Thomas, "Operation Rescue adviser helped Tiller suspect track doctor's court dates," McClatchy DC, https://www.mcclatchydc.com/news/nation-world/national/article24540694.html.

460   Dahlia Lithwick, "The Murderer Who Started a Movement," October 31, 2017, https://slate.com/news-and-politics/2017/10/michael-frederick-griffin-killed-an-abortion-doctor-he-could-soon-be-a-free-man.html.

461   Mike Littwin, "Are one's beliefs ever justification for taking a life?" Baltimore Sun, February 27, 1994, https://www.baltimoresun.com/news/bs-xpm-1994-02-27-1994058116-story.html.

462   Liam Zack, "A Brief History of Deadly Attacks on Abortion Providers," New York Times, November 29, 2015, https://www.nytimes.com/interactive/2015/11/29/us/30abortion-clinic-violence.html

463   Faludi, Susan. Backlash: The undeclared war against American women. Broadway Books, 2006.

464   Faludi, Susan. Backlash: The undeclared war against American women. Broadway Books, 2006.

465   Ron Elving, "Anita Hill's Challenge To Clarence Thomas: A Tale Of 2 Lives And 3 Elections," NPR, September 20, 2018, https://www.npr.org/2018/09/20/649721806/anita-hills-challenge-to-clarence-thomas-a-tale-of-2-lives-and-3-elections.

466   Ron Elving, "Anita Hill's Challenge To Clarence Thomas: A Tale Of 2 Lives And 3 Elections," NPR, September 20, 2018, https://www.npr.org/2018/09/20/649721806/anita-hills-challenge-to-clarence-thomas-a-tale-of-2-lives-and-3-elections.

467   Ron Elving, "Anita Hill's Challenge To Clarence Thomas: A Tale Of 2 Lives And 3 Elections," NPR, September 20, 2018, https://www.npr.org/2018/09/20/649721806/anita-hills-challenge-to-clarence-thomas-a-tale-of-2-lives-and-3-elections.

468   Ron Elving, "Anita Hill's Challenge To Clarence Thomas: A Tale Of 2 Lives And 3 Elections," NPR, September 20, 2018, https://www.npr.org/2018/09/20/649721806/anita-hills-challenge-to-clarence-thomas-a-tale-of-2-lives-and-3-elections.

469   Paul Blumenthal, "The Man Who Smeared Anita Hill Previews What Christine Blasey Ford Will Face in Senate," Huffington Post, September 26, 2018, https://www.huffpost.com/entry/brett-kavanaugh-christine-blasey-ford-hearing_n_5baab3b2e4b0f143d10e4873.

470   Jane Meyer, "What Joe Biden Hasn't Owned Up To About Anita Hill," April 27, 2019, New Yorker, https://www.newyorker.com/news/news-desk/what-joe-biden-hasnt-owned-up-to-about-anita-hill.

471   Arch Parsons, "Senate panel deadlocks on Thomas, 7-7 No recommendation made as nomination goes to full Senate," Baltimore Sun, September 28, 1991, https://www.baltimoresun.com/news/bs-xpm-1991-09-28-1991271006-story.html.

472   Helen Dewar, "SENATE CONFIRMS THOMAS BY 52 TO 48 TO SUCCEED MARSHALL ON SUPREME COURT," Washington Post, October 16, 1991, https://www.washingtonpost.com/archive/politics/1991/10/16/senate-confirms-thomas-by-52-to-48-to-succeed-marshall-on-supreme-court/ddbeeaba-bd5b-464a-b0bd-600ab2d0dfd7/.

473   Amanda Spake, "WOMEN CAN BE POWER BROKERS, TOO," Washington Post, June 5, 1988, https://www.washingtonpost.com/archive/lifestyle/magazine/1988/06/05/women-can-be-power-brokers-too/15916940-dbd9-459a-86a7-dfc94b41f469/.

474   "Ex-Christian Coalition Head Ralph Reed Resurfaces In Iowa," Americans United for the Separation of Church and State, May 2010, https://www.au.org/church-state/may-2010-church-state/people-events/ex-christian-coali-

tion-head-ralph-reed-resurfaces.

475   Dylan Matthews, "Paleoconservatism, the movement that explains Donald Trump, explained," Vox, May 6, 2016, https://www.vox.com/2016/5/6/11592604/donald-trump-paleoconservative-buchanan.

476   Howard Kurtz, "PAT BUCHANAN THE JEWISH QUESTION," Washington Post, September 20, 1990, https://www.washingtonpost.com/archive/lifestyle/1990/09/20/pat-buchanan-the-jewish-question/bfc8e956-316d-4abb-b33b-97aace0b80d0/.

477   Jim Dwyer, "The True Story of How a City in Fear Brutalized the Central Park Five," New York Times, May 30, 2019, https://www.nytimes.com/2019/05/30/arts/television/when-they-see-us-real-story.html.

478   Jack Nelson, "Bush Wins Georgia, but Buchanan Runs at 38% : Politics: The President also gets a victory in the Maryland primary and is running well in Colorado," Los Angeles Times, March 4, 1992, https://www.latimes.com/archives/la-xpm-1992-03-04-mn-3008-story.html.

479   Adam Nagourney, "From the Fringe in 1992, Patrick J. Buchanan's Words Now Seem Mainstream," The New York Times, August 30, 2012, https://www.nytimes.com/2012/08/30/us/politics/from-the-fringe-in-1992-patrick-j-buchanans-words-now-seem-mainstream.html.

480   Adam Nagourney, "From the Fringe in 1992, Patrick J. Buchanan's Words Now Seem Mainstream," The New York Times, August 30, 2012, https://www.nytimes.com/2012/08/30/us/politics/from-the-fringe-in-1992-patrick-j-buchanans-words-now-seem-mainstream.html.

481   Martin Pengelly, "'Laughter is the great unifier' – behind the incredible life of Molly Ivins," The Guardian, March 18, 2019, https://www.theguardian.com/film/2019/mar/18/molly-ivins-raise-hell-documentary.

482   Adam Nagourney, "From the Fringe in 1992, Patrick J. Buchanan's Words Now Seem Mainstream," The New York Times, August 30, 2012, https://www.nytimes.com/2012/08/30/us/politics/from-the-fringe-in-1992-patrick-j-buchanans-words-now-seem-mainstream.html.

483   Buckley Jr, William F. *Happy days were here again: reflections of a libertarian journalist.* Basic Books, 2008.

484   Susan Faludi, *Backlash: The undeclared war against American women*, Broadway Books, 2006.

485   Jessie Hellman, "SBA List seizing its moment," The Hill, June 20, 2017, https://thehill.com/business-a-lobbying/lobbyist-profiles/338501-sba-list-seizing-its-moment.

486   Valerie Richardson, "Feminist launches PAC for pro-lifers," Washington Times, November 7, 1992, Massachusetts Institute for Technology, http://web.mit.edu/~mkgray/afs/bar/afs/net/user/tytso/usenet/americast/twt/news/596.

487   Kelefa Sanneh, "The Intensity Gap," New Yorker, October 20, 2014, https://www.newyorker.com/magazine/2014/10/27/intensity-gap.

488   "The Insidious Power of the Anti-Choice Movement," NARAL Pro-Choice America, accessed May 13, 2020, https://www.prochoiceamerica.org/report/insidious-power-anti-choice-movement/.

489   Kate Sheppard, "Susan B. Anthony List Founder: Republicans Hijacked My PAC!," Mother Jones, February 22, 2012. https://www.motherjones.com/politics/2012/02/susan-b-anthony-list-sharp-right-turn-rachel-macnair/.

490   Kate Sheppard, "Susan B. Anthony List Founder: Republicans Hijacked My PAC!," Mother Jones, February 22, 2012. https://www.motherjones.com/politics/2012/02/susan-b-anthony-list-sharp-right-turn-rachel-macnair/.

491   Mason, Lilliana. Uncivil agreement: How politics became our identity. University of Chicago Press, 2018.

492   "Portrait of the Electorate: Table of Detailed Results," New York Times, November 6, 2010, https://archive.nytimes.com/www.nytimes.com/interactive/2010/11/07/weekinreview/20101107-detailed-exitpolls.html?_r=0.

493   "National Exit Polls Table," Election Results 2008, New York Times, https://www.nytimes.com/elections/2008/results/president/national-exit-polls.html.

494   Sarah Jacobs, "Kellyanne Conway gets a high White House salary, but she made a ton of money before joining Trump — here's how she made and spends her $39 million fortune," Business Insider, October 19, 2017. https://www.businessinsider.com/how-kellyanne-conway-became-rich-2017-7.

495   Ryan Lizza, "Kellyanne Conway's Political Machinations," New Yorker, October 8, 2016, https://www.newyorker.com/magazine/2016/10/17/kellyanne-conways-political-machinations.

496   Brittany Andres, "Frank Luntz's Tarnished Legacy," CBS News, January 19, 2007, https://www.cbsnews.com/news/frank-luntzs-tarnished-legacy/.

497   Steven Shepard, "Kellyanne Conway's polling firm sold to GOP PR shop," POLITICO, September 28, 2017, https://www.politico.com/story/2017/09/28/kellyanne-conway-polling-firm-sold-243256.

498   Ryan Lizza, "Kellyanne Conway's Political Machinations," New Yorker, October 8, 2016, https://www.newyorker.com/magazine/2016/10/17/kellyanne-conways-political-machinations.

499   Ed Kilgore, "Meet Kellyanne Conway, Trump's New Campaign Manager. She Specializes in Helping GOP Men Sound Less Piggish," Intelligencer, August 17, 2016, http://nymag.com/intelligencer/2016/08/meet-kellyanne-conway-trumps-new-campaign-manager.html.

500   Sarah Jacobs, "Kellyanne Conway gets a high White House salary, but she made a ton of money before joining Trump — here's how she made and spends her $39 million fortune," Business Insider, October 19, 2017. https://www.businessinsider.com/how-kellyanne-conway-became-rich-2017-7.

501   Paul Richter, "Clinton Picks Moderate Judge Breyer for Supreme Court Spot : Judiciary: President says the scholarly nominee has 'proven that he can build an effective consensus.' The federal jurist has wide bipartisan support in the Senate," Los Angeles Times, May 14, 1994, https://www.latimes.com/archives/la-xpm-1994-05-14-mn-57615-story.html.

502   "President Clinton impeached," History Channel, accessed June 9, 2020, https://www.history.com/this-day-in-history/president-clinton-impeached.

503   Randall Mikkelsen, "Clinton foe Gingrich admits impeachment-era affair," Reuters, March 9, 2007, https://www.reuters.com/article/us-usa-politics-gingrich/clinton-foe-gingrich-admits-impeachment-era-affair-idUSN0943442620070309.

504   Alison Mitchell and Eric Schmitt, "The 1998 Elections: Congress -- The Overview; G.O.P. In Scramble Over Blame for Poor Showing At The Polls," New York Times, November 5, 1998, https://www.nytimes.com/1998/11/05/us/1998-elections-congress-overview-gop-scramble-over-blame-for-poor-showing-polls.html.

505   Guy Gugliotta and Juliet Eilperin, "Gingrich Steps Down in Face of Rebellion," Washington Post, November 7, 1998, https://www.washingtonpost.com/wp-srv/politics/govt/leadership/stories/gingrich110798.htm.

506   Russell Goldman, "Laura Bush Reveals How George W. Stopped Drinking," ABC News, May 4, 2010, https://abcnews.go.com/Politics/laura-bush-reveals-george-stopped-drinking/story?id=10552148.

507   Michael Holmes, "Bush Wasn't Always a Front-Runner," Washington Post,

October 17, 1999, https://www.washingtonpost.com/wp-srv/aponline/19991017/ap-online114059_000.htm.

508   David Corn, "Bush's Abortion Flip-Flop?," *The Nation*, June 15, 2000, https://www.thenation.com/article/archive/bushs-abortion-flip-flop/.

509   David Corn, "Bush's Abortion Flip-Flop?," *The Nation*, June 15, 2000, https://www.thenation.com/article/archive/bushs-abortion-flip-flop/.

510   Abby Livingston, "Bus daughter headlines Planned Parenthood fundraiser," *Texas Tribune*, February 24, 2017, https://www.texastribune.org/2017/02/24/barbara-pierce-bush-headline-planned-p/.

511   David Corn, "Bush's Abortion Flip-Flop?," *The Nation*, June 15, 2000, https://www.thenation.com/article/archive/bushs-abortion-flip-flop/.

512   Tribune Staff, "CONTROVERSIAL ROBERTSON IS BACK," *Chicago Tribune*, February 27, 2000, https://www.dailypress.com/news/dp-xpm-20000227-2000-02-27-0002270102-story.html.

513   Richard L. Berke, "For Lamar Alexander, the End of the Line," *New York Times*, August 17, 1999, https://archive.nytimes.com/www.nytimes.com/library/politics/camp/081799wh-gop-alexander.html.

514   Chris Korzen, "McCain Attacked Bush in 2000 Over Anti-Catholic Endorsement," *HuffPost*, March 5, 2008, https://huffpost.com/entry/mccain-attacked-bush-in-2_b_90158.

515   Shailagh Murray and Perry Bacon Jr., "Key Constituency Is at Play At Candidates' Faith Forum," *Washington Post*, August 17, 2008, https://www.washingtonpost.com/wp-dyn/content/article/2008/08/16/AR2008081602322_pf.html.

516   "2000 Presidential Primary Election Results," Federal Election Commission, accessed May 12, 2020, https://transition.fec.gov/pubrec/fe2000/2000presprim.htm.

517   Christopher Klein, "Here's How Third-Party Candidates Have Changed Elections," *History Channel*, May 31, 2018, https://www.history.com/news/third-party-candidates-election-influence-facts.

518   Michael E. Miller, "'It's insanity!': How the 'Brooks Brothers Riot' killed the 2000 recount in Miami," Washington Post, November 15, 2018, https://www.washingtonpost.com/history/2018/11/15/its-insanity-how-brooks-brothers-riot-killed-recount-miami/.

519   "Bush v. Gore." Oyez. accessed May 12, 2020. https://www.oyez.org/cases/2000/00-949

520   Richard L. Hasen, "Election Hangover: The real legacy of Bush v. Gore," Slate, December 3, 2010, https://slate.com/news-and-politics/2010/12/the-real-legacy-of-bush-v-gore.html.

521   "Anti-Abortion Extremists," *National Abortion Federation*, accessed May 12, 2020, https://prochoice.org/education-and-advocacy/violence/anti-abortion-extremists/.

522
Julie Rovner, "'Partial-Birth Abortion': Separating Fact From Spin," NPR, February 21, 2006, https://www.npr.org/2006/02/21/5168163/partial-birth-abortion-separating-fact-from-spin.

523   Deborah Sontag, "Doctors Say It's Just One Way," New York Times, March 21, 1997.

524   Nick Baumann, "The Lobbyist File: Doug Johnson," *Mother Jones*, July/August 2011, https://www.motherjones.com/politics/2011/07/doug-johnson-national-right-to-life/.

525   Julie Rovner, "'Partial-Birth Abortion': Separating Fact From Spin," *National Public Radio*, February 21, 2006, https://www.npr.org/2006/02/21/5168163/

partial-birth-abortion-separating-fact-from-spin.

526   Julie Rovner, "'Partial-Birth Abortion': Separating Fact From Spin," *National Public Radio*, February 21, 2006, https://www.npr.org/2006/02/21/5168163/partial-birth-abortion-separating-fact-from-spin.

527   Alissa Rubin, "Partial Truths," The New Republic, March 4, 1996, via Nexis

528   Jennifer Gunter, "Term And Partial Birth Abortions: The Mythical Arch-Nemeses Of The Anti-Choice Movement," *HuffPost*, October 24, 2016, https://www.huffpost.com/entry/term-and-partial-birth-abortions-the-mythical-arch-nemeses-of-the-anti-choice-movement_b_580d4427e4b02444efa3f33a.

529   "Second-Trimester Abortion," ACOG Clinical Practice Bulletin 135, The American College of Obstetrics and Gynecology, June 2013, https://www.acog.org/clinical/clinical-guidance/practice-bulletin/articles/2013/06/second-trimester-abortion.

530   "Second-Trimester Abortion," ACOG Clinical Practice Bulletin 135, The American College of Obstetrics and Gynecology, June 2013, https://www.acog.org/clinical/clinical-guidance/practice-bulletin/articles/2013/06/second-trimester-abortion.

531   Mary Ziegler, "The Disability Politics of Abortion," Utah Law Review, Volume 2017, Number 3, Article 4, June 2017, https://dc.law.utah.edu/cgi/viewcontent.cgi?article=1054&context=ulr.

532   "Abortions Later in Pregnancy," Kaiser Family Foundation, December 5, 2019, https://www.kff.org/womens-health-policy/fact-sheet/abortions-later-in-pregnancy/.

533   Helen Dewar, "Late-Term Abortion Ban Passes Senate," *The Washington Post*, October 22, 1999, https://www.washingtonpost.com/wp-srv/politics/daily/oct99/senate22.htm.

534   "ABORTION BANS: IN THE STATES," ACLU, accessed June 9, 2020, https://www.aclu.org/other/abortion-bans-states.

535   Frank Bruni, "Transition In Washington: The Abortion Issue; Laura Bush Says Roe v. Wade Should Not Be Overturned," *New York Times*, January 19, 2001, https://www.nytimes.com/2001/01/19/us/transition-washingtion-abortion-issue-laura-bush-says-roe-v-wade-should-not-be.html.

536   George W. Bush, "President Bush Signs Partial Birth Abortion Ban Act of 2003," The White House (news release), November 5, 2003, https://georgewbush-whitehouse.archives.gov/news/releases/2003/11/20031105-1.html.

537   Richard W. Stevenson, "Bush Signs Ban On a Procedure For Abortions," *New York Times*, November 6, 2003, https://www.nytimes.com/2003/11/06/us/bush-signs-ban-on-a-procedure-for-abortions.html.

538   Richard W. Stevenson, "Bush Signs Ban On a Procedure For Abortions," *New York Times*, November 6, 2003, https://www.nytimes.com/2003/11/06/us/bush-signs-ban-on-a-procedure-for-abortions.html.

539   *Planned Parenthood Federation of America v. Ashcroft*, 320 F. Supp. 2d 957 (N.D. Cal. 2004), https://www.hortyspringer.com/HSM/Data/Cases/fulltext4/PlannedParenthood_v_Ashcroft_Jun2004.pdf.

540   *National Abortion Federation v. Ashcroft*, 330 F. Supp. 2d 436 (S.D.N.Y. 2004), https://www.courtlistener.com/opinion/2314185/national-abortion-federation-v-ashcroft/.

541   *Carhart v. Ashcroft*, 287 F. Supp. 2d 1015 (D. Neb. 2003), https://law.justia.com/cases/federal/district-courts/FSupp2/287/1015/2476006/.

542   "Carhart v. Margie Riley, et al., Amici on Behalf of Appellee," Find Law, accessed May 13, 2020, https://caselaw.findlaw.com/us-8th-circuit/1085636.html.

543   "Gonzales v. Carhart," Oyez, accessed May 12, 2020, https://www.oyez.org/

cases/2006/05-380.

544   David Montgomery, "Conquerors of the Courts," *Washington Post Magazine*, January, 2, 2019, https://www.washingtonpost.com/news/magazine/wp/2019/01/02/feature/conquerors-of-the-courts/.

545   Tamar Ziff, "JUDICIAL CRISIS NETWORK: THE CONSERVATIVE ORGANIZATION SHAPING THE SUPREME COURT," Citizens for Responsibility and Ethics in Washington, July 5, 2017, https://www.citizensforethics.org/judicial-crisis-network-conservative-organization-shaping-supreme-court/.

546   "Gonzales v. Carhart," Oyez, accessed May 12, 2020, https://www.oyez.org/cases/2006/05-380.

547   Karen Tumulty and Matthew Cooper, "Does Bush Owe the Religious Right?," *TIME*, February 7, 2005, http://content.time.com/time/specials/packages/article/0,28804,1993235_1993249_1993321,00.html.

548   Howard Kurtz, "Clintons Long Under Siege By Conservative Detractors," *The Washington Post*, January 28, 1998, https://www.washingtonpost.com/wp-srv/politics/special/clinton/stories/right012898.htm.

549   "Falwell apologizes to gays, feminists, lesbians," CNN, September 14, 2001, https://web.archive.org/web/20130401182609/http://archives.cnn.com/2001/US/09/14/Falwell.apology/.

550   David Grann, "Robespierre Of The Right," *The New Republic*, October 27, 1997, https://newrepublic.com/article/61338/robespierre-the-right.

551   Neil J. Young, "How George H.W. Bush enabled the rise of the religious right," *Washington Post*, December 5, 2018, https://www.washingtonpost.com/outlook/2018/12/05/how-george-hw-bush-enabled-rise-religious-right/.

552   Randall Blamer, *Thy Kingdom Come: How the Religious Right Distorts Faith and Threatens America*, (New York: Basic Books, 2007), page 13.

553   Richard Brookhiser, "Gravedigger of the Revolution," *The Atlantic*, October 1992, https://www.theatlantic.com/magazine/archive/1992/10/gravedigger-of-the-revolution/376353/.

554   David Grann, "Robespierre of the Right," New Republic, October 27, 1997, https://web.archive.org/web/19991011170703/http://magazines.enews.com/magazines/tnr/archive/10/102797/grann102797.html.

555   Eleanor Clift, "The Woman In The Middle," Newsweek, May 12, 1996, https://www.newsweek.com/woman-middle-178062.

556   David Grann, "Robespierre of the Right," New Republic, October 27, 1997, https://web.archive.org/web/19991011170703/http://magazines.enews.com/magazines/tnr/archive/10/102797/grann102797.html.

557   Paul Weyrich, interview by Peter Boyer, *Frontline: The Long March of Newt Gingrich, Public Broadcasting Service*, Accessed May 12, 2020, https://www.pbs.org/wgbh/pages/frontline/newt/newtintwshtml/weyrich2.html.

558   "Ralph Reed | May 15, 1995", *TIME Magazine*, May 15, 1995, http://content.time.com/time/covers/0,16641,19950515,00.html.

559   Jeffrey H. Birnbaum, "THE GOSPEL ACCORDING TO RALPH REED," *TIME Magazine*, May 15, 1995, http://content.time.com/time/magazine/article/0,9171,982929,00.html.

560   Thomas B. Edsall, "Newt Gingrich and the Future of the Right," Campaign Stops (blog), New York Times, January 29, 2012, https://campaignstops.blogs.nytimes.com/2012/01/29/newt-gingrich-and-the-future-of-the-right/.

561   Thomas B. Edsall, "Newt Gingrich and the Future of the Right," Campaign Stops (blog), New York Times, January 29, 2012, https://campaignstops.blogs.nytimes.com/2012/01/29/newt-gingrich-and-the-future-of-the-right/.

562   Katharine Q. Seelye, "Christian Coalition's Reed Quits for New Political Role," *The New York Times*, April 24, 1997, https://www.nytimes.com/1997/04/24/us/christian-coalition-s-reed-quits-for-new-political-role.html.

563   Peter Applebome, "Jerry Falwell, Moral Majority Founder, Dies at 73," *The New York Times*, May 16, 2007, https://www.nytimes.com/2007/05/16/obituaries/16falwell.html.

564   Bruce Weber, "Paul Weyrich, 66, a Conservative Strategist, Dies," *The New York Times*, Dec. 18, 2008, https://www.nytimes.com/2008/12/19/us/politics/19weyrich.html

565   "Data Points: Gender Gap in the 2008 Election," *U.S. News & World Report*, November 6, 2008, https://www.usnews.com/opinion/articles/2008/11/06/data-points-gender-gap-in-the-2008-election.

566   "Election Results 2008," *New York Times*, December 9, 2008, https://www.nytimes.com/elections/2008/results/president/votes.html.

567   Thomas Edsall, "A Permanent Democratic Majority?," *Real Clear Politics*, April 15, 2009, https://www.realclearpolitics.com/articles/2009/04/15/a_permanent_democratic_majority_48926.html.

568   Alex Koppelman, "A permanent Democratic majority?," *Salon*, November 13, 2008, https://www.salon.com/2008/11/13/new_mexico_6/.

569   Kyle Mantyla, "Conservative Action Project: A New Name For the Same Old Right-Wing Agenda," *Right Wing Watch*, February 1, 2010, https://www.rightwingwatch.org/post/conservative-action-project-a-new-name-for-the-same-old-right-wing-agenda/.

570   Amanda Terkel, "Why Didn't McCain Call Ralph Reed To Testify During Abramoff Investigation," *ThinkProgress*, August 15, 2008, https://thinkprogress.org/why-didnt-mccain-call-ralph-reed-to-testify-during-abramoff-investigation-d8618a54a5a/.

571   Erik Eckholm, "A Political Revival for Ralph Reed," *The New York Times*, May 31, 2011, https://www.nytimes.com/2011/06/01/us/politics/01reed.html

572   Jerry Markon, "New media help conservatives get their anti-Obama message out," Washington Post, February 1, 2010, http://www.washingtonpost.com/wp-dyn/content/article/2010/01/31/AR2010013102860.html?sid=ST2010020101258.

573   Anne Nelson, *Shadow Network: Media, Money, and the Secret Hub of the Radical Right* (Bloomsbury Publishing, 2019) https://books.google.com/books?id=al2SDwAAQBAJ&pg=PT167&lpg=PT167&dq=%22meese%22+%22Conway%22+%22conservative+action+project%22&source=bl&ots=5bLZiSiOSV&sig=ACfU3U1O7G8JDxEM2PsC0VlfuqQV7fT4Lg&hl=en&sa=X&ved=2ahUKEwj-v7TcjPXpAhVyVTABHb95AtgQ6AEwAXoECAoQAQ#v=onepage&q&f=false

574   Dan Diamond and Andrew Restuccia, "How Kellyanne Conway influenced a new Trump rule cheered by religious conservatives," Politico, May 9, 2019, https://www.politico.com/story/2019/05/09/kellyanne-conway-anti-abortion-doctors-1312316.

575   Louis Jacobson, "Obama says Heritage Foundation is source of health exchange idea," *Politifact*, April 1, 2010, https://www.politifact.com/factchecks/2010/apr/01/barack-obama/obama-says-heritage-foundation-source-health-excha/.

576   Alina Salganicoff, Laurie Sobel, and Amrutha Ramaswamy, "The Hyde Amendment and Coverage for Abortion Services," Kaiser Family Foundation, January 24, 2020, https://www.kff.org/womens-health-policy/issue-brief/the-hyde-amendment-and-coverage-for-abortion-services/.

577   Michelle Ye Hee Lee, "Does Obamacare provide federal subsidies for elective abortions?," Washington Post, January 26, 2015, https://www.washingtonpost.com/news/fact-checker/wp/2015/01/26/does-obamacare-provide-federal-subsi-

dies-for-elective-abortions/.

578   "Pro-lifers praise, pro-choicers condemn Stupak amendment," *The Hill*, November 8, 2009, https://thehill.com/blogs/blog-briefing-room/news/66891-pro-lifers-praise-pro-choicers-condemn-stupak-amendment.

579   "Attacks on Private Insurance Coverage of Abortion Care," NARAL Pro-Choice America, Accessed May 12, 2020, https://www.prochoiceamerica.org/wp-content/uploads/2017/01/3.-Attacks-on-Private-Insurance-Coverage-of-Abortion.pdf.

580   Alex Wayne, "House Adopts Stupak Amendment on Abortion," *Commonwealth Fund*, November 7, 2009, https://www.commonwealthfund.org/publications/newsletter-article/house-adopts-stupak-amendment-abortion.

581   "Pro-lifers praise, pro-choicers condemn Stupak amendment," *The Hill*, November 8, 2009, https://thehill.com/blogs/blog-briefing-room/news/66891-pro-lifers-praise-pro-choicers-condemn-stupak-amendment.

582   David G. Taylor, "Insurance companies required to cover preventive care," *Politifact*, September 1, 2011, https://www.politifact.com/truth-o-meter/promises/obameter/promise/519/reproductive-health-care-will-be-heart-health-care/.

583   Eugene Volokh "Anti-abortion group may proceed with its challenge to Ohio's ban on knowing/reckless false statements in election campaign," *The Washington Post*, June 16, 2014, https://www.washingtonpost.com/news/volokh-conspiracy/wp/2014/06/16/anti-abortion-group-may-proceed-with-its-challenge-to-ohios-ban-on-knowingreckless-false-statements-in-election-campaigns/.

584   U.S. Congress, House, Committee on Oversight and Reform, *Lines Crossed: Separation of Church and State. Has the Obama Administration Trampled on Freedom of Religion and Freedom of Conscience?* 112th Cong., 2nd sess., February 16, 2012, https://republicans-oversight.house.gov/hearing/lines-crossed-separation-of-church-and-state-has-the-obama-administration-trampled-on-freedom-of-religion-and-freedom-of-conscience/.

585   Laura Bassett and Amanda Terkel, "House Democrats Walk Out Of One-Sided Hearing On Contraception, Calling It An 'Autocratic Regime,'" HuffPost, Updated December 6, 2017, https://www.huffpost.com/entry/contraception-hearing-house-democrats-walk-out_n_1281730.

586   Elijah E. Cummings, "Why I demanded a voice for Sandra Fluke," *Baltimore Sun*, March 21, 2012, https://www.baltimoresun.com/opinion/bs-xpm-2012-03-21-bs-ed-cummings-fluke-20120321-story.html.

587   Laura Bassett and Amanda Terkel, "House Democrats Walk Out Of One-Sided Hearing On Contraception, Calling It An 'Autocratic Regime,'" *HuffPost*, Updated December 6, 2017, https://www.huffpost.com/entry/contraception-hearing-house-democrats-walk-out_n_1281730.

588   Maggie Fazeli Fard, "Sandra Fluke, Georgetown student called a 'slut' by Rush Limbaugh, speaks out," *Washington Post*, March 2, 2012, https://www.washingtonpost.com/blogs/the-buzz/post/rush-limbaugh-calls-georgetown-student-sandra-fluke-a-slut-for-advocating-contraception/2012/03/02/gIQAvjfSmR_blog.html.

589   Maggie Haberman, "Foster Friess: In my day, 'gals' put aspirin 'between their knees' for contraception," *Burns & Haberman* (blog), *Politico*, February 16, 2012, https://www.politico.com/blogs/burns-haberman/2012/02/foster-friess-in-my-day-gals-put-aspirin-between-their-knees-for-contraception-114730.

590   Jane Mayer, "Covert Operations," *The New Yorker*, August 23, 2010, https://www.newyorker.com/magazine/2010/08/30/covert-operations.

591   Angie Maxwell, "How Southern racism found a home in the Tea Party," *Vox*, July 7, 2016, https://www.vox.com/2016/7/7/12118872/southern-racism-tea-

party-trump.

592   Michelle Goldberg, "Tea Party, Meet the Religious Right," *American Prospect*, January 12, 2010, https://prospect.org/article/tea-party-meet-religious-right/.

593   Dana Goldstein, "Tea Party Embraces Pro-Life, Christian Conservative Ideals," *Daily Beast*, Updated July 14, 2017, https://www.thedailybeast.com/tea-party-embraces-pro-life-christian-conservative-ideals.

594   "Michael Steele Takes Center Stage at GOP Convention; Recession Recovery?," *John King, USA*, CNN, Aired August 6, 2010, https://edition.cnn.com/TRANSCRIPTS/1008/06/jkusa.01.html.

595   Kellyanne Conway, "The Power of Bachmann," *National Review*, June 20, 2011, https://www.nationalreview.com/corner/power-bachmann-kellyanne-conway/.

596   Stassa Edwards, "Trump Campaign Hires 'Gender Gap' Expert Kellyanne Conway, Who Touts 'Femininity, Not Feminism,'" *Jezebel*, July 1, 2016, https://theslot.jezebel.com/trump-campaign-hires-gender-gap-expert-kellyanne-conway-1782959310.

597   "The New "Women's Issues", Clare Boothe Luce Policy Institute and the Heritage Foundation, https://www.youtube.com/watch?v=0ULofK2quvs&feature=emb_title

598   Sarah Posner, "The Tea Party's religious roots exposed," *The Guardian*, October 12, 2010, https://www.theguardian.com/commentisfree/belief/2010/oct/12/tea-party-religious-right.

599   John Eligon and Michael Schwirtz, "Senate Candidate Provokes Ire With 'Legitimate Rape' Comment," *The New York Times*, August 19, 2012, https://www.nytimes.com/2012/08/20/us/politics/todd-akin-provokes-ire-with-legitimate-rape-comment.html.

600   Halimah Abdullah, "Akin's 'legitimate rape' comments trouble for GOP," *CNN*, August 20, 2012, https://www.cnn.com/2012/08/20/politics/akin-political-fallout/index.html.

601   Peter Hamby and Mark Preston, "Akin assessing candidacy with conservatives in Florida," *Political Ticker* (blog), CNN, August 23, 2012, http://politicalticker.blogs.cnn.com/2012/08/23/akin-assessing-candidacy-with-conservatives-in-florida/.

602   Catalina Camia, "Todd Akin retreats from 'legitimate rape' apology," *USA Today*, July 10, 2014, https://www.usatoday.com/story/news/politics/onpolitics/2014/07/10/todd-akin-legitimate-rape-book-apology/81596778/.

603   "Election 2012 Senate Map," *New York Times*, November 29, 2012, https://www.nytimes.com/elections/2012/results/senate.html.

604   "Election 2012 President Map," *New York Times*, November 29, 2012, https://www.nytimes.com/elections/2012/results/president.html.

605   "Election 2012 House Map," *New York Times*, November 29, 2012, https://www.nytimes.com/elections/2012/results/house.html.

606   Jeremy W. Peters, "Conservatives Hone Script to Light a Fire Over Abortion," *New York Times*, July 24, 2014, https://www.nytimes.com/2014/07/25/us/politics/republicans-abortion-midterm-elections.html.

607   Kathryn Smith, "Anti-abortion groups learn from NRA," *Politico*, January 21, 2013, https://www.politico.com/story/2013/01/anti-abortion-groups-take-page-from-nra-playbook-086531.

608   "Pro-life 'Freedom Rides' inspired by historic civil rights events," Culture Watch, July 23, 2010, https://issuu.com/catholicnewsherald/docs/cnh_issue_07_23_10.

609   "This Weekend's Pro-Life Freedom Ride Moved into High Gear by New

Survey Results," Priests for Life, July 20, 2010, https://www.priestsforlife.org/library/3248-this-weekends-pro-life-freedom-ride-moved-into-high-gear-by-new-survey-results.

610   P.R. Lockhart, "'Abortion as black genocide': inside the black anti-abortion movement," *Vox* January 19, 2018, https://www.vox.com/identities/2018/1/19/16906928/black-anti-abortion-movement-yoruba-richen-medical-racism.

611   Kellyanne Conway, "Singled Out," *National Review*, September 12, 2013, https://www.nationalreview.com/magazine/2013/09/30/singled-out/.

612   Penny Nance and Kellyanne Conway, "Roe and the Road Ahead," *Christian Post*, January 25, 2013, https://www.christianpost.com/news/roe-and-the-road-ahead.html.

613   "What Are Voters Thinking in 2014?; Good Omens for Democrats?," *CNN Crossfire*, Aired January 2, 2014, http://transcripts.cnn.com/TRANSCRIPTS/1401/02/cfr.01.html.

614   Peter Jesserer Smith, "Kellyanne Conway: President Trump's Pro-Life Counselor," *National Catholic Register*, January 27, 2017, http://www.ncregister.com/daily-news/kellyanne-conway-president-trumps-pro-life-counselor.

615   Sabrina Tavernise, "Planned Parenthood Awarded $2 Million in Lawsuit Over Secret Videos," The New York Times, November 15, 2019, https://www.nytimes.com/2019/11/15/us/planned-parenthood-lawsuit-secret-videos.html.

616   Time Staff, "Here's Donald Trump's Presidential Announcement Speech," *TIME*, JUNE 16, 2015, https://time.com/3923128/donald-trump-announcement-speech/.

617   Rupert Neate, "Donald Trump announces US presidential run with eccentric speech," *The Guardian*, June 16, 2015, https://www.theguardian.com/us-news/2015/jun/16/donald-trump-announces-run-president.

618   Alex Altman and Charlotte Alter, "Trump Launches Presidential Campaign With Empty Flair," *TIME*, June 16, 2015, https://time.com/3922770/donald-trump-campaign-launch/.

619   Max Read, "Maybe the Internet Isn't a Fantastic Tool for Democracy After All," *Intelligencer* (blog), *New York Magazine*, November 27, 2016, https://nymag.com/intelligencer/2016/11/maybe-the-internet-isnt-a-tool-for-democracy-after-all.html.

620   Adam Entous, Craig Timberg, and Elizabeth Dwoskin, "Russian operatives used Facebook ads to exploit America's racial and religious divisions," *Washington Post*, September 25, 2017, https://www.washingtonpost.com/business/technology/russian-operatives-used-facebook-ads-to-exploit-divisions-over-black-political-activism-and-muslims/2017/09/25/4a011242-a21b-11e7-ade1-76d061d56efa_story.html.

621   Michael Lerner, "Stop Shaming Trump Supporters," *New York Times*, 2016, https://www.nytimes.com/interactive/projects/cp/opinion/election-night-2016/stop-shaming-trump-supporters.

622   Tina Nguyen, "Gary Johnson and Jill Stein Handed the Presidency to Donald Trump," *Vanity Fair*, November 10, 2016, https://www.vanityfair.com/news/2016/11/gary-johnson-jill-stein-election-2016.

623   Lois Beckett, Rory Carroll, Carmen Fishwick, Amber Jamieson, and San Thielman, "The real 'shy Trump' vote - how 53% of white women pushed him to victory," The Guardian, November 10, 2016,https://www.theguardian.com/us-news/2016/nov/10/white-women-donald-trump-victory.

624   Michael Moore, "5 Reasons Why Trump Will Win," *MichaelMoore.com*, accessed June 5, 2020, https://michaelmoore.com/trumpwillwin/.

625   Weekend Edition Sunday, "As Trump Defies Expectations Of Faith, Might We Be Entering A New Era?," *NPR*, June 26, 2016, https://www.npr.org/2016/06/26/483506379/as-trump-defies-expectations-of-faith-might-we-be-entering-a-new-era.

626   Ben Schreckinger, "At Trump's victory party, hints of vengeance to come," *POLITICO*, November 9, 2016, https://www.politico.com/story/2016/11/trump-vengeance-victory-speech-2016-231084.

627   Adam Cancryn, "David Duke: Trump win a great victory for 'our people,'" *POLITICO*, November 9, 2016, https://www.politico.com/story/2016/11/david-duke-trump-victory-2016-election-231072.

628   Miranda Bryant, "Jerry Falwell's Liberty University dogged by growing claims of corruption," *The Guardian*, September 15, 2019, https://www.theguardian.com/us-news/2019/sep/14/jerry-falwell-liberty-university-corruption-trump.

629   Ben Schreckinger, "At Trump's victory party, hints of vengeance to come," *POLITICO*, November 9, 2016, https://www.politico.com/story/2016/11/trump-vengeance-victory-speech-2016-231084.

630   Jill Disis, "10 of Breitbart's most incendiary headlines," *CNN Business*, November 15, 2016, https://money.cnn.com/2016/11/14/media/breitbart-incendiary-headlines/.

631   Conor Friedersdorf, "The Decline and Fall of the Tea Party," *The Atlantic*, January 9, 2013, https://www.theatlantic.com/politics/archive/2013/01/the-decline-and-fall-of-the-tea-party/266972/.

632   "Family Research Council," Southern Poverty Law Center, accessed May 14, 2020. https://www.splcenter.org/fighting-hate/extremist-files/group/family-research-council.

633   "Family Research Council," Family Research Council, accessed May 14, 2020, https://web.archive.org/web/20100602184415/www.frc.org/issues.

634   "Tony Perkins," *Fox News*, accessed June 5, 2020, https://www.foxnews.com/person/p/tony-perkins.

635   "2014 Election Report," Susan B. Anthony List, accessed August 1, 2017, https://www.sba-list.org/2014-election-report.

636   "By the Numbers: 2014 Midterm Elections," Susan B. Anthony List, November 4, 2014, https://www.sba-list.org/newsroom/press-releases/numbers-2014-midterm-elections.

637   Rebecca R. Ruiz, Robert Gebeloff, Steve Eder and Ben Protess, "A Conservative Agenda Unleashed on the Federal Courts," *The New York Times*, March 16, 2020, https://www.nytimes.com/2020/03/14/us/trump-appeals-court-judges.html.

638   David G. Savage, "This Congress filled the fewest judgeships since 1952. That leaves a big opening for Trump," *Los Angeles Times*, December 31, 2016, https://www.latimes.com/politics/la-na-judges-trump-senate-20161231-story.html.

639   Sam Berger, "Conservative Court Packing," Center for American Progress, April 3, 2019, https://www.americanprogress.org/issues/democracy/news/2019/04/03/468234/conservative-court-packing/.

640   Carl Bialik, "How The Republican Field Dwindled From 17 To Donald Trump," *FiveThirtyEight*, May 5, 2016, https://fivethirtyeight.com/features/how-the-republican-field-dwindled-from-17-to-donald-trump/.

641   "Republican presidential nomination, 2016," *Ballotpedia*, accessed June 9, 2020, https://ballotpedia.org/Republican_presidential_nomination,_2016.

642   Ashley Parker and Steve Eder, "Inside the Six Weeks Donald Trump Was a Nonstop 'Birther,'" *New York Times*, July 2, 2016, https://www.nytimes.com/2016/07/03/us/politics/donald-trump-birther-obama.html.

643   "WorldNet Daily," Southern Poverty Law Center, accessed May 14, 2020, https://www.splcenter.org/fighting-hate/extremist-files/group/worldnetdaily.

644   Manuel Roig-Franzia, "Inside the spectacular fall of the granddaddy of right-wing conspiracy sites," *Washington Post*, April 2, 2019, https://www.washingtonpost.com/lifestyle/style/inside-the-spectacular-fall-of-the-granddaddy-of-right-wing-conspiracy-sites/2019/04/02/6ac53122-3ba6-11e9-a06c-3ec8ed509d15_story.html.

645   "Joseph Francis Farah," Southern Poverty Law Center, accessed June 5, 2020, https://www.splcenter.org/fighting-hate/extremist-files/individual/joseph-francis-farah.

646   Ashley Parker and Steve Eder, "Inside the Six Weeks Donald Trump Was a Nonstop 'Birther,'" *New York Times*, July 2, 2016, https://www.nytimes.com/2016/07/03/us/politics/donald-trump-birther-obama.html.

647   Ben Smith and Byron Tau, "Birtherism: Where it all began," *POLITICO*, April 22, 2011, https://www.politico.com/story/2011/04/birtherism-where-it-all-began-053563.

648   Ashley Parker and Steve Eder, "Inside the Six Weeks Donald Trump Was a Nonstop 'Birther,'" *New York Times*, July 2, 2016, https://www.nytimes.com/2016/07/03/us/politics/donald-trump-birther-obama.html.

649   Chris Megerian, "What Donald Trump has said through the years about where President Obama was born," *Los Angeles Times*, September 16, 2016, https://www.latimes.com/politics/la-na-pol-trump-birther-timeline-20160916-snap-htmlstory.html.

650   Richard Adams, "Donald Trump for president: a punchline looking for a joke," *The Guardian*, April 7, 2011, https://www.theguardian.com/world/richard-adams-blog/2011/apr/07/donald-trump-republican-president-candidate.

651   Chris Cillizza, "Trump won't run for president in 2012," The Washington Post, May 16, 2011, https://www.washingtonpost.com/blogs/the-fix/post/donald-trump-wont-run-for-president-in-2012/2011/05/16/AF14G14G_blog.html.

652   Davis Richardson, "Former Trump Advisor Admits to 'Peddling Birtherism' About Obama," *Observer*, August 3, 2018, https://observer.com/2018/08/former-trump-advisor-peddling-birtherism-about-obama/.

653   Amy Walter and Michael Falcone, "Donald Trump Runs Second in Poll: Can He Win Republican Nomination?," *ABC News*, April 7, 2011, https://abcnews.go.com/Politics/poll-donald-trump-catapults-place-2012-gop-field/story?id=13318814.

654   Ashley Parker and Steve Eder, "Inside the Six Weeks Donald Trump Was a Nonstop 'Birther,'" *New York Times*, July 2, 2016, https://www.nytimes.com/2016/07/03/us/politics/donald-trump-birther-obama.html.

655   Darren Samuelsohn, "Roger Stone sentenced to over 3 years in prison," *POLITICO*, February 20, 2020, https://www.politico.com/news/2020/02/20/roger-stone-sentenced-to-over-three-years-in-prison-116326.

656   Ashley Parker and Steve Eder, "Inside the Six Weeks Donald Trump Was a Nonstop 'Birther,'" *New York Times*, July 2, 2016, https://www.nytimes.com/2016/07/03/us/politics/donald-trump-birther-obama.html.

657   Byron York, "Evangelicals urged to support Trump," *Washington Examiner*, June 17, 2016, https://www.theintell.com/04b0ef14-1620-567e-b3e3-eb6919a8cd1d.html

658   McKay Coppins, "The Religious Right's Dangerous Bet On Trump," *Buzzfeed News*, August 1, 2016, https://www.buzzfeednews.com/article/mckaycoppins/the-religious-rights-dangerous-bet-on-trump.

659   Oliver Willis, "Donald Trump & Fox News: Timeline Of A Relationship," *Media Matters*, February 1, 2016, https://www.mediamatters.org/donald-trump/don-

ald-trump-fox-news-timeline-relationship

660   Emma Bazilian, "How Will Fox News Solve a Problem Like Donald Trump?," *Adweek*, April 1, 2011, https://www.adweek.com/tv-video/how-will-fox-news-solve-problem-donald-trump-126148/.

661   Tracie Egan Morrissey, "Donald Trump Hates Women as Much as He Loves Money," *Jezebel*, May 18, 2012, https://jezebel.com/donald-trump-hates-women-as-much-as-he-loves-money-5910904

662   Brandon Ambrosino, "How Trump Is Dividing Jerry Falwell's University," *POLITICO*, October 27, 2016, https://www.politico.com/magazine/story/2016/10/trump-evangelical-falwell-liberty-university-christian-conservatives-214394.

663   K.M. Calpin, "Business mogul Donald Trump visits Liberty," *Liberty Champion*, Liberty University, October 2, 2012, https://www.liberty.edu/champion/2012/10/business-mogul-donald-trump-visits-liberty/

664   Mitzi Bible, "Donald Trump addresses largest Convocation crowd, praises Liberty's growth," *Liberty News* (blog), *Liberty University*, September 24, 2012, http://www.liberty.edu/news/?PID=18495&MID=65182.

665   Mitzi Bible, "Donald Trump addresses largest Convocation crowd, praises Liberty's growth," *Liberty News* (blog), *Liberty University*, September 24, 2012, http://www.liberty.edu/news/?PID=18495&MID=65182.

666   Mitzi Bible, "Donald Trump addresses largest Convocation crowd, praises Liberty's growth," *Liberty News* (blog), *Liberty University*, September 24, 2012, http://www.liberty.edu/news/?PID=18495&MID=65182.

667   Philip Rucker, "Falwell Jr.'s Trump endorsement draws objections from late father's confidant," *The Washington Post*, March 1, 2016, https://www.newsadvance.com/news/local/falwell-jr-s-trump-endorsement-draws-objections-from-late-father/article_03ebfb52-dfe2-11e5-af71-3b333edd5687.html.

668   Philip Bump, "How Trump became an abortion hard-liner," *Washington Post*, May 15, 2019, https://www.washingtonpost.com/politics/2019/05/15/how-trump-became-an-abortion-hard-liner/.

669   "Trump in 1999: 'I am Very Pro-Choice'" *Meet the Press*, NBC News (video), 1:23, July 8, 2015, https://www.nbcnews.com/meet-the-press/video/trump-in-1999-i-am-very-pro-choice-480297539914.

670   "Donald Trump Sits Down With Bill O'Reilly," *Fox News*, March 30, 2011, https://www.foxnews.com/transcript/donald-trump-sits-down-with-bill-oreilly.

671   David Greene, "Trump Would Disrupt The Broken System In Washington, Ralph Reed Says," *Morning Edition*, NPR News, Washington, DC: NPR, June 22, 2016, https://www.npr.org/2016/06/22/483046602/ralph-reed-weighs-in-on-trumps-meeting-with-evangelicals.

672   Gabby Orr, "'He was in his face': Trump fumes over abortion, courts evangelicals," *POLITICO*, February 13, 2019, https://www.politico.com/story/2019/02/13/trump-evangelicals-1169394.

673   Thomas B. Edsall, "Newt Gingrich and the Future of the Right," *The New York Times*, January 29, 2012, https://campaignstops.blogs.nytimes.com/2012/01/29/newt-gingrich-and-the-future-of-the-right/.

674   Jake Tapper, "Gingrich Admits to Affair During Clinton Impeachment," *ABC News*, March 12, 2007, https://abcnews.go.com/Politics/story?id=2937633&page=1.

675   Amber Phillips, "'They're rapists.' President Trump's campaign launch speech two years later, annotated," *Washington Post*, June 16, 2017, https://www.washingtonpost.com/news/the-fix/wp/2017/06/16/theyre-rapists-presidents-trump-campaign-launch-speech-two-years-later-annotated/

676   Robert Jones, interview by Ezra Klein, "Behind the panic in white, Christian America," *Stitcher*, https://www.stitcher.com/podcast/vox/the-ezra-klein-

show/e/62281274

677 Daniel Marans, "Hate-Group Watchdog: Trump Has 'White Nationalist Positions,'" *Huffington Post*, August 26, 2015, https://www.huffpost.com/entry/trump-white-nationalist-positions_n_55dde385e4b0a40aa3acfab8.

678 Ben Schreckinger and Cate Martel, "The mystery of the Trump coalition," *POLITICO*, July 17, 2015, https://www.politico.com/story/2015/07/the-mystery-of-the-trump-coalition-120269.

679 America's Voice Press Release, "From a Memory Device to a Racist Rally Chant to a Damaging Government Shutdown, Trump's Border Wall Has Never Been About Policy," America's Voice, January 7, 2019, https://americasvoice.org/press_releases/from-a-memory-device-to-a-racist-rally-chant-to-a-damaging-government-shutdown-trumps-border-wall-has-never-been-about-policy/.

680 Evan Osnos, "The Fearful and the Frustrated," *The New Yorker*, August 24, 2015, https://www.newyorker.com/magazine/2015/08/31/the-fearful-and-the-frustrated.

681 Evan Osnos, "The Fearful and the Frustrated," *The New Yorker*, August 24, 2015, https://www.newyorker.com/magazine/2015/08/31/the-fearful-and-the-frustrated.

682 "IFA's Charlottesville Case: Sines v. Kessler - Defendants," Integrity First for America, accessed June 8, 2020, https://www.integrityfirstforamerica.org/our-work/case/charlottesville-case.

683 Evan Osnos, "The Fearful and the Frustrated," *The New Yorker*, August 24, 2015, https://www.newyorker.com/magazine/2015/08/31/the-fearful-and-the-frustrated.

684 Andrew Kaczynski "David Duke On Trump: He's 'Certainly The Best Of The Lot' Running For President," *BuzzFeed News*, August 25, 2015, https://www.buzzfeednews.com/article/andrewkaczynski/david-duke-on-trump-hes-certainly-the-best-of-the-lot-runnin#.lnZAeRKwQZ.

685 Evan Osnos, "The Fearful and the Frustrated," *The New Yorker*, August 24, 2015, https://www.newyorker.com/magazine/2015/08/31/the-fearful-and-the-frustrated.

686 "From Alt Right to Alt Lite: Naming the Hate," Anti-Defamation League, accessed MAy 14, 2020, https://www.adl.org/resources/backgrounders/from-alt-right-to-alt-lite-naming-the-hate.

687 Matthew N. Lyons, "CTRL-ALT-DELETE," *Political Research Associates*, January 20, 2017, https://www.politicalresearch.org/2017/01/20/ctrl-alt-delete-report-on-the-alternative-right

688 Joseph Goldstein, "Alt-Right Gathering Exults in Trump Election With Nazi-Era Salute," *New York Times*, November 20, 2016, https://www.nytimes.com/2016/11/21/us/alt-right-salutes-donald-trump.html.

689 "Richard Bertrand Spencer," Southern Poverty Law Center, accessed June 9, 2020, https://www.splcenter.org/fighting-hate/extremist-files/individual/richard-bertrand-spencer-0.

690 Evan Osnos, "The Fearful and the Frustrated," *The New Yorker*, August 24, 2015, https://www.newyorker.com/magazine/2015/08/31/the-fearful-and-the-frustrated.

691 Glenn Kessler, "Donald Trump and David Duke: For the record," *Washington Post*, March 1, 2016, https://www.washingtonpost.com/news/fact-checker/wp/2016/03/01/donald-trump-and-david-duke-for-the-record/.

692 Alison Lefkovitz, "Jordan Peterson and the return of the men's rights movement," *Washington Post*, July 24, 2018, https://www.washingtonpost.com/news/made-by-history/wp/2018/07/24/before-jordan-peterson-there-were-

mens-rights-activists/.

693   Pierce Alexander Dignam and Deana A. Rohlinger, "Misogynistic Men On-line: How the Red Pill Helped Elect Trump," *Signs: Journal of Women in Culture and Society* 44, no. 3 (Spring 2019): 589-612. https://doi.org/10.1086/701155.

694   Caitlin Dewey, "The only guide to Gamergate you will ever need to read," *Washington Post*, October 14, 2014, https://www.washingtonpost.com/news/the-intersect/wp/2014/10/14/the-only-guide-to-gamergate-you-will-ever-need-to-read/.

695   Matt Lees, "What Gamergate should have taught us about the 'alt-right'" *The Guardian*, December 1, 2016, https://www.theguardian.com/technology/2016/dec/01/gamergate-alt-right-hate-trump.

696   Tim Colwill, "GamerGate Supporters Hopeful Continued Harassment Will Prove They Don't Support Harassment," *Point and Clickbait*, March 24, 2016, https://www.pointandclickbait.com/2016/03/gamergate-harassment-campaign/.

697   Emma Grey Ellis, "How Red-Pill Culture Jumped the Fence and Got to Kanye West," Wired, April 27, 2018, https://www.wired.com/story/kanye-west-red-pill/.

698   Marissa G. Muller and Krystin Arneson, "A Timeline of Donald Trump's Inappropriate History With Women," *Glamour,* June 22, 2019, https://www.glamour.com/story/a-history-timeline-of-donald-trump-sexual-assault.

699   Daniel Marans, "Hate-Group Watchdog: Trump Has 'White Nation-alist Positions,'" HuffPost, August 26, 2015, https://www.huffpost.com/entry/trump-white-nationalist-positions_n_55dde385e4b0a40aa3acfab8.

700   Claire Cohen, "Donald Trump sexism tracker: Every offensive comment in one place," *The Telegraph,* July 14, 2017, https://www.telegraph.co.uk/women/politics/donald-trump-sexism-tracker-every-offensive-comment-in-one-place/.

701   Michael D. Shear and Eileen Sullivan,"'Horseface,' 'Lowlife,' 'Fat, Ugly': How the President Demeans Women," *New York Times*, October 16, 2018, https://www.nytimes.com/2018/10/16/us/politics/trump-women-insults.html.

702   Jeva Lange, "61 things Donald Trump has said about women," *The Week*, October 16, 2018, https://theweek.com/articles/655770/61-things-donald-trump-said-about-women.

703   Pierce Alexander Dignam and Deana A. Rohlinger, "Misogynistic Men On-line," *Journal of Women in Culture and Society Volume,* 44, Number 3, Spring 2019, https://www.journals.uchicago.edu/doi/full/10.1086/701155.

704   Ryan Mac, "A Troll Outside Trump Tower Is Helping To Pick Your Next Government," *Forbes,* January 9, 2017, https://www.forbes.com/sites/mattdrange/2017/01/09/chuck-johnson-troll-trump-transition-team/.

705   "Quiz: Who Said It, Donald Trump or a Men's Rights Activist?" The Cut, *New York Magazine,* May 11, 2016, https://www.thecut.com/2016/05/who-said-it-donald-trump-or-an-mra.html.

706   Charlotte Alter, "Sexist Hillary Clinton Attacks Are Best Sellers," *TIME*, June 6, 2016, https://time.com/4357406/hillary-clinton-sexist-donald-trump/.

707   Charlotte Alter, "Sexist Hillary Clinton Attacks Are Best Sellers," *TIME*, June 6, 2016, https://time.com/4357406/hillary-clinton-sexist-donald-trump/.

708   Stephanie Mencimer, "'The Left Can't Meme': How Right-Wing Groups Are Training the Next Generation of Social Media Warriors," *Mother Jones*, April 2, 2019, https://www.motherjones.com/politics/2019/04/right-wing-groups-are-training-young-conservatives-to-win-the-next-meme-war/.

709   Stephanie Mencimer, "'The Left Can't Meme': How Right-Wing Groups Are Training the Next Generation of Social Media Warriors," *Mother Jones*, April 2, 2019, https://www.motherjones.com/politics/2019/04/right-wing-groups-are-training-

young-conservatives-to-win-the-next-meme-war/.

710   Stephanie Mencimer, "'The Left Can't Meme': How Right-Wing Groups Are Training the Next Generation of Social Media Warriors," *Mother Jones*, April 2, 2019, https://www.motherjones.com/politics/2019/04/right-wing-groups-are-training-young-conservatives-to-win-the-next-meme-war/.

711   Jennifer Rubin, "The mainstreaming of racism on Fox News," *Washington Post*, October 26, 2016, https://www.washingtonpost.com/blogs/right-turn/wp/2016/10/26/the-mainstreaming-of-racism-on-fox-news/?tid=hybrid_experimentrandom_2_na&utm_term=.ad52f8b26b0e.

712   "Boycott List," Gamergate Wiki, accessed June 8, 2020, http://ggwiki.deepfreeze.it/index.php?title=Boycott_List.

713   Thomas B. Edsall, "Newt Gingrich and the Future of the Right," *New York Times*, January 29, 2012, https://campaignstops.blogs.nytimes.com/2012/01/29/newt-gingrich-and-the-future-of-the-right/.

714   Thomas B. Edsall, "Newt Gingrich and the Future of the Right," *New York Times*, January 29, 2012, https://campaignstops.blogs.nytimes.com/2012/01/29/newt-gingrich-and-the-future-of-the-right/.

715   National Right to Life News, National Right to Life, accessed May 15, 2020, http://www.nrlc.org/news/.

716   "Choose Life," *National Right to Life,* accessed May 15, 2020, http://www.nrlc.org/outreach/chooselife/.

717   "All the facts you ever need to know about ABORTION," *Life Site News*, accessed May 15, 2020, https://www.lifesitenews.com/resources/abortion.

718   "Feelings after abortion: Post-Abortion Syndrome," *Life Site News*, accessed May 15, 2020, https://www.lifesitenews.com/resources/abortion/abortion-risks/feelings-after-abortion-post-abortion-syndrome.

719   Fr. Mark Hodges, "The U.S. must release all illegal immigrants claiming to be gay, bisexual, or transgender: Homosexual activists," *Life Site News*, May 28, 2015, https://www.lifesitenews.com/news/the-u.s.-must-release-all-illegal-immigrants-claiming-to-be-gay-bisexual-or.

720   K.V. Turley, "Ireland's new pro-life party leader: Abortion is 'stain' that 'should be removed'," *Life Site News*, January 28, 2019, https://www.lifesitenews.com/news/hermann-kelly.

721   Sharon Kann and Julie Tulbert, "Other networks are letting Fox News poison abortion-related coverage with dangerous lies," *Media Matters,* September 23, 2019. https://www.mediamatters.org/fox-news/other-networks-are-letting-fox-news-poison-abortion-related-coverage-dangerous-lies.

722   Ashley Parker and Steve Eder, "Inside the Six Weeks Donald Trump Was a Nonstop 'Birther'," *The New York Times*, July 2, 2016, https://www.nytimes.com/2016/07/03/us/politics/donald-trump-birther-obama.html.

723   "Hon. Ted Cruz," The Federalist Society, accessed June 9, 2020, https://fedsoc.org/contributors/ted-cruz.

724   Patricia Murphy, "The Only Republicans Man Enough to Stop Trump Are Women," *Roll Call*, January 26, 2016, https://www.rollcall.com/2016/01/26/the-only-republicans-man-enough-to-stop-trump-are-women/.

725   CWALAC Staff, "Was Donald Trump Mistreated? Penny Nance Responds to CNN Reporter Regarding the First GOP Debate," *Concerned Women for America*, August 8, 2015. https://concernedwomen.org/was-donald-trump-mistreated-penny-nance-responds-to-cnn-reporter-regarding-the-first-gop-debate/?fbclid=IwAR22LQ2-MsDhYmoY1dVYOyV7sxBaVM1Yj1D8n47644SW_2nsvBNUUQl817M.

726   Marjorie Dannenfelser and Penny Nance, "Feminists Are Total Hypocrites When It Comes to Carly Fiorina," *TIME*, December 2, 2015, https://time.

com/4132649/carly-fiorina-women-voters/.

727   Marjorie Dannenfelser, "Carly Fiorina's principled campaign," *Washington Times*, May 14, 2015, https://www.washingtontimes.com/news/2015/may/14/marjorie-dannenfelser-carly-fiorinas-pro-life-camp/.

728   "SBA List: Carly Fiorina is the Ideal VP Pick," SBA List, April 27, 2016, https://www.sba-list.org/newsroom/press-releases/sba-list-carly-fiorina-ideal-vp-pick.

729   Leonardo Blair, "Paula White says President Trump's opposition to late-term abortion is personal conviction," *Christian Post,* March 30, 2019. https://www.christianpost.com/news/paula-white-confirms-president-trumps-opposition-late-term-abortion-personal-conviction.html.

730   Gabby Orr, "'He was in his face': Trump fumes over abortion, courts evangelicals," *POLITICO*, February 13, 2019, https://www.politico.com/story/2019/02/13/trump-evangelicals-1169394.

731   Eric Bradner, "Trump blames Tony Perkins for '2 Corinthians,'" *CNN politics,* January 21, 2016, https://www.cnn.com/2016/01/20/politics/donald-trump-tony-perkins-sarah-palin/index.html.

732   David Brody and Scott Lamb, *The Faith of Donald J. Trump: A Spiritual Biography,* (New York: Harper Collins, 2018): 163, via Amazon Kindle.

733   Tim Alberta, "Why Trump Is Growing on Social-Conservative Leaders," *National Review*, October 23, 2015, https://www.nationalreview.com/2015/10/donald-trump-woos-social-conservative-leaders/.

734   Tim Alberta, "Why Trump Is Growing on Social-Conservative Leaders," *National Review*, October 23, 2015, https://www.nationalreview.com/2015/10/donald-trump-woos-social-conservative-leaders/.

735   Tim Alberta, "Why Trump Is Growing on Social-Conservative Leaders," *National Review*, October 23, 2015, https://www.nationalreview.com/2015/10/donald-trump-woos-social-conservative-leaders/.

736   Tim Alberta, "Why Trump Is Growing on Social-Conservative Leaders," *National Review*, October 23, 2015, https://www.nationalreview.com/2015/10/donald-trump-woos-social-conservative-leaders/.

737   Tim Alberta, "Why Trump Is Growing on Social-Conservative Leaders," *National Review*, October 23, 2015, https://www.nationalreview.com/2015/10/donald-trump-woos-social-conservative-leaders/.

738   Tim Alberta, "Why Trump Is Growing on Social-Conservative Leaders," *National Review*, October 23, 2015. https://www.nationalreview.com/2015/10/donald-trump-woos-social-conservative-leaders/.

739   David Brody and Scott Lamb, *The Faith of Donald J. Trump: A Spiritual Biography,* (New York: Harper Collins, 2018): 179-81.

740   Hank Berrien, "Donald Trump Botched A Biblical Reference. Now He's Blaming Someone Else. Just Like Jesus Would," *Daily Wire*, January 21, 2016, https://www.dailywire.com/news/donald-trump-botched-biblical-reference-now-hes-hank-berrien

741   David Brody, "Just In: Brody File Exclusive: Donald Trump Comes Out In Support Of 20 Week Abortion Ban," *The Brody File* (blog), *CBN News*, July 22, 2015, https://www1.cbn.com/thebrodyfile/archive/2015/07/22/just-in-brody-file-exclusive-donald-trump-comes-out-in.

742   Betsy Woodruff, "Donald Trump Is Planned Parenthood's Favorite Republican," *Daily Beast,* August 11, 2015, https://www.thedailybeast.com/donald-trump-is-planned-parenthoods-favorite-republican
n.

743   Betsy Woodruff, "Donald Trump Is Planned Parenthood's Favorite Republican," *Daily Beast,* August 11, 2015, https://www.thedailybeast.com/don-

ald-trump-is-planned-parenthoods-favorite-republican
n.

744   Betsy Woodruff, "Donald Trump Is Planned Parenthood's Favorite Republican," *Daily Beast,* August 11, 2015, https://www.thedailybeast.com/don-
ald-trump-is-planned-parenthoods-favorite-republican
n.

745   Dick Polman, "Wait - Donald Trump is defending Planned Parenthood?: Dick Polman," *Penn Live*, August 17, 2015, https://www.pennlive.com/opin-
ion/2015/08/wait_-_donald_trump_is_defendi.html

746   Betsy Swan, "Donald Trump Is Planned Parenthood's Favorite Republican," *Daily Beast,* April 14, 2017, https://www.thedailybeast.com/don-
ald-trump-is-planned-parenthoods-favorite-republican

747   "Pro-life Women Sound the Alarm: Donald Trump is Unacceptable," Susan B. Anthony List, January 26, 2016. https://www.sba-list.org/home/pro-life-
women-sound-the-alarmdonald-trump-is-unacceptable.

748   Donald Trump, "Donald Trump op-ed: My vision for a culture of life,"
Washington Examiner, January 23, 2016, https://www.washingtonexaminer.com/
donald-trump-op-ed-my-vision-for-a-culture-of-life.

749   Jennifer Haberkorn, "Anti-abortion groups say they distrust Trump," *PO-
LITICO*, January 26, 2016, https://www.politico.com/story/2016/01/donald-trump-
anti-abortion-group-distrust-218258.

750   Jennifer Haberkorn, "Anti-abortion groups say they distrust Trump," *PO-
LITICO*, January 26, 2016, https://www.politico.com/story/2016/01/donald-trump-
anti-abortion-group-distrust-218258.

751   Phillip Bump, "How Trump became an abortion hard-liner," *Washington
Post*, May 15, 2019,   https://www.washingtonpost.com/politics/2019/05/15/how-
trump-became-an-abortion-hard-liner/.

752   Miranda Blue, "Anti-Choice Leader Offers Dubious Strategy For Preventing Back-Alley Abortions," *Right Wing Watch*, March 31, 2016. https://www.right-
wingwatch.org/post/anti-choice-leader-offers-dubious-strategy-for-prevent-
ing-back-alley-abortions/.

753   Ally Boguhn, "'She's One of Us': Trump Official Kellyanne Conway's Two
Decades of Anti-Choice Advocacy," *ReWire*, January 18, 2017, https://rewire.news/
article/2017/01/18/shes-one-us-trump-official-kellyanne-conways-two-decades-
anti-choice-advocacy/

754   Matt Flegenheimer and Maggie Haberman, "Donald Trump, Abortion Foe,
Eyes 'Punishment' for Women, Then Recants," *New York Times,* March 30, 2016,
https://www.nytimes.com/2016/03/31/us/politics/donald-trump-abortion.html?_
r=0.

755   Brian Philips, (@RealBPhil), "Don't overthink it: Trump doesn't understand
the pro-life position because he's not pro-life." Twitter, March 30, 2016, https://
twitter.com/RealBPhil/status/715250339373576192.

756   "Wisconsin Primary Results," *New York Times*, accessed May 15, 2020,
https://www.nytimes.com/elections/2016/results/primaries/wisconsin

757   "Wisconsin Exit Polls," *New York Times*, April 5, 2016, https://www.nytimes.
com/interactive/2016/04/05/us/elections/wisconsin-republican-primary-ex-
it-polls.html

758   Betsy Woodruff, "Trump Blows Off Pro-Life Leaders," *Daily Beast,* published April 6, 2016, last updated April 13, 2017. https://www.thedailybeast.com/
trump-blows-off-pro-life-leaders.

759   Jennifer Haberkorn, "Anti-abortion groups say they distrust Trump," *PO-
LITICO*, January 26, 2016, https://www.politico.com/story/2016/01/donald-trump-

anti-abortion-group-distrust-218258.

760   Matt Taibbi, "Why Trump's Endorsements Should Scare Your Pants Off," *Rolling Stone*, March 11, 2016, https://www.rollingstone.com/politics/politics-news/why-trumps-endorsements-should-scare-your-pants-off-51938/.

761   Mario Moretto, "LePage courts women voters, says he opposes 'killing babies as a form of contraception,'" *Bangor Daily News*, September 26, 2014, https://bangordailynews.com/2014/09/26/politics/elections/lepage-courts-women-voters-blasts-planned-parenthood-for-killing-babies/.

762   Michael Pollard and Joshua Mendelsohn, "RAND Kicks Off 2016 Presidential Election Panel Survey," January 27, 2016, https://www.rand.org/blog/2016/01/rand-kicks-off-2016-presidential-election-panel-survey.html.

763   Derek Thompson, "Who Are Donald Trump's Supporters, Really?," *The Atlantic*, March 1, 2016, https://www.theatlantic.com/politics/archive/2016/03/who-are-donald-trumps-supporters-really/471714/.

764   Michael Pollard and Joshua Mendelsohn, "RAND Kicks Off 2016 Presidential Election Panel Survey," January 27, 2016, https://www.rand.org/blog/2016/01/rand-kicks-off-2016-presidential-election-panel-survey.html.

765   James Fallows, "The Daily Trump: Filling a Time Capsule," *The Atlantic*, October 11, 2016, https://www.theatlantic.com/notes/2016/10/trump-time-capsule-140-lock-her-up/503684/.

766   Jennifer Steinhauer, "You Mean It's Next Week? Why Some G.O.P. Senators Will Skip the Convention," *New York Times*, July 15, 2016, https://www.nytimes.com/2016/07/17/us/politics/republican-senators-convention-cleveland.html.

767   Gabe Ortiz, "Buzzfeed, HP, Coca-Cola, Microsoft Dump Republican National Convention Over Donald Trump," *America's Voice*, June 7, 2016, https://americasvoice.org/blog/buzzfeed-hp-coca-cola-microsoft-dump-republican-national-convention-donald-trump/.

768   Peter Schroeder, "No Trump endorsement from Cruz: 'Vote your conscience,'" *The Hill*, July 20, 2016, https://thehill.com/blogs/ballot-box/presidential-races/288607-no-trump-endorsement-from-cruz-who-tells-gop-vote-your.

769   Anna Giaritelli, "Heidi Cruz removed from RNC floor for her safety," *Washington Examiner*, July 20, 2016, https://www.washingtonexaminer.com/heidi-cruz-removed-from-rnc-floor-for-her-safety.

770   "FULL SPEECH: Willie Robertson of Duck Dynasty at Republican National Convention," *ABC15 Arizona*, accessed via YouTube, July 18, 2016, https://www.youtube.com/watch?v=3Gg2dTFu2sc.

771   "Full list: 2016 Republican convention speakers," *POLITICO*, July 14, 2016, https://www.politico.com/story/2016/07/full-list-2016-republican-convention-speakers-225526.

772   "Sheriff Joe Arpaio RNC FULL Speech 7/21/16 Republican National Convention," LesGrossman News, accessed via YouTube, July 21, 2016, https://www.youtube.com/watch?v=ayr3a_2su9U.

773   Tribune News Services, "GOP speakers fault Clinton on Benghazi deaths," *Los Angeles Times*, July 18, 2016, https://www.latimes.com/nation/ct-gop-speakers-blame-clinton-for-benghazi-deaths-20160718-story.html.

774   "Pastor Mark Burns at the RNC: 'All Lives Matter,'" *ABC News*, accessed via YouTube, July 21, 2016, https://www.youtube.com/watch?v=GIA1OAC8SVQ.

775   "Republican Platform 2016," 2016 Republican National Convention, accessed May 15, 2016, https://prod-cdn-static.gop.com/media/documents/DRAFT_12_FINAL%5B1%5D-ben_1468872234.pdf.

776   Steve Benen, "Republican platform reflects the party's far-right evolu-

tion," *MSNBC*, July 13, 2016, http://www.msnbc.com/rachel-maddow-show/republican-platform-reflects-the-partys-far-right-evolution.

777   Jeremy W. Peters, "Emerging Republican Platform Goes Far to the Right," *New York Times*, July 12, 2016, https://www.nytimes.com/2016/07/13/us/politics/republican-convention-issues.html.

778   "Republican Platform 2016," 2016 Republican National Convention, accessed May 15, 2016, https://prod-cdn-static.gop.com/media/documents/DRAFT_12_FINAL%5B1%5D-ben_1468872234.pdf.

779   Pema Levy, "The Porn Crisis, Gay Conversion Therapy, and Other Notable Elements of the GOP Platform," *Mother Jones*, July 13, 2016, https://www.motherjones.com/politics/2016/07/republican-platform-lurches-right/.

780   Dawn Ennis, "Republican National Committee Endorses Anti-Trans 'Bathroom Bills," *The Advocate*, February 25, 2016, https://www.advocate.com/transgender/2016/2/25/republican-national-committee-endorses-anti-trans-bathroom-bills.

781   "Republican Platform 2016," 2016 Republican National Convention, accessed May 15, 2016, https://prod-cdn-static.gop.com/media/documents/DRAFT_12_FINAL%5B1%5D-ben_1468872234.pdf.

782   Jeremy W. Peters, "Emerging Republican Platform Goes Far to the Right," *New York Times*, July 12, 2016, https://www.nytimes.com/2016/07/13/us/politics/republican-convention-issues.html.

783   Sean Sullivan, "Trump hires ex-Cruz super PAC strategist Kellyanne Conway," *Washington Post*, July 1, 2016, https://www.washingtonpost.com/news/post-politics/wp/2016/07/01/trump-hires-ex-cruz-super-pac-strategist-kellyanne-conway/.

784   Phillip Elliott, "How Donald Trump Hired and Fired Paul Manafort," *TIME*, October 30, 2017, https://time.com/5003298/paul-manafort-indictment-donald-trump/.

785   "Conway: Press Secretary Gave 'Alternative Facts'," *NBC News*, January 22, 2017, https://www.nbcnews.com/meet-the-press/video/conway-press-secretary-gave-alternative-facts-860142147643.

786   David Weigel, "Phyllis Schlafly faces coup over Trump endorsement," The Washington Post, April 11, 2016, https://www.washingtonpost.com/news/post-politics/wp/2016/04/11/phyllis-schlafly-endorses-trump-then-faces-coup/.

787   David Weigel and Jose A. Del Real, "Phyllis Schlafly endorses Trump in St. Louis," The Washington Post, March 11, 2016, https://www.washingtonpost.com/news/post-politics/wp/2016/03/11/phyllis-schlafly-endorses-trump-in-st-louis/.

788   David A. Graham, "There Is No Trump Campaign," *The Atlantic*, June 9, 2016, https://www.theatlantic.com/politics/archive/2016/06/there-is-no-trump-campaign/486380/.

789   David A. Graham, "There Is No Trump Campaign," *The Atlantic*, June 9, 2016, https://www.theatlantic.com/politics/archive/2016/06/there-is-no-trump-campaign/486380/.

790   Ron Elving, "What Happened With Merrick Garland In 2016 And Why It Matters Now," *National Public Radio*, June 29, 2018, https://www.npr.org/2018/06/29/624467256/what-happened-with-merrick-garland-in-2016-and-why-it-matters-now.

791   Yi Zhou and Archie Tse, "How Republican Senators Voted on Sotomayor," *New York Times*, August 6, 2009, https://archive.nytimes.com/www.nytimes.com/interactive/2009/07/31/us/politics/0731-sotomayor-vote.html?em.

792   "Senate Vote 229 - Confirms Elena Kagan to the Supreme Court," *Pro-Publica*, August 5, 2010, https://projects.propublica.org/represent/votes/111/senate/2/229.

793   Ron Elving, "What Happened With Merrick Garland In 2016 And Why It Matters Now," *National Public Radio*, June 29, 2018, https://www.npr.org/2018/06/29/624467256/what-happened-with-merrick-garland-in-2016-and-why-it-matters-now.

794   Ron Elving, "What Happened With Merrick Garland In 2016 And Why It Matters Now," *National Public Radio*, June 29, 2018, https://www.npr.org/2018/06/29/624467256/what-happened-with-merrick-garland-in-2016-and-why-it-matters-now.

795   Marjorie Dannenfelser and Frank Pavone, "Dear pro-lifers: Trump absolutely worth your vote," *The Washington Examiner*, November 5, 2016, https://www.washingtonexaminer.com/dear-pro-lifers-trump-absolutely-worth-your-vote.

796   Rebecca Harrington and Sonam Sheth, "Here's where Trump stands on abortion and other women's health issues," *Business Insider*, November 9, 2016, https://www.businessinsider.com/donald-trump-abortion-womens-health-platforms-positions-2016-11.

797   "Media Advisory: House Will Vote on Five Month Abortion Limit," Susan B. Anthony List (news release), September 25, 2017. https://www.sba-list.org/newsroom/press-releases/media-advisory-house-will-vote-five-month-abortion-limit.

798   "Election 2016: Life on the Line," Susan B. Anthony List, Accessed July 31, 2019, https://www.sba-list.org/trump-vs-clinton.

799   Susheela Singh, Lisa Remez, Gilda Sedgh, Lorraine Kwok, and Tsuyoshi Onda, "Abortion Worldwide 2017: Uneven Progress and Unequal Access," Guttmacher Institute, March 2018, https://www.guttmacher.org/report/abortion-worldwide-2017#.

800   "Election 2016: Life on the Line," Susan B. Anthony List, Accessed July 31, 2019, https://www.sba-list.org/trump-vs-clinton.

801   National Pro Life Alliance, *2016 Federal Candidates Region 5*, PDF file, accessed May 13, 2020, http://nationalprolifealliance.com/2016/Region5Roster.pdf.

802   Dave Andrusko, "On the eve of Super Tuesday, more on Trump and abortion," *NRL News Today*, February 29, 2016, https://www.nationalrighttolifenews.org/2016/02/on-the-eve-of-super-tuesday-more-on-trump-and-abortio/.

803   David Brody, "Exclusive: Donald Trump Tells Brody File: Roe v. Wade Was Wrongly Decided," *The Brody File* (blog), CBN News, February 18, 2016, https://www1.cbn.com/thebrodyfile/archive/2016/02/18/exclusive-donald-trump-tells-brody-file-roe-v.-wade-was.

804   "Presidential Candidates Pledge to Advance Pro-Life Issues In Office," Susan B. Anthony List (news release), June 17, 2011, https://www.sba-list.org/newsroom/press-releases/presidential-candidates-pledge-advance-pro-life-issues-office.

805   Mitt Romney, "My Pro-Life Pledge," *National Review*, June 18, 2011, https://www.nationalreview.com/corner/my-pro-life-pledge-mitt-romney/.

806   Jane Coaston, "'Borking,' explained: why a failed Supreme Court nomination in 1987 matters," *Vox*, September 27, 2018, https://www.vox.com/2018/9/26/17896126/bork-kavanaugh-supreme-court-conservatives-republicans.

807   Peter Sullivan, "Trump promises to appoint anti-abortion Supreme Court justices," *The Hill*, May 11, 2016, https://thehill.com/policy/healthcare/279535-trump-on-justices-they-will-be-pro-life.

808   Alan Rappeport and Charlie Savage, "Donald Trump Releases List of Pos-

sible Supreme Court Picks," *New York Times*, May 18, 2016, https://www.nytimes.com/2016/05/19/us/politics/donald-trump-supreme-court-nominees.html.

809   Alan Rappeport and Charlie Savage, "Donald Trump Releases List of Possible Supreme Court Picks," *New York Times*, May 18, 2016, https://www.nytimes.com/2016/05/19/us/politics/donald-trump-supreme-court-nominees.html.

810   Dan McLaughlin, "Three Thoughts on Donald Trump's Supreme Court List," *National Review*, May 18, 2016, https://www.nationalreview.com/corner/donald-trumps-supreme-court-list-too-little-too-late/.

811   "SBA List Responds to Trump's SCOTUS List," Susan B. Anthony List (news release), May 18, 2016, https://www.sba-list.org/newsroom/press-releases/sba-list-responds-trumps-scotus-list.

812   Anugrah Kumar, "Has Donald Trump Accepted Christ? James Dobson Says 'Yes,'" *Christian Post*, June 27, 2016, https://www.christianpost.com/news/has-donald-trump-accepted-jesus-christ-james-dobson-says-yes.html

813   Penny Young Nance, "The Question Trump Never Answered at His Meeting With Evangelicals," *Christian Post*, June 29, 2016, https://www.christianpost.com/news/the-question-trump-never-answered-at-his-meeting-with-evangelicals.html?page=1.

814   Richard Ducayne, "Trump Meets With Christian Leaders," *Church Militant*, June 21, 2016, https://www.churchmilitant.com/news/article/trump-meets-with-christian-leaders.

815   "The Insidious Power of the Anti-Choice Movement," NARAL Pro-Choice America, 2018, https://www.prochoiceamerica.org/wp-content/uploads/2018/01/NARAL-Research-Report_FINAL-LINKS.pdf.

816   Sarah Posner, "How Donald Trump Divided and Conquered Evangelicals," *Rolling Stone*, July 21, 2016, https://www.rollingstone.com/politics/politics-features/how-donald-trump-divided-and-conquered-evangelicals-107456/.

817   Penny Young Nance, "The Question Trump Never Answered at His Meeting With Evangelicals," *The Christian Post*, June 29, 2016, https://www.christianpost.com/news/the-question-trump-never-answered-at-his-meeting-with-evangelicals.html?page=2.

818   Penny Young Nance, "The Question Trump Never Answered at His Meeting With Evangelicals," *The Christian Post*, June 29, 2016, https://www.christianpost.com/news/the-question-trump-never-answered-at-his-meeting-with-evangelicals.html?page=2.

819   Irin Carmon, "Trump appeals to social conservatives with his hire of John Mashburn," *MSNBC*, May 5, 2016, http://www.msnbc.com/msnbc/trump-appeals-social-conservatives-his-hire-john-mashburn.

820   "The Helms Amendment," Population Connection Action Fund, accessed May 14, 2020, https://www.populationconnectionaction.org/the-helms-amendment/.

821   Irin Carmon, "Trump appeals to social conservatives with his hire of John Mashburn," *MSNBC*, May 5, 2016, http://www.msnbc.com/msnbc/trump-appeals-social-conservatives-his-hire-john-mashburn.

822   Sean Sullivan, "Trump hires ex-Cruz super PAC strategist Kellyanne Conway," The Washington Post, July 1, 2016, https://www.washingtonpost.com/news/post-politics/wp/2016/07/01/trump-hires-ex-cruz-super-pac-strategist-kelly-anne-conway/.

823   Amy Trend "Falwell backs Trump's choice for VP, says evangelicals will 'enthusiastically' embrace Pence," *News & Advance*, July 15, 2016, https://www.newsadvance.com/news/local/falwell-backs-trump-s-choice-for-vp-says-evangelicals-will/article_98f58d10-4ac9-11e6-bc49-bf6e50ca1453.html.

824   Matthew Nussbaum, "Trump flirts with unpopular Pence," *Politico*, July 12, 2016, https://www.politico.com/story/2016/07/trump-mike-pence-vice-president-225387.

825   Matthew Nussbaum, "Trump flirts with unpopular Pence," *Politico*, July 12, 2016, https://www.politico.com/story/2016/07/trump-mike-pence-vice-president-225387.

826   Eric Bradner, Dana Bash, and MJ Lee, "Donald Trump selects Mike Pence as VP," *CNN*, July 16, 2016, https://www.cnn.com/2016/07/14/politics/donald-trump-vice-presidential-choice/index.html.

827   Paul Bedard, "Falwell Jr. calls Trump/Pence most faith-friendly White House 'ever,'" *Washington Secrets* (blog), *Washington Examiner,* May 10, 2019, https://www.washingtonexaminer.com/washington-secrets/falwell-calls-trump-pence-most-faith-friendly-white-house-ever.

828   Ralph Ellis, Ashley Fantz, Faith Karimi, and Eliott C. McLaughlin, "Orlando shooting: 49 killed, shooter pledged ISIS allegiance," *CNN*, June 13, 2016, https://www.cnn.com/2016/06/12/us/orlando-nightclub-shooting/index.html.

829   Jennifer Jacobs, "Trump Goes Traditional With Florida Meeting of Evangelical Leaders," *Bloomberg*, August 9, 2016, https://webcache.googleusercontent.com/search?q=cache:VOu4CzC-gdkJ:https://www.bloomberg.com/news/articles/2016-08-09/trump-to-meet-privately-with-700-evangelical-leaders-in-florida-this-week+&cd=1&hl=en&ct=clnk&gl=us.

830   Kurtis Lee, "Donald Trump polling stronger with evangelicals than Mitt Romney four years ago," *Baltimore Sun*, July 13, 2016, https://www.baltimoresun.com/la-na-trailguide-updates-1468439539-htmlstory.html.

831   "Trump Letter on Pro-Life Coalition," Susan B. Anthony List, accessed May 14, 2020, https://www.sba-list.org/wp-content/uploads/2016/09/Trump-Letter-on-ProLife-Coalition.pdf.

832   "Trump Letter on Pro-Life Coalition," Susan B. Anthony List, accessed May 14, 2020, https://www.sba-list.org/wp-content/uploads/2016/09/Trump-Letter-on-ProLife-Coalition.pdf.

833   "Trump Outlines Pro-Life Commitments, Taps SBA List's Dannenfelser to Chair Pro-Life Coalition," Susan B. Anthony List (news release), September 16, 2016, https://www.sba-list.org/newsroom/press-releases/trump-outlines-pro-life-commitments-taps-sba-lists-dannenfelser-chair-pro-life-coalition.

834   Katie Glueck, "Trump taps top abortion foe to chair anti-abortion coalition," *Politico*, September 16, 2016, https://www.politico.com/story/2016/09/donald-trump-marjorie-dannenfelser-abortion-228252.

835   Matt Bowman, "Donald Trump Sets New Pro-Life Standard," *National Pulse*, November 6, 2016, https://thenationalpulse.com/commentary/donald-trump-sets-new-pro-life-standard/.

836   Ben Tinker, "Reality Check: Trump on Clinton allowing abortions 'in the 9th month, on the final day,'" *CNN*, October 20, 2016, https://www.cnn.com/2016/10/20/politics/donald-trump-hillary-clinton-abortion-fact-check/index.html.

837   Carimah Townes, "Donald Trump spews incorrect facts about late-term abortion during final debate," *Think Progress*, October 20, 2016, https://thinkprogress.org/trump-debate-roe-wade-290089ed4734/.

838   Pam Belluck, "Trump Said Women Get Abortions Days Before Birth. Doctors Say They Dont," *New York Times*, October 20, 2016, https://www.nytimes.com/2016/10/21/health/donald-trump-debate-late-abortion-remarks.html.

839   Kelly Cervantes, "Why I Had a Late-Term Abortion," *Cosmopolitan*, March 8, 2016, https://www.cosmopolitan.com/politics/news/a54680/why-i-had-a-late-term-abortion/.

840   Jeremy W. Peters, "Trump on Their Side, Conservatives See Hope in Lengthy Abortion Fight," *New York Times,* January 26, 2017, https://www.nytimes.com/2017/01/26/us/politics/democrats-republicans-planned-parenthood.html.

841   Jeremy W. Peters, "Trump on Their Side, Conservatives See Hope in Lengthy Abortion Fight," *New York Times,* January 26, 2017, https://www.nytimes.com/2017/01/26/us/politics/democrats-republicans-planned-parenthood.html.

842   Bradford Richardson, "Pro-life groups struggle against Planned Parenthood funding in Virginia politics," *Washington Times*, October 25, 2017, https://www.washingtontimes.com/news/2017/oct/25/virginia-pro-life-message-muffled-by-planned-paren/.

843   Meabh Ritchie, "Meet Marjorie Dannenfelser: The woman set to make Donald Trump's anti-abortion policies a reality," *The Telegraph,* September 26, 2016, https://www.telegraph.co.uk/women/politics/donald-trump-abortion-row-meet-marjorie-dannenfelser-the-woman-s/.

844   Matea Gold and Anu Narayanswamy, "GOP donors, fearful of Trump-fueled electoral rout, direct big money down-ballot," *Washington Post*, August 11, 2016, https://www.washingtonpost.com/politics/gop-donors-fearful-of-trump-fueled-electoral-rout-direct-big-money-down-ballot/2016/08/11/bb1a2826-5fda-11e6-af8e-54aa2e849447_story.html.

845   Janet Hook, Beth Reinhard, and Reid J. Epstein, "GOP Scrambles to Salvage Election After Donald Trump's Latest Imbroglio," *Wall Street Journal*, October 8, 2016, https://www.wsj.com/articles/gop-scrambles-to-salvage-election-after-donald-trumps-latest-imbroglio-1475969203.

846   Reid Wilson and Joe Disipio, "Clinton holds huge ground game advantage over Team Trump," *The Hill*, October 22, 2016, https://thehill.com/campaign/302231-clinton-holds-huge-ground-game-advantage-over-team-trump.

847   David A. Graham, "There Is No Trump Campaign," *The Atlantic*, June 9, 2016, https://www.theatlantic.com/politics/archive/2016/06/there-is-no-trump-campaign/486380/.

848   *"By the Numbers: 2014 Midterm Elections," Susan B. Anthony List, November 4, 2014, https://www.sba-list.org/newsroom/press-releases/numbers-2014-midterm-elections.*

849   "About," Susan B. Anthony List, Accessed July 15, 2019, https://www.sba-list.org/about-susan-b-anthony-list.

850   Susan B. Anthony List, "Dannenfelser: The Way Forward for the Pro-Life Movement," YouTube (video), 04:05, November 9, 2016, https://www.youtube.com/watch?v=JpDpbmWCWNw.

851   "Victory: Judge Gorsuch Confirmed to the Supreme Court," Susan B. Anthony List (blog), April 7, 2017, https://www.sba-list.org/suzy-b-blog/victory-judge-gorsuch-confirmed-supreme-court.

852   "Pro-Life Victory: Judge Joan Larsen Confirmed," Susan B. Anthony List (news release), November 1, 2017, https://www.sba-list.org/newsroom/press-releases/pro-life-victory-judge-joan-larsen-confirmed.

853   "SBA List Election Night HQ," Susan B. Anthony List, accessed October 10, 2017, https://www.sba-list.org/electionhq.

854   Federal Election Commission, "Women Speak Out Political Action Committee," Spending 2015-2016 (Raw Data), accessed November 12, 2017, https://www.fec.gov/data/committee/C00530766/?tab=spending&cycle=2016.

855   "Victory: Judge Gorsuch Confirmed to the Supreme Court," Susan B. Anthony List (Blog), April 7, 2017, https://www.sba-list.org/suzy-b-blog/victory-judge-gorsuch-confirmed-supreme-court.

856   "SBA List Knocks 1 Million+ Doors in Battleground States, Expands Digital

Campaign," Susan B. Anthony List (news release), October 31, 2016, https://www.sba-list.org/newsroom/press-releases/sba-list-knocks-1-million-doors-battle-ground-states-expands-digital-campaign.

857   "Women Speak Out PAC - Summary," *Open Secrets,* Center for Responsive Politics, accessed December 6, 2017, https://www.opensecrets.org/pacs/lookup2.php?strID=C00530766&cycle=2016.

858   Susan B. Anthony List, "TV Ad: Micah," YouTube (video), 01:00, August 2, 2016, https://www.youtube.com/watch?v=fw7bMhkguGM.

859   *Claire Chretien, "Pro-life group reaches twice as many voters as Planned Parenthood with roughly half the budget," Life Site News, October 31, 2016, https://www.lifesitenews.com/news/pro-life-group-reaches-twice-as-many-voters-as-planned-parenthood-with-roug.*

860   Claire Chretien, "Pro-life group reaches twice as many voters as Planned Parenthood with roughly half the budget," *Life Site News,* October 31, 2016, https://www.lifesitenews.com/news/pro-life-group-reaches-twice-as-many-voters-as-planned-parenthood-with-roug.

861   Paul DuPont, "WATCH: Pro-Life Group Releases New Ad Supporting Trump," *National Pulse,* November 7, 2016, https://thenationalpulse.com/politics/watch-pro-life-group-releases-new-ad-supporting-trump/.

862   Susan B. Anthony List, "Election 2016 Ad: 'Not Okay,'" YouTube (video), 0:15, November 4, 2016, https://www.youtube.com/watch?v=0QgIjhqSqW0.

863   Susan B. Anthony List, "The difference between Trump and Clinton on abortion couldn't be clearer," Facebook (video), 0:15, accessed November 2, 2016, https://www.facebook.com/watch/?v=10153780447361370.

864   Susan B. Anthony List, "EWTN: Dannenfelser on Efforts to Mobilize Pro-life Voters," YouTube (video), 2:41, November 7, 2016, https://www.youtube.com/watch?v=V7g1oS4GYLA.

865   Barbara Saldivar, "Kansas Election Resources and More!" Concerned Women for America, October 26, 2016, https://concernedwomen.org/kansas-election-resources-and-more/.

866   Terri Johannessen, "Merry Christmas from CWA of Florida and Looking Forward to 2017," Concerned Women for America, December 18, 2016, https://concernedwomen.org/merry-christmas-from-cwa-of-florida-and-looking-forward-to-2017/.

867   "Judges," Concerned Women for America PAC, YouTube, 2:20, September 14, 2016, https://www.youtube.com/watch?v=0ub8jK73uDk.

868   "National Right to Life Congratulates Donald Trump," *National Right to Life* (news release), November 9, 2016, https://www.nrlc.org/communications/releases/2016/national-right-to-life-congratulates-donald-trump/.

869   "National Right to Life - Summary," *Open Secrets,* Center for Responsive Politics, accessed July 31, 2019, https://www.opensecrets.org/pacs/lookup2.php?strID=C00111278&cycle=2012.

870   "About the Faith and Freedom Coalition" Faith & Freedom Coalition, accessed May 14, 2020, https://www.ffcoalition.com/about/.

871   "About the Faith and Freedom Coalition" Faith & Freedom Coalition, accessed May 14, 2020, https://www.ffcoalition.com/about/.

872   "Activities of Priests for Life - Election 2016," *Political Responsibility Center,* Priests for Life, accessed May 14, 2020, https://www.priestsforlife.org/vote/2016-activities.aspx.

873   "Vote Pro-Life Coalition," Vote Pro-Life Coalition, accessed May 14, 2020, http://voteprolifecoalition.com/.

874   Kate Kaye, "Data-Driven Targeting Creates Huge 2016 Political Ad Shift:

Broadcast Down 20%, Cable and Digital Way Up," *AdAge*, January 3, 2017, https://ad-age.com/article/media/2016-political-broadcast-tv-spend-20-cable-52/307346.

875   Emma Roller, "Willie Horton's Heirs," *New York Times*, January 12, 2016, https://www.nytimes.com/2016/01/12/opinion/campaign-stops/ads-from-donald-trump-and-ted-cruz-play-to-racist-fears.html.

876   "Trump's Racist Ad Depicts Wrong Country," *Cheat Sheet* (blog), *Daily Beast*, updated April 13, 2017, https://www.thedailybeast.com/cheats/2016/01/04/trump-s-racist-ad-depicts-wrong-country.

877   Emily Stewart, "Most Russian Facebook ads sought to divide Americans on race," Vox, May 13, 2018, https://www.vox.com/policy-and-politics/2018/5/13/17349670/facebook-russia-ads-race-house-democrats.

878   "Exit Polls 2016," *Election 2016*, CNN, November 15, 2016, https://www.cnn.com/election/2016/results/exit-polls/ohio/president.

879   Tiffany Stanley, "The Revival of the Old Religious Right," Religion and Politics, November 11, 2016, https://religionandpolitics.org/2016/11/11/the-revival-of-the-old-religious-right/.

880   Susan B. Anthony List, "Marjorie Dannenfelser on PBS: 2016 Election Revolutionized the Politics of Abortion," YouTube (video), 6:08, January 30, 2017, https://www.youtube.com/watch?v=P2TrhfZJ4xc.

881   Amanda Marcotte, "Pickup artists don't just sound like Trump, they worship the very ground he walks on," *Salon*, June 4, 2016, https://www.salon.com/2016/06/04/pickup_artists_dont_just_sound_like_trump_they_worship_the_very_ground_he_walks_on/.

882   Andrew Buncombe, "Controversial pick-up artist Roosh V celebrates Donald Trump's victory: 'If the President can say it then you can say it,'" *The Independent*, Nov 16, 2016, https://www.independent.co.uk/news/people/controversial-pick-up-artist-roosh-v-celebrates-donald-trump-s-victory-if-the-president-can-say-it-a7421161.html.

883   James Allsup via Twitter.com, October 6, 2017, Account suspended. For more information, see NARAL Research.

884   Chad Sokol, "WSU College Republicans leader says he was attacked amid D.C. inauguration protests," The Spokane Spokesman-Review, January 20, 2017, https://www.spokesman.com/stories/2017/jan/20/wsu-college-republicans-leader-says-he-was-attacke/.

885   James Allsup via Twitter, October 6, 2017, Account suspended. For more information, see NARAL Research.

886   Tara Bahrampour and Scott Clement, "White working-class men increasingly falling behind as college becomes the norm," *Washington Post*, October 5, 2016, https://www.washingtonpost.com/local/social-issues/white-working-class-men-increasingly-falling-behind-as-college-becomes-the-norm/2016/10/05/95610130-8a51-11e6-875e-2c1bfe943b66_story.html.

887   "Megyn Kelly Calls Out Trump for Sexism," *Cheat Sheet* (blog), *Daily Beast*, updated April 14, 2017, https://www.thedailybeast.com/cheats/2015/08/06/megyn-kelly-call-out-trump-for-sexism.

888   "Trump: Megyn Kelly Has 'Blood Coming Out of Her Wherever,'" *Cheat Sheet* (blog), *Daily Beast,* updated April 14, 2017, https://www.thedailybeast.com/cheats/2015/08/07/trump-megyn-kelly-has-blood-coming-out-of-somewhere-else.

889   Tufayel Ahmed, "Megyn Kelly Reflects on 'Scary' Time When Trump Attacked Her for Questioning His Treatment of Women," *Newsweek*, December 14, 2019, https://www.newsweek.com/megyn-kelly-interview-scary-trump-breitbart-attacks-1477262.

890   Tom Liddy, "Newt Gingrich Tells Megyn Kelly 'You Are Fascinated With Sex' When She Mentions Trump's Accusers," *ABC News*, October 25, 2016, https://abc-news.go.com/Politics/newt-gingrich-tells-megyn-kelly-fascinated-sex-mentions/story?id=43060668.

891   Zoe Todd, "'Cull Her Out': How Megyn Kelly went from Fox News Star to Alt-Right Target," *Frontline, Public Broadcasting Service*, December 13, 2019, https://www.pbs.org/wgbh/frontline/article/cull-her-out-how-megyn-kelly-went-from-fox-news-star-to-alt-right-target/.

892   "Donald Trump Mocks Accusers, Calls Them Unattractive and Liars," *Fortune*, October 15, 2016, https://fortune.com/2016/10/15/donald-trump-sexual-assault-women/.

893   Libby Nelson and Emily Crockett, "Sexual assault allegations against Donald Trump: 15 women say he groped, kissed, or assaulted them," *Vox*, updated January 19, 2017, https://www.vox.com/2016/10/12/13265206/trump-accusations-sexual-assault.

894   David A. Fahrenthold, "Trump recorded having extremely lewd conversation about women in 2005," *Washington Post*, October 8, 2016, https://www.washingtonpost.com/politics/trump-recorded-having-extremely-lewd-conversation-about-women-in-2005/2016/10/07/3b9ce776-8cb4-11e6-bf8a-3d26847eeed4_story.html?itid=lk_inline_manual_2.

895   Alex Isenstadt, "RNC halts Victory project work for Trump," *Politico*, October 8, 2016, https://www.politico.com/story/2016/10/rnc-halts-all-victory-project-work-for-trump-229363.

896   Alan Yuhas, "The growing list of Republicans withdrawing support for Donald Trump," *THe Guardian*, October 9, 2016, https://www.theguardian.com/us-news/2016/oct/08/donald-trump-list-of-republicans-reject-support-endorsement.

897   David A. Fahrenthold, "Trump recorded having extremely lewd conversation about women in 2005," *Washington Post*, October 8, 2016, https://www.washingtonpost.com/politics/trump-recorded-having-extremely-lewd-conversation-about-women-in-2005/2016/10/07/3b9ce776-8cb4-11e6-bf8a-3d26847eeed4_story.html?itid=lk_inline_manual_2.

898   Andrea Mitchell and Alastair Jamieson, "Trump Planned Debate 'Stunt,' Invited Bill Clinton Accusers to Rattle Hillary," *NBC News*, October 10, 2016, https://www.nbcnews.com/storyline/2016-presidential-debates/trump-planned-debate-stunt-invited-bill-clinton-accusers-rattle-hillary-n663481.

899   David Brody and Scott Lamb, *The Faith of Donald J. Trump: A Spiritual Biography,* (New York: Harper Collins, 2018), p 181 (Kindle ed.).

900   Yousef Saba, "Falwell censored anti-Trump column, Liberty U student editor says," *Politico*, October 18, 2016, https://www.politico.com/story/2016/10/jerry-falwell-donald-trump-liberty-229964.

901   Alex Rohr, "Falwell stands with Trump, believes GOP leaked video," *News & Advance*, October 11, 2016, https://www.newsadvance.com/archives/falwell-stands-with-trump-believes-gop-leaked-video/article_a5dc66c7-e967-5c81-81e7-794987e517e7.html.

902   Will E. Young, "Inside Liberty University's 'culture of fear,'" *Washington Post*, July 24, 2019, https://www.washingtonpost.com/outlook/2019/07/24/inside-liberty-universitys-culture-fear-how-jerry-falwell-jr-silences-students-professors-who-reject-his-pro-trump-politics/?arc404=true.

903   Jim Galloway, "Ralph Reed, Jerry Falwell unshaken by Donald Trump video," *Political Insider* (blog), *Atlanta Journal Constitution*, October 10, 2016, https://www.ajc.com/blog/politics/ralph-reed-jerry-falwell-unshaken-donald-trump-vid-

eo/OlxxFocljn5JgyWJXSrCRK/.

904   Ralph Reed, "Here is my statement on Donald Trump's comments made off-camera during an Access Hollywood interview in 2005," Facebook, October 8, 2016, https://www.facebook.com/ralphreedjr/posts/here-is-my-statement-on-donald-trumps-comments-made-off-camera-during-an-access-/525672827635710/.

905   Sarah Pulliam Bailey, "Standing by Donald Trump, Pat Robertson calls lewd video 'macho talk,'" Washington Post, October 10, 2016, https://www.washingtonpost.com/news/acts-of-faith/wp/2016/10/10/pat-robertson-what-donald-trump-said-in-lewd-video-was-macho/.

906   Sarah Cliff, "No, Donald Trump, abortions do not happen at 9 months pregnant," Vox, October 19, 2016, https://www.vox.com/2016/10/19/13341532/abortion-9-months-trump.

907   David Brody and Scott Lamb, The Faith of Donald J. Trump: A Spiritual Biography, (New York: Harper Collins, 2018).

908   David Brody, "Exclusive: Donald Trump Tells Brody File: Roe v. Wade Was Wrongly Decided," The Brody File (blog), CBN News, February 18, 2016, https://www1.cbn.com/thebrodyfile/archive/2016/02/18/exclusive-donald-trump-tells-brody-file-roe-v.-wade-was.

909   Jill Filipovic, "A new poll shows what really interests 'pro-lifers': controlling women," The Guardian, August 22, 2019, https://www.theguardian.com/commentisfree/2019/aug/22/a-new-poll-shows-what-really-interests-pro-lifers-controlling-women.

910   Marjorie Dannenfelser and Frank Pavone, "Dear pro-lifers: Trump absolutely worth your vote," Washington Examiner, November 5, 2016, https://www.washingtonexaminer.com/dear-pro-lifers-trump-absolutely-worth-your-vote.

911   Julia Hahn, "Exclusive—Phyllis Schlafly Makes the Case for President Trump: 'Only Hope to Defeat the Kingmakers,'" Breitbart, January 10, 2016, https://www.breitbart.com/politics/2016/01/10/phyllis-schlafly-makes-the-case-for-president-trump/.

912   Julia Hahn, "Exclusive—Phyllis Schlafly Makes the Case for President Trump: 'Only Hope to Defeat the Kingmakers,'" Breitbart, January 10, 2016, https://www.breitbart.com/politics/2016/01/10/phyllis-schlafly-makes-the-case-for-president-trump/.

913   Douglas Martin, "Phyllis Schlafly, 'First Lady' of a Political March to the Right, Dies at 92," New York Times, September 5, 2016, https://www.nytimes.com/2016/09/06/obituaries/phyllis-schlafly-conservative-leader-and-foe-of-era-dies-at-92.html.

914   Phyllis Schlafly, Ed Martin, and Brett M. Decker, The Conservative Case for Trump (Washington D.C.: Regnery Publishing, 2016).

915   Amber Jamieson, Simon Jeffery, and Nicole Puglise, "A timeline of Donald Trump's alleged sexual misconduct: who, when and what," The Guardian, October 27, 2016, https://www.theguardian.com/us-news/2016/oct/13/list-of-donald-trump-sexual-misconduct-allegations.

916   Art Buchwald, "Yes, We Have No Harassment," Washington Post, April 30, 1981, https://www.washingtonpost.com/archive/lifestyle/1981/04/30/yes-we-have-no-harassment/504bca10-7b5a-486b-8329-34aa4cc567b4/.

917   Eugene Scott, "When Phyllis Schlafly made the case for DoOnald Trump," CNN, September 7, 2016, https://www.cnn.com/2016/09/07/politics/phyllis-schlafly-donald-trump-book/index.html.

918   Philip Bump, "Donald Trump will be president thanks to 80,000 people in three states," The Washington Post, December 1, 2016, https://www.washington-

post.com/news/the-fix/wp/2016/12/01/donald-trump-will-be-president-thanks-to-80000-people-in-three-states/.

919   "Exit Polls - National President," *Election 2016, CNN*, November 23, 2016, https://www.cnn.com/election/2016/results/exit-polls/national/president.

920   W. Scott Lamb, "5 questions with congressional candidate Chad Connelly," *Washington Times*, March 22, 2017, https://www.washingtontimes.com/news/2017/mar/22/5-questions-with-congressional-candidate-chad-conn/.

921   "Exit Polls - National President," *Election 2016, CNN*, November 23, 2016, https://www.cnn.com/election/2016/results/exit-polls/national/president.

922   Faith & Freedom Coalition, " FFC 2016 Election Impact," YouTube (video), 35:36, December 6, 2016, https://www.youtube.com/watch?v=9Sgxa4jLOIM.

923   Kristan Hawkins, "Our time is now," *Students for Life* (blog), November 9, 2016, https://studentsforlife.org/2016/11/09/our-time-is-now-5/.

924   Kristan Hawkins, "Our time is now," *Students for Life* (blog), November 9, 2016, https://studentsforlife.org/2016/11/09/our-time-is-now-5/.

925   Donald J. Trump, "The Inaugural Address," WhiteHouse.gov, January 20, 2017, https://www.whitehouse.gov/briefings-statements/the-inaugural-address/.

926   Tess Owen, "The Women's March turnout is at 3.2 million and counting," Vice News, January 23, 2017, https://www.vice.com/en_ca/article/a3jbpp/womens-march-turnout-is-at-3-2-million-and-counting.

927   Meghan Keneally, "More Than 1 Million Rally at Women's Marches in US and Around World," ABC News, January 22, 2017, https://abcnews.go.com/Politics/womens-march-heads-washington-day-trumps-inauguration/story?id=44936042.

928   Erica Chenoweth and Jeremy Pressman, "This is what we learned by counting the women's marches," Monkey Cage, The Washington Post, February 7, 2017, https://www.washingtonpost.com/news/monkey-cage/wp/2017/02/07/this-is-what-we-learned-by-counting-the-womens-marches/

929   Tess Owen, "The Women's March turnout is at 3.2 million and counting," Vice News, January 23, 2017, https://www.vice.com/en_ca/article/a3jbpp/womens-march-turnout-is-at-3-2-million-and-counting.

930   Alanna Vagianos and Damon Dahlen, "89 Badass Feminist Signs From The Women's March On Washington," HuffPost, January 21, 2017, https://www.huffpost.com/entry/89-badass-feminist-signs-from-the-womens-march-on-washington_n_5883ea28e4b070d8cad310cd.

931   Masuma Ahuja, "Yes, even people in Antarctica are joining the Women's March movement," CNN Politics, January 21, 2017, https://www.cnn.com/2017/01/21/politics/womens-march-antarctica/index.html.

932   Tess Owen, "The Women's March turnout is at 3.2 million and counting," Vice News, January 23, 2017, https://www.vice.com/en_ca/article/a3jbpp/womens-march-turnout-is-at-3-2-million-and-counting.

933   Elle Hunt, "Trump's inauguration crowd: Sean Spicer's claims versus the evidence," The Guardian, January 22, 2017, https://www.theguardian.com/us-news/2017/jan/22/trump-inauguration-crowd-sean-spicers-claims-versus-the-evidence.

934   Rebecca Davis O'Brien, Rebecca Ballhaus, and Aruna Viswanatha, "Trump Inauguration Spending Under Criminal Investigation by Federal Prosecutors," The Wall Street Journal, December 13, 2018, https://www.wsj.com/articles/trump-inauguration-spending-under-criminal-investigation-by-federal-prosecutors-11544736455.

935   Russ Choma, "New Court Documents Reveal That Corruption at the Trump Inaugural Fund Went to the Very Top," Mother Jones, January 24, 2020, https://www.motherjones.com/politics/2020/01/lawsuit-trump-inaugural-com-

mittee-corruption-top-ivanka/.

936   David Smith, "Chris Christie dropped as head of Trump's White House transition team," The Guardian, November 11, 2016, https://www.theguardian.com/us-news/2016/nov/11/chris-christie-dropped-trump-transition-team.

937   Andrew Restuccia and Nancy Cook, "Trump advisers steamroll Christie's transition," Politico, November 15, 2016, https://www.politico.com/story/2016/11/trump-christie-transition-231390.

938   T.A. Frank, "Trump's Dark, Raw Inauguration Speech Shocks Washington," Hive, Vanity Fair, January 20, 2017, https://www.vanityfair.com/news/2017/01/trump-inauguration-speech-shocks-washington.

939   Glenn Kessler and Michelle Ye Hee Lee "Fact-checking President Trump's inaugural address," Fact Checker, The Washington Post, January 20, 2017, https://www.washingtonpost.com/news/fact-checker/wp/2017/01/20/fact-checking-president-trumps-inaugural-address/.

940   Alexandra Jaffe, "Kellyanne Conway: WH Spokesman Gave 'Alternative Facts' on Inauguration Crowd," NBC News, January 22, 2017, https://www.nbcnews.com/storyline/meet-the-press-70-years/wh-spokesman-gave-alternative-facts-inauguration-crowd-n710466.

941   Eric Bradner, "Conway: Trump White House offered 'alternative facts' on crowd size," CNN, January 23, 2017, https://www.cnn.com/2017/01/22/politics/kellyanne-conway-alternative-facts/index.html

942   Alexandra Jaffe, "Kellyanne Conway: WH Spokesman Gave 'Alternative Facts' on Inauguration Crowd," NBC News, January 22, 2017, https://www.nbcnews.com/storyline/meet-the-press-70-years/wh-spokesman-gave-alternative-facts-inauguration-crowd-n710466.

943   Ally Boguhn, "Trump Reinstates Anti-Choice 'Global Gag Rule' Restriction," Rewire.News, January 23, 2017, https://rewire.news/article/2017/01/23/trump-reinstates-anti-choice-global-gag-rule-restriction/.

944   Katelyn Burns, "Trump Administration Announces New Expansion of Global 'Gag Rule,'" Rewire.News, March 26, 2019, https://rewire.news/article/2019/03/26/trump-administration-announces-new-expansion-of-global-gag-rule/.

945   Molly Redden, "Trump expands policy that bans US aid for overseas abortion providers," The Guardian, May 15, 2017, https://www.theguardian.com/world/2017/may/15/trump-abortion-rule-mexico-city-policy.

946   Tess Sohngen, "This Is the Best Way to Lift Women Out of Poverty, According to Melinda Gates," Global Citizen, September 20, 2017, https://www.globalcitizen.org/en/content/melinda-gates-urges-congress-to-fund-family-planni/?fb_comment_id=1632122793485999_1633233800041565.

947   Anna North, "The domestic gag rule on abortion, explained," Vox, May 15, 2018, https://www.vox.com/2018/5/11/17319614/trump-abortion-planned-parenthood-domestic-gag-rule-title-x.

948   Molly Redden, "Trump expands policy that bans US aid for overseas abortion providers," The Guardian, May 15, 2017, https://www.theguardian.com/world/2017/may/15/trump-abortion-rule-mexico-city-policy.

949   Sneha Barot and Susan A. Cohen, "The Global Gag Rule and Fights over Funding UNFPA: The Issues That Won't Go Away," Guttmacher, Spring 2015, https://www.guttmacher.org/sites/default/files/article_files/gpr1802715.pdf.

950   Ali Vitali, Kasie Hunt, and Frank Thorp V, "Trump referred to Haiti and African nations as 'shithole' countries," NBC News, January 11, 2018, https://www.nbcnews.com/politics/white-house/trump-referred-haiti-african-countries-shithole-nations-n836946.

951   Salvador Rizzo, "President Trump's shifting claim that 'we got rid' of the

Johnson Amendment," Fact Checker, The Washington Post, May 9, 2019, https://www.washingtonpost.com/politics/2019/05/09/president-trumps-shifting-claim-that-we-got-rid-johnson-amendment/.

952   Ali Vitali, "Trump Signs 'Religious Liberty' Executive Order Allowing for Broad Exemptions," NBC News, May 4, 2017 https://www.nbcnews.com/news/us-news/trump-signs-religious-liberty-executive-order-allowing-broad-exemptions-n754786

953   Salvador Rizzo, "President Trump's shifting claim that 'we got rid' of the Johnson Amendment," Fact Checker, The Washington Post, May 9, 2019, https://www.washingtonpost.com/politics/2019/05/09/president-trumps-shifting-claim-that-we-got-rid-johnson-amendment/.

954   Jeff Sessions, MEMORANDUM: Federal Law Protections for Religious Liberty, PDF File, via the Office of the Attorney General, October 6, 2017, https://www.justice.gov/opa/press-release/file/1001891/download

955   Sharita Gruberg, Frank J. Bewkes, Elizabeth Platt, Katherine Franke, and Claire Markham, "Religious Liberty for a Select Few," Center for American Progress, April 3, 2018, https://www.americanprogress.org/issues/lgbtq-rights/reports/2018/04/03/448773/religious-liberty-select/.

956   Donald J. Trump, "Numerous states introducing...," Twitter, January 28, 2019, https://twitter.com/realDonaldTrump/status/1089876055224184833.

957   Audie Cornish, "New 'Religious Liberty Task Force' Highlights Sessions, DOJ Priorities," All Things Considered, NPR News, Washington, DC: NPR, August 2, 2018, https://www.npr.org/2018/08/02/635047680/new-religious-liberty-task-force-highlights-sessions-doj-priorities.

958   Emma Green, "Health and Human Services and the Religious-Liberty War," The Atlantic via Google WebCache, May 7, 2019, https://webcache.googleusercontent.com/search?q=cache:YNtWZjCe8YkJ:https://www.theatlantic.com/politics/archive/2019/05/hhs-trump-religious-freedom/588697/+&cd=1&hl=en&ct=clnk&gl=us.

959   Taylor Berglund, "President Trump Calls Abortion 'Execution' During Conference Call With Evangelical Leaders," Charisma Magazine, 2019, https://www.charismamag.com/life/culture/40415-president-trump-calls-abortion-execution-during-conference-call-with-evangelical-leaders.

960   Lorraine Woellert, "I love him so much I can hardly explain it': Evangelical leaders praise Trump after pastor's release," Politico, October 12, 2018, https://www.politico.com/story/2018/10/12/brunson-evangelical-leaders-trump-898396.

961   Michael Lewis, "'This guy doesn't know anything': the inside story of Trump's shambolic transition team," The Guardian, September 27, 2018, https://www.theguardian.com/news/2018/sep/27/this-guy-doesnt-know-anything-the-inside-story-of-trumps-shambolic-transition-team.

962   Tamar Lewin, "In Bitter Abortion Debate, Opponents Learn to Reach for Common Ground," The New York Times, February 17, 1992, https://www.nytimes.com/1992/02/17/us/in-bitter-abortion-debate-opponents-learn-to-reach-for-common-ground.html?pagewanted=all.

963   Chuck Raasch, "Trump to nominate former St. Louis lawyer Puzder as labor secretary," St. Louis Post-Dispatch, December 8, 2016, https://www.stltoday.com/news/local/govt-and-politics/trump-to-nominate-former-st-louis-lawyer-puzder-as-labor/article_5a259060-6f37-5722-8068-a7f43c33ea60.html.

964   Joni Kantor and Jennifer Medina, "Workers Say Andrew Puzder Is 'Not the One to Protect' Them, but He's Been Chosen To," The New York Times, January 15, 2017, https://www.nytimes.com/2017/01/15/us/politics/andrew-puzder-labor-secretary.html.

965   "6 Things to Know About... Andrew Puzder," Washington Week, PBS, https://www.pbs.org/weta/washingtonweek/blog-post/6-things-know-about-andrew-puzder.

966   Joni Kantor and Jennifer Medina, "Workers Say Andrew Puzder Is 'Not the One to Protect' Them, but He's Been Chosen To," The New York Times, January 15, 2017, https://www.nytimes.com/2017/01/15/us/politics/andrew-puzder-labor-secretary.html.

967   Claire Landsbaum, "Ex–Labor Secretary Nominee Says Sexist Ads 'Saved a Lot of Jobs,'" The Cut, March 9, 2017, https://www.thecut.com/2017/03/andrew-puzder-says-sexist-ads-saved-a-lot-of-jobs.html.

968   Noam Scheiber, "Democrats and Allies Wage Fight to Derail Labor Secretary Pick," The New York Times, January 12, 2017, https://www.nytimes.com/2017/01/12/business/andrew-puzder-labor-senate.html.

969   Alan Rappeport, "Andrew Puzder, Trump's Labor Pick, Admits to Hiring Undocumented Maid," The New York Times, February 7, 2017, https://www.nytimes.com/2017/02/07/us/politics/andrew-puzder-labor-trump-undocumented.html.

970   Burgess Everett and Marianne Levine, "Oprah gives tape with Puzder abuse allegations to Senate," Politico, February 13, 2017, https://www.politico.com/story/2017/02/susan-collins-andrew-puzder-oprah-tape-allegations-234964.

971   Manu Raju, "Puzder's ex-wife defends Labor nominee against abuse allegations," CNN Politics, February 7, 2017, https://www.cnn.com/2017/02/07/politics/andy-puzder-ex-wife-labor-nominee-abuse-allegations/index.html.

972   Lisa Baertlein and Sarah N. Lynch, "Fast-food workers protest Trump's labor secretary nominee," Reuters, January 12, 2017, https://www.reuters.com/article/us-usa-congress-puzder/fast-food-workers-protest-trumps-labor-secretary-nominee-idUSKBN14W25A.

973   Burgess Everett, Tara Palmeri, and Marianne Levine, "Labor nominee Puzder withdraws," Politico, February 15, 2017, https://www.politico.com/story/2017/02/senate-republicans-tell-white-house-to-withdraw-puzder-nomination-235062.

974   Michael W. Chapman, "Pastor Robison: Trump Still Standing, Given All the Liberal Attacks, 'Is a Miracle of God,'" CNS News, September 18, 2019, https://www.cnsnews.com/blog/michael-w-chapman/pastor-robison-trump-still-standing-despite-liberal-attacks-miracle-god.

975   Ariel Levy, "Prodigal Son," The New Yorker, June 28, 2010, https://www.newyorker.com/magazine/2010/06/28/prodigal-son.

976   Bud Kennedy, "Texas' James Robison wants 'open door' for Trump spiritual advisers," Fort Worth, Star-Telegram, May 20, 2017, https://www.star-telegram.com/opinion/bud-kennedy/article151763962.html.

977   Marci McDonald, "The Armageddon Factor: The Rise of Christian Nationalism in Canada," Vintage Canada, 2020, pg. 422 https://www.google.com/books/edition/The_Armageddon_Factor/vDDwk6U6o98C?hl=en&gbpv=1&dq=%22james+robison%22+%22tea+party%22+%222010%22&pg=PA422&printsec=frontcover.

978   Kayleigh McEnany, "The New American Revolution: The Making of a Populist Movement," Simon & Schuster,   pg. 249, https://books.google.com/books?id=M52nDwAAQBAJ&pg=PA249&lpg=PA249&dq=%22james+robison%22+%22access+hollywood%22&source=bl&ots=FU2MMUM9KN&sig=ACfU3U3VHiyFNrQri7H1_ypKKtpxYHcyww&hl=en&sa=X&ved=2ahUKEwjK9uG-Fj9fpAhV2gnIEHT-QAM4Q6AEwAnoECAkQAQ#v=onepage&q=%22james%20robison%22%20%22access%20hollywood%22&f=false.

979   David Brody and Scott Lamb, "The Faith of Donald J. Trump," (New York: HarperCollins Publishers, 2018), 261.

980   David Brody and Scott Lamb, "The Faith of Donald J. Trump," (New York: HarperCollins Publishers, 2018), 261.

981   David Brody and Scott Lamb, "The Faith of Donald J. Trump," (New York: HarperCollins Publishers, 2018), 261.

982   "Trump narrows down Supreme Court nominee list to 3," Associated Press, January 24, 2017, https://www.dailynews.com/2017/01/24/trump-narrows-down-supreme-court-nominee-list-to-3/.

983   Robert O'Harrow Jr. and Shawn Boburg, "A conservative activists's campaign to remake the nation's courts," The Washington Post, May 21, 2019, https://www.washingtonpost.com/graphics/2019/investigations/leonard-leo-federal-ists-society-courts/.

984   Robert O'Harrow Jr. and Shawn Boburg, "A conservative activists's campaign to remake the nation's courts," The Washington Post, May 21, 2019, https://www.washingtonpost.com/graphics/2019/investigations/leonard-leo-federal-ists-society-courts/.

985   Robert O'Harrow Jr. and Shawn Boburg, "A conservative activists's campaign to remake the nation's courts," The Washington Post, May 21, 2019, https://www.washingtonpost.com/graphics/2019/investigations/leonard-leo-federal-ists-society-courts/.

986   "Our Board," Student's For Life, Accessed May 14, 2020, https://students-forlife.org/about/boardofdirectors/.

987   Ian Millhiser, "Trump's top domestic policy adviser: being gay is a 'lifestyle' that 'can be changed,'" ThinkProgress, November 11, 2016, https://thinkprogress.org/trumps-top-domestic-policy-adviser-being-gay-is-a-lifestyle-that-can-be-changed-b4d876e0ce31/.

988   The Leadership Institute, "Key Talento," Accessed May 14, 2020, https://www.leadershipinstitute.org/training/contact.cfm?FacultyID=646772.

989   Reay Earhart, "The Real Housewives of Gilead," Advocate, December 2, 2017, https://www.advocate.com/commentary/2017/6/27/real-housewives-gilead.

990   Reay Earhart, "The Real Housewives of Gilead," Advocate, December 2, 2017, https://www.advocate.com/commentary/2017/6/27/real-housewives-gilead.

991   Katy French Talento, "Miscarriage Of Justice: Is Big Pharma Breaking Your Uterus?" The Federalist, January 22, 2015, https://thefederalist.com/2015/01/22/miscarriage-of-justice-is-big-pharma-breaking-your-uterus/.

992   Catherine Pearson, "It's Time To End The 'Birth Control Causes Miscarriage' Myth," HuffPost, January 7, 2017, https://www.huffpost.com/entry/myth-birth-con-trol-miscarriage_n_586fd1cde4b02b5f858891cd.

993   The American College of Obstetricians and Gynecologists, "FAQ: Pregnancy," PDF file, August 2015, https://www.acog.org/-/media/For-Patients/faq090.pdf.

994   Ally Boguhn, "Trump's HHS Installs Fake Clinic Leader to Oversee Family Planning Funds," Rewire News, May 30, 2018. https://rewire.news/article/2018/05/30/trumps-hhs-installs-fake-clinic-leader-oversee-family-planning-funds/.

995   Ally Boguhn, "Trump's HHS Installs Fake Clinic Leader to Oversee Family Planning Funds." https://rewire.news/article/2018/05/30/trumps-hhs-installs-fake-clinic-leader-oversee-family-planning-funds/.

996   Rosie McCall, "From 'Smoking Doesn't Kill' To Conversion Therapy—Mike Pence's Most Controversial Science Remarks," Newsweek, February 27, 2020, https://www.newsweek.com/mike-pence-coronavirus-science-hiv-aids-smoking-evolution-climate-change-1489458.

997   Fiona Hearst, "What are Mike Pence's Irish roots?" RTÉ News, Septer 2, 2019, https://www.rte.ie/news/ireland/2019/0902/1073317-mike-pence/.

998   Jane Mayer, "The Danger of President Pence," The New Yorker, October 16, 2017, https://webcache.googleusercontent.com/search?q=cache:uqtwzC-2JahUJ:https://www.newyorker.com/magazine/2017/10/23/the-danger-of-president-pence+&cd=3&hl=en&ct=clnk&gl=us.

999   "Michael R. Pence," WhiteHouse.gov, Accessed May 14, 2020, https://www.whitehouse.gov/people/mike-pence/.

1000   Catherine Garcia, "Mike Pence: 'I'm a Christian, a conservative, and a Republican — in that order,'" The Week, July 20, 2016, https://theweek.com/speedreads/637487/mike-pence-im-christian-conservative-republican--that-order.

1001   Julie Zauzmer, "By picking Mike Pence, Trump sends conservative evangelicals a mixed message," The Washington Post, July 15, 2016, https://www.washingtonpost.com/news/acts-of-faith/wp/2016/07/14/pence-defines-himself-as-a-christian-above-all-else-do-christians-want-him-for-vp/.

1002   Jane Mayer, "The Danger of President Pence," The New Yorker, October 23, 2017, https://www.newyorker.com/magazine/2017/10/23/the-danger-of-president-pence.

1003   Dwight Adams, "RFRA: Why the 'religious freedom law' signed by Mike Pence was so controversial," IndyStar, April 25, 2018, https://www.indystar.com/story/news/2018/04/25/rfra-indiana-why-law-signed-mike-pence-so-controversial/546411002/.

1004   Monica Davey, "In Diluting Measure to Ban Gay Marriage, Indiana Shows a Shift," The New York Times, February 18 2014, https://www.nytimes.com/2014/02/18/us/politics/in-diluting-measure-to-ban-gay-marriage-indiana-shows-a-shift.html.

1005   Tyler Trykowski, "Mike Pence, Trump's VP Pick, Is Pretty Damn Homophobic," Vice, July 15, 2016, https://www.vice.com/en_us/article/exkd5w/everything-you-need-to-know-about-mike-pences-homophobia.

1006   Will Drabold, "Here's What Mike Pence Said on LGBT Issues Over the Years," Time, July 15, 2016, https://time.com/4406337/mike-pence-gay-rights-lgbt-religious-freedom/.

1007   Emma Brown and Mandy McLaren, "How Indiana's school voucher program soared, and what it says about education in the Trump era," The Washington Post, December 26, 2016, https://www.washingtonpost.com/local/education/how-indianas-school-voucher-program-soared-and-what-it-says-about-education-in-the-trump-era/2016/12/26/13d1d3ec-bc97-11e6-91ee-1adddfe36cbe_story.html?utm_term=.508d14b40674&tid=lk_inline_manual_2&itid=lk_inline_manual_2.

1008   "What bills has Gov. Pence signed into law?" IndyStar, May 8, 2015, https://www.indystar.com/story/news/politics/2015/05/08/bills-gov-pence-signed-law/26977175/.

1009   Ariane de Vogue, "Federal court blasts Pence on Syrian refugees," CNN, October 3, 2016, https://www.cnn.com/2016/10/03/politics/mike-pence-syrian-refugees/index.html.

1010   Emily Crockett, "Mike Pence is one of the most anti-abortion Republicans in Washington. Here's his record." Vox, January 27, 2017, https://www.vox.com/identities/2017/1/27/14412660/mike-pence-record-abortion-reproductive-rights-march-for-life.

1011   Theodore Schleifer, "Indiana Gov. Mike Pence signs new abortion restrictions into law," CNN, March 24, 2016, https://www.cnn.com/2016/03/24/politics/mike-pence-indiana-disability-abortion/index.html.

1012   "Even some abortion foes balking at tough Indiana bill," CBS News, March 10, 2016, https://www.cbsnews.com/news/even-some-abortion-foes-balking-at-tough-indiana-bill/.

1013   Steven W. Thrasher, "Mike Pence Is Still to Blame for an HIV Outbreak in Indiana—but for New Reasons," The Nation, October 4, 2018, https://www.thenation.com/article/archive/mike-pence-is-still-to-blame-for-an-hiv-outbreak-in-indiana-but-for-new-reasons/.

1014   Paul Demko, "How Pence's slow walk on needle exchange helped propel Indiana's health crisis," Politico, August 7, 2016, https://www.politico.com/story/2016/08/under-pences-leadership-response-to-heroin-epidemic-criticized-as-ineffective-226759.

1015   Paul Demko, "How Pence's slow walk on needle exchange helped propel Indiana's health crisis," Politico, August 7, 2016, https://www.politico.com/story/2016/08/under-pences-leadership-response-to-heroin-epidemic-criticized-as-ineffective-226759.

1016   Sharon Lerner, "Cronyism and Conflicts of Interest in Trump's Coronavirus Task Force," The Intercept, February 29, 2020, https://theintercept.com/2020/02/29/cronyism-and-conflicts-of-interest-in-trumps-coronavirus-task-force/.

1017   Juliet Eilperin, Amy Goldstein, and John Wagner, "HHS Secretary Tom Price resigns amid criticism for taking charter flights at taxpayer expense," The Washington Post, September 29, 2017, https://www.washingtonpost.com/news/post-politics/wp/2017/09/29/trump-to-decide-friday-night-whether-to-fire-hhs-secretary-price/.

1018   Matt Hadro, "HHS Secretary says he is proud to lead 'Department of Life,'" Catholic News Agency, January 24, 2020, https://www.catholicnewsagency.com/news/hhs-secretary-says-he-is-proud-to-lead-department-of-life-91508.

1019   Mark Osborne, "'Make American health great again': Pence swears in new surgeon general," ABC News, September 6, 2017, https://abcnews.go.com/US/make-american-health-great-pence-swears-surgeon-general/story?id=49645025.

1020   Mark Osborne, "'Make American health great again': Pence swears in new surgeon general," ABC News, September 6, 2017, https://abcnews.go.com/US/make-american-health-great-pence-swears-surgeon-general/story?id=49645025.

1021   U.S. Department of Health & Human Services, "ASL Offices," HHS.gov, Accessed May 14, 2020, https://www.hhs.gov/about/agencies/asl/about-asl/asl-offices/index.html.

1022   Rachana Pradhan and Alice Miranda Ollstein, "How Mike Pence's 'Indiana mafia' took over health care policy," Politico, May 20, 2019, https://www.politico.com/story/2019/05/20/mike-pence-health-care-1331705.

1023   Anna North, "What Mike Pence's public health record says about his ability to lead on coronavirus," Vox, February 28, 2020, https://www.vox.com/2020/2/28/21156158/mike-pence-coronavirus-trump-administration-hiv-science.

1024   Rachana Pradhan and Alice Miranda Ollstein, "How Mike Pence's 'Indiana mafia' took over health care policy," Politico, May 20, 2019, https://www.politico.com/story/2019/05/20/mike-pence-health-care-1331705.

1025   Amy Littlefield, "Thanks to Pence, Indiana Now Has One Less Abortion Clinic," Rewire.News, July 26, 2017, https://rewire.news/article/2017/07/26/thanks-pence-indiana-now-one-less-abortion-clinic/.

1026   David R Boulware, "Defunding of Women's Health and Rising Maternal Mortality in Indiana," HHS Public Access, U.S. Department of Health & Human Services, February 2017, https://www.ncbi.nlm.nih.gov/pmc/articles/PMC6445540/.

1027   Rachel Siegel, "The Trump official who tried to stop a detained immigrant from getting an abortion," The Washington Post, October 26, 2017, https://www.washingtonpost.com/news/post-nation/wp/2017/10/26/the-trump-official-who-tried-to-stop-a-detained-immigrant-from-getting-an-abortion/.

1028   Hannah Levintova, "The Trump Official Who Failed to Reunify Dozens of Separated Children Is Getting a New Role," Mother Jones, January/February 2019, https://www.motherjones.com/politics/2018/11/scott-lloyd-abortion-child-migrants-office-of-refugee-resettlement/.

1029   Anna North, "What would America look like without Roe v. Wade? These teenagers are finding out." Vox, February 2, 2018, https://www.vox.com/identities/2018/2/2/16957378/scott-lloyd-trump-unaccompanied-minors-abortion-pill-reversal-teenager.

1030   Fernando Peinado, "Scott Lloyd, the devout government official on a mission to prevent undocumented minors from having abortions," Univision News, October 25, 2017, https://www.univision.com/univision-news/politics/scott-lloyd-the-devout-government-official-on-a-mission-to-prevent-undocumented-minors-from-having-abortions.

1031   Adam Cancryn and Renuka Rayasam, "Meet the anti-abortion Trump appointee taking care of separated kids," Politico, June 21, 2018, https://www.politico.com/story/2018/06/21/scott-lloyd-anti-abortion-separated-kids-642094.

1032   Dan Diamond, "Trump appointee under scrutiny for handling of child separations," Politico, February 26, 2019, https://www.politico.com/story/2019/02/26/trump-refugee-director-family-separations-1211032.

1033   Colby Itkowitz, "The Health 202: Trump officials ignored HHS advice on two big issues," The Washington Post, August 1, 2018, https://www.washingtonpost.com/news/powerpost/paloma/the-health-202/2018/08/01/the-health-202-trump-officials-ignored-hhs-advice-on-two-big-issues/5b6076fc1b326b0207955e70/.

1034   Dan Diamond, "HHS reviews refugee operations as Trump calls for border crackdown," Politico, October 23, 2018, https://www.politico.com/story/2018/10/23/trump-caravan-border-hhs-873152.

1035   Nathaniel Weixel, "Former Trump refugee director did not notify superiors about family separation warnings," The Hill, February 26, 2019, https://thehill.com/policy/healthcare/431721-former-trump-refugee-director-did-not-notify-superiors-about-family.

1036   Emily Alford, "Despite Being Unable to Spell Menstrual, Scott Lloyd's ORR Tracked Teens' Periods on a Spreadsheet," Jezebel, March 16, 2019, https://theslot.jezebel.com/despite-being-unable-to-spell-menstrual-scott-lloyds-o-1833348219.

1037   Liz Posner, "For Months, the Trump Administration Has Illegally Stopped Undocumented Women From Obtaining Abortions," AlterNet, October 18, 2017, https://www.alternet.org/2017/10/trump-illegally-stopped-undocumented-women-obtaining-abortions/.

1038   Maria Sacchetti and Sandhya Somashekhar, "An undocumented teen is pregnant and in custody. Can the U.S. stop her from getting an abortion?" The Washington Post, October 17, 2017, https://www.washingtonpost.com/local/immigration/an-undocumented-teen-is-pregnant-and-in-custody-can-the-us-stop-her-from-getting-an-abortion/2017/10/17/6b548cda-b34b-11e7-9e58-e6288544af98_story.html.

1039   Anna North,"What would America look like without Roe v. Wade? These teenagers are finding out," Vox, February 2, 2019, https://www.vox.com/identities/2018/2/2/16957378/scott-lloyd-trump-unaccompanied-minors-abortion-pill-reversal-teenager.

1040   "Who is Scott Lloyd?" Planned Parenthood, Accessed May 14, 2020, https://www.plannedparenthoodaction.org/tracking-trump/player/scott-lloyd.

1041   Hannah Levintova, "The Trump Official Who Failed to Reunify Dozens of Separated Children Is Getting a New Role," Mother Jones, January/February 2019, https://www.motherjones.com/politics/2018/11/scott-lloyd-abortion-child-migrants-office-of-refugee-resettlement/.

1042   Rachel Siegel, "The Trump official who tried to stop a detained immigrant from getting an abortion," The Washington Post, October 26, 2017, https://www.washingtonpost.com/news/post-nation/wp/2017/10/26/the-trump-official-who-tried-to-stop-a-detained-immigrant-from-getting-an-abortion/.

1043   Rebecca Harrington, "Trump's official behind the Jane Doe case urged 'savvy' lawmakers to make women get men's permission before getting abortions," Business Insider, October 29, 2017, https://www.businessinsider.com/scott-lloyd-jane-doe-abortion-case-controversial-past-2017-10.

1044   Mark Joseph Stern"Trump Administration: We Bar Abortions for Raped Minors Because It's in Their 'Best Interest,'" Slate, December 21, 2017, https://slate.com/news-and-politics/2017/12/trump-administration-bars-abortion-for-raped-minors-because-its-in-their-best-interest.html.

1045   Stacy Sullivan, "Jane Doe Wants an Abortion but the Government Is Hell Bent on Stopping Her," ACLU, October 19, 2017, https://www.aclu.org/blog/immigrants-rights/immigrants-rights-and-detention/jane-doe-wants-abortion-government-hell-bent.

1046   Stacy Sullivan, "Jane Doe Wants an Abortion but the Government Is Hell Bent on Stopping Her," ACLU, October 19, 2017, https://www.aclu.org/blog/immigrants-rights/immigrants-rights-and-detention/jane-doe-wants-abortion-government-hell-bent.

1047   Stacy Sullivan, "Jane Doe Wants an Abortion but the Government Is Hell Bent on Stopping Her," ACLU, October 19, 2017, https://www.aclu.org/blog/immigrants-rights/immigrants-rights-and-detention/jane-doe-wants-abortion-government-hell-bent.

1048   Mark Joseph Stern, "D.C. Circuit's Dubious Compromise Won't Guarantee Undocumented Minor's Abortion Rights," Slate, October 20, 2017, https://slate.com/news-and-politics/2017/10/d-c-circuit-s-dubious-compromise-won-t-guarantee-undocumented-minor-s-abortion-rights.html.

1049   Mark Joseph Stern, "Appeals Court Rebukes Brett Kavanaugh, Grants Abortion Access to Undocumented Minors," Slate, June 14, 2019, https://slate.com/news-and-politics/2019/06/brett-kavanaugh-abortion-undocumented-minors-appeals-court.html.

1050   Mark Joseph Stern, "Appeals Court Rebukes Brett Kavanaugh, Grants Abortion Access to Undocumented Minors," Slate, June 14, 2019, https://slate.com/news-and-politics/2019/06/brett-kavanaugh-abortion-undocumented-minors-appeals-court.html.

1051   Mark Joseph Stern, "Appeals Court Rebukes Brett Kavanaugh, Grants Abortion Access to Undocumented Minors," Slate, June 14, 2019, https://slate.com/news-and-politics/2019/06/brett-kavanaugh-abortion-undocumented-minors-appeals-court.html.

1052   Debra Cassens Weiss, "Trump adds 5 names to his Supreme Court shortlist, including former Kennedy clerk Kavanaugh," ABA Journal, November 20, 2017, https://www.abajournal.com/news/article/trump_adds_five_names_to_his_supreme_court_shortlist_including_former_kenne.

1053   Jessie Hellmann, "Trump appointee who oversaw refugee children office to leave administration," The Hill, May 29, 2019, https://thehill.com/policy/healthcare/445920-controversial-trump-appointee-who-oversaw-refugee-children-office-leaving.

1054   U.S. Department of Health & Human Services, "Strategic Plan FY 2018 - 2022," HHS.gov, accessed July 14, 2019. https://www.hhs.gov/about/strategic-plan/index.html.

1055   Stephanie Armour, "Trump Appointee Harnesses Civil-Rights Law to Protect Anti-Abortion Health Workers," *Wall Street Journal,* April 13, 2018. https://www.wsj.com/articles/health-workers-new-advocate-sees-objection-to-abortion-as-a-civil-right-1523611801.

1056   Katherine Burgess, "HHS official to abortion opponents: 'We're just getting started,'" *The Wichita Edge,* June 29, 2018, https://www.kansas.com/news/politics-government/article214071619.html.

1057   Steve Benen, "Another step backwards: Trump sharply curtails fetal-tissue research," *The MaddowBlog* (Blog), *MSNBC,* June 16, 2019, http://www.msnbc.com/rachel-maddow-show/another-step-backwards-trump-sharply-curtails-fetal-tissue-research.

1058   Yasmeen Abutaleb, " Trump administration moves to end U.S. research using fetal tissue from abortions," *Reuters,* June 5, 2019, https://www.reuters.com/article/us-usa-health-fetus/trump-administration-moves-to-end-u-s-research-using-fetal-tissue-from-abortions-idUSKCN1T6251.

1059   U.S. Department of Health & Human Services, "HHS Proposes to Revise ACA Section 1557 Rule to Enforce Civil Rights in Healthcare, Conform to Law, and Eliminate Billions in Unnecessary Costs," news release, May 24, 2019, https://www.hhs.gov/about/news/2019/05/24/hhs-proposes-to-revise-aca-section-1557-rule.html.

1060   SAGE staff, "Sexual Orientation Questions Added Back Into National Survey of LGBT Older Adults," *SAGE in the news, SAGE USA,* June 23, 2017, archived December 28, 2017. https://web.archive.org/web/20171228001801/https://www.sageusa.org/newsevents/news.cfm?ID=453.

1061   Kathrin F. Stanger-Hall and David W. Hall, "Abstinence-Only Education and Teen Pregnancy Rates: Why We Need Comprehensive Sex Education in the U.S.," PLoS One, 2011 https://www.ncbi.nlm.nih.gov/pmc/articles/PMC3194801/.

1062   Jonathan Allen, "Trump administration pauses new rule limiting abortion referrals: report," Reuters, July 21, 2019. https://www.reuters.com/article/us-usa-abortion/trump-administration-pauses-new-rule-limiting-abortion-referrals-report-idUSKCN1UG0IW.

1063   Kenneth Vogel and Robert Pear, "Trump Administration Gives Family Planning Grant to Anti-Abortion Group," The New York Times, March 29, 2019, https://www.nytimes.com/2019/03/29/us/politics/trump-grant-abortion.html.

1064   The Obria Group, accessed Oct. 25, 2018, https://www.obriagroup.org/.

1065   Miriam Berg, "Obama Administration Protects Access to Health Care for Millions of People," *Blog, Planned Parenthood,* December 14, 2016, https://www.plannedparenthoodaction.org/blog/obama-administration-protects-access-to-health-care-for-millions-of-people.

1066   Sara Ganim, "Democrats: Anti-abortion group helped draft HHS letter rescinding Planned Parenthood policy," CNN, February 13, 2018, https://www.cnn.com/2018/02/12/politics/house-democrats-hhs-letter/index.html.

1067   Yasmeen Abutaleb and Joseph Tanfani, "As Trump rewrites public health rules, Pence sees conservative agenda born again," *Reuters Investigates* (blog), *Reuters,* May 30, 2019. https://www.reuters.com/investigates/special-report/usa-pence-hhs/.

1068   The Times Editorial Board, "Editorial: Trump's new 'religious freedom' rule looks like a license to discriminate," Los Angeles Times, August 20, 2019, https://www.latimes.com/opinion/story/2019-08-19/editorial-trumps-new-religious-freedom-rule-looks-like-a-license-to-discriminate.

1069   Yasmeen Abutaleb and Joseph Tanfani, "Special Report: As Trump rewrites health rules, Pence sees conservative agenda born again," Reuters, March

30, 2019, https://ru.reuters.com/article/idUSKCN1T0176.

1070   Elizabeth Dias, "Inside Mike Pence's Private Meeting with March for Life Leaders," Time, January 27, 2017, https://time.com/4651781/mike-pence-march-life-meeting-abortion/.

1071   Katie Franklin, "4 Brave Moms Tell VP Mike Pence Their Incredible Pro-life Stories," Pregnancy Help News, January 18, 2019, https://pregnancyhelpnews.com/4-brave-moms-tell-vp-mike-pence-their-incredible-pro-life-stories.

1072   Robert Barnes, "Trump picks Colo. appeals court judge Neil Gorsuch for Supreme Court," The Washington Post, January 31, 2017, https://www.washingtonpost.com/politics/trump-picks-colo-appeals-court-judge-neil-gorsuch-for-supreme-court/2017/01/31/2b08a226-e55e-11e6-a547-5fb9411d332c_story.html?hpid=hp_rhp-banner-main_gorsuch805p%3Ahomepage%2Fstory&utm_term=.f2598ce0eb3e.

1073   "Doing What He Said He Would: President Trump's Transparent, Principled and Consistent Process for Choosing a Supreme Court Nominee," WhiteHouse.gov, January 31, 2017, https://www.whitehouse.gov/briefings-statements/said-president-trumps-transparent-principled-consistent-process-choosing-supreme-court-nominee/.

1074   "Hon. Neil M. Gorsuch," The Federalist Society, accessed January 25, 2017, http://www.fed-soc.org/experts/detail/neil-gorsuch.

1075   Aaron Blake, "Neil Gorsuch, Antonin Scalia and originalism, explained," The Washington Post, February 1, 2017, https://www.washingtonpost.com/news/the-fix/wp/2017/02/01/neil-gorsuch-antonin-scalia-and-originalism-explained/.

1076   Mark Fahey, "Donald Trump's top court nominee is young, but '50 year' term is a serious long shot," CNBC, The Big Crunch (blog), February 1, 2017, https://www.cnbc.com/2017/02/01/gorsuch-age-donald-trumps-scotus-nominee-is-the-youngest-since-1991.html.

1077   "Doing What He Said He Would: President Trump's Transparent, Principled and Consistent Process for Choosing a Supreme Court Nominee," WhiteHouse.gov, January 31, 2017, https://www.whitehouse.gov/briefings-statements/said-president-trumps-transparent-principled-consistent-process-choosing-supreme-court-nominee/.

1078   Mark Fahey, "Donald Trump's top court nominee is young, but '50 year' term is a serious long shot," CNBC, The Big Crunch (blog), February 1, 2017, https://www.cnbc.com/2017/02/01/gorsuch-age-donald-trumps-scotus-nominee-is-the-youngest-since-1991.html.

1079   Alex Swoyer, "Federalist Society becomes progressives' new bogeyman," The Washington Times, June 18, 2017, http://www.washingtontimes.com/news/2017/jun/18/federalist-society-seen-as-danger-to-progressives/.

1080   Jeffrey Toobin, "The Conservative Pipeline to the Supreme Court," The New Yorker, April 10, 2017, https://www.newyorker.com/magazine/2017/04/17/the-conservative-pipeline-to-the-supreme-court.

1081   "Judicial Crisis Network Launches $10 Million Campaign to Preserve Justice Scalia's Legacy, Support President-Elect Trump Nominee," Judicial Crisis Network, January 9, 2017, https://judicialnetwork.com/jcn-press-release/judicial-crisis-network-launches-10-million-campaign-preserve-justice-scalias-legacy-support-president-elect-trump-nominee/.

1082   "The Insidious Power of the Anti-Choice Movement," NARAL Pro-Choice America, January 2018, https://www.prochoiceamerica.org/report/insidious-power-anti-choice-movement/.

1083   "The Insidious Power of the Anti-Choice Movement," NARAL Pro-Choice America, January 2018, https://www.prochoiceamerica.org/report/insidious-power-anti-choice-movement/.

1084   Josh Gerstein, "Gorsuch takes victory lap at Federalist dinner," Politico, November 16, 2017, https://www.politico.com/story/2017/11/16/neil-gorsuch-federalist-society-speech-scotus-246538.

1085   Syllabus, National Institute of Family and Life Advocates v. Becerra, U.S. No. 16–1140 (2018), https://www.supremecourt.gov/opinions/17pdf/16-1140_5368.pdf.

1086   Emma Green, "The Supreme Court Hands a Win to the Pro-Life Movement," The Atlantic, June 26, 2018, https://www.theatlantic.com/politics/archive/2018/06/the-supreme-court-hands-a-win-to-the-pro-life-movement/563738/.

1087   Jacob Pramuk and Marty Steinberg, "Anthony Kennedy retiring from Supreme Court," CNBC, June 27, 2018, https://www.cnbc.com/2018/06/27/anthony-kennedy-retiring-from-supreme-court.html.

1088   Adam Liptak and Maggie Haberman, "Inside the White House's Quiet Campaign to Create a Supreme Court Opening," The New York Times, June 28, 2018, https://www.nytimes.com/2018/06/28/us/politics/trump-anthony-kennedy-retirement.html.

1089   Kevin Daley and Saagar Enjeti, "Pro-Life Leader Says Judges Amy Barrett and Thomas Hardiman are Trump's Best Possible SCOTUS Picks," Little Bytes News, via Google WebCache, February 17, 2020, https://webcache.googleusercontent.com/search?q=cache:wel-mGrfZC0J:https://www.littlebytesnews.com/news/pro-life-leader-says-judges-amy-barrett-and-thomas-hardiman-are-trumps-best-possible-scotus-picks/+&cd=1&hl=en&ct=clnk&gl=us.

1090   Mark Barrett, "'Hold your nose and vote,' Graham tells Christians," Citizen Times, October 15, 2016, https://www.citizen-times.com/story/news/politics/elections/2016/10/15/hold-your-nose-and-vote-graham-tells-christians/92139852/.

1091   Mark Landler and Maggie Haberman, "Brett Kavanaugh Is Trump's Pick for Supreme Court," The New York Times, July 9, 2018, https://www.nytimes.com/2018/07/09/us/politics/brett-kavanaugh-supreme-court.html.

1092   Zeke Miller, "The Latest: Liberals rally on court steps against Kavanaugh," Associated Press, July 9, 2018, https://apnews.com/ae9330694da8476e82a97b-4cd472d8e2.

1093   Maggie Haberman and Jonathan Martin, "McConnell Tries to Nudge Trump Toward Two Supreme Court Options," The New York Times, July 7, 2018, https://www.nytimes.com/2018/07/07/us/politics/trump-mcconnell-supreme-court.html.

1094   "Sen. Coons: 'We have to confront an uncomfortable, but important question about whether President Trump may have selected you, Judge Kavanaugh, with an eye towards protecting himself,'" Chris Coons, Senate.gov, September 4, 2018, https://www.coons.senate.gov/news/press-releases/video-sen-coons-we-have-to-confront-an-uncomfortable-but-important-question-about-whether-president-trump-may-have-selected-you-judge-kavanaugh-with-an-eye-towards-protecting-himself.

1095   Corey Brettschneider, "Brett Kavanaugh's Radical View of Executive Power," Politico, September 4, 2018, https://www.politico.com/magazine/story/2018/09/04/kavanaugh-trump-mueller-executive-power-219634.

1096   Senate Judiciary Committee, James Ho to Brett Kavanaugh, March 24, 2003, RE: Pro-choice op-eds in support of Justice Owen? PDF File, via The New York Times, https://int.nyt.com/data/documenthelper/269-kavanaugh-email-re-whether-roe/e6dbbda94dd204fe02af/optimized/full.pdf#page=1.

1097   Senate Judiciary Committee, James Ho to Brett Kavanaugh, March 24, 2003, RE: Pro-choice op-eds in support of Justice Owen? PDF File, via The New York

Times, https://int.nyt.com/data/documenthelper/269-kavanaugh-email-re-wheth-er-roe/e6dbbda94dd204fe02af/optimized/full.pdf#page=1.

1098   Garza v. Hargan, D.C. App, No. 17-5236 (2017), https://www.cadc.us-courts.gov/internet/opinions.nsf/C81A5EDEADAE82F2852581C30068AF6E/$-file/17-5236-1701167.pdf.

1099   John Bowden, "Who top conservatives want Trump to pick for Supreme Court," The Hill, July 7, 2018, https://thehill.com/homenews/administration/395960-who-top-conservatives-want-trump-to-pick-for-supreme-court.

1100   Amy Howe, "Potential nominee profile: Amy Coney Barrett," Scotus-Blog, July 4, 2018,https://www.scotusblog.com/2018/07/potential-nominee-pro-file-amy-coney-barrett/

1101   "Amy Coney Barrett is the favorite of social conservatives, but Democrats are already taking aim," Los Angeles Times, July 9, 2018, https://www.latimes.com/politics/la-na-pol-amy-barrett-supreme-court-20180709-story.html.

1102   KC Johnson, "Returning Due Process to Campus," City Journal, July 17, 2019, https://www.city-journal.org/john-doe-v-purdue-univ.

1103   NARAL Pro-Choice Virginia via Twitter, Jul 11, 2018, https://twitter.com/i/web/status/1017181744737472517.

1104   Lawrence Hurley and Andrew Chung, "Abortion looms over Senate fight on Supreme Court nominee," Reuters, August 31, 2018, https://www.reuters.com/article/us-usa-court-abortion/abortion-looms-over-senate-fight-on-supreme-court-nominee-idUSKCN1LG17A.

1105   Monica Hesse, "'Civility' vs 'hysteria' at the Kavanaugh hearings, and what they truly mean," The Washington Post, September 7, 2018, https://www.washing-tonpost.com/lifestyle/style/civility-vs-hysteria-at-the-kavanaugh-hearings-and-what-they-truly-mean/2018/09/07/52e5769a-b1de-11e8-9a6a-565d92a3585d_story.html.

1106   Michael McConnell, "Brett Kavanaugh will bring middle principles to our polarized nation," The Hill, September 1, 2018, https://thehill.com/opinion/judicia-ry/404670-brett-kavanaugh-will-bring-middle-principles-to-our-polarized-nation.

1107   Robert O'Harrow Jr. and Shawn Boburg, "A conservative activist's behind-the-scenes campaign to remake the nation's courts," The Washington Post, May 21, 2019, https://www.washingtonpost.com/graphics/2019/investigations/leon-ard-leo-federalists-society-courts/.

1108   Alayna Treene, "Heritage Action to spend bulk of $11.5 million budget on confirming Kavanaugh," Axios, July 16, 2018, https://www.axios.com/heritage-action-brett-kavanaugh-supreme-court-ec321cf1-9647-4322-a444-9ecbf9186361.html.

1109   Jane Mayer, "Red-State Democrats' Fears Over Kavanaugh Vote May Be Overblown," The New Yorker, July 14, 2018, https://www.newyorker.com/news/news-desk/red-state-democrats-fears-over-kavanaugh-vote-may-be-overblown.

1110   "Kavanaugh's Conservative, Anti-Choice Backers Have Not Been Able To Translate Their Millions Into Grassroots Energy," NARAL Pro-Choice America Research, August 20, 2018, https://www.prochoiceamerica.org/wp-content/up-loads/2017/06/Memo_-False-Equivalencies-in-Kavanaugh-Campaigns-8.20.18.pdf.

1111   Katarina Sostaric, "At Contentious Grassley Town Hall, Iowans Split Over Supreme Court Nominee," Iowa Public Radio, September 11, 2018, https://www.iowapublicradio.org/post/contentious-grassley-town-hall-iowans-split-over-su-preme-court-nominee.

1112   Kathryn Rubino, "The Historically Unpopular Brett Kavanaugh," Above The Law, August 17, 2018, https://abovethelaw.com/2018/08/the-historically-unpopu-lar-brett-kavanaugh/.

1113   Cheyenne Haslett, "'The Handmaid's Tale' protesters target Kavanaugh," ABC News, September 4, 2018, https://abcnews.go.com/Politics/handmaids-tale-protesters-target-kavanaugh/story?id=57592706.

1114   Eli Watkins and Ariane de Vogue, "Washington Post: Kavanaugh accuser comes forward," CNN, September 16, 2018, https://www.cnn.com/2018/09/16/politics/christine-blasey-ford-brett-kavanaugh/index.html.

1115   "Christine Ford," Center for Advanced Study in the Behavioral Sciences, Stanford University, https://casbs.stanford.edu/people/christine-ford.

1116   Lisa Miller, "The Entitled Rage of Brett Kavanaugh," The Cut, September 28, 2018, https://www.thecut.com/2018/09/brett-kavanaugh-and-his-entitled-rage.html.

1117   Li Zhou and Tara Golshan, "The 6 key themes of Kavanaugh's first day of confirmation hearings," Vox, September 4, 2018, https://www.vox.com/2018/9/4/17819710/supreme-court-nominee-brett-kavanaugh-hearing.

1118   Sabrina Siddiqui and David Smith, "Hundreds arrested at anti-Kavanaugh protest: 'It's time for women to be heard'," The Guardian, October 5, 2018, https://www.theguardian.com/us-news/2018/oct/04/kavanaugh-supreme-court-protests-washington.

1119   Justin Wise, "Yale Law students stage sit-in to demand Kavanaugh investigation," The Hill, September 24, 2018, https://thehill.com/blogs/blog-briefing-room/news/408111-yale-students-stage-sit-in-to-demand-investigation-into-sexual.

1120   Anita Hill, "Anita Hill: How to Get the Kavanaugh Hearings Right," The New York Times, September 18, 2018, https://www.nytimes.com/2018/09/18/opinion/anita-hill-brett-kavanaugh-clarence-thomas.html.

1121   Michelle Clark, "Ronald Reagan's daughter Patti Davis says she was sexually assaulted and can't remember certain details — just like Christine Blasey Ford," Business Insider, September 21, 2018, https://www.businessinsider.com/patti-davis-sexual-assault-defends-christine-blasey-ford-kavanaugh-accuser-2018-9.

1122   "Trump mocks Dr. Christine Blasey Ford's Senate testimony," CBS News via YouTube, October 2, 2018, https://www.youtube.com/watch?v=AWv1ipoi-c8.

1123   Mark Gongloff, "With Kavanaugh, the GOP Could Win by Losing," Bloomberg, September 24, 2018, https://www.bloomberg.com/opinion/articles/2018-09-24/with-brett-kavanaugh-the-gop-could-win-by-losing.

1124   "Tearful woman confronts Senator Flake on elevator," CNN via YouTube,September 28, 2018, https://www.youtube.com/watch?v=bshgOZ8QQxU.

1125   Abby Vesoulis, "Meet One of the Women Who Helped Change Jeff Flake's Mind in a Senate Elevator," Time, October 2, 2018, https://time.com/5412444/jeff-flake-elevator-protester/.

1126   David Smith, "Rape survivors' powerful rebuke to Jeff Flake a key moment on day of drama," The Guardian, September 28, 2018, https://www.theguardian.com/us-news/2018/sep/28/jeff-flake-elevator-rape-survivors-brett-kavanaugh.

1127   Fox News Staff, "FOX NEWS FIRST: Kavanaugh, Ford face the hot seat in Supreme battle; Kavanaugh a victim of mistaken identity?" Fox News, September 27, 2018, https://www.foxnews.com/us/fox-news-first-kavanaugh-ford-face-the-hot-seat-in-supreme-battle-kavanaugh-a-victim-of-mistaken-identity.

1128   Brett M. Kavanaugh, "I Am an Independent, Impartial Judge," Wall Street Journal, October 4, 2018, https://www.wsj.com/articles/i-am-an-independent-impartial-judge-1538695822.

1129   Jenna Johnson and Robert Costa, "'It's the culture war on steroids.' Kavanaugh fight takes on symbolism in divided era," Washington Post, September 24, 2018, https://www.washingtonpost.com/politics/its-the-culture-war-on-steroids-kavanaugh-fight-takes-on-symbolism-in-divided-era/2018/09/24/15ccc792-c028-11e8-be77-516336a26305_story.html.

1130   Tim Marcin, "Sexual Assault Should Not Disqualify Kavanaugh if Proven, Majority of Republicans Believe: Poll," Newsweek, September 27, 2018, https://www.newsweek.com/sexual-assault-should-not-disqualify-kavanaugh-proven-majority-republicans-1141877.

1131   Sheryl Gay Stolberg, "Kavanaugh Is Sworn In After Close Confirmation Vote in Senate," New York Times, October 6, 2018, https://www.nytimes.com/2018/10/06/us/politics/brett-kavanaugh-supreme-court.html.

1132   Tessa Berenson, "Inside Brett Kavanaugh's First Term on the Supreme Court," TIME, June 28, 2019, https://time.com/longform/brett-kavanaugh-supreme-court-first-term/.

1133   Li Zhou, "It's official: Brett Kavanaugh just became the least popular Supreme Court justice in modern history," Vox, October 6, 2018, https://www.vox.com/2018/10/6/17942468/brett-kavanaugh-confirmation-partisan.

1134   Ted Hesson, "Trump has whipped up a frenzy on the migrant caravan. Here are the facts." Politico, October 23, 2018,   https://www.politico.com/story/2018/10/23/migrant-caravan-facts-trump-border-881006.

1135   Kevin Breuninger, "Republicans credit the 'Kavanaugh effect' for Senate wins against red-state Democrats," CNBC, November 7, 2018, https://www.cnbc.com/2018/11/07/gop-credits-kavanaugh-effect-for-senate-wins-against-red-state-democrats.html.

1136   Chuck Todd, Mark Murray and Carrie Dann, "Midterms 2018: It was the Year of the Woman — for Democrats, not Republicans," NBC News, November 20 2018,   https://www.nbcnews.com/politics/first-read/it-was-year-woman-not-republican-side-n938341.

1137   Kristen Bialik, "For the fifth time in a row, the new Congress is the most racially and ethnically diverse ever," Pew Research, February 8, 2019, https://www.pewresearch.org/fact-tank/2019/02/08/for-the-fifth-time-in-a-row-the-new-congress-is-the-most-racially-and-ethnically-diverse-ever/.

1138   Julie Hirschfield Davis, "Nancy Pelosi Elected Speaker as Democrats Take Control of House," The New York Times, January 3, 2019,
        https://www.nytimes.com/2019/01/03/us/politics/nancy-pelosi-speaker-116th-congress.html.

1139   "FACT SHEET: More Than 45 Leading National Advocacy Organizations Endorse Nancy Pelosi for Speaker," Newsroom, Speaker.gov, November 18, 2018, https://www.speaker.gov/newsroom/111819.

1140   Tara Golshan, "The reason Republican women are on the decline in the House," Vox, December 4, 2018, https://www.vox.com/policy-and-politics/2018/12/4/18125631/house-republican-women-decline-identity-politics

1141   Ried Wilson, "Abortion battles heat up with Kavanaugh on Supreme Court," The Hill, May 7, 2019, https://thehill.com/homenews/state-watch/442358-abortion-battles-heat-up-with-kavanaugh-on-supreme-court.

1142   Sarah McCammon, "With Kavanaugh Confirmed, Both Sides Of Abortion Debate Gear Up For Battle," All Things Considered, NPR, October 10, 2018, https://www.kvcrnews.org/post/kavanaugh-confirmed-both-sides-abortion-debate-gear-battle#stream/0.

1143   Sarah McCammon, "With Kavanaugh Confirmed, Both Sides Of Abortion Debate Gear Up For Battle," All Things Considered, NPR, October 10, 2018, https://www.npr.org/2018/10/10/656017613/with-kavanaugh-confirmed-both-sides-of-abortion-debate-gear-up-for-battle.

1144   Ried Wilson, "Abortion battles heat up with Kavanaugh on Supreme

Court," The Hill, May 7, 2019, https://thehill.com/homenews/state-watch/442358-abortion-battles-heat-up-with-kavanaugh-on-supreme-court.

1145   Ried Wilson, "Abortion battles heat up with Kavanaugh on Supreme Court," The Hill, May 7, 2019, https://thehill.com/homenews/state-watch/442358-abortion-battles-heat-up-with-kavanaugh-on-supreme-court.

1146   Philip Schwadel and Gregory A. Smith, Evangelical approval of Trump remains high, but other religious groups are less supportive," *FACT TANK* (Blog), *PEW Research Center*, March 18, 2019, https://www.pewresearch.org/fact-tank/2019/03/18/evangelical-approval-of-trump-remains-high-but-other-religious-groups-are-less-supportive/.

1147   Emma Green, "Nothing Will Persuade White Evangelicals to Support Impeachment," The Atlantic, October 21, 2019, https://www.theatlantic.com/politics/archive/2019/10/trump-white-evangelical-impeachment/600376/.

1148   Amy Littlefield, "'Pro-Life' Groups Praise Trump But Are Silent on Charlottesville (Updated)," ReWire, August 15, 2017, https://rewire.news/article/2017/08/15/pro-life-groups-praise-trump-silent-charlottesville/.

1149   Charles C. Camosy, "Pro-life groups have an obligation to call out Trump on immigration," America Magazine, June 22, 2018, https://www.americamagazine.org/politics-society/2018/06/22/pro-life-groups-have-obligation-call-out-trump-immigration.

1150   Rachael Rettner, "How does the new coronavirus compare with the flu?," *Live Science*, May 14, 2020, https://www.livescience.com/new-coronavirus-compare-with-flu.html.

1151   Vince McLeod, "COVID-19: A History of Coronavirus," Lab Manager, March 16, 2020, https://www.labmanager.com/lab-health-and-safety/covid-19-a-history-of-coronavirus-22021.

1152   Silvia Amaro, "How bad could it get? Economists predict how the coronavirus could hurt the global economy," *CNBC*, March 10, 2020, https://www.cnbc.com/2020/03/10/coronavirus-analysts-cut-global-growth-forecasts-as-epidemic-spreads.html

1153   Max Greenwood, "Tuesday primary turnout slumps amid coronavirus anxiety," *The Hill*, March 18, 2020, https://thehill.com/homenews/campaign/488294-tuesday-primary-turnout-slumps-amid-coronavirus-anxiety

1154   NARAL Pro-Choice America, Interested Parties Memo, NARAL Pro-Choice America, April 2020, https://www.prochoiceamerica.org/wp-content/uploads/2020/04/Re_-Ad-Campaign-to-Expose-Trump-for-Exploiting-COVID-1-2.pdf

1155   Andrew Blake, "Former Rep. Ron Paul: Trump should fire Dr. Fauci, 'fraud' leading coronavirus response," *Washington Times*, April 10, 2020, https://www.washingtontimes.com/news/2020/apr/10/ron-paul-former-gop-congressman-trump-should-fire-/

1156   Alex Seitz-Wald and Sahil Kapur, "Coronavirus has ignited a battle over voting by mail. Here's why it's so controversial.," *NBC News*, April 7, 2020, https://www.nbcnews.com/politics/2020-election/coronavirus-has-ignited-battle-over-voting-my-mail-here-s-n1178531.

1157   Morgan Chalfant and Niv Elis, "Trump steps up effort to blame China for coronavirus," *The Hill*, May 4, 2020, https://thehill.com/homenews/administration/496047-trump-steps-up-effort-to-blame-china-for-coronaviru.

1158   Nancy Cook, "Trump revs up for a state-by-state fight over coronavirus shutdowns," *POLITICO*, April 20, 2020, https://www.politico.com/news/2020/04/20/trump-revs-up-state-fight-coronavirus-shutdowns-195443.

1159   Lev Facher, "Fact-checking Trump's claims about hydroxychloroquine, the antimalarial drug he's touting as a coronavirus treatment," *STAT*, April 6, 2020, https://www.statnews.com/2020/04/06/trump-hydroxychloroquine-fact-check/.

1160   NARAL Pro-Choice America, Interested Parties Memo, NARAL Pro-Choice America, April 29, 2020, https://www.prochoiceamerica.org/wp-content/uploads/2020/04/Pro-Life-Hypocrisy-During-Covid-Memo_4.29.2020_.pdf.

1161   Tamara Keith, "Pence, As Coronavirus Task Force Head, Aims To Show He Can Manage A Crisis," *NPR*, April 28, 2020, https://www.npr.org/2020/04/28/846919781/pence-as-coronavirus-task-force-head-aims-to-show-he-can-manage-a-crisis.

1162   Gregg Gonsalves and Forrest Crawford, "How Mike Pence Made Indiana's HIV Outbreak Worse," *POLITICO*, March 2, 2020, https://www.politico.com/news/magazine/2020/03/02/how-mike-pence-made-indianas-hiv-outbreak-worse-118648.

1163   Lev Facher, "'A number of new stars': The definitive guide to the Trump administration's coronavirus response team," *STAT*, March 20, 2020, https://www.statnews.com/2020/03/20/guide-to-trump-administration-coronavirus-response-team/.

1164   Lee Fang, "TRUMP CABINET BIBLE TEACHER BLAMES CORONAVIRUS PANDEMIC ON GOD'S WRATH — SOMEHOW IT INVOLVES CHINA, GAY PEOPLE, AND ENVIRONMENTALISTS," The Intercept, March 24, 2020, https://theintercept.com/2020/03/24/trump-cabinet-bible-studies-coronavirus/.

1165   Eugene Scott, "A White House faith adviser is under fire for appearing to suggest coronavirus is due to God's wrath over homosexuality, environmentalism," *Washington Post*, March 27, 2020, https://www.washingtonpost.com/politics/2020/03/27/top-white-house-faith-adviser-is-under-fire-suggesting-that-coronavirus-is-due-gods-wrath-over-homosexuality-environmentalism/

1166   Lee Fang, "TRUMP CABINET BIBLE TEACHER BLAMES CORONAVIRUS PANDEMIC ON GOD'S WRATH — SOMEHOW IT INVOLVES CHINA, GAY PEOPLE, AND ENVIRONMENTALISTS," *The Intercept*, March 24 2020, https://theintercept.com/2020/03/24/trump-cabinet-bible-studies-coronavirus/.

1167   Eric Lutz, "Trump In Talks to Sideline Fauci, Birx During Coronavirus Briefings," *Vanity Fair*, April 27, 2020, https://www.vanityfair.com/news/2020/04/trump-in-talks-to-sideline-fauci-brix-during-coronavirus-briefings.

1168   Anne Gearan and John Wagner, "Trump expresses support for angry anti-shutdown protesters as more states lift coronavirus lockdowns," *Washington Post*, May 1, 2020, https://www.washingtonpost.com/politics/trump-expresses-support-for-angry-anti-shutdown-protesters-as-more-states-lift-coronavirus-lockdowns/2020/05/01/25570dbe-8b9f-11ea-8ac1-bfb250876b7a_story.html.

1169   Jaweed Kaleem, "Megachurch pastors defy coronavirus pandemic, insisting on right to worship," *Los Angeles Times*, March 31, 2020, https://www.latimes.com/world-nation/story/2020-03-31/coronavirus-megachurches-meeting-pastors.

1170   Reuters, "The Americans Defying Palm Sunday Quarantines: 'Satan's Trying to Keep Us Apart'," *Reuters*, April 4, 2020, https://www.reuters.com/article/us-health-coronavirus-usa-palmsunday/the-americans-defying-palm-sunday-quarantines-satans-trying-to-keep-us-apart-idUSKBN21M0OP

1171   Ruth Graham, "People at Liberty University Aren't Happy About Falwell Jr.'s Decision to Reopen Campus," *Slate*, March 25, 2020, https://slate.com/human-interest/2020/03/people-at-liberty-university-arent-happy-about-jerry-falwell-jrs-decision-to-reopen-campus.html.

1172   Tim Fitzsimons, "Group behind Central Park's COVID-19 field hospital run by antigay evangelist," *NBC News*, March 31, 2020, https://www.nbcnews.com/feature/nbc-out/group-behind-central-park-s-covid-19-field-hospital-run-n1173396.

1173   John Haltiwanger, "Trump said he 'always' took the coronavirus seriously. Here's what he was actually doing," *Business Insider*, April 6, 2020, https://www.businessinsider.com/heres-what-trump-was-doing-as-coronavirus-was-rapidly-spreading-2020-4.

1174   Maggie Haberman, "Trade Adviser Warned White House in January of Risks of a Pandemic," *New York Times*, April 6, 2020, https://www.nytimes.com/2020/04/06/us/politics/navarro-warning-trump-coronavirus.html.

1175   Caroline Kelly, "Washington Post: Trump downplayed coronavirus despite more than a dozen warnings in daily briefings," *CNN*, April 27, 2020, https://www.cnn.com/2020/04/27/politics/trump-presidential-daily-briefings-coronavirus/index.html.

1176   Chris Cillizza, "The last 'daily' White House press briefing was 170 days ago," *CNN*, August 28, 2019, https://www.cnn.com/2019/08/28/politics/trump-white-house-daily-press-briefing/index.html.

1177   Jim Acosta and Kaitlan Collins, "Heated disagreement breaks out in Situation Room over hydroxychloroquine," *CNN*, April 7, 2020, https://www.cnn.com/2020/04/05/politics/white-house-malaria-drug-hydroxychloroquine-disagreement/index.html.

1178   Lev Facher, "Fact-checking Trump's claims about hydroxychloroquine, the antimalarial drug he's touting as a coronavirus treatment," *STAT*, April 6, 2020, https://www.statnews.com/2020/04/06/trump-hydroxychloroquine-fact-check/.

1179   Jim Acosta and Kaitlan Collins, "Heated disagreement breaks out in Situation Room over hydroxychloroquine," *CNN*, April 7, 2020, https://www.cnn.com/2020/04/05/politics/white-house-malaria-drug-hydroxychloroquine-disagreement/index.html.

1180   Jonathan Swan, "Scoop: Inside the epic White House fight over hydroxychloroquine." *Axios*, updated April 5, 2020, https://www.axios.com/coronavirus-hydroxychloroquine-white-house-01306286-0bbc-4042-9bfe-890413c6220d.html

1181   Nate Raymond, "Oklahoma, Ohio can't bar abortions during coronavirus crisis, courts hold," Reuters, April 6, 2020, https://www.reuters.com/article/health-abortion/oklahoma-ohio-cant-bar-abortions-during-coronavirus-crisis-courts-hold-idUSL1N2BU2TH.

1182   Patrice A. Harris, "AMA statement on government interference in reproductive health care," American Medical Association, March 30, 2020, https://www.ama-assn.org/press-center/ama-statements/ama-statement-government-interference-reproductive-health-care.

1183   Liz Ford, "Coronavirus crisis may deny 9.5 million women access to family planning," *The Guardian*, April 3, 2020, https://www.theguardian.com/global-development/2020/apr/03/coronavirus-crisis-may-deny-95-million-women-access-to-family-planning.

1184   Editorial Board, "Make Abortion More Available During the Pandemic—Not Less," *New York Times*, March 26, 2020, https://www.nytimes.com/2020/03/26/opinion/abortion-law-coronavirus.html.

1185   Christine Grimaldi, "Abortion Pill Restrictions Won't Be Lifted During Pandemic, FDA Says," *VICE*, March 19, 2020, https://www.vice.com/en_us/article/ep-g85a/fda-refuses-to-improve-abortion-pill-access-under-coronavirus

1186   Amy Goldstein, "Trump ban on fetal tissue research blocks coronavirus treatment effort," *Washington Post*, March 18, 2020, https://www.washingtonpost.com/health/trump-ban-on-fetal-tissue-research-blocks-coronavirus-treatment-effort/2020/03/18/ddd9f754-685c-11ea-abef-020f086a3fab_story.html.

1187   Sarah McCammon, "Anti-Abortion Rights Groups Ask HHS To Urge End

To Abortion During Pandemic," *National Public Radio*, March 24, 2020, https://www.npr.org/sections/coronavirus-live-updates/2020/03/24/820730777/anti-abortion-rights-groups-ask-hhs-to-urge-end-to-abortion-during-pandemic.

1188   Susan Dunlap, "As pandemic continues, abortion groups feel greater strain," *NM Political Report*, April 3, 2020, https://nmpoliticalreport.com/2020/04/03/as-pandemic-continues-abortion-groups-feel-greater-strain/.

1189   Carol Robinson, "Alabama woman loses unborn child after being shot, gets arrested; shooter goes free," *AL.com*, updated June 27, 2019, https://www.al.com/news/birmingham/2019/06/woman-indicted-in-shooting-death-of-her-unborn-child-charges-against-shooter-dismissed.html.

1190   Carol Robinson, "Alabama woman loses unborn child after being shot, gets arrested; shooter goes free," *AL.com*, updated June 27, 2019, https://www.al.com/news/birmingham/2019/06/woman-indicted-in-shooting-death-of-her-unborn-child-charges-against-shooter-dismissed.html.

1191   Gheni Platenburg and Michael Brice-Saddler, "A bullet, a miscarriage and an unthinkable question: Who's the victim, and who is to blame?," *Washington Post*, June 29, 2019, https://www.washingtonpost.com/nation/2019/06/29/bullet-miscarriage-an-unthinkable-question-whos-victim-who-is-blame/.

1192   Tiffany Diane Tso, "When A Fetus' Life Is Valued Over The Mother's, Women Like Marshae Jones Are Punished," *Refinery 29*, July 2, 2019, https://www.refinery29.com/en-us/2019/07/236840/marshae-jones-alabama-charged-manslaughter-fetus-personhood.

1193   Tiffany Diane Tso, "When A Fetus' Life Is Valued Over The Mother's, Women Like Marshae Jones Are Punished," *Refinery 29*, July 2, 2019, https://www.refinery29.com/en-us/2019/07/236840/marshae-jones-alabama-charged-manslaughter-fetus-personhood.

1194   Darran Simon and Susan Scutti, "DA drops all charges against a pregnant woman indicted in her baby's death after shooting in Alabama, " *CNN*, July 3, 2019, https://www.cnn.com/2019/07/03/us/pregnant-alabama-woman-manslaughter-indictment/index.html.

1195   Jerry Iannelli, "Florida Lawmaker Doubles Down on White Supremacist, Anti-Abortion Talking Point," *Miami New Times*, May 30, 2019, https://www.miaminewtimes.com/news/florida-state-senator-dennis-baxley-doubles-down-on-racist-abortion-comments-11184157.

1196   Jerry Iannelli, "Florida Lawmaker Doubles Down on White Supremacist, Anti-Abortion Talking Point," *Miami New Times*, May 30, 2019, https://www.miaminewtimes.com/news/florida-state-senator-dennis-baxley-doubles-down-on-racist-abortion-comments-11184157.

1197   Nellie Bowles, "'Replacement Theory,' a Racist, Sexist Doctrine, Spreads in Far-Right Circles," *New York Times*, March 18, 2019, https://www.nytimes.com/2019/03/18/technology/replacement-theory.html.

1198   Ilyse Hogue, Twitter post, December 28, 2019, 12:24 PM, https://twitter.com/ilyseh/status/1210974701905989634.

1199   Callum Paton, "Florida Senator's 'Racist' Replacement Theory Stance Against Abortion Slammed By Reproductive Rights Supporters," *Newsweek*, May 30, 2019, https://www.newsweek.com/florida-senators-racist-replacement-theory-stance-against-abortion-slammed-1439253.

1200   Marianne Goodland, "GOP lawmaker: Planned Parenthood is the 'real culprit' in the shooting." *Colorado Independent*, December 1, 2015, https://www.coloradoindependent.com/2015/12/01/gop-lawmaker-planned-parenthood-is-the-real-culprit-in-the-shooting/.

1201   Brian Fisher, "New York is Celebrating Abortion up to Birth," Human Coalition, accessed May 20, 2020, https://www.humancoalition.org/2019/02/01/new-york-is-celebrating-abortion-up-to-birth/.

1202   Penny Nance, Twitter post, January 30, 2019, 3:17 PM, https://twitter.com/PYNance/status/1090705564634619909.

1203   Kevin McCarthy, Twitter post, January 30, 2019, 10:18 PM, https://twitter.com/GOPLeader/status/1090811460366798849.

1204   Username BadAndyPandy, Twitter post, January 27, 2019, 5:17 PM, https://twitter.com/Badandypandy/status/1089648591155605504.

1205   Lauren Enriquez, Twitter post, January 29, 2019, 12:56 PM, https://twitter.com/LNEnriquez/status/1090307820904501253.

1206   Maureen Ferguson, "Survivors of late-term abortion are grwon up and speaking out," *Washington Examiner,* May 20, 2020, https://www.washingtonexaminer.com/opinion/survivors-of-late-term-abortion-are-grown-up-and-speaking-out.

1207   Life News, Twitter post, February 4, 2019, 11:00 PM, https://twitter.com/LifeNewsHQ/status/1092633923052548096.

1208   Lauren Enriquez, Twitter post, February 15, 2019, 12:26 PM, https://twitter.com/LNEnriquez/status/1096460799139344389.

1209   Steven Ertelt, "Her Father Repeatedly Raped Her, What He Did to Her When She Became Pregnant Was Even Worse, *LifeNews.com*, February 23, 2015, https://www.lifenews.com/2015/02/23/her-father-repeatedly-raped-her-what-he-did-to-her-when-she-became-pregnant-was-even-worse/.

1210   Kristan Hawkins, Twitter post, March 15, 2019, 10:37 PM, https://twitter.com/KristanHawkins/status/1106565096233467905.

1211   Wesley Lowery, Danielle Paquette, and Jerry Markon, "'No more baby parts,' suspect in attack at Colo. Planned Parenthood clinic told official," *Washington Post*, November 28, 2015, https://www.washingtonpost.com/politics/no-more-baby-parts-suspect-in-attack-at-colo-planned-parenthood-clinic-told-official/2015/11/28/e842b2cc-961e-11e5-8aa0-5d0946560a97_story.html.

1212   Wesley Lowery, Danielle Paquette, and Jerry Markon, "'No more baby parts,' suspect in attack at Colo. Planned Parenthood clinic told official," *Washington Post*, November 28, 2015, https://www.washingtonpost.com/politics/no-more-baby-parts-suspect-in-attack-at-colo-planned-parenthood-clinic-told-official/2015/11/28/e842b2cc-961e-11e5-8aa0-5d0946560a97_story.html.

1213   Nora Caplan-Bricker, "2015 Was the Most Violent Year in Recent Memory for Abortion Providers," *Slate*, April 6, 2016, https://slate.com/human-interest/2016/04/for-abortion-providers-2015-was-the-most-violent-year-in-recent-memory.html.

1214   Mary Emily O'Hara, "Abortion Clinics Report Threats of Violence on the Rise," *NBC News*, updated February 14, 2017, https://www.nbcnews.com/news/us-news/abortion-clinics-report-threats-violence-rise-n719426.

1215   Eric Lichtblau and Matt Flegenheimer, "Jeff Sessions Confirmed as Attorney General, Capping Bitter Battle," *New York Times*, February 8, 2017, https://www.nytimes.com/2017/02/08/us/politics/jeff-sessions-attorney-general-confirmation.html.

1216   Mary Emily O'Hara, "Abortion Clinics Report Threats of Violence on the Rise," *NBC News*, updated February 14, 2017, https://www.nbcnews.com/news/us-news/abortion-clinics-report-threats-violence-rise-n719426.

1217   Josh Dawsey, "Porn star was paid $130,000 to keep quiet about a relationship with Trump, Wall Street Journal reports," *Washington Post*, January 12, 2018, https://www.washingtonpost.com/politics/porn-star-was-paid-130000-to-keep-quiet-about-a-relationship-with-trump-wall-street-journal-reports/2018/01/12/

fde75e72-f7ef-11e7-91af-31ac729add94_story.html.

1218   Donald J. Trump, "Remarks by President Trump to March for Life Partic-ipants and Pro-Life Leaders," (speech, 2018 March for Life, Washington, D.C., Jan-uary 19, 2018), https://www.whitehouse.gov/briefings-statements/remarks-presi-dent-trump-march-life-participants-pro-life-leaders/.

1219   Eileen Sullivan, "Thousands March in Washington at Annual Anti-Abortion Rally," New York Times, January 18, 2019, https://www.nytimes.com/2019/01/18/us/politics/march-for-life-dc.htm.

1220   Donald J. Trump, "Remarks by President Trump to March for Life Partic-ipants and Pro-Life Leaders," (speech, 2018 March for Life, Washington, D.C., Jan-uary 19, 2018), https://www.whitehouse.gov/briefings-statements/remarks-presi-dent-trump-march-life-participants-pro-life-leaders/.

1221   Matt Apuzzo, "F.B.I. Raids Office of Trump's Longtime Lawyer Michael Cohen; Trump Calls It 'Disgraceful,'" New York Times, April 9, 2018, https://www.nytimes.com/2018/04/09/us/politics/fbi-raids-office-of-trumps-longtime-lawyer-michael-cohen.html.

1222   Ally Boguhn, "Trump Offers Obamacare Exemption to Foes of Abortion Rights," Rewire News, April 10, 2018, https://rewire.news/article/2018/04/10/trump-offers-obamacare-exemption-foes-abortion-rights/.

1223   Byron Tau, Rebecca Ballhaus, and Erica Orden, "Senate Intelligence Com-mittee Backs Conclusion That Moscow Attempted to Boost Trump," Wall Street Jour-nal, updated May 16, 2018, https://www.wsj.com/articles/senate-intelligence-com-mittee-backs-conclusion-that-moscow-attempted-to-boost-trump-1526488842.

1224   Matt Apuzzo, "F.B.I. Raids Office of Trump's Longtime Lawyer Michael Cohen; Trump Calls It 'Disgraceful,'" New York Times, April 9, 2018, https://www.nytimes.com/2018/04/09/us/politics/fbi-raids-office-of-trumps-longtime-lawyer-michael-cohen.html.

1225   "Title X & The Gag Rule," Planned Parenthood of Western Pennsylvania, Planned Parenthood, accessed May 20, 2020, https://www.plannedparenthood.org/planned-parenthood-western-pennsylvania/stay-informed/title-x.

1226   John T. Bennett, "For first time in 2020 cycle, Trump makes abortion a reelection issue," Roll Call, June 26, 2019, https://www.rollcall.com/news/white-house/for-first-time-in-2020-cycle-trump-makes-abortion-a-reelection-issue.

1227   Donald J. Trump, "Republican Retreat in Philadelphia," (speech, Phila-delphia, PA, January 26, 2017), via FactBase, https://factba.se/transcript/don-ald-trump-speech-philadelphia-pa-january-26-2017.

1228   "Abortion," Factbase, accessed May 20, 2020, https://factba.se/search#abortion.

1229   "Abortion," Factbase, accessed May 20, 2020, https://factba.se/search#abortion.

1230   "Abortion," Factbase, accessed May 20, 2020, https://factba.se/search#abortion.

1231   Donald J. Trump, "Donald Trump Holds a Political Rally in Fayetteville, North Carolina," (speech, Fayetteville, NC, September 9, 2019), via FactBase, https://factba.se/transcript/donald-trump-speech-kag-rally-fayetteville-nc-septem-ber-9-2019.

1232   Donald J. Trump, "Donald Trump Holds a Political Rally in Manchester, New Hampshire," (speech, Manchester, NH, August 15, 2019), via FactBase, https://factba.se/transcript/donald-trump-speech-maga-rally-manchester-nh-au-gust-15-2019.

1233   Donald J. Trump, "Donald Trump Holds a Political Rally in Cincinnati, Ohio," (speech, Cincinnati, OH, August 1, 2019), via FactBase, https://factba.se/transcript/donald-trump-speech-maga-rally-cincinnati-oh-august-1-2019.

1234   Donald J. Trump, "Donald Trump Holds a Political Rally in Greenville, North Carolina," (speech, Greenville, NC, July 17, 2019), via FactBase, https://factba.se/transcript/donald-trump-speech-maga-rally-greenville-nc-july-17-2019.

1235   Donald J. Trump, "Donald Trump Holds a Political Rally in Panama City Beach, Florida," (speech, Panama City Beach, FL, May 8, 2019), via FactBase, https://factba.se/transcript/donald-trump-speech-maga-rally-panama-city-beach-flori-da-may-8-2019.

1236   "Exit Polls 2018," *CNN*, accessed May 20, 2020, https://www.cnn.com/election/2018/exit-polls.

1237   "Exit Polls 2018," *CNN*, accessed May 20, 2020, https://www.cnn.com/election/2018/exit-polls.

1238   "U.S. House Election Results 2018," *New York Times*, updated May 15, 2019, https://www.nytimes.com/interactive/2018/11/06/us/elections/results-house-elections.html.

1239   Ramsey Touchberry, "House Democrats Who Flipped Trump Districts Raked In 3 Times More Campaign Cash Than GOP Challengers," *Newsweek*, April 16, 2020, https://www.newsweek.com/house-democrats-who-flipped-trump-districts-raked-3-times-more-campaign-cash-gop-challengers-1498371.

1240   Jay Cost, "Republicans Remain in a Strong Position in State Legislatures," *National Review*, November 12, 2018, https://www.nationalreview.com/2018/11/midterm-elections-republicans-strong-position-state-legislatures/.

1241   "Governor Election Results 2018," *New York Times*, updated May 15, 2019, https://www.nytimes.com/interactive/2018/11/06/us/elections/results-governor-elections.html.

1242   Jon Kamp and Scott Calvert, "Democrats Win Some State Legislatures, but GOP Maintains Majority," *Wall Street Journal*, November 7, 2018, https://www.wsj.com/articles/democrats-win-some-state-legislatures-but-gop-maintains-majority-1541618643.

1243   Travis Fain, "Democrats break veto-proof majority in General Assembly," @NCCapitol (blog), *WRAL*, updated November 7, 2018, https://www.wral.com/democrats-break-veto-proof-majority-in-general-assembly/17974495/.

1244   Politico Staff, "Trump's State of the Union address," *POLITICO*, February 8, 2019, https://www.politico.com/interactives/2019/trump-state-of-the-union-2019-live-fact-check-transcript-2/5/19/

1245   Donald J. Trump, Twitter post, February 25, 2019, 8:50 PM, https://twitter.com/realDonaldTrump/status/1100211495223218176.

1246   PolitiFact Staff, "Fact-checking Donald Trump's two-hour speech at CPAC," PolitiFact, March 4, 2019, https://www.politifact.com/truth-o-meter/article/2019/mar/04/fact-checking-donald-trump-two-hour-speech/

1247   Steven Ertelt, "President Trump Meets With Woman Who Survived Abortion and Pro-Life Advocate Alveda King," *LifeNews.com*, February 14, 2019, https://www.lifenews.com/2019/02/14/president-trump-meets-with-woman-who-survived-abortion-and-pro-life-advocate-alveda-king/.

1248   National Pro-Life Conference Call, via NARAL Research Department

1249   Donald J. Trump, "President Trump at Conservative Political Action Conference," (speech, CPAC 2019, National Harbor, MD, March 2, 2019), via *CSPAN*, https://www.c-span.org/video/?458390-1/president-trump-criticizes-russia-investigation-democrats-hour-long-speech-cpac.

1250   PolitiFact Staff, "Fact-checking Donald Trump's two-hour speech at CPAC," *PolitiFact*, March 4, 2019, https://www.politifact.com/truth-o-meter/article/2019/mar/04/fact-checking-donald-trump-two-hour-speech/

1251   PolitiFact Staff, "Fact-checking Donald Trump's two-hour speech at CPAC," *PolitiFact*, March 4, 2019, https://www.politifact.com/truth-o-meter/article/2019/mar/04/fact-checking-donald-trump-two-hour-speech/

1252   Kevin Drum, "It's Time to Stop Repeating Donald Trump's Lies," *Mother Jones*, April 29, 2019, https://www.motherjones.com/kevin-drum/2019/04/its-time-to-stop-repeating-donald-trumps-lies/.

1253   Human Coalition, Twitter post, July 9, 2018, 9:16 PM, https://twitter.com/HumanCoalition/status/1016491246326632448.

1254   Amy Hagstrom Miller, "Virginia's abortion fight shows how conservatives will weaponize reproductive rights in 2020," *Washington Post*, February 22, 2019, https://www.washingtonpost.com/opinions/localopinions/virginias-abortion-fight-shows-how-conservatives-will-weaponize-reproductive-rights-in-2020/2019/02/22/44d93ec6-353a-11e9-af5b-b51b7ff322e9_story.html.

1255   "Governor Cuomo Signs Legislation Protecting Women's Reproductive Rights," Governor Andrew M. Cuomo, New York State (news release), January 22, 2019, https://www.governor.ny.gov/news/governor-cuomo-signs-legislation-protecting-womens-reproductive-rights.

1256   Abraham Kenmore, "N.Y. removes abortion from criminal code," *Adirondack Daily Enterprise*, January 23, 2019, https://www.adirondackdailyenterprise.com/news/local-news/2019/01/n-y-removes-abortion-from-criminal-code/.

1257   Christina Cauterucci, "It's Both Difficult and Incredibly Important to Make the Case for Third-Trimester Abortions," Slate, February 1, 2019, https://slate.com/news-and-politics/2019/02/virginia-abortion-third-trimester-law-kathy-tran.html.

1258   Christina Cauterucci, "It's Both Difficult and Incredibly Important to Make the Case for Third-Trimester Abortions," Slate, February 1, 2019, https://slate.com/news-and-politics/2019/02/virginia-abortion-third-trimester-law-kathy-tran.html.

1259   Devan Cole, "Virginia governor faces backlash over comments supporting late-term abortion bill," CNN Politics, January 31, 2019, https://www.cnn.com/2019/01/31/politics/ralph-northam-third-trimester-abortion/index.html.

1260   Susan B. Anthony List, Twitter Post, February 2, 2019, 10:00 p.m., https://twitter.com/SBAList/status/1091894280216629249.

1261   Reggie Littlejohn, "New York's new abortion law is more barbaric than China's. Here's how," https://www.lifesitenews.com/opinion/new-yorks-new-abortion-law-is-more-barbaric-than-chinas.-heres-how?utm_content=buffere83d9&utm_medium=LSN&utm_source=lifesitenews%2Btwitter&utm_campaign=LSN

1262   Faith & Freedom, Twitter Post, January 31, 2019, 4:25 p.m., https://twitter.com/FaithandFreedom/status/1091084959673212928.

1263   Alexandra DeSanctis, "Virginia Governor Defends Letting Infants Die," NationL Review, January 30, 2019, https://www.nationalreview.com/corner/virginia-governor-defends-letting-infants-die/.

1264   Marjorie Dannenfelser, Twitter Post, January 30, 2019, 2:37 p.m., https://twitter.com/marjoriesba/status/1090695525190508544.

1265   Alexandra DeSanctis, "Virginia Governor Defends Letting Infants Die," NationL Review, January 30, 2019, https://www.nationalreview.com/corner/virginia-governor-defends-letting-infants-die/.

1266   Brad Wenstrup, "We've Asked for a Vote 18 Times to Ban Infanticide. Democrats Have Blocked Us," The Daily Signal, March 13, 2019, https://www.dailysignal.com/2019/03/13/weve-asked-for-a-vote-18-times-to-ban-infanticide-democrats-have-blocked-us/.

1267   Warren Fiske, "Trump falsely claims Northam said he'd let doctors 'execute' newborns," Politifact, Poynter Institute, February 20, 2019, https://www.politifact.com/factchecks/2019/feb/20/donald-trump/trump-wrongly-claims-northam-said-he-would-execute/.

1268   Courtney Hagle et al, "Right-wing media are flat-out lying about later abortions being 'infanticide,'" Media Matters, January 31, 2019, https://www.media-matters.org/sean-hannity/right-wing-media-are-flat-out-lying-about-later-abortions-being-infanticide.

1269   "The Anti-Choice Propaganda Playbook: Five Tactics To Look Out For in 2020," NARAL, Medium, January 15, 2020, https://medium.com/@NARAL/the-anti-choice-propaganda-playbook-five-tactics-to-look-out-for-in-2020-4a30b5e016aa.

1270   Gabby Orr, "Trump White House to screen anti-abortion movie Friday," POLITICO, April 11, 2019, https://www.politico.com/story/2019/04/11/trump-white-house-anti-abortion-movie-1271824.

1271   Gabby Orr, "Trump White House to screen anti-abortion movie Friday," POLITICO, April 11, 2019, https://www.politico.com/story/2019/04/11/trump-white-house-anti-abortion-movie-1271824.

1272   Philip Rucker, Josh Dawsey, and Toluse Olorunnipa, "'A watershed moment': Trump faces crossroads amid mounting threats on all sides," The Washington Post, February 3, 2019, https://www.washingtonpost.com/politics/a-watershed-moment-trump-faces-crossroads-amid-mounting-threats-on-all-sides/2019/02/02/0f019554-2587-11e9-81fd-b7b05d5bed90_story.html?utm_term=.927de3f21b59&wpisrc=nl_daily202&wpmm=1.

1273   Mary Ann Ahern, "Who Is Dick Uihlein, Ives' Bankroller in the GOP Race for Governor?" NBC 5 Chicago, February 5, 2018, https://www.nbcchicago.com/news/local/dick-uihlein-illinois-governor-primary-ives-rauner/139996/.

1274   Mary Ann Ahern, "Who Is Dick Uihlein, Ives' Bankroller in the GOP Race for Governor?" NBC 5 Chicago, February 5, 2018, https://www.nbcchicago.com/news/local/dick-uihlein-illinois-governor-primary-ives-rauner/139996/.

1275   Rick Pearson, "Wheaton lawmaker Ives looks at primary challenge of Rauner," Chicago Tribune, October 22, 2017, https://www.chicagotribune.com/politics/ct-met-jeanne-ives-bruce-rauner-primary-20171022-story.html.

1276   Bernard Schoenburg, "Rauner 'marriage' ad includes profane clergyman," State Journal-Register, October 23, 2018, https://www.sj-r.com/news/20181023/rauner-marriage-ad-includes-profane-clergyman.

1277   Greg Hinz, "Here's the pol who really deserves LGBTQ voters' ire," Crain's Chicago Business, October 24, 2018, https://www.chicagobusiness.com/greg-hinz-politics/heres-pol-who-really-deserves-lgbtq-voters-ire.

1278   "Illinois Results," New York Times, August 1, 2017, https://www.nytimes.com/elections/2016/results/illinois.

1279   "Bill Status of HJR0102," 98th General Assembly, Illinois General Assembly, accessed May 20, 2020, http://www.ilga.gov/legislation/billstatus.asp?DocNum=102&GAID=12&GA=98&DocTypeID=HJR&LegID=82471&SessionID=85.

1280   House Roll Call, House Joint Resolution 102, State of Illinois Ninety-Eighth General Assembly, May 30, 2014, http://ilga.gov/legislation/votehistory/98/house/09800HJ0102_05302014_005000.pdf.

1281   "Illinois House Shoots Down Ban On Gay Conversion Therapy," CBS Chicago, April 11, 2014, https://chicago.cbslocal.com/2014/04/11/illinois-house-shoots-down-ban-on-gay-conversion-therapy/.

1282   Natasha Korecki, "Incendiary ad fuels primary challenge to Illinois governor," POLITICO, February 5, 2018, https://www.politico.com/story/2018/02/05/illinois-governor-rauner-ives-ad-392258.

1283   Chuck Sweeny, "Chuck Sweeny: State Rep. Litesa Wallace's speech goes viral: 4.4 million views!" JournalStandard.com, September 16, 2015, https://www.

journalstandard.com/article/20150916/NEWS/150919572/1999/1.

1284   Curtis M. Wong, "Illinois GOP Rep. Doesn't Get Why Transphobic Ad Upset People," HuffPost, February 7, 2018, https://www.huffpost.com/entry/jeanne-ives-transphobic-campaign-ad_n_5a7b2078e4b07af4e820047c.

1285   Rick Pearson and Kim Geiger, "Ives' anti-Rauner ad ripped as 'racist, sexist, homophobic,'" Chicago Tribune, February 3, 2018, https://www.chicagotribune.com/politics/ct-met-jeanne-ives-bruce-rauner-transgender-ad-cps-20180202-story.html.

1286   "Illinois Primary Election Results," New York Times, March 21, 2018, https://www.nytimes.com/interactive/2018/03/20/us/elections/results-illinois-primary-elections.html.

1287   "Illinois Governor," Illinois Election Results 2018, POLITICO, accessed May 20, 2020, https://www.politico.com/election-results/2018/illinois/.

1288   "Home," Jeanne for Congress, accessed May 20, 2020, https://www.jeanneforcongress.com/.

1289   Rick Pearson, "Freshman Democratic U.S. Rep. Sean Casten builds up war chest of more than $1.4 million in advance of GOP challenge from Jeanne Ives," Chicago Tribune, October 15, 2019, https://www.chicagotribune.com/politics/ct-sean-casten-congressional-fundraising-20191015-xncrdflmlbgbld2fp4qg7jy6o4-story.html

1290   Benjamin Wallace Wells, "Roy Moore and the Republican Reckoning," New Yorker, September 27, 2017, https://www.newyorker.com/news/benjamin-wallace-wells/roy-moore-and-the-republican-reckoning.

1291   Benjamin Wallace Wells, "Roy Moore and the Republican Reckoning," New Yorker, September 27, 2017, https://www.newyorker.com/news/benjamin-wallace-wells/roy-moore-and-the-republican-reckoning.

1292   Joan Biskupic, "Roy Moore: The judge who fought the law," CNN Politics, September 27, 2017, https://www.cnn.com/2017/09/27/politics/roy-moore-judicial-fight/index.html.

1293   Jonathan Martin and Alan Blinder, "Luther Strange, Newest Senator, Is Ex-Lobbyist Who Thrived in 'Swamp,'" New York Times, February 9, 2017, https://www.nytimes.com/2017/02/09/us/politics/luther-strange-senate-jeff-sessions-alabama.html.

1294   David Weigel, Michael Scherer, and Robert Costa, "McConnell allies declare open warfare on Bannon," Washington Post, October 25, 2017, https://www.washingtonpost.com/powerpost/gops-insurgents-step-up-campaign-against-mcconnell/2017/10/25/ec3a5af4-b9a0-11e7-9e58-e6288544af98_story.html.

1295   Louis Nelson, "Trump: I originally backed Luther Strange because Moore couldn't win," POLITICO, December 13, 2017, https://www.politico.com/story/2017/12/13/trump-responds-alabama-senate-election-2017-294168.

1296   Scott Detrow, "RNC Restores Financial Support For Roy Moore As Trump Gives Full Endorsement," NPR, December 4, 2017, https://www.npr.org/2017/12/04/568274917/removing-any-qualifications-trump-endorses-roy-moore.

1297   "Roy Moore: Republican accused of sexual misconduct to run for Senate," The Guardian, June 20, 2019, https://www.theguardian.com/us-news/2019/jun/20/roy-more-alabama-senate-launch-2020-sexual-misconduct-allegations.

1298   Stephanie McCrummen, Beth Reinhard, and Alice Crites, "Woman says Roy Moore initiated sexual encounter when she was 14, he was 32," Washington Post, November 9, 2017, https://www.washingtonpost.com/investigations/woman-says-roy-moore-initiated-sexual-encounter-when-she-was-14-he-was-32/2017/11/09/1f495878-c293-11e7-afe9-4f60b5a6c4a0_story.html.

1299   Sonam Sheth, "Roy Moore's former colleague: It was 'common knowledge' that Moore 'dated high school girls,'" Business Insider, November 11, 2017, https://www.businessinsider.com/roy-moore-former-colleague-common-knowledge-hedated-high-school-girls-2017-11.

1300   Graham Lester, "Roy Moore - What Voters Need to Know," Daily Kos, December 10, 2017, https://www.dailykos.com/stories/2017/12/10/1723014/-Roy-Moore-What-Voters-Need-to-Know.

1301   "Roy Moore says he never dated young girls without their mother's permission," The Week, November 10, 2017, https://theweek.com/5things/736854/roy-moore-says-never-dated-young-girls-without-mothers-permission.

1302   Christina Wilkie, "Republicans pull endorsements of Roy Moore after he acknowledges relationships with teens," CNBC, November 10, 2017, https://www.cnbc.com/2017/11/10/republicans-pull-endorsements-of-roy-moore-after-he-admits-to-multiple-relationships-with-teens.html.

1303   Philip Wegmann, "Alabama state auditor defends Roy Moore against sexual allegations, invokes Mary and Joseph," Washington Examiner, November 9, 2017, https://www.washingtonexaminer.com/alabama-state-auditor-defends-roy-moore-against-sexual-allegations-invokes-mary-and-joseph.

1304   Summer Meza, "Roy Moore Pursued Young Girls For Their 'Purity' And Because After Vietnam War It Was Hard To Get A Date, Pastor Says," Newsweek, November 22, 2017, https://www.newsweek.com/roy-moore-liked-young-girls-their-purity-and-vietnam-war-719654.

1305   Carlos Ballesteros, "Alabama Evangelicals More Likely To Support Roy Moore After Sexual Assault Allegations, Poll Shows," Newsweek, November 12, 2017, https://www.newsweek.com/roy-more-sexual-assault-alabama-evangelicals-709015.

1306   Ian Lovett, "Roy Moore Relying on Evangelical Christians to Keep Campaign Afloat," Wall Street Journal, November 19, 2017, https://www.wsj.com/articles/roy-moore-relying-on-evangelical-christians-to-keep-campaign-afloat-1511103647.

1307   Oliver Darcy, "Breitbart went all out for Roy Moore. Now its top editor says he was a 'weak candidate,'" CNN Business, December 20, 2017, https://money.cnn.com/2017/12/20/media/breitbart-alex-marlow-roy-moore/index.html.

1308   Carlos Ballesteros, "Alabama Evangelicals More Likely To Support Roy Moore After Sexual Assault Allegations, Poll Shows," Newsweek, November 12, 2017, https://www.newsweek.com/roy-more-sexual-assault-alabama-evangelicals-709015.

1309   Oliver Darcy, "Breitbart went all out for Roy Moore. Now its top editor says he was a 'weak candidate,'" CNN Business, December 20, 2017, https://money.cnn.com/2017/12/20/media/breitbart-alex-marlow-roy-moore/index.html.

1310   Matthew Bloch et al, "Alabama Election Results: Doug Jones Defeats Roy Moore in U.S. Senate Race," New York Times, December 12, 2017, https://www.nytimes.com/elections/results/alabama-senate-special-election-roy-moore-doug-jones.

1311   Ella Nilsen, "Doug Jones is the first Democrat to win an Alabama Senate seat in 25 years," Vox, December 13, 2017, https://www.vox.com/policy-and-politics/2017/12/13/16770668/doug-jones-roy-moore-alabama-senate.

1312   Chris Cillizza, "Here's why Roy Moore will never concede," CNN, December 28, 2017, https://www.cnn.com/2017/12/28/politics/roy-moore-analysis/index.html.

1313   "Live results: 2020 Alabama Senate primaries," Washington Post, March 28, 2020, https://www.washingtonpost.com/elections/election-results/alabama-senate-primary-live-results/.

1314   "Governor Election Results 2018," New York Times, May 15, 2019, https://www.nytimes.com/interactive/2018/11/06/us/elections/results-governor-elections.html.

1315   Maya T. Prabhu, "Kemp signs anti-abortion 'heartbeat' legislation, sets up legal fight," Atlanta Journal-Constitution, May 7, 2019, https://www.ajc.com/news/state--regional-govt--politics/kemp-signs-anti-abortion-heartbeat-legislation-sets-legal-fight/XPcrtRcYypWRdF1pATTyiP/.

1316   Alexandra Glorioso, "Putnam and DeSantis vow to sign abortion-ban law if elected," POLITICO, June 28, 2018, https://www.politico.com/states/florida/story/2018/06/28/putnam-and-desantis-vow-to-sign-abortion-ban-law-if-elected-494539.

1317   Jessica Taylor, "In Florida And Georgia, Heated Campaigns For Governor Boil Over In Controversies," NPR, October 23, 2018, https://www.npr.org/2018/10/23/660025757/in-florida-and-georgia-heated-campaigns-for-governor-boil-over-in-controversies.

1318   Patricia Mazzei and Alan Blinder, "What Happens When Politicians Who Oversee Elections Are Also the Candidates?" New York Times, November 14, 2018, https://www.nytimes.com/2018/11/14/us/florida-georgia-scott-kemp.html.

1319   "Racist robocall targets Abrams and Oprah as Trump heads to Georgia," Guardian, November 3, 2018, https://www.theguardian.com/us-news/2018/nov/03/racist-robocall-stacey-abrams-oprah-winfrey-georgia.

1320   Khushbu Shah, "'Textbook voter suppression': Georgia's bitter election a battle years in the making," Guardian, November 10, 2018, https://www.theguardian.com/us-news/2018/nov/10/georgia-election-recount-stacey-abrams-brian-kemp.

1321   Jeffrey Cook, "Georgia's next governor remains unclear as Abrams scraps for votes," ABC News, November 13, 2018, https://abcnews.go.com/Politics/georgias-governor-remains-unclear-abrams-scraps-votes/story?id=59166302.

1322   Cat Schuknecht, "Georgia's 'Uneasy Truce' On Abortion Ends," NPR, March 30, 2019, https://www.npr.org/2019/03/30/708365446/georgias-uneasy-truce-on-abortion-ends.

1323   "The states with the highest (and lowest) maternal mortality, mapped," Advisory Board, November 9, 2018, https://www.advisory.com/daily-briefing/2018/11/09/maternal-mortality.

1324   Erick Eckholm, "Anti-Abortion Groups Are Split on Legal Tactics," New York Times, December 4, 2011, https://www.nytimes.com/2011/12/05/health/policy/fetal-heartbeat-bill-splits-anti-abortion-forces.html.

1325   Adam Rogers, "'Heartbeat' Bills Get the Science of Fetal Heartbeats All Wrong," Wired, Marcch 14, 2019, https://www.wired.com/story/heartbeat-bills-get-the-science-of-fetal-heartbeats-all-wrong/.

1326   Bonnie Meibers, "Supreme Court shift prompts questions over Roe v. Wade's future," Bismarck Tribune, October 14, 2018, https://bismarcktribune.com/news/state-and-regional/supreme-court-shift-prompts-questions-over-roe-v-wade-s-future/article_2ab1da51-e290-54d1-a6c4-672cfc0c03fb.html.

1327   Bonnie Meibers, "Supreme Court shift prompts questions over Roe v. Wade's future," Bismarck Tribune, October 14, 2018, https://bismarcktribune.com/news/state-and-regional/supreme-court-shift-prompts-questions-over-roe-v-wade-s-future/article_2ab1da51-e290-54d1-a6c4-672cfc0c03fb.html.

1328   Jessie Balmert, "Who is Roy Moore's spokeswoman? An Ohioan with roots in state's abortion fights," Cincinnati Enquirer, updated December 7, 2017, https://www.cincinnati.com/story/news/politics/2017/12/06/roy-moores-new-spokeswoman-ohioan-roots-states-abortion-fights/926355001/.

1329   Chris Cillizza, "Roy Moore's 'non-accusers' and 15 other outrageous quotes on the Alabama Senate race," *The Point* (blog), *CNN*, December 5, 2017, https://www.cnn.com/2017/12/05/politics/roy-moore-poppy-harlow-cnntv/index.html.

1330   Tasneem Nashrulla, "Roy Moore's Spokeswoman Said His Opponent Would Support Killing A CNN Anchor's 'Unborn Child,'" *BuzzFeed News*, December 5, 2017, https://www.buzzfeednews.com/article/tasneemnashrulla/roy-moores-spokeswoman-defended-him-by-saying-he-would-not.

1331   Eliza Relman, "CNN's Anderson Cooper grills Roy Moore spokeswoman about controversial past positions on homosexuality, 9/11, and Muslims," *Business Insider*, December 7, 2017, https://www.businessinsider.com/roy-moore-janet-porter-cnn-anderson-cooper-2017-12.

1332   Leada Gore, "Janet Porter, spokesperson for Roy Moore, alleges plots and lies in combative interviews," *AL.com*, updated March, 7, 2019, https://www.al.com/news/2017/12/janet_porter_spokesperson_for.html.

1333   Zoë Carpenter, "Meet the Fringe Zealot Behind One of the Country's Most Extreme Anti-Abortion Measures," *The Nation*, December 3, 2019, https://www.thenation.com/article/archive/janet-porter-abortion-ban/.

1334   "Active Hate Groups 2016," *Intelligence Report*, Southern Poverty Law Center, February 15, 2017, https://www.splcenter.org/fighting-hate/intelligence-report/2017/active-hate-groups-2016.

1335   Rachel Janik, "Far-right conspiracies abound at Phyllis Schlafly Eagle Council in St. Louis," *Hatewatch* (blog), Southern Poverty Law Center, October 9, 2017, https://www.splcenter.org/hatewatch/2017/10/09/far-right-conspiracies-abound-phyllis-schlafly-eagle-council-st-louis.

1336   Nina Liss-Schultz, "The Mastermind Behind Ohio's New 'Heartbeat' Abortion Bill Is Too Extreme for Christian Talk Radio," *Mother Jones*, December 9, 2016, https://www.motherjones.com/politics/2016/12/ohio-heartbeat-abortion-janet-porter/.

1337   Jessica Glenza, "The anti-gay extremist behind America's fiercely strict abortion bans," *The Guardian*, April 25, 2019, https://www.theguardian.com/world/2019/apr/25/the-anti-abortion-crusader-hopes-her-heartbeat-law-will-test-roe-v-wade.

1338   Nina Liss-Schultz, "The Mastermind Behind Ohio's New 'Heartbeat' Abortion Bill Is Too Extreme for Christian Talk Radio," *Mother Jones*, December 9, 2016, https://www.motherjones.com/politics/2016/12/ohio-heartbeat-abortion-janet-porter/.

1339   Nina Liss-Schultz, "The Mastermind Behind Ohio's New 'Heartbeat' Abortion Bill Is Too Extreme for Christian Talk Radio," *Mother Jones*, December 9, 2016, https://www.motherjones.com/politics/2016/12/ohio-heartbeat-abortion-janet-porter/.

1340   Michelle Cottle, "Janet Folger Porter, Abortion Warrior, on Her Heartbeat Crusade," *Daily Beast*, updated July 11, 2017, https://www.thedailybeast.com/janet-folger-porter-abortion-warrior-on-her-heartbeat-crusade.

1341   Mary Mogan Edwards, "Abortion foe Janet Porter's zealous tactics divide, inspire," *Columbus Dispatch*, updated December 11, 2016, https://www.dispatch.com/content/stories/local/2016/12/11/1-janet-porter-abortion-foes-zealous-tactics-divide-inspire.html.

1342   Tom Dodge, "'Heartbeat bill' divides Ohio anti-abortion leaders," *Columbus Dispatch*, September 27, 2011, https://www.dispatch.com/article/20110927/NEWS/309279739

1343   Jessica Glenza, interviewed by Michael Martin, *All Things Considered*, National Public Radio, May 18, 2019, https://www.npr.org/2019/05/18/724656375/who-is-heartbeat-bill-author-janet-porter.

1344   Michelle Cottle, "Janet Folger Porter, Abortion Warrior, on Her Heartbeat Crusade," *Daily Beast*, updated July 11, 2017, https://www.thedailybeast.com/janet-folger-porter-abortion-warrior-on-her-heartbeat-crusade.

1345   Jeremy Pelzer, "Gov. John Kasich OKs tighter abortion restrictions, vetoes 'heartbeat' bill and pay raises," *Cleveland.com*, December 21, 2018, https://www.cleveland.com/politics/2018/12/gov-john-kasich-vetoes-anti-abortion-heartbeat-bill-legislative-pay-raises.html.

1346   "Governor Election Results 2018," *The New York Times*, May 15, 2019, https://www.nytimes.com/interactive/2018/11/06/us/elections/results-governor-elections.html.

1347   Gabe Rosenberg, "A Bill Banning Most Abortions Becomes Law In Ohio," *NPR*, April 11, 2019, https://www.npr.org/2019/04/11/712455980/a-bill-banning-most-abortions-becomes-law-in-ohio.

1348   Sabrina Tavernise, "'The Time Is Now': States Are Rushing to Restrict Abortion, or to Protect It," *The New York Times*, May 15, 2019, https://www.nytimes.com/2019/05/15/us/abortion-laws-2019.html.

1349   Deanna Paul and Emily Wax-Thibodeaux, "Could miscarriages land women in jail? Let's clarify these Georgia and Alabama abortion bills.," *The Washington Post*, May 12, 2019, https://www.washingtonpost.com/health/2019/05/11/could-miscarriages-land-women-jail-lets-clarify-these-georgia-alabama-abortion-bills/.

1350   Michelle Lou, "Alabama doctors who perform abortions could face up to 99 years in prison -- the same as rapists and murderers," *CNN*, May 15, 2019, https://www.cnn.com/2019/05/15/us/alabama-abortion-law-felony-trnd/index.html.

1351   Anna North, "A Texas bill would allow the death penalty for patients who get abortions," *Vox*, April 11, 2019, https://www.vox.com/policy-and-politics/2019/4/11/18304825/abortion-texas-tony-tinderholt-death-penalty-bill.

1352   Anna North, "The new bill that would create a crime called "abortion murder," explained," *Vox*, December 9, 2019, https://www.vox.com/2019/12/5/20994296/ohio-abortion-murder-hb-413-reimplant-ectopic.

1353   Anna North, "The new bill that would create a crime called "abortion murder," explained," *Vox*, December 9, 2019, https://www.vox.com/2019/12/5/20994296/ohio-abortion-murder-hb-413-reimplant-ectopic.

1354   Jenn Conti Tweet, Twitter, May 8, 2019, https://twitter.com/doctorjenn/status/1126153493918523393.

1355   Carter Sherman, "Giving Fetuses Legal Rights Could Be a Nightmare for Women, Advocates Say," *Vice*, May 22 2019, https://www.vice.com/en_us/article/wjvzew/giving-fetuses-legal-rights-could-be-a-nightmare-for-women-advocates-say.

1356   Bill Rankin, "DIGGING DEEPER: Could Georgia abortion law challenge Roe v. Wade?," *Atlanta Journal Constitution*, April 26, 2019, https://www.ajc.com/news/local/could-georgia-abortion-law-challenge-roe-wade/WiipMbWRW8DC6l-rl8qzksJ/.

1357   Avery Wilks, "GOP lawmaker shared story of her rape. Now she says she's under attack in abortion debate," *Charlotte Observer*, May 10, 2019, https://www.charlotteobserver.com/news/state/south-carolina/article230258089.html.

1358   Daisy Stein and Natalie Green, "Poll: 77% of Americans Want Abortion to Remain Safe and Legal," Planned Parenthood, July 22, 2019, https://www.plannedparenthoodaction.org/blog/73-of-americans-want-abortion-to-remain-safe-and-legal.

1359   Laurel Wamsley, "Across The Country, Protesters Rally To Stop States' Abortion Bans," NPR, May 21, 2019, https://www.npr.org/2019/05/21/725410050/across-the-country-protesters-rally-to-stop-states-abortion-bans.

1360   "Almost 200 CEOs in the US join the fight against abortion bans," Women's Agenda, accessed May 20, 2020, https://womensagenda.com.au/latest/almost-200-ceos-in-the-us-join-the-fight-against-abortion-bans/.

1361   Robyn Curnow, "Battle lines are drawn between the film industry and Georgia over controversial 'heartbeat bill'," CNN, August 21, 2019, https://www.cnn.com/2019/08/21/us/georgia-heartbeat-law-film-industry/index.html.

1362   "Reclaim Georgia 2020 Pledge," NARAL Pro-Choice America, accessed May 20, 2020, https://prochoicegeorgia.org/issues/reclaim-georgia-2020-pledge/.

1363   Richard Elliot, "Heartbeat Bill protests expected on final day of General Assembly," WSB-TV 2, April 1, 2019, https://www.wsbtv.com/news/politics/heartbeat-bill-protests-expected-on-final-day-of-general-assembly/936091014/.

1364   Greg Bluestein, "Kemp to sign anti-abortion 'heartbeat' bill on Tuesday," Atlanta Journal-Constitution, May 06, 2019, https://www.ajc.com/blog/politics/breaking-kemp-sign-anti-abortion-heartbeat-bill-tuesday/SMN1lGQHqWBEsn-RhXPGa7I/.

1365   Mark Osborne, "President Trump denounces restrictive abortion bans, compares himself to Ronald Reagan," ABC News, May 19, 2019, https://abcnews.go.com/Politics/president-donald-trump-opposes-highly-restrictive-alabama-abortion/story?id=63133310

1366   Mark Osborne, "President Trump denounces restrictive abortion bans, compares himself to Ronald Reagan," ABC News, May 19, 2019, https://abcnews.go.com/Politics/president-donald-trump-opposes-highly-restrictive-alabama-abortion/story?id=63133310

1367   Rachana Pradhan, "Abortion could decide Kentucky's close governor's race," POLITICO, November 4, 2019, https://www.politico.com/news/2019/11/04/abortion-could-decide-kentuckys-close-governors-race-065382.

1368   Ed Kilgore, "Beshear Beats Trump-Loving Bevin in Kentucky," Intelligencer, November 6, 2019, https://nymag.com/intelligencer/2019/11/andy-beshear-beats-trump-loving-matt-bevin-as-kentucky-gov.html.

1369   Lisa Gillespie, "Here's A Rundown Of Kentucky's New Anti-Abortion Laws — And What's Next," 89.3 WFPL, April 1, 2019, https://wfpl.org/heres-a-rundown-of-kentuckys-new-anti-abortion-laws-and-whats-next/.

1370   Bruce Schreiner, "Bevin plays up immigration, abortion in new ads," Associated Press, September 17, 2019, https://apnews.com/d03fd836f544405b-b3a205420a7bee86.

1371   Rick Klein and Kendall Karson, "Suburban revolt boosts Democrats on Election Day in the age of Trump: ANALYSIS," ABC News, November 6, 2019, https://abcnews.go.com/US/suburban-revolt-boosts-democrats-age-trump-analysis/story?id=66791338.

1372   Andrew O'Reilly, "Sasse says Virginia Gov. Northam should 'get the hell out of office' in wake of abortion comments," Fox News, January 31, 2019, https://www.foxnews.com/politics/sasse-tells-virginia-gov-northam-to-get-the-hell-of-office-in-wake-of-abortion-comments.

1373   John McCormack, "Will Virginia Vote for Abortion Extremism?," National Review, October 30, 2019, https://www.nationalreview.com/2019/10/virginia-state-elections-gop-warns-of-democrat-abortion-extremism/.

1374   Aída Chávez, "THE GOP'S FEARMONGERING OVER ABORTION FLOPPED IN KENTUCKY AND VIRGINIA," The Intercept, November 6 2019, https://theintercept.com/2019/11/06/election-results-virginia-kentucky-abortion/.

1375   Pomidor Quixote, "MOLOCH: New York Legalizes "Any Time" Abortions if Mothers' Lives are in Danger," *Daily Stormer*, January 25, 2019, https://dailystormer.su/moloch-new-york-legalizes-any-time-abortions-if-mothers-lives-are-in-danger/.

1376   Pomidor Quixote, "MOLOCH: New York Legalizes "Any Time" Abortions if Mothers' Lives are in Danger," *Daily Stormer*, January 25, 2019, https://dailystormer.su/moloch-new-york-legalizes-any-time-abortions-if-mothers-lives-are-in-danger/.

1377   Students for Life Tweet, Twitter, January 31, 2019, https://twitter.com/StudentsforLife/status/1090984346574602240.

1378   Vegas Tenold, "Extremists Are Winning the War on Abortion," *Vice*, May 20, 2019, https://news.vice.com/en_us/article/qv73p5/extremists-are-winning-the-war-on-abortion?utm_campaign=sharebutton.

1379   Emily Glazer, "Facebook to Keep Targeted Political Ads but Give Users More Control," *The Wall Street Journal*, January 9, 2020, https://www.wsj.com/articles/facebook-to-keep-targeted-political-ads-but-will-give-users-more-control-11578567603.

1380   Anna Massoglia and Karl Evers-Hillstrom, "2020 presidential candidates top $100M in digital ad spending as Twitter goes dark," *Open Secrets*, November 14, 2019, https://www.opensecrets.org/news/2019/11/digital-ad-spending-2020-presidential-candidates-top-100m/.

1381   Mike Isaac and Cecilia Kang, "Facebook Says It Won't Back Down From Allowing Lies in Political Ads," *The New York Times*, January 9, 2020, https://www.nytimes.com/2020/01/09/technology/facebook-political-ads-lies.html.

1382   Thomas Kaplan and Sarah Almukhtar, "How Trump Is Outspending Every 2020 Democrat on Facebook," May 21, 2019, https://www.nytimes.com/interactive/2019/05/21/us/politics/trump-2020-facebook-ads.html.

1383   Ben Gilbert, "Facebook refuses to fact-check political ads, and it's infuriating employees and lawmakers. Here's why the issue continues to dog the company." *Business Insider*, December 14, 2019, https://www.businessinsider.com/facebook-political-ads-fact-check-policy-explained-2019-11#facebook-is-reportedly-considering-a-label-for-political-ads-that-spells-out-when-theyre-not-fact-checked-5.

1384   Mariah Blake, "Mad Men: Inside the Men's Rights Movement—and the Army of Misogynists and Trolls It Spawned," *Mother Jones*, January 2015, https://www.motherjones.com/politics/2015/01/warren-farrell-mens-rights-movement-feminism-misogyny-trolls/2/

1385   Emmett Rensin, "The internet is full of men who hate feminism. Here's what they're like in person.," Vox, August 18, 2015, https://www.vox.com/2015/2/5/7942623/mens-rights-movement

1386   Alex Kotch, "Secretive Right-Wing Nonprofit Plays Role in COVID-19 Organizing," *PR Watch*, May 15, 2020, https://www.prwatch.org/news/2020/05/13581/secretive-right-wing-nonprofit-plays-role-covid-19-organizing.

1387   NARAL Pro-Choice America, "Research Roundup: Pro-Life Hypocrisy on COVID-19," NARAL Pro-Choice America, accessed May 20, 2020, https://www.prochoiceamerica.org/report/research-roundup-covid-hypocrisy/.

1388   Trip Gabriel and Jonathan Martin, "Gretchen Whitmer Isn't Backing Down," *The New York Times*, April 18, 2020, https://www.nytimes.com/2020/04/18/us/politics/gretchen-whitmer-michigan-protests.html.

1389   Rory Sullivan, "Man who 'threatened to kill' Michigan governor Gretchen Whitmer faces terrorism charge," *The Independent*, May 16, 2020, https://www.independent.co.uk/news/world/americas/michigan-governor-gretchen-whitmer-death-threat-terrorism-detroit-a9518066.html

1390   David Welch, "Michigan Cancels Legislative Session to Avoid Armed Protesters," *Bloomberg*, May 14, 2020, https://www.bloomberg.com/news/articles/2020-05-14/michigan-cancels-legislative-session-to-avoid-armed-protesters.

1391   Valerie Edwards, "Michigan Gov Gretchen Whitmer is target of death threats from vigilante Facebook groups with 400,000 members ahead of an armed protest at state Capitol," *Daily Mail*, May 11, 2020, https://www.dailymail.co.uk/news/article-8309667/Michigan-Gov-Gretchen-Whitmer-target-numerous-threats-Facebook.html,

1392   Jeremy W. Peters, "Republicans' Messaging on Abortion Puts Democrats on the Defensive," *The New York Times*, May 16, 2019, https://www.nytimes.com/2019/05/16/us/politics/abortion-republicans-democrats.html.

1393   Jeremy W. Peters, "Republicans' Messaging on Abortion Puts Democrats on the Defensive," *The New York Times*, May 16, 2019, https://www.nytimes.com/2019/05/16/us/politics/abortion-republicans-democrats.html.

1394   "S.311 - Born-Alive Abortion Survivors Protection Act," 116th Congress, January 31, 2019, https://www.congress.gov/bill/116th-congress/senate-bill/311/text.

1395   "S.220 - Born-Alive Abortion Survivors Protection Act," 115th Congress, January 24, 2017, https://www.congress.gov/bill/115th-congress/senate-bill/220?q=%7B%22search%22%3A%5B%22born+alive+abortion+survivors+protection+act%22%5D%7D&s=2&r=3.

1396   "BORN-ALIVE ABORTION SURVIVORS PROTECTION ACT," Congressional Record Vol. 164, No. 12, January 19, 2018, https://www.congress.gov/congressional-record/2018/1/19/house-section/article/h560-1?s=1&r=8.

1397   Alan Fram, "Dems block Senate GOP bill on infants surviving abortions," *Associated Press*, February 25, 2019, https://apnews.com/cafdaef4411c49ee9b-17838d3c338eee.

1398   "S.220 - Born-Alive Abortion Survivors Protection Act," 115th Congress, January 24, 2017, https://www.congress.gov/bill/115th-congress/senate-bill/220?q=%7B%22search%22%3A%5B%22born+alive+abortion+survivors+protection+act%22%5D%7D&s=2&r=3.

1399   Press Release, "Senate Will Have Roll Call Vote on Born-Alive Abortion Survivors Protection Act," Senator Ben Sasse, February 14, 2019, https://www.sasse.senate.gov/public/index.cfm/2019/2/senate-will-have-roll-call-vote-on-born-alive-abortion-survivors-protection-act.

1400   "Fact Checking Rhetoric On Infants Surviving Abortions: Babies Are Rarely Born Alive And When They Are Doctors Don't Kill Them," *Kaiser Health News*, February 27, 2019, https://khn.org/morning-breakout/fact-checking-rhetoric-on-infants-surviving-abortions-babies-are-rarely-born-alive-and-when-they-are-doctors-dont-kill-them/.

1401   "Roll Call Vote # 58," United States Senate, 116th Congress, February 25, 2020, https://www.senate.gov/legislative/LIS/roll_call_lists/roll_call_vote_cfm.cfm?congress=116&session=2&vote=00058.

1402   Todd Dorman, "Your friendly neighborhood super PAC is bankrolling ads in Iowa's 1st District," *The Gazette*, November 18, 2019, https://www.thegazette.com/subject/opinion/staff-columnist/finkenauer-hinson-20191118

1403   "What About 'Whataboutism'?" *Merriam-Webster*, accessed May 20, 2020, https://www.merriam-webster.com/words-at-play/whataboutism-origin-meaning.

1404   Sarah Grant, "Watch John Oliver Break Down Trump's Three Dangerous

Manipulation Tactics," *Rolling Stone*, November 13, 2017, https://www.rollingstone. com/tv/tv-news/watch-john-oliver-break-down-trumps-three-dangerous-manipulation-tactics-116113/.

1405   Kevin Liptak, Daniella Diaz and Sophie Tatum, "Trump pardons former Sheriff Joe Arpaio," *CNN*, August 27, 2017, https://www.cnn.com/2017/08/25/politics/sheriff-joe-arpaio-donald-trump-pardon/index.html.

1406   "Trump defends Charlottesville comments by praising Confederate general," *Times of Israel*, April 26, 2019, https://www.timesofisrael.com/trump-defends-charlottesville-comments-by-praising-confederate-general/.

1407   Laurel Wamsley and Bobby Allyn, "Neo-Nazi Who Killed Charlottesville Protester Is Sentenced To Life In Prison," *NPR*, June 28, 2019, https://www.npr. org/2019/06/28/736915323/neo-nazi-who-killed-charlottesville-protester-is-sentenced-to-life-in-prison

1408   Philip Bump, "The whataboutism at the heart of Trump's focus on antifa," *The Washington Post*, August 21, 2019, https://www.washingtonpost.com/politics/2019/08/21/whataboutism-heart-trumps-focus-antifa/.

1409   Derek Hawkins, "Arizona congressman repeats bogus claim that Charlottesville violence was left-wing plot," *The Washington Post*, October 6, 2017, https://www.washingtonpost.com/news/morning-mix/wp/2017/10/06/arizona-congressman-repeats-bogus-claim-that-charlottesville-violence-was-left-wing-plot/

1410   Patrick O'Connor and John Bresnahan, "Tears, tempers fly in Pelosi campaign," *Pittsburgh Post-Gazette*, November 8, 2009, https://www.post-gazette. com/news/politics-politico/2009/11/08/Tears-tempers-fly-in-Pelosi-campaign/stories/200911080254.

1411   Jessica Washington, "House Republicans Tried to Capitalize on Coronavirus to Sneak Anti-Abortion Language Into Law," *Mother Jones*, March 13, 2020, https://www.motherjones.com/politics/2020/03/house-republicans-tried-to-capitalize-on-coronavirus-to-sneak-anti-abortion-language-into-law/.

1412   SBA List Tweet, Twitter, February 2, 2019, https://twitter.com/SBAList/status/1091894280216629249.

1413   Elizabeth Dias and Lisa Lerer, "How a Divided Left Is Losing the Battle on Abortion," *The New York Times*, December 1, 2019, https://www.nytimes. com/2019/12/01/us/politics/abortion-planned-parenthood.html.

1414   "Why Strongmen Attack Women's Rights," *Freedom House*, June 18, 2019, https://freedomhouse.org/article/why-strongmen-attack-womens-rights.

1415   Peter Beinart, "The New Authoritarians Are Waging War on Women," *The Atlantic*, January 2019, https://www.theatlantic.com/magazine/archive/2019/01/authoritarian-sexism-trump-duterte/576382/.

1416   Krizsan, Andrea & Roggeband, Conny. (2018). Towards a Conceptual Framework for Struggles over Democracy in Backsliding States: Gender Equality Policy in Central Eastern Europe. Politics and Governance. 6. 90. 10.17645/pag. v6i3.1414, https://www.researchgate.net/publication/327657292_Towards_a_Conceptual_Framework_for_Struggles

1417   Norman Eisen, Andrew Kenealy, Susan Corke, Torrey Taussig, and Alina Polyakova, "The Democracy Playbook: Preventing and Reversing Democratic Backsliding", Governance Studies, *The Brookings Institution*, November 2019, https:// www.brookings.edu/wp-content/uploads/2019/11/The-Democracy-Playbook_Preventing-and-Reversing-Democratic-Backsliding.pdf

1418 Domenico Montenaro, "Poll: Majority Want To Keep Abortion Legal, But They Also Want Restrictions," *NPR*, June 7, 2019, https://www.npr.org/2019/06/07/730183531/poll-majority-want-to-keep-abortion-legal-but-they-also-want-restrictions.

1419   "Only 9% of Americans Support a Full Abortion Ban," Change Research via Medium, June 3, 2019, https://medium.com/change-research/only-9-of-americans-support-a-full-abortion-ban-9e03bcfc29cb.

1420   "The Abortion Debate in the United States," NPR/PBS NewsHour/Marist Poll Results, June 7, 2019, http://maristpoll.marist.edu/npr-pbs-newshour-marist-poll-results-6/#sthash.w2Wyo12l.dpbs.

1421   Amy Gardner, Shawn Boburg and Josh Dawsey, "As Trump attacks voting by mail, GOP builds 2020 strategy around limiting its expansion," *The Washington Post*, May 31, 2020, https://www.washingtonpost.com/politics/as-trump-attacks-voting-by-mail-gop-builds-2020-strategy-around-limiting-its-expansion/2020/05/31/a17ccfa0-a00d-11ea-b5c9-570a91917d8d_story.html.

1422   Miles Parks, "Expert Warns Of 'Real Festival Of Partisan Gerrymandering' In 2021," *NPR*, April 19, 2020, https://www.npr.org/2020/04/19/836260800/expert-warns-of-real-festival-of-partisan-gerrymandering-in-2021.

1423   Alvin Chang, "How Republicans are undermining the 2020 census, explained with a cartoon," *Vox*, May 7, 2018, https://www.vox.com/2018/5/7/17286692/census-republicans-funding-undercount-data-chart.

1424   Sarah D. Wire, "GOP is accused of sending misleading 'census' forms ahead of the actual count," *Los Angeles Times*, February 2, 2020, https://www.latimes.com/politics/story/2020-02-20/gop-is-accused-of-sending-misleading-census-forms.

CPSIA information can be obtained
at www.ICGtesting.com
Printed in the USA
FSHW011250250920
74138FS